Lecture Notes in Computer

T0238115

Commenced Publication in 1973
Founding and Former Series Editors:
Gerhard Goos, Juris Hartmanis, and Jan van Leeuwen

Roberto Gorrieri   Heike Wehrheim (Eds.)

Formal Methods for Open Object-Based Distributed Systems

8th IFIP WG 6.1 International Conference, FMOODS 2006
Bologna, Italy, June 14-16, 2006
Proceedings

 Springer

Volume Editors

Roberto Gorrieri
Università di Bologna
Dipartimento di Scienze dell'Informazione
Mura A. Zamboni, 7, 40127 Bologna, Italy
E-mail: gorrieri@cs.unibo.it

Heike Wehrheim
Universität Paderborn
Institut für Informatik
Warburger Str. 100, 33098 Paderborn, Germany
E-mail: wehrheim@uni-paderborn.de

Library of Congress Control Number: 2006926884

CR Subject Classification (1998): C.2.4, D.1.3, D.2, D.3, F.3, D.4

LNCS Sublibrary: SL 2 – Programming and Software Engineering

ISSN   0302-9743
ISBN-10   3-540-34893-X Springer Berlin Heidelberg New York
ISBN-13   978-3-540-34893-1 Springer Berlin Heidelberg New York

Springer is a part of Springer Science+Business Media

springer.com

© Springer-Verlag Berlin Heidelberg 2006
Printed in Germany

Typesetting: Camera-ready by author, data conversion by Scientific Publishing Services, Chennai, India
Printed on acid-free paper   SPIN: 11768869   06/3142   5 4 3 2 1 0

Preface

This volume contains the proceedings of the 8th IFIP International Conference on Formal Methods for Open Object-based Distributed Systems (FMOODS 2006). The conference was held in Bologna, Italy, 14-16 June 2006, as part of the federated multiconference DisCoTec (Distributed Computing Techniques), together with the 8th International Conference on Coordination Models and Languages (COORDINATION) and the 6th IFIP International Conference on Distributed Applications and Interoperable Systems (DAIS). DisCoTec was organized by the Department of Computer Science of the University of Bologna.

Established in 1996, the FMOODS series of conferences aims to provide an integrated forum for research on formal aspects of open object-based distributed systems. The FMOODS 2006 especially attracted novel contributions reflecting recent developments in the area, such as component- and model-based design, service-oriented computing, and software quality. Some more specific topics of interest were: semantics and implementation of object-oriented programming and (visual) modelling languages; formal techniques for specification, design, analysis, verification, validation and testing; formal methods for service-oriented computing; and integration of quality of service requirements into formal models.

These proceedings contain a selection of 16 research contributions, out of 51 submissions, which went through a rigorous review process by international reviewers. We therefore owe special thanks to all members of the Program Committee, and their sub-referees, for the excellent work they have done in the short time they had.

Additionally, these proceedings include three invited papers by Pierpaolo Degano (University of Pisa), José Luiz Fiadeiro (University of Leicester) and Davide Sangiorgi (University of Bologna).

Finally, our thanks go to the Organizing Committee of the DisCoTec federated conference, chaired by Gianluigi Zavattaro, for the excellent work done and for the support they gave in managing the submission system by Philippe Rigaux. We also gratefully acknowledge the financial support of the Department of Computer Science of the University of Bologna and from the EU-project SENSORIA.

June 2006

Roberto Gorrieri
Heike Wehrheim

Organization

General Chair	Gianluigi Zavattaro (University of Bologna, Italy)
Program Chairs	Roberto Gorrieri (University of Bologna, Italy)
	Heike Wehrheim (University of Paderborn, Germany)
Publicity Chair	Martin Steffen (University of Kiel, Germany)

Steering Committee

John Derrick (University of Sheffield, UK)
Roberto Gorrieri (University of Bologna, Italy)
Elie Najm (ENST, Paris, France)

Program Committee

Lynne Blair (U. of Lancaster, UK)
Eerke Boiten (U. of Kent, UK)
Nadia Busi (U. of Bologna, Italy)
John Derrick (U. of Sheffield, UK)
Alessandro Fantechi (U. of Florence, Italy)
Colin Fidge (U. of Queensland, Australia)
Robert France (Colorado State U., USA)
Roberto Gorrieri (U. of Bologna, Italy)
Reiko Heckel (U. of Leicester, UK)
Einar Broch Johnsen (U. of Oslo, Norway)
Doug Lea (State U. of New York, USA)
Elie Najm (ENST Paris, France)
Uwe Nestmann (TU Berlin, Germany)
Erik Poll (U. of Nijmegen, Netherlands)
Arend Rensink (U. Twente, Netherlands)
Ralf Reussner (U. of Karlsruhe, Germany)
Bernhard Rumpe (TU Braunschweig, Germany)
Martin Steffen (U. of Kiel, Germany)
Carolyn Talcott (SRI International, USA)
Andrzej Tarlecki (Warsaw University, Poland)
Vasco Vasconcelos (U. of Lisbon, Portugal)
Heike Wehrheim (U. of Paderborn, Germany)
Elena Zucca (U. of Genova, Italy)

Organizing Committee

Claudio Guidi
Ivan Lanese
Roberto Lucchi
Luca Padovani
Elisa Turrini
Stefano Zacchiroli

Referees

Davide Ancona
Michele Banci
Laura Bocchi
Edoardo Bonta
Mario Bravetti
Manuel Breschi
Barbara Catania
Walter Cazzola
Antonio Cerone
Giorgio Delzanno
Piergiorgio Di Giacomo
Luca Durante
Karsten Ehrig
Harald Fecher
Maurizio Gabbrielli
Geri Georg
Hans Grönniger
Andreas Gruener
Christian Haack
Jan Hendrik Hausmann
Marcel Kyas
Giovanni Lagorio

Grzegorz Marczyński
Francisco Martins
Viviana Mascardi
Peter Iveczky
Wiesław Pawłowski
Holger Rasch
Antonio Ravara
Dirk Reiß
Paolo Rosso
Murat Sahingöz
Luigi Sassoli
Martin Schindler
Gerardo Schneider
Aleksy Schubert
Graeme Smith
Mark Stein
Gabriele Taentzer
Simone Tini
Hugo Vieira
Steven Voelkel
Gianluigi Zavattaro
Artur Zawłocki

Table of Contents

Part I

Invited Speakers

Security Issues in Service Composition

Massimo Bartoletti, Pierpaolo Degano, and Gian Luigi Ferrari

Dipartimento di Informatica, Università di Pisa, Italy
{bartolet, degano, giangi}@di.unipi.it

Abstract. We use a distributed, enriched λ-calculus for describing networks of services. Both services and their clients can protect themselves, by imposing security constraints on each other's behaviour. Then, service interaction results in a call-by-property mechanism, that matches the client requests with service's. A static approach is also described, that determines how to compose services while guaranteeing that their execution is always secure, without resorting to any dynamic check.

1 Introduction

Service-oriented computing (SOC) is an emerging paradigm to design distributed applications [31, 30, 19]. In this paradigm, applications are built by assembling together independent computational units, called *services*. A service is a stand-alone component distributed over a network, and made available through standard interaction mechanisms. An important aspect is that services are *open*, in that they are built with little or no knowledge about their operating environment, their clients, and further services therein invoked. Composition of services may require peculiar mechanisms to handle complex interaction patterns (e.g. to implement transactions), while enforcing non-functional requirements on the system behaviour (e.g. security and service level agreement). Web Services [3, 34, 38] built upon XML technologies are possibly the most illustrative and well developed example of the SOC paradigm. Indeed, a variety of XML-based technologies already exists for describing, discovering and invoking web services [18, 14, 5, 39]. There are also several standards for defining and enforcing non-functional requirements of services, e.g. WS-Security [6], WS-Trust [4] and WS-Policy [15] among the others.

1.1 Security and Service Composition

The *orchestration* of services consists of their composition and coordination. Languages for that have been recently proposed, e.g. BPEL4WS [5, 25]. Service composition heavily depends on which information about a service is made public, on how to choose those services that match the user's requirements, and on their actual run-time behaviour. Security makes service composition even harder. Services may be offered by different providers, which only partially trust each other. On the one hand, providers have to guarantee the delivered service to respect a given security policy, in any interaction with the operational

R. Gorrieri and H. Wehrheim (Eds.): FMOODS 2006, LNCS 4037, pp. 1–16, 2006.

environment, and regardless of who actually called the service. On the other hand, clients may want to protect their sensible data from the services invoked.

A typical approach consists in endowing the network infrastructure with authentication mechanisms, so to certify the identity of services. However, security may be breached even by trusted services, either because of unintentional behaviour (e.g. bugs), or because the composition of the client and the services exhibits some behaviour unwanted by the client (e.g. leakage of information).

We have addressed the problem of security in a linguistic framework. In our approach, clients may protect from their callers by wrapping security-critical portions of their own code into *safety framings*. These framings enforce the given security policy on the execution of the wrapped piece of code, aborting it whenever about to violate the policy, thus offering additional flexibility with respect to monolithic *global* policies, and relieving the programmer of guarding each use of security-critical resources.

On their side, callers may constrain the behaviour of the called services, by supplying a security policy at the moment of invocation. We push further this invocation mechanism, by allowing callers to request services that not only do obey the imposed security constraints, but that also respect a given contract on their functional behaviour. The implementation of this so-called *call-by-property* invocation mechanism requires that services are published together with a *certified* abstraction of their behaviour.

1.2   The Planning Problem

Call-by-property invocation and safety framings make service composition secure. A *plan* orchestrates the execution of a service-based application, by associating the sequence of run-time service requests with a corresponding sequence of selected services. A major problem is still left open: how to construct a plan that guarantees no executions will abort because of some action attempting to violate security.

Determining such a viable plan amounts to selecting from the network those services that accomplish the requested task, while respecting the security constraints on demand. Those services that locally obey the property imposed by a request are not always good candidates, because their behaviour may affect security of the whole composition. For example, consider a device with a limited computational power. Suppose it downloads an applet from the network, and then delegates a remote service to run it. Although the contract between the device and the code provider is fulfilled, the applet may violate a security policy imposed by the executer. To determine the viable plans, one has to check the effects of all the available applets against the security policies of all the remote executers.

As a matter of fact, there might be several different kinds of plans, each with a different expressive power. Among them, one may consider plans that attach a selection of services to each program point representing a service request. The expressive power varies according to the nature of the information associated with each request. *Simple plans* associate a single service with each request, *multi-choice plans* map requests into sets of services, and *dependent plans* also convey the dependence of a service selection with the choices made in the past (a sort of continuation-passing plan). These kinds of plans have been studied in [9]. *Dependent multi-choice* plans are a mix of the last two kinds. Further expressive power is gained when relaxing the assumption of associating service selections to the program points where requests are made. *Regular plans* drive the execution of a program, by providing it with the possible patterns of service selections, in the form of a regular expression. *Dynamic plans* can be updated at run-time, according to the evaluation of some conditions on the program execution (e.g. boolean guards in conditionals, number of iterations in a loop, etc.).

1.3   A Static Approach to Secure Service Composition

We have proposed a solution to the planning problem, within a distributed framework [10]. Services are functional units in an enriched λ-calculus, they are explicitly located at network sites, and they have a published public interface. Unlike standard syntactic signatures, this interface includes an abstraction of the service behaviour, in the form of annotated types. To obtain a service with a specific behaviour, a client queries the network for a published interface matching the requirements. Security is implemented by wrapping the critical blocks of code inside safety framings (with local scopes, possibly nested), that enforce the relevant policies during the execution of the block. In the spirit of history-based security [1], a security policy can inspect the whole execution history at a given site. Since our framework is fully distributed, our policies cannot span over multiple sites.

We have introduced a type and effect system for our calculus [21, 28, 35]. The type of a service describes its functional behaviour, while the effect is a *history expression*, representing those histories of events relevant to security. History expressions extend regular expressions with information about the selection of services, coupled with their corresponding effect.

We have then devised a way of extracting from a history expression all the *viable* plans, i.e. those that successfully drive secure executions. This is a two-stage construction. A first transformation of history expressions makes them model-checkable for validity [7]. Valid history expressions guarantee that the services they come from never go wrong at run-time. From valid histories it is then immediate to obtain the viable plans, that make any execution monitor unneeded.

1.4   Trusted Orchestration

Our planning technique acts as a *trusted orchestrator* of services. It provides a client with the plans guaranteeing that the invoked services always respect the required properties. Thus, in our framework the only trusted entity is the orchestrator, and neither clients nor services need to be such. In particular, the orchestrator infers functional and behavioural types of each service. Also, it is responsible for certifying the service code, for publishing its interface, and for guaranteeing that services will not arbitrarily change their code on the fly: when this happens, services need to be certified again.

When an application is injected in the network, the orchestrator provides it with a viable plan (if any), constructed by composing and analysing the certified interfaces of the available services. The trustworthiness of the orchestrator relies upon formal grounds. We proved the soundness of our type and effect system, and the correctness of the static analysis and model-checking technique that infers viable plans.

The orchestrator constructs the plans for a client, by considering the view of the network at the moment the application is injected. To be more dynamic, one would like to manage the discovering of new services, as well as the case when existing ones are no longer available.

Both these problems require a special treatment. Multi-choice plans are a first solution to deal with disappearing services, because they offer many choices for the same request. Publication of new services poses instead a major problem. To cope with that, one has to reconfigure plans at run-time, by exploiting the new interfaces. However, incrementally checking viability of plans is an open problem. A possible solution is to enrich history expressions with *hooks* where new services can be attached. The orchestrator then needs to check the validity of the newly discovered plans, hopefully in an incremental manner.

1.5   Related Work

The secure composition of components underlies the design of Sewell and Vitek's box-π [33], an extension of the π-calculus that allows for expressing safety policies in the form of *security wrappers*. These are programs that encapsulate a component to control the interactions with other (possibly untrusted) components. A type system that statically captures the allowed causal information flows between components. Our safety framings are closely related to wrappers.

Gorla, Hennessy and Sassone [23] consider a calculus for agents which may migrate between sites in a controlled manner. Each site has a *membrane*, representing both a security policy and a classification of the levels of trust of external sites. A membrane guards the incoming agents before allowing them to execute.

Recently, increasing attention has been devoted to express service contracts as behavioural (or session) types. These synthetise the essential aspects of the interaction behaviour of services, while allowing efficient static verification of properties of composed systems. Session types [24] have been exploited to formalize compatibility of components [37] and to describe adaptation of web services [16]. Security issues have been recently considered in terms of session types, e.g. in [13], which proves the decidability of type-checking in an extension of the π-calculus with session types and correspondence assertions [40].

Other works have proposed type-based methodologies to check security properties of distributed systems. For instance, Gordon and Jeffrey [22] use a type and effect system to prove authenticity properties of security protocols. Web service authentication has been recently modelled and analysed in [11, 12] through a process calculus enriched with cryptographic primitives.

The problem of discovering and composing Web Services by taking advantage of semantic information has been the subject of a considerable amount of research and development, [2, 17, 27, 29, 32, 36] to cite a few. The idea is to extend the primitives of service description languages with basic constructs for specifying properties of the published interface. We can distinguish between semantic-web descriptions [2, 29, 32, 36] in which service interfaces are annotated with parameter ontologies, and behavioural description [17, 27] in which the annotation details the ordering of service actions. A different solution to planning service composition has been proposed in [26], where the problem of composing services in order to achieve a given goal is expressed as a constraint satisfaction problem. Our approach extends and complements those based on behavioral descriptions, with an eye to security. Indeed, our methodology fully automates the process of discovering services and planning their composition in a secure way.

2   Planning Secure Service Compositions

To illustrate our approach, consider the scenario in the figure below. The boxes model services, distributed over a network. Each box encloses the service code, and is decorated with the location ℓ_i where the service is published.

Assume that the client at site ℓ_0 is a device with limited computational capabilities, wanting to execute some code downloaded from the network. To do that, the client issues two requests in sequence. The request labelled r_1 asks for a piece of mobile code (e.g. an applet), and it can be served by two code providers at ℓ_1 and ℓ_2. The request type $\tau \rightarrow (\tau \rightarrow \tau)$ means that, upon receiving a value of type τ (which can be an arbitrary base type, immaterial here) the invoked service replies with a function from τ to τ, with no security constraints.

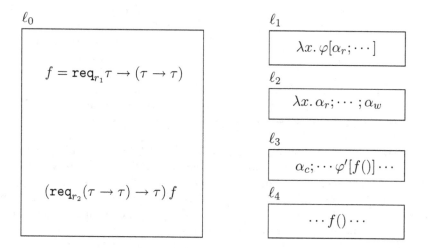

Fig. 1. One client (ℓ_0), two code providers (ℓ_1, ℓ_2), and two code executers (ℓ_3, ℓ_4)

The service at ℓ_1 returns a function that protects itself with a policy φ, permitting its use in certified sites only (modelled by the event α_c). Within the function body, the only security-relevant operation is a read α_r on the file system where the delivered code is run. The code provided by ℓ_2 first reads (α_r) some local data, and eventually writes them (α_w) back to ℓ_2.

Since ℓ_0 has a limited computational power, the code f obtained by the request r_1 is passed as a parameter to the service invoked by the request r_2. This request can be served by ℓ_3 and ℓ_4. The service at ℓ_3 is certified (α_c), and runs the provided code f under a "Chinese Wall" security policy φ', requiring that no data can be written (α_w) after reading them (α_r). The service at ℓ_4 is not certified, and it simply runs f.

2.1 Programming Model

Clients and services are modelled as expressions in a λ-calculus enriched with primitives for security and service requests. Security-relevant operations are rendered as side-effects in the calculus, and they are called *access events* (e.g. $\alpha_c, \alpha_r, \alpha_w$). A *security policy* is a regular property over a sequence η of access events, namely a *history*. A piece of code e framed within a policy φ (written $\varphi[e]$) must respect φ at each step of its execution. A *service request* has the form $\mathtt{req}_r\rho$. The label r uniquely identifies the request, while the *request type* ρ is the query pattern to be matched by the invoked service. For instance, the request type $\tau \xrightarrow{\varphi[\bullet]} \tau'$ matches services with functional type $\tau \to \tau'$, and whose behaviour respects the policy φ. The abstract syntax of services follows.

Syntax of Services

e, e'	$::=$	x	variable
		α	access event
		$\mathtt{if}\ b\ \mathtt{then}\ e\ \mathtt{else}\ e$	conditional
		$\lambda_z x.\, e$	named abstraction
		$e\, e'$	application
		$\varphi[e]$	safety framing
		$\mathtt{req}_r\rho$	service request
		$\mathtt{wait}\ \ell$	wait reply

The stand-alone evaluation of a service is much alike the call-by-value semantics of the λ-calculus; additionally, it enforces all the policies within their framings. More precisely, assume that, starting from the current history η, an expression e may evolve to e' and extend the history to η'. Then, a framing $\varphi[e]$ may evolve to $\varphi[e']$ if η' satisfies φ — otherwise the evaluation gets stuck. Eventually, values leave the scope of framings.

When a service is plugged into a network, a plan is used to resolve the requests therein, acting as an orchestrator. For brevity, we consider here only the case of *simple* plans, that have the following syntax:

Syntax of Simple Plans

$$\pi, \pi' \quad ::= \quad 0 \quad | \quad r[\ell] \quad | \quad \pi \mid \pi'$$

The empty plan 0 has no choices. The plan $r[\ell]$ associates the service e published at site ℓ with the request labelled r. The composition operator $|$ is associative, commutative and idempotent, with identity 0. We require plans to have a single choice for each request, i.e. $r[\ell] \mid r[\ell']$ implies $\ell = \ell'$.

A service e is plugged into a network by publishing it at a site ℓ, together with its interface τ. Hereafter, $\ell\langle e : \tau \rangle$ denotes such a *published service*. We assume that each site publishes a single service, and that interfaces are certified, e.g. they are inferred by the type system in [10]. Also, we assume that services cannot invoke each other circularly, because this would make little sense. A *network* is a set of clients and published services.

The state of a published service $\ell\langle e : \tau \rangle$ is denoted by $\ell\langle e : \tau \rangle : \eta, e'$ — abbreviated as $\ell : \eta, e'$ when unambiguous. The component η is the history generated so far at site ℓ, and e' models the code in execution. We assume here that services are *stateless*, i.e. the history of a service is cleared at each instantiation. A network configuration has the form $\ell_1 : \eta_1, e'_1 \parallel \cdots \parallel \ell_k : \eta_k, e'_k$.

A request r, resolved by the current plan with the service ℓ', can be served if the service ℓ' is available (written $\ell' : \star$). In this case, a new instance of the service is generated: the service code (a function) is applied to the received argument. The invoker waits until ℓ' has produced a value. When this happens, the value is returned to the invoker, and the service becomes available again.

Back to our example, consider the plan $\pi = r_1[\ell_2] \mid r_2[\ell_3]$. Then, π drives the following computation (for brevity, we omit the types in requests):

$$\ell_0 : \varepsilon, (\lambda f.\, \mathsf{req}_{r_2} f)\, \mathsf{req}_{r_1} \parallel \ell_1 : \star \parallel \ell_2 : \star \parallel \ell_3 : \star \parallel \ell_4 : \star$$

$$\rightarrow_\pi \ell_0 : \varepsilon, (\lambda f.\, \mathsf{req}_{r_2} f)\, \mathsf{wait}\, \ell_2 \parallel \ell_1 : \star \parallel \ell_2 : \varepsilon, \lambda x.\, \alpha_r; \cdots ; \alpha_w \parallel \ell_3 : \star \parallel \ell_4 : \star$$

$$\rightarrow_\pi \ell_0 : \varepsilon, (\lambda f.\, \mathsf{req}_{r_2} f)\, (\lambda x.\, \alpha_r; \cdots ; \alpha_w) \parallel \ell_1 : \star \parallel \ell_2 : \star \parallel \ell_3 : \star \parallel \ell_4 : \star$$

$$\rightarrow_\pi \ell_0 : \varepsilon, \mathsf{req}_{r_2}(\lambda x.\, \alpha_r; \cdots ; \alpha_w) \parallel \ell_1 : \star \parallel \ell_2 : \star \parallel \ell_3 : \star \parallel \ell_4 : \star$$

$$\rightarrow_\pi \ell_0 : \varepsilon, \mathsf{wait}\, \ell_3 \parallel \ell_1 : \star \parallel \ell_2 : \star \parallel \ell_3 : \varepsilon, \alpha_c; \cdots ; \varphi'[(\lambda x.\, \alpha_r; \cdots ; \alpha_w)()] \parallel \ell_4 : \star$$

$$\rightarrow_\pi \ell_0 : \varepsilon, \mathsf{wait}\, \ell_3 \parallel \ell_1 : \star \parallel \ell_2 : \star \parallel \ell_3 : \alpha_c, \varphi'[(\lambda x.\, \alpha_r; \cdots ; \alpha_w)()] \parallel \ell_4 : \star$$

$$\rightarrow_\pi \ell_0 : \varepsilon, \mathsf{wait}\, \ell_3 \parallel \ell_1 : \star \parallel \ell_2 : \star \parallel \ell_3 : \alpha_c, \varphi'[\alpha_r; \cdots ; \alpha_w] \parallel \ell_4 : \star$$

$$\rightarrow_\pi \ell_0 : \varepsilon, \mathsf{wait}\, \ell_3 \parallel \ell_1 : \star \parallel \ell_2 : \star \parallel \ell_3 : \alpha_c \alpha_r, \varphi'[\alpha_w] \parallel \ell_4 : \star$$

The computation at site ℓ_3 is now aborted, because the history $\alpha_c \alpha_r \alpha_w$ would otherwise violate the Chinese-Wall policy φ'. We have then discovered that the plan $r_1[\ell_2] \mid r_2[\ell_3]$ is *not* viable. As we will see in a while, our static machinery infers that also the plan $r_1[\ell_1] \mid r_2[\ell_4]$ is not viable (it violates the policy φ). There are two further plans to consider: $r_1[\ell_1] \mid r_2[\ell_3]$ and $r_1[\ell_2] \mid r_2[\ell_4]$. These plans will be shown viable by our static analysis, and they will drive secure executions that never abort.

2.2   Types and Effects

We stipulated that the services published in the network have certified interfaces. To do that, in [10] we have defined a type and effect system, that will also be used to infer an over-approximation of client behaviour.

Types τ, τ' are either base types, or they have the form $\tau \xrightarrow{H} \tau'$. The annotation H over the arrow is a *history expression*. It describes the latent effect associated with the function: one of the histories represented by H is generated when a value is applied to a function with that type. History expressions have the following abstract syntax:

Syntax of History Expressions

$$
\begin{array}{lll}
H, H' & ::= & \varepsilon & \text{empty} \\
 & & h & \text{variable} \\
 & & \alpha & \text{access event} \\
 & & H \cdot H' & \text{sequence} \\
 & & H + H' & \text{choice} \\
 & & \varphi[H] & \text{safety framing} \\
 & & \mu h.H & \text{recursion} \\
 & & \ell : H & \text{localization} \\
 & & \{\pi_i \rhd H_i\}_{i \in I} & \text{planned selection}
\end{array}
$$

Access events represent the program actions where sensible resources are accessed; the constructors $\cdot$ and $+$ correspond to sequentialization of code and conditionals, respectively; safety framings model blocks of code subject to security policies; recursion is for loops and recursive functions. The construct $\ell : H$ localizes the behaviour H to the site ℓ. E.g., $\ell : \alpha \cdot (\ell' : \alpha') \cdot \beta$ denotes two histories: $\alpha\beta$ occurring at location ℓ, and α' occurring at ℓ'. A planned selection abstracts the behaviour of service requests. E.g., $\{r[\ell_1] \rhd H_1 \cdots r[\ell_k] \rhd H_k\}$ says that a request r can be resolved into one of the services provided by the sites $\ell_1, \ldots, \ell_k$, which may generate a history represented by $H_1, \ldots, H_k$, respectively.

A typing judgment $\Gamma, H \vdash_\ell e : \tau$ means that the service e at site ℓ evaluates to a value of type τ, and produces a history denoted by the effect H. Typing judgments are similar to those of the simply-typed λ-calculus. To give the flavour of how the effects are inferred, consider first the rule to type applications:

$$
\frac{\Gamma, H \vdash_\ell e : \tau \xrightarrow{H''} \tau' \quad \Gamma, H' \vdash_\ell e' : \tau}{\Gamma, H \cdot H' \cdot H'' \vdash_\ell e\, e' : \tau'}
$$

The rule says that e is an expression whose evaluation will generate a history in H. It will reduce to a value which is a function (from τ to τ') with latent effect H''. The evaluation of the argument e' with type τ will generate a history in H'. The overall effect of e applied to e' is $H \cdot H' \cdot H''$, thus respecting the evaluation order of the call-by-value semantics (function, argument, latent effect).

To give a type to service requests, some auxiliary technical notation is needed: the interested reader can find all the definitions in [7]. Just to give the intuition, the typing judgement for a request $\mathbf{req}_r\rho$ has the following schema:

$$\frac{\tau = \uplus\{\,\rho \boxplus_{r[\ell']} \tau' \mid \emptyset, \varepsilon \vdash_{\ell'} e : \tau' \quad \ell \prec \ell' \langle e : \tau' \rangle \quad \rho \approx \tau'\,\}}{\Gamma, \varepsilon \vdash_\ell \mathbf{req}_r\rho : \tau}$$

Requests have an empty actual effect, and a functional type τ. The latent effect is a planned selection that picks from the network those services known by ℓ and matching the request type ρ. The relation $\rho \approx \tau$ models ρ being compatible with τ; the partial order $\prec$ represents visibility among services (e.g. $\ell \prec \ell'$ when ℓ' is visible by ℓ). The operator $\boxplus$ combines the request type with a service interface; the operator $\uplus$ suitably assembles such combinations into a planned selection.

Back to our running example, the types inferred for the services are shown in the figure below (they are displayed as decorations of the boxes). The public interface of the client is the base type *unit*, meaning that it cannot be invoked by other services. The interfaces of the services are as expected; for instance, the type of ℓ_3 is a function that, when applied to a function with latent effect h, will produce a value of type τ, and a history denoted by $\alpha_c \cdot \varphi'[h]$.

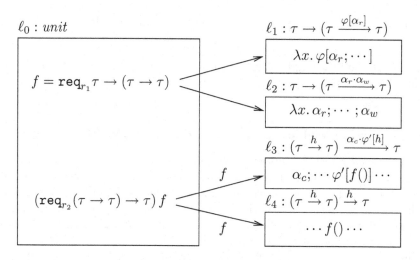

Fig. 2. One client, four services, and their (certified) published interfaces

To obtain an over-approximation to the behaviour of the network upon the injection of a client, our type and effect system suitably combines the abstract behaviour of the client with the certified interfaces of the services it can invoke.

The inferred history expression approximates the run-time behaviour of *each* site in the network. For our running example, the abstract behaviour of the whole network is rendered by the following history expression H:

$$\{r_2[\ell_3] \rhd \ell_3 : \alpha_c \cdot \varphi'[\{r_1[\ell_1] \rhd \varphi[\alpha_r], r_1[\ell_2] \rhd \alpha_r \cdot \alpha_w\}]$$
$$r_2[\ell_4] \rhd \ell_4 : \{r_1[\ell_1] \rhd \varphi[\alpha_r], r_1[\ell_2] \rhd \alpha_r \cdot \alpha_w\}\}$$

The intuitive meaning of H is that, under the plan $r_2[\ell_3]$ — i.e. if r_2 is served by ℓ_3 — the event α_c is generated at site ℓ_3, followed by a safety framing φ'. This framing wraps $\varphi[\alpha_r]$ if ℓ_1 is chosen for r_1, or $\alpha_r \alpha_w$ if ℓ_2 is chosen instead. Otherwise, if r_2 is served by ℓ_4, then the behaviour (on site ℓ_4) depends on the former choice for r_1: if ℓ_1 was selected, then $\varphi[\alpha_r]$, otherwise $\alpha_r \alpha_w$. Note also that no event is generated by the client at site ℓ_0.

Say that a computation *goes wrong at* ℓ when it reaches a configuration whose state at ℓ is stuck. For example, a configuration $\eta, \varphi[e]$ is stuck if a step of e would violate φ. Say a plan π *viable* for e at ℓ when the evolution of e within a network, under plan π, does not go wrong at ℓ. Then, we say that a history expression H is π-*valid* when the plan π is viable for all the histories produced by H under π.

For example, consider the history expression $H_1 = \alpha_c \cdot \varphi'[\alpha_r \cdot \alpha_w]$, where φ' requires that no write α_w occurs after a read α_r. Then, H_1 is *not* 0-valid. Indeed, under the empty plan 0, the event α_w occurs within a safety framing enforcing φ', and the history $\alpha_c \alpha_r \alpha_w$ does not obey φ'.

We have proved two fundamental results about our type and effect system. First, it correctly over-approximates the actual run-time histories. Second, it enjoys the following type safety property.

Theorem 1. *Let $\{\ell_i\langle e_i : \tau_i\rangle\}_{i \in I}$ be a network, and let $\emptyset, H_i \vdash e_i : \tau_i$ for all $i \in I$. If H_i is π_i-valid, then π_i is viable for e_i at ℓ_i.*

Therefore, to find the viable plans for a client, one has to infer the effect H of the client injected in the network, and then find the plans π_i that make H π_i-valid. The following sections show how to do that.

2.3   Extracting Viable Plans I: Linearizing History Expressions

Once extracted a history expression H from a client e, we analyse H to find if there is any viable plan for the execution of e. This issue is not trivial, because the effect of selecting a given service for a request is not confined to the execution of that service. Since each service selection affects the *whole* execution of a network, we cannot simply devise a viable plan by selecting services that satisfy the constraints imposed by the requests, only.

This is actually shown by our running example. Consider again the aborting computation with plan $r_1[\ell_2] \mid r_2[\ell_3]$, here slightly abridged:

$$\ell_0 : \varepsilon, (\lambda f. \mathtt{req}_{r_2} f) \, \mathtt{req}_{r_1} \parallel \ell_2 : \star \parallel \ell_3 : \star$$
$$\rightarrow_\pi \ell_0 : \varepsilon, (\lambda f. \mathtt{req}_{r_2} f) \, \mathtt{wait} \, \ell_2 \parallel \ell_2 : \varepsilon, \lambda x. \, \alpha_r; \cdots ; \alpha_w \parallel \ell_3 : \star$$
$$\rightarrow_\pi^* \ell_0 : \varepsilon, \mathtt{req}_{r_2} (\lambda x. \, \alpha_r; \cdots ; \alpha_w) \parallel \ell_2 : \star \parallel \ell_3 : \star$$
$$\rightarrow_\pi \ell_0 : \varepsilon, \mathtt{wait} \, \ell_3 \parallel \ell_2 : \star \parallel \ell_3 : \varepsilon, \alpha_c; \cdots ; \varphi'[(\lambda x. \, \alpha_r; \cdots ; \alpha_w)()]$$
$$\rightarrow_\pi^* \ell_0 : \varepsilon, \mathtt{wait} \, \ell_3 \parallel \ell_2 : \star \parallel \ell_3 : \alpha_c \alpha_r, \varphi'[\alpha_w]$$

The choice of the service ℓ_2 for the request r_1 results in downloading an applet from site ℓ_2. This seems correct, until the plan chooses the service ℓ_3 to execute the applet. The computation aborts because the applet provided by ℓ_2 attempts to violate the policy φ', that becomes active after the service ℓ_2 has returned.

As a matter of fact, the tree-shaped structure of planned selections makes it difficult to determine the plans under which a history expression is valid. To cope with this problem, we have devised a static analysis that "linearizes" such a tree structure into a set of history expressions, forming an equivalent planned selection $\{\pi_1 \rhd H_1 \cdots \pi_k \rhd H_k\}$, where no H_i has further planned selections.

In our running example, we find that H is equivalent to the following H':

$$\begin{aligned}
H' = \{ &r_1[\ell_1] \mid r_2[\ell_3] \rhd \ell_3 : \alpha_c \cdot \varphi'[\varphi[\alpha_r]], \\
&r_1[\ell_2] \mid r_2[\ell_4] \rhd \ell_4 : \alpha_r \cdot \alpha_w, \\
&r_1[\ell_1] \mid r_2[\ell_4] \rhd \ell_4 : \varphi[\alpha_r], \\
&r_1[\ell_2] \mid r_2[\ell_3] \rhd \ell_3 : \alpha_c \cdot \varphi'[\alpha_r \cdot \alpha_w] \}
\end{aligned}$$

Every element of H' clearly separates the plan from the associated abstract behaviour. This piece of behaviour has no further plans within, and so it is easier to model-check its validity.

For instance, under the plan $r_1[\ell_1] \mid r_2[\ell_3]$, the overall abstract behaviour is $\alpha_c \cdot \varphi'[\varphi[\alpha_r]]$ at site ℓ_3. As already seen, the first two plans in H' are viable, while the others give rise to non-valid behaviour. The plan $r_1[\ell_2] \mid r_2[\ell_4]$ is *not* viable, because the policy φ would be violated when the obtained code f is run on a non certified site; instead, the plan $r_1[\ell_2] \mid r_2[\ell_3]$ would violate φ'.

Given a history expression H, we obtain its linearization as follows. First, we define an equational theory of history expressions: an equation $H \equiv H'$ means that H and H' represent the same histories, under all plans. Roughly, our equations say that each history expression $\mathcal{C}(H)$ is equivalent to some planned selection H'. For instance, when $\mathcal{C}(H) = \varphi[H]$, we have that:

$$\varphi[\{\pi_1 \rhd H_1 \cdots \pi_k \rhd H_k\} \equiv \{\pi_1 \rhd \varphi[H_1] \cdots \pi_k \rhd \varphi[H_k]\}$$

If $\mathcal{C}(H)$ is already a planned selection, then either it is linear, or it has one level of nesting more than H'. For instance, if $\mathcal{C}(H) = \{\pi_0 \rhd H\}$, then:

$$\{\pi_0 \rhd \{\pi_1 \rhd H_1 \cdots \pi_k \rhd H_k\}\} \equiv \{\pi_0 \mid \pi_1 \rhd H_1 \cdots \pi_0 \mid \pi_k \rhd H_k\}$$

When oriented from left to right, these equations give rise to a rewriting system that is easily proved finitely terminating and confluent – up to the equational laws (commutativity, associativity, idempotence, and zero) of the algebra of plans. The resulting planned selection is linear.

For instance, the linearization of the history expression H inferred for our client is constructed as follows:

$$\{r_2[\ell_3] \rhd \ell_3 : \alpha_c \cdot \varphi'[\{r_1[\ell_1] \rhd \varphi[\alpha_r], r_1[\ell_2] \rhd \alpha_r \cdot \alpha_w\}]$$
$$r_2[\ell_4] \rhd \ell_4 : \{r_1[\ell_1] \rhd \varphi[\alpha_r], r_1[\ell_2] \rhd \alpha_r \cdot \alpha_w\}\}$$
$$\equiv \{r_2[\ell_3] \rhd \ell_3 : \alpha_c \cdot \{r_1[\ell_1] \rhd \varphi'[\varphi[\alpha_r]], r_1[\ell_2] \rhd \varphi'[\alpha_r \cdot \alpha_w]\}]$$
$$r_2[\ell_4] \rhd \{r_1[\ell_1] \rhd \ell_4 : \varphi[\alpha_r], r_1[\ell_2] \rhd \ell_4 : \alpha_r \cdot \alpha_w\}\}$$
$$\equiv \{r_2[\ell_3] \rhd \{r_1[\ell_1] \rhd \ell_3 : \alpha_c \cdot \varphi'[\varphi[\alpha_r]], r_1[\ell_2] \rhd \ell_3 : \alpha_c \cdot \varphi'[\alpha_r \cdot \alpha_w]\}]$$
$$r_2[\ell_4] \rhd \{r_1[\ell_1] \rhd \ell_4 : \varphi[\alpha_r], r_1[\ell_2] \rhd \ell_4 : \alpha_r \cdot \alpha_w\}\}$$
$$\equiv \{r_1[\ell_1] \mid r_2[\ell_3] \rhd \ell_3 : \alpha_c \cdot \varphi'[\varphi[\alpha_r]], \; r_1[\ell_2] \mid r_2[\ell_4] \rhd \ell_4 : \alpha_r \cdot \alpha_w,$$
$$r_1[\ell_1] \mid r_2[\ell_4] \rhd \ell_4 : \varphi[\alpha_r], \; r_1[\ell_2] \mid r_2[\ell_3] \rhd \ell_3 : \alpha_c \cdot \varphi'[\alpha_r \cdot \alpha_w]\}$$

The technical role of linearization is unveiled by the following theorem, that will enable us to detect the viable plans for service composition.

Theorem 2. *If $H = \{\pi_1 \rhd H_1 \cdots \pi_k \rhd H_k\}$ is linear, and H_i is 0-valid for some $i \in 1..k$, then H is π_i-valid.*

Summing up, we extract from an client e a history expression H, we linearize it into $\{\pi_1 \rhd H_1 \cdots \pi_k \rhd H_k\}$, and if some H_i is valid, then we can deduce that H is π_i-valid. By Theorem 1, the plan π_i safely drives the execution of e, without resorting to any run-time monitor.

2.4   Extracting Viable Plans II: Verifying Validity

To verify the validity of history expressions that have no planned selections, it suffices to apply the verification technique of [7], briefly described below. Our technique consists in smoothly transforming history expressions in procesess of Basic Process Algebras (BPAs), and in model checking them with Finite State Automata (FSA). The standard decision procedure for verifying that a BPA process p satisfies a (ω-regular) property φ amounts to constructing the pushdown automaton for p and the Büchi automaton for the negation of φ. Then, the property holds if the (context-free) language accepted by the conjunction of the above, which is still a pushdown automaton, is empty. This problem is decidable, and several algorithms and tools show this approach feasible [20]. Since our execution histories are always finite and our properties are regular, it turns out that we can simplify this procedure by using FSA, instead of Büchi automata.

However, our notion of validity is *non-regular*, because of the arbitrary nesting of framings. As an example, language denoted by $H = \mu h. \alpha + h \cdot h + \varphi[h]$ is context-free and non-regular, because it contains unbounded nesting of framings (technically, it is equivalent to the language of balanced parentheses). Since context-free languages are not closed under intersection, the emptiness problem is undecidable. To apply the procedure sketched above, we then manipulate history expressions in order to make validity a regular property.

The intuition is that non-regularity is a consequence of *redundant framings*, i.e. vacuous nesting of the same framing. For example, the history $\eta = \alpha\varphi[\alpha'\varphi'[\varphi[\alpha'']]]$ has an inner redundant safety framing φ around α''. Since α'' is already under the scope of the outermost φ-framing, it happens that η is valid if and only if $\alpha\varphi[\alpha'\varphi'[\alpha'']]$ is valid.

In [8], we have defined a validity-preserving transformation that, given a history expression H, yields a $H\!\downarrow$ that does not generate redundant safety framings. Also, for each policy φ, we have defined a formula $\varphi_{[]}$ to be used in verifying the validity (w.r.t. φ) of histories with no redundant framings.

For instance, consider again φ' saying that no event α_w can occur after α_r. The finite state automata enforcing φ and $\varphi_{[]}$ are shown below, where the special events $[_\varphi$ and $]_\varphi$ denote the opening and closing of the scope of φ, respectively. It is immediate to check that the history $[_\varphi\alpha_r]_\varphi\alpha_w$ is accepted by $A_{\varphi_{[]}}$, while $\alpha_c[_\varphi\alpha_r\alpha_w]_\varphi$ is not.

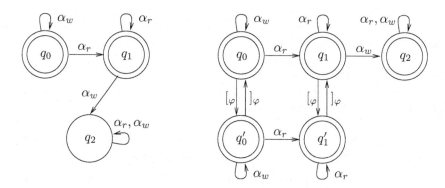

Validity of history expression H with no planned selections can be decided by showing that the BPA generated by the regularization of H (written $BPA(H\!\downarrow)$) satisfies a suitably constructed regular formula.

Together with Theorem 1, this dispenses us from using an execution monitor to enforce the security policies on demand.

Theorem 3. *A history expression H with no planned selections is 0-valid iff:*

$$[\![BPA(H\!\downarrow)]\!] \models \bigwedge_{\varphi\in H}\varphi_{[]}$$

Back to our running example, we have that:

$$\alpha_c[_{\varphi'}[_\varphi\alpha_r]_\varphi]_{\varphi'} \models \varphi_{[]}\wedge\varphi'_{[]} \implies r_1[\ell_1]\mid r_2[\ell_3]\quad\text{viable,}$$
$$\alpha_r\alpha_w \models tt \implies r_1[\ell_2]\mid r_2[\ell_4]\quad\text{viable,}$$
$$[_\varphi\alpha_r]_\varphi \not\models \varphi_{[]} \implies r_1[\ell_1]\mid r_2[\ell_4]\quad\text{not viable}$$
$$\alpha_c[_{\varphi'}\alpha_r\alpha_w]_{\varphi'} \not\models \varphi'_{[]} \implies r_1[\ell_2]\mid r_2[\ell_3]\quad\text{not viable}$$

2.5   Beyond Simple Plans

Recall that so far we have only considered *simple* plans that associate a single service with each request. Indeed, planning service composition can be more complex, as we will show in a while.

Assume first that the two requests r_1 and r_2 in the client are repeatedly performed in a loop. Then, suppose that a new service for r_2 is discovered at site ℓ_5, offering to run the code f without any constraints. Note that, if we stick to simple plans, then we must choose once and for all one among the viable plans, i.e. $r_1[\ell_1] \mid r_2[\ell_3]$, $r_1[\ell_2] \mid r_2[\ell_4]$, and $r_1[\ell_2] \mid r_2[\ell_5]$. Consequently, at each iteration of the loop the *same* service is taken for the request r_2. To be more flexible (i.e. in case the service chosen for r_2 becomes unavailable), we would like to accept as valid also the plan $r_1[\ell_2] \mid r_2[\ell_4, \ell_5]$, where r_2 can be served by either ℓ_4 or ℓ_5. This is just an example of *multi-choice* plans, where a request can be resolved by a set of services. In our running example, this has the advantage of permitting to select for r_2 between ℓ_4 and ℓ_5 at each iteration of the loop.

Consider now another slight extension of our example, where the client is billed for the services it has invoked. To do that, assume that an argument g is passed to the request r_1, to invoke a billing service through a request r_3, and so let the code provider invoice the customer ℓ_0 for the service. The same function g is also passed later on the service which will actually run the code f, to charge ℓ_0 for the cost of the execution.

A billing service acts as a function that takes as input an invoice (of some type τ', immaterial here) and delivers back a payment certification, i.e. a function of type $\tau' \xrightarrow{\alpha_{paid}} \tau'$ that generates α_{paid} to signal successful transaction. Let $\tau_b = \tau' \to (\tau' \xrightarrow{\alpha_{paid}} \tau')$ be the type of billing services. Then, the request types of r_1 and r_2 would have the following form:

$$\rho_1 = \tau \times \tau_b \xrightarrow{\psi} (\tau \to \tau) \qquad \rho_2 = (\tau \to \tau) \times \tau_b \xrightarrow{\psi} \tau$$

where the property ψ on demand requires that payment is accomplished before the control returns back to the client.

Assume now that two billing services ℓ_6 and ℓ_7 are discovered in the network. The service ℓ_6 can be used by certified users only, while ℓ_7 imposes no constraints. Clearly, the service which provides the code and the one which runs it can choose different billing services. However, neither simple nor multi-choice plans can render adequately this situation. The simple plan (yet ill-formed) that seems to solve the problem is $r_1[\ell_1] \mid r_2[\ell_3] \mid r_3[\ell_6] \mid r_3[\ell_7]$. However, this plan cannot express the linkage between the choice for r_3 within code providers, and that within code executers.

We therefore extend plans to keep track of dependencies among choices. The *dependent* plan $r_1[\ell_1.r_3[\ell_7]] \mid r_2[\ell_3.r_3[\ell_6]]$ is viable: the request r_3 is resolved with ℓ_7 within the service ℓ_1 chosen for r_1, while it is resolved with ℓ_6 within the service ℓ_3 chosen for r_2. In [9] we have shown how to extract viable plans from history expressions, also in the case of multi-choice and dependent plans.

3   Conclusions

A static approach has been proposed to study secure orchestration of services. We have surveyed a distributed calculus with an explicit notion of location and of located executions. Our calculus has primitives for enforcing local security policies, and for invoking services that respect given security requirements.

We have devised a way of statically constructing the plans that drive successful, secure executions. The actual histories that can occur at run-time are over-approximated by a type and effect system. These approximations are then model-checked to find the plans that guarantee secure executions, without the need of execution monitoring.

Acknowledgments

Research partially supported by the EU, within the FETPI Global Computing, Project IST-2005-16004 SENSORIA (Software Engineering for Service-Oriented Overlay Computers).

References

1. M. Abadi and C. Fournet. Access control based on execution history. In *Proc. 10th Annual Network and Distributed System Security Symposium*, 2003.
2. R. Akkiraju et al. *Web Service Semantics*. WSDL-S technical note (version 1.0), 2005.
3. G. Alonso, F. Casati, H. Kuno, and V. Machiraju. *Web Services: Concepts, Architectures and Applications*. Springer-Verlag, 2004.
4. S. Anderson et al. *Web Services Trust Language (WS-Trust)*, 2005.
5. T. Andrews et al. *Business Process Execution Language for Web Services (BPEL4WS), Version 1.1*, 2003.
6. B. Atkinson et al. *Web Services Security (WS-Security)*, 2002.
7. M. Bartoletti, P. Degano, and G. L. Ferrari. Enforcing secure service composition. In *Proc. 18th Computer Security Foundations Workshop (CSFW)*, 2005.
8. M. Bartoletti, P. Degano, and G. L. Ferrari. History based access control with local policies. In *Proc. Fossacs*, 2005.
9. M. Bartoletti, P. Degano, and G. L. Ferrari. Plans for service composition. In *Workshop on Issues in the Theory of Security (WITS)*, 2006.
10. M. Bartoletti, P. Degano, and G. L. Ferrari. Types and effects for secure service orchestration. In *To appear in Proc. 19th Computer Security Foundations Workshop (CSFW)*, 2006.
11. K. Bhargavan, R. Corin, C. Fournet, and A. D. Gordon. Secure sessions for web services. In *Proc. ACM Workshop on Secure Web Services*, 2004.
12. K. Bhargavan, C. Fournet, and A. D. Gordon. A semantics for web services authentication. In *Proc. ACM Symposium on Principles of Programming Languages*, 2004.
13. E. Bonelli, A. Compagnoni, and E. Gunter. Typechecking safe process synchronization. In *Proc. Foundations of Global Ubiquitous Computing*, 2004.
14. D. Box et al. *Simple Object Access Protocol (SOAP) 1.1*. WRC Note, 2000.
15. D. Box et al. *Web Services Policy Framework (WS-Policy)*, 2002.
16. A. Brogi, C. Canal, and E. Pimentel. Behavioural types and component adaptation. In *Proc. AMAST*, 2004.
17. A. Brogi and R. Popescu. Towards semi-automated workflow-based aggregation of web services. In *Proc. ICSOC*, 2005.

18. R. Chinnici, M. Gudgina, J. Moreau, and S. Weerawarana. *Web Service Description Language (WSDL), Version 1.2*, 2002.
19. F. Curbera, R. Khalaf, N. Mukhi, S. Tai, and S. Weerawarane. The next step in web services. *Communications of the ACM*, 46(10), 2003.
20. J. Esparza. On the decidability of model checking for several μ-calculi and Petri nets. In *Proc. 19th Int. Colloquium on Trees in Algebra and Programming*, 1994.
21. D. K. Gifford and J. M. Lucassen. Integrating functional and imperative programming. In *ACM Conference on LISP and Functional Programming*, 1986.
22. A. Gordon and A. Jeffrey. Types and effects for asymmetric cryptographic protocols. In *Proc. IEEE Computer Security Foundations Workshop*, 2002.
23. D. Gorla, M. Hennessy, and V. Sassone. Security policies as membranes in systems for global computing. In *Proc. FGUC*, 2004.
24. K. Honda, V. Vansconcelos, and M. Kubo. Language primitives and type discipline for structures communication-based programming. In *Proc. ESOP*, 1998.
25. R. Khalaf, N. Mukhi, and S. Weerawarana. Service oriented composition in BPEL4WS. In *Proc. WWW*, 2003.
26. A. Lazovik, M. Aiello, and R. Gennari. Encoding requests to web service compositions as constraints. In *Constraint Programming CP*, 2005.
27. S. B. Mokhtar, N. Georgantas, and V. Issarny. Ad hoc composition of user tasks in pervasive computing environment. In *Software Composition*, 2005.
28. F. Nielson and H. R. Nielson. Type and effect systems. In *Correct System Design*, 1999.
29. M. Paolucci, T. Kawamura, T. Payne, and K. Sycara. Semantic matchmaking of web services capabilities. In *First International Semantic Web Conference on The Semantic Web*, 2002.
30. M. P. Papazoglou. Service-oriented computing: Concepts, characteristics and directions. In *WISE*, 2003.
31. M. Papazouglou and D. Georgakopoulos. Special issue on service oriented computing. *Communications of the ACM*, 46(10), 2003.
32. P. Rajasekaran, J. A. Miller, K. Verma, and A. P. Sheth. Enhancing web services description and discovery to facilitate composition. In *Semantic Web Services and Web Process Composition*, 2005.
33. P. Sewell and J. Vitek. Secure composition of untrusted code: box-π, wrappers and causality types. *Journal of Computer Security*, 11(2), 2003.
34. M. Stal. Web services: Beyond component-based computing. *Communications of the ACM*, 55(10), 2002.
35. J.-P. Talpin and P. Jouvelot. The type and effect discipline. *Information and Computation*, 2(111), 1994.
36. P. Traverso and M. Pistore. Automated composition of semantic web services into executable processes. In *Proc. ISWC*, 2004.
37. A. Vallecillo, V. Vansconcelos, and A. Ravara. Typing the behaviours of objects and components using session types. In *Proc. of FOCLASA*, 2002.
38. W. Vogels. Web services are not distributed objects. *IEEE Internet Computing*, 7(6), 2003.
39. W3C. *UDDI Technical White Paper*, 2000.
40. T. Woo and S. Lam. A semantic model for authentication protocols. In *IEEE Symposium on Security and Privacy*, 1993.

Separating Distribution from Coordination and Computation as Architectural Dimensions

José Luiz Fiadeiro

Department of Computer Science, University of Leicester
University Road, Leicester LE1 7RH, UK
jose@mcs.le.ac.uk

The power of architectural modelling approaches in addressing the complexity of software systems derives, to a large extent, from the way they are able to separate coordination from computation concerns. However, distribution has become a key factor of complexity in the modelling of ubiquitous, software-intensive systems. Distribution interferes with both the way computations are performed and interactions are coordinated. Can we separate it as a third architectural dimension? If so, how can we derive the joint behaviour that emerges when the three dimensions are brought together?

In this talk, we provide an overview of our joint work with Dr. Antónia Lopes, from the University of Lisbon, around CommUnity – a prototype language for architectural description that provides a formal framework in which the questions above can be formulated and answered in general mathematical terms.

R. Gorrieri and H. Wehrheim (Eds.): FMOODS 2006, LNCS 4037, p. 17, 2006.
© IFIP International Federation for Information Processing 2006

The Bisimulation Proof Method: Enhancements and Open Problems

Davide Sangiorgi

Università di Bologna, Italy
http://www.cs.unibo.it/~sangio/

Bisimulation (and, more generally, co-induction) can be regarded as one of the most important contributions of Concurrency Theory to Computer Science. Nowadays, bisimulation and the co-inductive techniques developed from the idea of bisimulation are widely used, not only in Concurrency, but, more broadly, in Computer Science, in a number of areas: functional languages, object-oriented languages, type theory, data types, domains, databases, compiler optimisations, program analysis, verification tools, etc.. For instance, in type theory bisimulation and co-inductive techniques have been used: to prove soundness of type systems; to define the meaning of equality between (recursive) types and then to axiomatise and prove such equalities; to define co-inductive types and manipulate infinite proofs in theorem provers. Also, the development of Final Semantics, an area of Mathematics based on co-algebras and category theory and that gives us a rich and deep perspective on the meaning of co-induction and its duality with induction, has been largely motivated by the interest in bisimulation.

In my talk I will discuss the bisimulation proof method – an instance of the co-induction proof method – that is at the heart of the success of bisimulation. I will discuss a number of enhancements of the method and some open problems.

The objective of enhancements is to relieve the work involved with the bisimulation proof method. Thus proving a bisimulation result becomes simpler. Such enhancements can sometimes be extremely important. They seem to be even *essential* in calculi for mobility such as the π-calculus [Mil99, SW01], and in higher-order languages (that is, languages where substitutions can involve the replacement of variables with arbitrary terms of the language) such as Higher-Order π-calculus [San92], Ambients [CG98], or even sequential languages such as the λ–calculus.

References

[CG98]   L. Cardelli and A.D. Gordon. Mobile ambients. In Nivat. M., editor, *Proc. FoSSaCS '98*, volume 1378 of *Lecture Notes in Computer Science*, pages 140–155. Springer Verlag, 1998.

[Hir99] D. Hirschkoff. *Mise en oeuvre de preuves de bisimulation*. PhD thesis, Phd Thesis, Ecole Nationale des Ponts et Chausses, 1999.

[HPS05] Daniel Hirschkoff, Damien Pous, and Davide Sangiorgi. A correct abstract machine for safe ambients. In *COORDINATION*, pages 17–32, 2005.

R. Gorrieri and H. Wehrheim (Eds.): FMOODS 2006, LNCS 4037, pp. 18–19, 2006.

[Mil89]   R. Milner. *Communication and Concurrency*. Prentice Hall, 1989.

[Mil99]   R. Milner. *Communicating and Mobile Systems: the π-Calculus*. Cambridge University Press, 1999.

[MZN05]   M. Merro and F. Zappa Nardelli. Behavioural theory for mobile ambients. Journal of the ACM. To appear, 2005.

[Pou05]   Damien Pous. Up-to techniques for weak bisimulation. In *ICALP*, pages 730–741, 2005.

[San98]   D. Sangiorgi. On the bisimulation proof method. *Journal of Mathematical Structures in Computer Science*, 8:447–479, 1998.

[SM92]   D. Sangiorgi and R. Milner. The problem of "Weak Bisimulation up to". In W.R. Cleveland, editor, *Proc. CONCUR '92*, volume 630 of *Lecture Notes in Computer Science*, pages 32–46. Springer Verlag, 1992.

[San92]   D. Sangiorgi. *Expressing Mobility in Process Algebras: First-Order and Higher-Order Paradigms*. PhD thesis CST–99–93, Department of Computer Science, University of Edinburgh, 1992.

[SW01]   D. Sangiorgi and D. Walker. *The π-calculus: a Theory of Mobile Processes*. Cambridge University Press, 2001.

An Approach to Quality Achievement at the Architectural Level: AQUA

Heeseok Choi[1], Keunhyuk Yeom[2], Youhee Choi[3], and Mikyeong Moon[2]

[1] NTIS Organization, Korea Institute of Science and Technology Information
Eoeun-dong 52-11, Yuseong-gu, Daejeon, 305-806, South Korea
choihs@kisti.re.kr
[2] Department of Computer Engineering, Pusan National University
30 Changjeon-dong, Keumjeong-gu, Busan, 609-735, South Korea
{yeom, mkmoon}@pusan.ac.kr
[3] Embedded S/W Research Division, Electronics and Telecommunications
Research Institute, 161 Gajeong-dong, Yuseong-gu, Daejeon, 305-700, South Korea
yhchoi@etri.re.kr

Abstract. Architecture-based software development plays an important role in successfully developing and managing large and complex software systems. Recently, there have been a number of studies for designing, evaluating, or transforming architectures. However, there is not much work being done for closely connecting an architectural evaluation with an architectural transformation in order to achieve quality attributes during the architecture-based software development. For this reason, it is still difficult to achieve consistently quality attributes at the architectural level. This paper presents an approach to quality achievement in architecture-based software development, which is called AQUA. The AQUA involves two distinctive activities, which are architectural evaluation and transformation, but these activities can be seamlessly combined through producing relevant artifacts based on the design decisions that led to the architecture. Due to the proposed approach, we can expect to achieve quality attributes in architecture-based software development.

1 Introduction

Quality attributes of large software systems are principally determined by the system's software architecture, which represents a common high-level abstraction of the system [1,2]. Therefore, architecture-based software development plays an important role in successfully developing and managing large and complex software systems [1,3,4].

Recently, there have been a number of studies for designing, evaluating, or transforming an architecture. Namely, methods for designing software architectures for developing quality softwares[1], methods for evaluating software architectures with respect to software quality attributes (e.g.[2],[3],[4],[5]), or methods for transforming a software architecture in order to improve one or more of its quality attributes (e.g.[3],[6],[7]) have been studied. There is, however, not much work being done for closely connecting architectural evaluation with architectural transformation in order to achieve quality attributes during the architecture-based software development. For this reason, it is still difficult to achieve consistently quality attributes at the architectural level.

R. Gorrieri and H. Wehrheim (Eds.): FMOODS 2006, LNCS 4037, pp. 20–32, 2006.

This paper presents an approach to quality achievement in architecture-based software development, which is called AQUA afterwards. The AQUA involves two distinctive activities, which are architectural evaluation and transformation. However, these activities can be seamlessly combined through allowing the evaluation artifacts to be effectively utilized for architectural transformation centering around design decisions acquired from architectural evaluation. Furthermore, activities for architectural evaluation in the AQUA play a significant role in revealing any potential defects or assessing the fulfillment of required quality requirements, and activities for architectural transformation play a significant role in reducing defects in the architecture or making changes to the architecture.

2 Overview of AQUA Process

In this paper, we present an approach to quality achievement in architecture-based software development, which is called AQUA. The AQUA provides software architects with a mean for achieving quality attributes at the architectural level. For the purpose of achieving quality attributes during architecture-based software development, it is necessary to transform architectures based on the evaluation results as well as to evaluate them. Therefore, the AQUA involves two kinds of distinctive activities, which are architectural evaluation and transformation. Namely, the AQUA integrates activities for providing insights of an architecture with respect to its desired qualities with activities for making changes to the architecture within a framework. Due to the AQUA, it can be easily performed to achieve quality attributes at the architectural level without difficulties of bridging heterogeneous approaches. In other words, the information acquired from architectural evaluation can be effectively utilized in making changes to the architecture for quality achievement.

Figure 1 presents an overview of the AQUA. The AQUA first needs the generation of an evaluation contract for scoping software requirements and identifying the desired quality attributes of an architecture. Then the AQUA requires characterizing each quality attribute for specializing explicitly the characteristics of quality attributes. Next, the AQUA includes the identification of architectural design decisions having an important impact on the achievement of quality attributes. Such design decisions can be identified by characterizing key designs relevant to quality achievement in the presented architecture with considering the characteristics of quality attributes. Based on the decisions, the AQUA includes the generation of an architecture profile representing the quality achievement of the architecture, and gets to generate a prediction facility helpful in understanding the traceability between quality attributes and architectural designs. Namely, it provides insights concerned with the quality achievement of the architecture with respect to its desired qualities.   According to the insights about quality achievement, it is necessary to make changes to the architecture for the purpose of achieving quality attributes. Furthermore, the changes should be able to be planned for avoiding unnecessary changes. For this reason, the impact on other design decisions should be considered before applying the changes to the

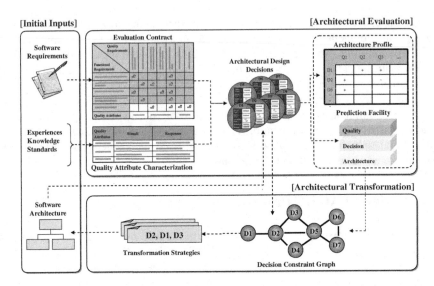

Fig. 1. The AQUA process

architecture. Therefore, the AQUA includes the generation of a decision constraint graph for representing explicitly the dependencies among design decisions, then for tracing easily the impacts of a decision change. Through using the decision constraint graph, the AQUA guides the establishment of transformation strategies that lead to a new architecture. Finally, the activities of the AQUA for conducting an evaluation and transformation of an architecture can be repeatedly performed until reaching the desired levels of quality attributes in the architecture. Therefore, the AQUA provides software architects with a mean that supports achieving quality attributes during architecture-based software development. In the sections below, these artifacts are discussed in more detail.

3   Quality Achievement Activities of the AQUA Process

3.1   Understanding Quality Achievement Goals Using Evaluation Contract

The evaluation contract means the consensus between users and software architects about expectations from the evaluation for quality achievement. Namely, expectations from the evaluation can be concluded and negotiated. This contract includes the lists of quality and functional requirements, their relationship, and identifies quality goals of architecture.

Figure 2 represents generating an evaluation contract. To generate an evaluation contract, software architects first document quality requirements and functional requirements of a system separately. In general, functional requirements have relations to one or more quality requirements. Subsequently software architects determine the scope of functional requirements, then software architects determine the scope of quality requirements. Finally, software architects identify the quality attributes representing the goals of an architectural evaluation for quality achievement.

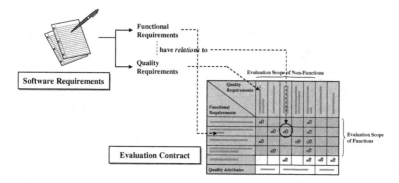

Fig. 2. Generating an evaluation contract

3.2 Finding Architectural Design Decisions

Software architecture is composed of architectural design decisions, which are the aspects of an architecture that have a significant impact on achieving quality attributes, such as components, connectors, and configuration. Namely, architectural decisions are made from an overall system perspective. Essentially, these decisions identify the system's key structural elements, the externally visible properties of these elements, and their relationships, and they define how to achieve the architecturally significant requirements[3]. Since architectural design decisions represent decisions on various design alternatives applicable to design problems during architectural design, these decisions can be interpreted as pairs of decision variable and decision value. The following are to illustrate the concepts of decision variables and decision values, respectively:

- A *decision value* describes a design itself applied to the current architecture as the selected solution out of design alternatives applicable to each design issue. The decision values can be easily conceived from a well presented software architecture. More specifically, parts of designs relevant to functional requirements within the evaluation scope for quality achievement should be first identified. Next, each design is summarized in terms of design elements, relationships, and their properties. Finally, the decision values describing meaningfully key designs are identified in the presented architecture through characterizing such design summaries.
- A *decision variable* describes the architectural design issue that each selected solution is addressing, such as "What are the big parts of the system?" and/or "How are they connected?". Such decision issue can be found by analyzing decision values based on architectural knowledge such as design patterns, styles, and architectural views. Namely, the decision variables can be determined by asking questions about why the decision values have resulted from software requirements.

Figure 3 represents the finding of architectural design decisions. As in the above illustrations about a decision variable and a decision value, software architects should first identify design areas relevant to functional requirements within the evaluation

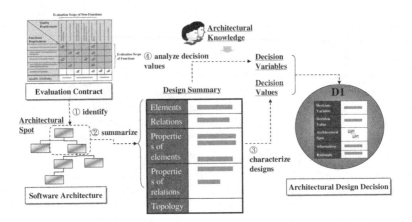

Fig. 3. Finding architectural design decisions

scope (① in Figure 3). Subsequently, key designs should be summarized (② in Figure 3). Then decision values can be identified through characterizing design summaries (③ in Figure 3). Finally, decision variables are determined by identifying one or more design issues that each decision value involves (④ in Figure 3).

3.3 Generating Decision Constraint Graph

Architectural design decisions also have relations to other decisions in terms of the consistency among designs. For instance, a decision for determining elements of a system should be consistent with a decision for structuring the system. The decision constraint graph is a graph for maintaining the consistency among design decisions. The graph helps in representing explicitly the dependencies among design decisions, and in tracing easily the impacts of a decision change. Here, architectural design decisions introduce two kinds of design constraints, which are unary and binary constraints. The following are to illustrate unary constraints and binary constraints:

- A *unary constraint* captures any constraint to the design that the chose alternative (the decision value) might pose, which restricts design alternatives applicable to each design issue (the decision variable). In order to determine unary constraints, software architects should first analyze the characteristics of decision values at various points in the design. For example, if the design elements support the concurrency of system, it can be considered that there is the constraint equal to concurrency support. Next, software architects should determine whether the characteristics are closely related to the requirements specified in previous evaluation contract. Finally, the characteristics irrelevant to requirements should be excluded.

- A *binary constraint* captures any constraint for design consistency that two decision values might pose each other, which represents a condition restricting design alternatives applicable to relevant decision variables. In order to determine binary constraints, software architects should analyze only the characteristics causing consistency problems between two decision values.

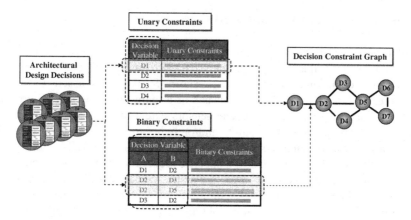

Fig. 4. Generating a decision constraint graph

Figure 4 represents the generation of a decision constraint graph. Each node in the graph represents a decision variable, and each edge in the graph represents constraint relationship between two decision variables. To generate a decision constraint graph, software architects should first document two kinds of constraints according to the above illustration; unary constraints and binary constraints. Based on the identified constraints, the relationships among design decisions are determined with respect to design consistency. As a result, nodes and edges of decision constraint graph are defined.

3.4 Applying Architectural Changes for Quality Achievement

Software architects can apply various changes in order to reduce any potential defects, or to make changes to the architecture. Each change leads to a new version of the architecture that has the same functionality, but different satisfaction for desired quality attributes. However, applying a change to a specific design area may have an impact an adjacent design area or whole architecture. Therefore, it is necessary to analyze how a change to the specific area affected on other areas and to determine applicable design alternatives for the target area needs to be changed.

To do this, software architects first find architectural alternatives. To find architectural alternatives, we can utilize various design theories or refer to other alternatives from candidate architectures or architect's experience. To select appropriate architectural options, we should analyze the architectural options with respect to the scope and impacts of applying them. In particular, architectural options must be consistently selected against other architectural decisions. To achieve this goal, we propose checking the following consistencies based on the decision constraint graph.

- *Node consistency* means the satisfaction of unary constraints restricting the decision values applicable to a decision variable. This also means that all architectural alternatives unsatisfying unary constraints on a decision variable would be pruned from the candidate solutions of the variable.
- *Arc consistency* is the satisfaction of binary constraints representing a condition between two decision variables. Namely, architectural alternatives applicable to the specific design should satisfy arc consistency between the designs.

4 An Example: House Alarm System

To address the practical applicability and features of our approach, we have chosen an example that is familiar but rich with interesting design and architectural problems, that of the House Alarm System (discussed in [8] and elsewhere). A house alarm system consists of a main unit to which a number of sensors and alarms are connected. The sensors detect movements in the guarded area, and the alarms generate sounds and/or lights to scare off an intruder. The total area that can be guarded is divided into cells, where a cell contains some sensors and some alarms that guard a specific area. Since the house alarm system is included in real-time systems, there are some special concerns when modeling the system. Naturally, concurrency, communication, and synchronization are the most important factors, but fault tolerance, performance optimization, and distribution must also be dealt with when modeling a house alarm system.

In this example, we focused on illustrating that the AQUA seamlessly supports two distinctive activities centering around architectural design decisions. For this reason, we omitted some artifacts such as quality attribute characterization and architecture profile in this paper. Furthermore, this paper introduced only architectural designs necessary for understanding the proposed approach. As shown in Figure 5 through Figure 7, partial software architecture of a house alarm system was presented with the 4+1 view model in UML. Firstly, Figure 5 represents a set of key abstractions for the system and their logical relationships. Sensors and alarms are connected to a cell handler, which is an active class that handles a specific cell. The cell handler is connected to the system handler, which is an active class that handles the user communication. Next, Figure 6 represents a partially logical organization between sensors and alarms in the system. The house alarm system is structured based on the shared memory style. Finally, Figure 7 shows the interaction when a sensor detectssomething. It then sends an asynchronous alarm signal to the cell handler. Subse-uently, the cell handler sends in parallel synchronous trigger signals to all alarms and an asynchronous alarm signal to the system handler. Inside the system handler, the alarm signal is handled synchronously.

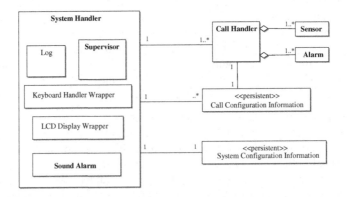

Fig. 5. A set of key abstractions for the system and their logical relationships

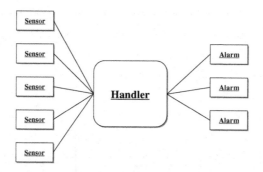

Fig. 6. An architecture of house alarm system based on the shared memory style

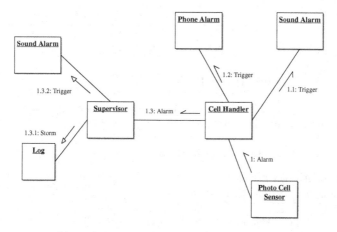

Fig. 7. The interaction when a sensor detects something

4.1 Understanding Quality Achievement Goals Using Evaluation Contract

In this example, we first defined the evaluation contract. We found that the house alarm system had the functionality such as activity detection, alarm generation, user communication, and system monitoring. In addition, we found that the system had non-functionality relevant to quality attributes such as performance, concurrency, and fault tolerance. When we defined the evaluation contract, we first placed the functional requirements and non-functional requirements in a row and column of the evaluation contract, respectively. The relationships between functional requirements and non-functional requirements were naturally determined. Here, we restricted theevaluation scope for evaluating the quality achievement of current architecture within the requirements listed in the oblique area of Figure 8. As a result, two kinds of quality attributes (i.e. performance, concurrency) were identified as the things to be dealt with in this example. In this way, we could start quality achievement at architectural level with the generated evaluation contract.

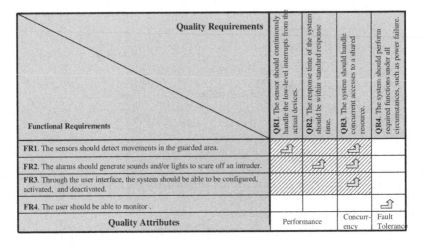

Fig. 8. Evaluation contract

4.2 Finding Architectural Design Decisions

In this example, we identified some design decisions necessary for illustrating our approach. Table 1 summarized architectural design decisions of a house alarm system.

Table 1. Architectural design decisions

Architectural design decision		Brief Description
Decision Variable	**Decision Value**	
Design Elements (D1)	Three Kinds of Logical Elements	-The system consists of three kinds of logical elements such as sensors, alarms, and handlers.
Roles of Elements (D2)	-User Communication -Cell Handling -Activity Detection -Sound/Light Effects	-The system handler handles the user communication. -The cell handlers handle a specific cell consisting of sensors and alarms. -The sensors handle the low-level interrupts from the actual device, then detect activity in a specific area. -The alarms handle the low-level communication with the device, then generate sound and light effects.
Properties of Elements (D3)	Active Class	-The main elements are designed as active classes.
Structure of System (D4)	Shared Memory Style	-The system is structured based on the shared memory style.
Task Partition (D5)	Unit of Active Class	-The task is modeled as the unit of active class.
Message Types (D6)	Use of Synchronous & Asynchronous Messages	-Inside the system handler, the synchronous messages are used. But outside the system handler, the asynchronous messages are used.
Task Interaction (D7)	Event-based Communication	-The interaction among tasks is performed via event-based communication
Task Synchronization (D8)	Task Monitoring	-The system monitors concurrently trying to modify or access a shared resource.

There were the decisions that identify the system's key structural elements, their properties, and their relationships. In addition, there were the interesting decisions such as choosing patterns and message types. They became a leverage to help us understand the architecture in practice.

4.3 Generating Decision Constraint Graph

For the generation of a decision constraint graph, we identified unary and binary constraints on the design decisions summarized in Table 1. As results, Table 2 summarized unary constraints to each decision, and Table 3 summarized binary constraints between the design decisions. Furthermore, the consistency relationships among design decisions were naturally found by determining binary constraints.

Table 2. Unary constraints

Decision Variable	Unary Constraints
Design Elements	The inputs of system should be different from the outputs of system.
Roles of Elements	Assigned roles should support the concurrency of system.
Properties of Elements	Real-time properties of system should be supported.
Structure of System	Relevant data among elements should be shared.
Task Partition	Real-time properties of system should be supported.
Message Types	Both synchronous and asynchronous properties should be supported.
Task Interaction	The system should be run in terms of external events.
Task Synchronization	The tasks concurrently trying to access a shared resource should be synchronized.

Table 3. Binary constraints

Architectural Design Decisions		Binary Constraints
Decisions	Decisions	
Design Elements	Roles of Elements	Design elements should have the independent roles.
Design Elements	Structure of System	There should be an element for sharing data.
Roles of Elements	Properties of Elements	The concurrency among elements should be satisfied.
Roles of Elements	Structure of System	An element should have a role for sharing data.
Task Partition	Design Elements	The elements having independent roles should be identified as concurrent tasks
Task Partition	Task Synchronization	The tasks concurrently trying to access a shared resource should be synchronized.
Task Interaction	Message Types	The tasks should interact with each other by transmitting any type of message.
Task Synchronization	Structure of System	The tasks concurrently trying to access a shared resource should be synchronized.

Using the decisions and constraints described in Table 1 through Table 3, we generated the decision constraint graph as shown in Figure 9. Though a few decisions were considered in this example, the relationship among them was more complex in

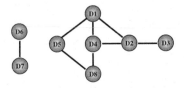

Fig. 9. Decision constraint graph

practice. Therefore, we found that the decision constraint graph would be useful for showing complex relationships among the decisions. In other words, the graph showed that the decision had the consistent relationship with one or more of them.

4.4 Applying Architectural Changes for Quality Achievement

As an example, we tried to transform the current decision for synchronization among the tasks concurrently trying to access a shared resource according to the previous evaluation results. Namely, we considered applying a periodic execution mechanism using a scheduler [3] to the design area of D8(Task Synchronization). Prior to applying an alternative to a design area, however, it is necessary to analyze its impact on an architecture. To do this, we gradually performed impact analysis starting from change of D8. Figure 10 represents the result of impact analysis for architectural transformation. As shown in Figure 10, some nodes of a graph were traversed during impact analysis by checking both node consistency and arc consistency. Since the change to the D8 doesn't violate unary and binary constraint for D4(Structure of System), the change to the D8 doesn't have impact on D4. However, the adjacent node D5(Task Partition) is affected for reasons of consistency violation. Then additional changes for the nodes D1(Design Elements) and D4(Structure of System) were needed by adding a scheduler to the system. As a result, we easily established a transformation strategy consisting of D5, D1, and D4 by the sequence of ☐ through ☐ in Figure 10. Through transforming the presented architecture according to the transformation strategy, we expect to reduce the possibility of errors, but it can reduce performance. Finally, it is necessary to validate the correctness of the transformations performed. It can be achieved by performing iteratively the AQUA process.

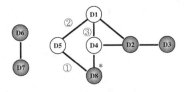

Fig. 10. Establishing a transformation strategy

5   Comparison with Existing Methods

We compared the AQUA with the existing methods in terms of activities necessary for achieving qualities at the architectural level. To do this, we first identified the

Table 4. Comparison with existing methods

Methods / Activities for Quality Achievement	Architecture Evaluation			Architecture Transformation			Architecture Evaluation & Transformation
	ATAM[4]	SAAM[4]	ARID[4]	Bosch's Approach[3]	Carriere's Approach[6]	Krikhaar's Approach[7]	AQUA
Identifying desired qualities	Scenarios	Scenarios	Scenarios	Activity only	Not defined	Not defined	Evaluation contract
Specializing quality attributes	Utility tree	Scanarios	Not defined	Quality profiles	Not defined	Quality metrics	Quality attribute characterizations
Analyzing an architecture	Sensitivity points &Trade-off points	Sensitivity points	Activity only	Activity only	Features	Not defined	Architectural decisions Architecture profile
Analyzing change impacts	Not defined	Not defined	Not defined	Activity only	Not defined	RPA model	Decision constraint graph
Modifying an architecture	Not defined	Not defined	Not defined	Activity only	Activity only	RPA model	Transformation strategy
Validating an architecture	Not defined	Not defined	Not defined	Activity only	Activity only	Not defined	Architecture profile (by iteration)

activities through analyzing existing studies on architectural evaluation and transformation. When we analyzed them, we particularly focused on understanding the full process from quality identification to quality achievement. As a result, we identified six key activities to be handled at the architectural level for quality achievement as described in Table 4. The activities are as follows:

- *Identifying desired qualities* is an activity to determine the kinds of quality attributes to be dealt with during the quality achievement of an archi-ecture. Due to this activity, the goal for quality achievement can be clearly defined.
- *Specializing quality attributes* contributes in acquiring more informative characteristics of quality attributes. In addition, it contributes in identifying architectural decisions having a significant impact on achieving quality attributes.
- *Analyzing an architecture* is an activity to determine quality achievement of current architecture with respect to its desired qualities. It provides insights concerned with the quality achievement of architecture.
- *Analyzing change impacts* is an activity to analyze the effects of making changes to the architecture on the other quality attributes or other designs. In particular, it helps make sure the design is consistent with one or more of them.
- *Modifying an architecture* leads to a new version of the architecture with the same functionality, but with different values for its desired qualities.
- *Validating an architecture* is an activity to validate the correctness of the transformations performed. Through validating the architecture, the quality achievement can be confirmed.

Then we analyzed whether the existing methods and the AQUA effectively supported the activities necessary for quality achievement or not. To do this, we summarized the artifacts closely related to the activities through analyzing some methods including the AQUA as described in Table 4. The artifacts mean that the methods effectively support the described activity. As illustrated in Table 4, the existing methods fail to support the activities for quality achievement consistently. Compared with the methods described in Table 4, however, the AQUA can effectively support quality achievement in architecture-based software development through producing explicitly the artifacts relevant to quality achievement at the architectural level based on the design decisions.

6 Conclusions and Future Work

We presented an approach to quality achievement in architecture-based software development, which is called the AQUA. In addition, we applied the proposed approach to the House Alarm system to illuminate the approach. The AQUA involves two distinctive activities, which are architectural evaluation and transformation. Here, architectural evaluation plays a significant role in revealing any potential defects or assessing the fulfillment of required quality requirements, and architectural transformation plays a significant role in reducing defects in the architecture or making changes to the architecture. However, the AQUA effectively integrates the activities for providing insights of an architecture with respect to its desired qualities with the activities for making changes to the architecture within a framework. Furthermore, the AQUA seamlessly supports the activities relevant to quality achievement centering around the architectural design decisions by explicitly documenting them. Through following the AQUA, it can be easily performed to achieve quality attributes at the architectural level without difficulties of bridging heterogeneous approaches.

In the future, we expect that this approach may be more complemented and extended as a result of ongoing researches. Presently, we are interested in several issues in supporting architecture-based software development. In particular, the development of mechanisms for process automation is considered to be important. We believe our approach will be effectively involved at the early stages of a software development lifecycle.

References

1. Bass, L., Clements, P., and Kazman, R., *Software Architecture in Practice, 2/E*, Addison-Wesley, 2003.
2. Kazman, R. et al., "The Architecture Tradeoff Analysis Method", *Proceedings of the 4th IEEE International Conference on Engineering of Complex Computer Systems*, August 1998, pp.68-78.
3. Bosch, J., *Design and Use of Software Architecture*, Addison-Wesley, 2000.
4. Clements, P., Kazman, R., and Klein, M., *Evaluating Software Architectures*, Addison-Wesley, 2002.
5. Dobrica, L. and Niemela, E., "A Survey on Software Architecture Analysis Methods", *IEEE Transactions on Software Engineering*, IEEE Computer Society, Vol. 28, No. 7, July 2002, pp.638-653.
6. Carriere, S.J., Woods, S., and Kazman, R., "Software Architectural Transformation", *Proceedings of the 6th Working Conference on Reverse Engineering*, October 1999, pp.13-23.
7. Krikhaar, R., et al., "A Two-phase Process for Software Architecture Improvement", *Proceedings of the International Conference on Software Maintenance*, August 1999, pp.371-380.
8. Eriksson, H.E. and Penker, M., UML Toolkit, John Wiley & Sons, 1998.

Bounded Analysis and Decomposition for Behavioural Descriptions of Components

Pascal Poizat[1,*], Jean-Claude Royer[2,**], and Gwen Salaün[3]

[1] IBISC - FRE 2873 CNRS
Tour Évry 2, 523 place des terrasses de l'Agora, F-91000 Évry Cedex
Pascal.Poizat@ibisc.univ-evry.fr
[2] OBASCO Group, EMN - INRIA, LINA
4 rue Alfred Kastler, BP 20722, F-44307 Nantes Cedex 3
Jean-Claude.Royer@emn.fr
[3] VASY Project, INRIA Rhône-Alpes
655 Avenue de l'Europe, F-38330 Montbonnot Saint-Martin
Gwen.Salaun@inrialpes.fr

Abstract. Explicit behavioural interfaces are now accepted as a mandatory feature of components to address architectural analysis. Behavioural interface description languages should be able to deal with data types and with rich communication means. Symbolic Transition Systems (STS) support the definition of component models which take into account control, concurrency, communication and data types. However, verification of components described with protocol modelled by STS, especially model-checking, is difficult since they possibly involve different sources of infinity. In this paper, we propose the notions of *bounded analysis* and *bounded decomposition*. They can be used to test boundedness of systems and to generate finite simulations for them so that standard model-checking techniques may be applied for verification purposes.

1 Introduction

Behavioural interface description languages and protocol descriptions are needed in component models to address architectural analysis and verification issues such as checking component behavioural compatibility, detecting architectural deadlocks or building adaptors to compensate incompatible component interfaces, but also to relate efficiently design models and implementation ones. In this context, different behavioural models have been used, such as process algebras [1, 8, 20] or automata-based formalisms [4, 24]. In the context of a national project, ACI DISPO, our researches are interested in checking components and resources or services availability.

Components may exchange data with service requests, or may internally compute data values on which behaviours depend, yielding compositions which deadlock only for some specific values (*e.g.,* think of an arithmetic component which

---

* Supported by the French national project RNRT STACS on abstract and compositional techniques for model-based testing.
** Supported by the French national project ACI DISPO on component availability.

R. Gorrieri and H. Wehrheim (Eds.): FMOODS 2006, LNCS 4037, pp. 33–47, 2006.

accepts two integers, x and y and denies service when y is 0). Therefore, there is a need for component models integrating data types within behaviours. Unfortunately, this is known to yield state explosion problems when verifying models, especially with model-checking. Research on Symbolic Transition Systems (STS) [10, 18, 19] aims at providing a model and dedicated verification techniques to deal with these issues.

In this paper we develop a model of communicating components based on STS, together with specific analysis techniques. First, we formalise our notion of communicating and concurrent STS, with a proper semantics based on configuration graphs. We also link our STS with LTS using interpretations and we state properties relating interpretations and STS composition. This provides a unified framework where STS and LTS can be both defined and composed. Second, we present a decidable boundedness procedure (*bounded analysis*) which tests the boundedness of communicating components architectures (called systems). Model-checking techniques can be used thereafter to prove properties. It is common that a system handles both bounded variables and unbounded variables. Enumerative model-checking will arbitrarily bound all the variables. Whenever the bounds set by model-checking tools are reached, the specifier does not know if the system is either too big for the tool or really unbounded. For instance, a system which deadlocks for every n smaller than 10, does not imply anything about the behaviour for greater values of n. Bounded analysis may therefore be viewed as a complementary debugging means to detect possible flaws that model-checking may miss in the presence of data types. Next, we develop a decomposition technique (*bounded decomposition*) that is used to split systems into parts which can be separately tested for boundedness and if so, checked separately. This approach may not solve every problem related to infinite data types, but it is especially worthy with the (numerous) systems involving bounded resources (*i.e.,* where parts associated to the resources are bounded) and with systems where the number of components is bounded.

The paper is organised as follows. Section 2 formally defines STS, configuration graphs, relations between STS and LTS, and communication between STS. Sections 3 and 4 present, respectively, boundedness analysis and bounded decomposition and illustrate them on examples. Section 5 reviews related work. Finally, Section 6 draws up some concluding remarks. More details about our approach and formal definitions can be consulted in [26].

2 Formalising Components as Symbolic Transition Systems

This section states some definitions we use thereafter to introduce our approach. First of all, we consider algebraic specifications as an abstraction of concrete implementation languages like Java, C++, or Python. A *signature* (or static interface) Σ is a pair $(\mathcal{S}, F)$ where $\mathcal{S}$ is a set of *sorts* (type names) and F a set of function names equipped with *profiles* over these sorts. X is used to denote the set of all variables, it contains a distinguished variable, $Self_D$, whose goal is much like explicit receivers in Object-Oriented languages (*e.g.,* this in Java). From a signature Σ and from X, one may obtain *terms,* denoted by $T_{\Sigma,X}$. An *algebraic specification* is a pair (Σ, Ax) where Ax is a set of axioms between terms of $T_{\Sigma,X}$. Let r be a ground term, $r \downarrow$ denotes the normal form or normalization (assumed to be unique) of r. $v : R$ means that v has type R and $v(u)$ denotes the application of v to term u.

2.1   Symbolic Transition Systems

Symbolic Transition Systems [10, 18, 19] have initially been developed as a solution to the state and transition explosion problem in value-passing process algebras using substitutions associated to states and symbolic values in transition labels.

Definition 1 (STS). *An STS is a tuple* $(D,\ (\Sigma, Ax),\ S,\ L,\ s^0,\ T)$ *where:* (Σ, Ax) *is an algebraic specification,* D *is a sort called* sort of interest *defined in* (Σ, Ax), $S = \{s_i\}$ *is a countable set of states,* $L = \{l_i\}$ *is a countable set of event labels,* $s^0 \in S$ *is the initial state, and* $T \subseteq S \times T_{\Sigma_{Boolean}, X} \times Event \times T_{\Sigma_D, X} \times S$ *is a set of transitions.*

Note that *countable* means that the set may be infinite but can be enumerated. *Events* denote atomic activities that occur in the components. Events are either: *i)* hidden (or internal) events: τ, *ii)* silent events: l, with $l \in L$, *iii)* emissions: $l!e$, with $e \in T_{\Sigma, \{Self_D\}}$, or *iv)* receptions: $l?x : R$ with $x \in X \backslash \{Self_D\}$. Internal events denote internal actions of the components which may have an effect on its behaviour yet without being observable from its context. Silent events are pure synchronising events, while emissions and receptions naturally correspond, respectively, to requested and provided services of the components. To simplify we only consider binary communications here, but emissions and receptions may be extended to n-ary emissions and receptions. STS transitions are tuples $(s,\ \mu,\ \epsilon,\ \delta,\ t)$ for which s is called the source state, t the target state, μ the guard, ϵ the event and δ the action. Each action is denoted by a term with variables where at least $Self_D$ occurs. A do-nothing action is simply denoted by $Self_D$. In forthcoming figures, transitions will be labelled as follows: $[\mu]\ \epsilon\ /\ \delta$.

2.2   Configuration Graphs

The semantics of STS is formalised using configuration graphs. They are obtained applying jointly the unfolding of receptions and the reduction of ground terms to their normal forms.

Definition 2 (Unfolding). *The unfolding of an STS* $(D,\ (\Sigma, Ax),\ S,\ L,\ s^0,\ T)$, *in* $v^0 \in T_{\Sigma_D}$, *is the STS* $(D,\ (\Sigma, Ax),\ S',\ L,\ (s^0, v^0 \downarrow),\ T')$. *The sets* $S' \subseteq S \times D$ *and* T' *are inductively defined by:* $(s^0, v^0 \downarrow) \in S'$ *and for each* $(s, v) \in S'$:

- *if* $(s,\ \mu,\ \tau,\ \delta,\ t) \in T$ *and* $\mu(v) \downarrow = true$ *then* $s' = (t,\ \delta(v) \downarrow) \in S'$ *and* $((s, v),\ true,\ \tau,\ Self_D,\ s') \in T'$,

- if $(s, \mu, l, \delta, t) \in T$ and $\mu(v){\downarrow}= true$ then $s' = (t, \delta(v){\downarrow}) \in S'$ and $((s,v), true, l, Self_D, s') \in T'$,
- if $(s, \mu, l!e, \delta, t) \in T$ and $\mu(v){\downarrow}= true$ then $s' = (t, \delta(v){\downarrow}) \in S'$ and $((s,v), true, l!e(v){\downarrow}, Self_D, s') \in T'$, and iv) if $(s, \mu, l?x : R, \delta, t) \in T$ then for each $r : R$ such that $\mu(v,r){\downarrow}= true$, there is $s' = (t, \delta(v,r){\downarrow})) \in S'$ and $((s,v), true, l!r, Self_D, s') \in T'$.

Pairs (s, v) are *configurations* where s is the *control state*. Let d be an STS. Its unfolding in a v^0 term, $G(d, v^0)$, is called a *configuration graph*. A configuration graph is a particular STS without reception, where guards are all equal to *true*, emission terms are in normal form and actions are do-nothing actions denoted by $Self_D$.

2.3 Interpretations

Configuration graphs and STS can be interpreted as LTS[1]. Such mappings enable one to use existing model-checkers, such as SPIN [17] or CADP [16], to verify these models. We introduce two LTS interpretations based on the following rules:

- $(rule_1)$ any STS transition $(x, \mu, \epsilon, \delta, y)$ is reduced to an LTS transition (x, l, y), where l is the label of the event ϵ;
- $(rule_2)$ any configuration (s, v) is reduced to its *control state* s, and any STS transition $((s, v), \mu, \epsilon, \delta, (t, u))$ is reduced to a LTS one (s, l, t).

Definition 3 (LTS Interpretations). *The standard interpretation, I_{LTS}, of an STS, is an LTS computed with $rule_1$ and discarding D and (Σ, Ax). The weak interpretation, W_{LTS}, of an STS, is an LTS computed with $rule_2$ and discarding D and (Σ, Ax).*

We use $\supseteq$ for the transition relation inclusion and $\sqsupseteq$ for the trace inclusion of two LTSs. $d_1 \supseteq d_2$ means that d_1 and d_2 share the same set of states but the set of transitions of d_2 is a subset of the transitions of d_1. $d_1 \sqsupseteq d_2$ means that any d_2 trace is also a d_1 trace. As defined in [2] for LTS, $B = (S_B, L, b^0, T_B)$ is a *simulation* of $A = (S_A, L, a^0, T_A)$, noted $B \succeq A$, iff there is a relation $\mathcal{R}$ included in $S_A \times S_B$ such that: i) $\forall s_A \in S_A, \exists s_B \in S_B$ such that $s_A \mathcal{R} s_B$, ii) if s_A is initial then $\exists s_B \in S_B$ such that $s_A \mathcal{R} s_B$ and s_B is initial, and iii) $\forall (s_A, l, t_A) \in T_A, \forall s_B \in S_B, s_A \mathcal{R} s_B \Rightarrow (\exists t_B \in S_B, \exists (s_B, l, t_B) \in T_B \wedge t_A \mathcal{R} t_B)$.

Proposition 1. *Let d be an STS:*

1. $W_{LTS}(d) \supseteq W_{LTS}(G(d, v^0))$,
2. $I_{LTS}(d) \succeq I_{LTS}(G(d, v^0))$,
3. $I_{LTS}(d) \sqsupseteq I_{LTS}(G(d, v^0))$.

Point 2 above defines a simulation which in turn implies trace inclusion (point 3). Previous works [22, 12] have shown that simulation preserves a subset of μ-calculus, namely safety properties. The above relations could be later extended to other existing abstractions, such as [11, 22, 12, 5].

---

[1] We recall that an LTS is a structure (S, L, s^0, T) with $T \subseteq S \times L \times S$.

2.4   Concurrency and Communication

Concurrent communicating components can be described with protocols modelled by STS, and synchronous products adapted from the LTS related definition [2] can be used to obtain the resulting global system. Given two STS with sets of labels L_1 and L_2, a set V of synchronisation vectors is a set of pairs (l_1, l_2), called synchronous labels, such that $l_1 \in L_1$ and $l_2 \in L_2$. Hidden events cannot participate in a synchronisation. Two components synchronise at some transition if their respective labels are synchronous (*i.e.*, belong to the vector) and if the *label offers* are compatible. Offer compatibility follows simple rules: type equality and emission/reception matching. A label l such that there is no pair in V which contains l is said to be non-synchronised or *asynchronous*. Corresponding transitions are triggered independently and have independent running steps. The formal definition of the synchronous product of STS can be found in [26]. The synchronous product operator is noted $\otimes_V$ and is extended to a n-ary product and to any depth.

The configuration graph and the standard interpretation have compatibility properties with the synchronous product, which are formalised below.

Proposition 2. *Let d_1 and d_2 be two STS, V a synchronisation vector, $v_1 \in T_{\Sigma_{D_1}}$ and $v_2 \in T_{\Sigma_{D_2}}$:*

    1. $G(d_1 \otimes_V d_2, (v_1, v_2)) \equiv G(G(d_1, v_1) \otimes_V d_2, v_2) \equiv (G(d_1, v_1) \otimes_V G(d_2, v_2))$.
    2. $I_{LTS}(d_1 \otimes_V d_2) \succeq I_{LTS}(G(d_1, v_1) \otimes_V d_2) \succeq I_{LTS}(G(d_1 \otimes_V d_2, (v_1, v_2)))$.

Proposition 2.1 gives three ways to compute the configuration graph of an STS product. Proposition 2.2 shows that the interpretation of $G(d_1, v_1) \otimes_V d_2$ is a finer simulation for $I_{LTS}(G(d_1 \otimes_V d_2, (v_1, v_2)))$ than $I_{LTS}(d_1 \otimes_V d_2)$. These results are used in Section 4 to apply the standard interpretation to composite systems.

3   Bounded Analysis

Enumerative model-checking works on state spaces which are generated from specifications written in high-level languages such as process algebras. Symbolic model-checking techniques rely on different techniques (such as BDD encodings) to deal with big state spaces. However this is not sufficient when components encapsulate or exchange data. Possibly infinite data type domains must be restricted and free variables bound to avoid state explosion. For instance, reasoning on LOTOS specifications using CADP may be performed in different ways. The underlying global LTS can be first generated and then verified. On-the-fly techniques can also be used, in presence of concurrency, to avoid the generation of the whole global system [23]. However, a shortcoming of all these approaches is that model-checking is applied to a restricted finite state system and full correctness cannot be ensured. Accordingly we present in the sequel of this section an approach preserving symbolic values. Our objective is not to replace existing model-checking techniques and tools. Bounded analysis has to be viewed as a complementary debugging means to detect possible flaws that model-checking may miss.

3.1 Principle

It is common that a system handles both bounded variables and unbounded variables. Enumerative model-checking will arbitrarily bound all the variables and it may be insufficient to assert properly a given property for the whole system. Bounded analysis begins by checking if a system is bounded, *i.e.*, testing if its configuration graph is finite or not. The system taken into account may be either made up of a single component or several communicating components. Whenever the system is bounded, bounds for variables can be computed or at least estimated (see [21] for example) and the configuration graph may thereafter be generated. Boundedness checking mainly traverses the system configuration graph to seek accumulating cycles, *i.e.*, a cycle of control states with a greater data value at the end. When bounds are known, the generation of the bounded system can be tuned such that the entire system can be computed. We experimented the previous case with CADP, see [26] for an example. If the system is not bounded, verification techniques developed for infinite systems are relevant, see [5, 14, 13, 3, 7] for example. In the sequel we describe another way to abstract infinite component systems using boundedness analysis. This approach is particularly relevant on component systems, because of Proposition 2. This proposition states that a composite system may be abstracted by checking the boundedness of one component and if bounded, the synchronous product of the bounded configuration graph with other components is computed. This approach is illustrated in the next subsection and extended in Section 4 with a notion of decomposition.

Definition 4 (Bounded STS). *An STS is bounded, for an initial value v_0, iff its configuration graph is finite.*

Checking boundedness is a semi-decidable problem and a semi-algorithm computing the configuration graph has been implemented in our prototype. This algorithm completely unfolds the system and merges identical configurations. However boundedness is decidable for some specific classes of STS. Our prototype therefore implements a decision procedure for one of them, *counter STS*, which are an adequate abstraction for many systems, see [15, 3] for related definitions. They are particularly convenient in the context of component availability properties since counter STS can describe dynamic systems allocating finite amounts of resources.

Definition 5 (Counter STS). *A counter STS, is an STS where: i) the data type is restricted to natural numbers (counters) c_i $1 \leq i \leq m$, ii) guards are boolean conjunctions of the following atoms: true, false, $c_i > n_i$, or $c_i \geq n_i$, where n_i is a natural, and iii) actions are $c_i := \Sigma_{j=1}^{m} a_j * c_j \pm p_i$, where a_j, p_i are natural numbers and at least one a_j is greater than 0.*

Counter STS are as powerful as generalized transfer nets [15] which extend Petri nets with both duplication and transfer arcs. They admit neither reseting nor equality testing, since their boundedness would then not be decidable.

Proposition 3. *The boundedness test of counter STS is decidable.*

The principle of the procedure is to find an accumulating cycle in the configuration graph. The proof relies on the following fact: the effect of all the transitions may be viewed as an affine increasing function on the vector of counters. This defines a well-structured transition system and boundedness is therefore decidable following a general theorem for them [15].

3.2   Application: A Resource Allocator (V1)

This subsection describes the application of bounded analysis to an infinite system. Whenever the bounds set by model-checking tools are reached, the specifier does not know if the system is either too big for the tool or really unbounded. For instance a system which deadlocks for every n smaller than 10, does not imply anything about the behaviour for greater values of n. In such a case, bounded analysis is successful and complements model-checking. Let us consider an infinite global system in which some components are finite (bounded), which has been proved using the method introduced above. Indeed, we compute the configuration graph of the bounded STS, the product with the other STS, then the LTS interpretation of the finite resulting system. We recall with reference to Proposition 2.2 that it is a finer interpretation than simply computing the product and interpreting it afterwards.

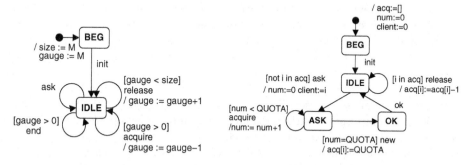

Fig. 1. Resource allocator system (left: allocator, right: client system)

As an illustration, let us take a resource allocator system with two components: the allocator and the client system. Figure 1 presents the STS descriptions of these components. The *allocator* can start (`init`), accept a request for a quantity (`ask`), send a resource unit (`acquire`), release a quantity (`release`), fulfill a request (`end`). The maximal amount of resources shared by the allocator is M. Variable `gauge` is used to keep track of the allocated resources. On the other hand, one *client system* centralizes the management of all the clients which are requiring resources. To simplify the presentation, we have omitted the client actions of entering and leaving the system. The client system can start (init), send a request for a quantity (ask) and related to client i, accept a resource unit (acquire), release a resource acquired by the client i (release), terminate the request (new), return to the idle state (ok). The amount requested by one client is identified by the QUOTA constant (with QUOTA$\leq$M). Variable num stores the current number of resources while acquiring them, and the acq vector stores the acquired resources for the clients. Synchronisations are (init,init), (release,release), (acquire,acquire), (ask,ask) and (end,ok).

Under the hypotheses of a given M and a given QUOTA, the system is not finite since the number of clients is not known. Model-checking techniques must set this number, and hence find a deadlock. Indeed, after a while, resources will lack since resources acquired by the clients are not all released before starting a new request. Thus we can only assert that the allocator deadlocks for a given number of clients. However, bounded analysis can be performed, since the allocator is bounded (M is a constant and gauge$\leq$M is a global constraint). In this example the weak interpretation of the STS ($W_{LTS}(allocator \otimes_V client\ system)$) resulting from the synchronous product of the allocator and the client system STS, and the configuration graph of the allocator STS ($G(allocator, M)$) are deadlock free. Finally, we can detect that the synchronous product of the allocator configuration graph and the client STS ($G(allocator, M) \otimes_V client\ system$) deadlocks without choosing arbitrarily a specific number of clients.

4   Bounded Decomposition

Results of the previous section are extended by a notion of decomposition which allows in a first step to generate finite representations of bounded parts of a system, and to check them in a second step.

4.1   Principle

The idea is to choose a subset of the data and to do a partial evaluation of STS using it. The computation of the configuration graph is adjusted to only evaluate guards and actions related to the selected data. One can then analyse parts of an STS which can be bounded and then build an abstraction. This requires the STS to be decomposable. In this section, we introduce our definitions on a binary decomposition, even though the decomposition can be extended to $n > 2$ and can be iterated several times.

Definition 6 (Decomposable STS). *An STS $(D, (\Sigma, Ax), S, L, s^0, T)$ is decomposable if and only if: i) D can be decomposed into $D_1 \times D_2$, ii) for each $(s, \mu, \epsilon, \delta, t)$ in T, for each $v = (v_1, v_2) : D$, $\mu(v) \equiv \mu_1(v_1) \land \mu_2(v_2)$, with μ_i a guard for D_i, iii) for each $(s, \mu, \epsilon, \delta, t)$ in T, for each $v = (v_1, v_2) : D$, $\delta(v) \equiv (\delta_1(v_1), \delta_2(v_2))$, with δ_i a function on D_i.*

When d is decomposable we may define two successive partial unfoldings, G_1 and G_2. G_1 simulates the system relatively to D_1 and keeps unchanged information related to D_2. G_1 can be viewed as a partial evaluation of the configuration graph. We focus here on emissions, however the principle extends to other kinds of events. G_1 applies to transitions $(s, \mu, l!e, \delta, t)$ and values $v_1 : D_1$. If $\mu_1(v1)\downarrow = true$, G_1 generates a transition $((s, v_1), \mu_2, l!e, (Self_{D_1}, \delta_2), (t, \delta_1(v_1)\downarrow))$. G_2 simulates $G_1(d, v_1^0)$ relatively to D_2. Hence, it applies to transitions generated by G_1 and values $v_2 : D_2$. If $\mu_2(v_2)\downarrow = true$, G_2 generates a transition $((s, (v_1, v_2)), true, l!e((v_1, v_2))\downarrow, (Self_{D_1}, Self_{D_2}), (t, (\delta_1(v_1)\downarrow, \delta_2(v_2)\downarrow)))$. During the G_1 step, internal communications and (external) emissions are evaluated. However, receptions from D_2 must be delayed until the G_2 step takes place.

Proposition 4. *Let d be a decomposable STS. The configuration graph G of d can be computed as follows: $G(d, (v_1^0, v_2^0)) \equiv G_2(G_1(d, v_1^0), v_2^0)$.*

On the left hand side, a transition such as $(s, \mu, l!e, \delta, t)$ with $v = (v_1, v_2)$, becomes $((s, (v_1, v_2)), true, l!e((v_1, v_2))\downarrow, (Self_{D_1}, Self_{D_2}), (t, (\delta(v_1, v_2)\downarrow)))$. On the right hand side, the transition is $((s, v_1), v_2), true, l!e((v_1, v_2)) \downarrow, (Self_{D_1}, Self_{D_2}), (t, (\delta_1(v_1)\downarrow, \delta_2(v_2)\downarrow))$ if $\mu_1(v_1)\downarrow = true$ and $\mu_2(v_2)\downarrow = true$. Both results are equivalent taking into account the decomposition properties of d and the state isomorphism from $S_1 \times (D_1 \times D_2)$ to $(S_1 \times D_1) \times D_2$.

Definition 7 (Bounded Decomposition). *If d is a decomposable STS and $G_1(d, v_1^0)$ is finite then it is a bounded decomposition of d.*

Bounded decompositions define abstractions of STS which yet preserve interesting properties with reference to the initial STS. These properties ensure that some analysis for the initial STS can be undertaken on one of its bounded decompositions. Propositions 1.2 and 4 ensure that the standard interpretation of the bounded decomposition $G_1(d, v_1^0)$ is a simulation of the standard interpretation of $G(d, (v_1^0, v_2^0))$.

Proposition 5. *If d and d' are decomposable STS then $d \otimes_V d'$ is decomposable.*

There are several possible decompositions for $d \otimes_V d'$. Note that the STS synchronous product naturally yields decomposable STS. However, a nontrivial decomposition is the following. If $D = D_1 \times D_2$ and $D' = D_1' \times D_2'$ then the data type of $d \otimes_V d'$ is $(D_1 \times D_2) \times (D_1' \times D_2')$ which is isomorphic to $(D_1 \times D_1') \times (D_2 \times D_2')$. d and d' being decomposable, this isomorphism may guide a new decomposition of $d \otimes_V d'$.

4.2   Application: The Ticket Mutual Exclusion Protocol

We illustrate first the decomposition principle on a mutual exclusion protocol inspired by the ticket protocol as described in [13]. However, our version differs from that one since we deal with distributed components communicating by messages, and not processes operating on a shared memory. We also distinguish entering (**use**) and leaving (**end**) the critical section. Finally, a counter C and a guard C=0 are added to the server which computes the number of processes in their critical section. This counter is used to check the mutual exclusion property. STS associated to process and server are described in Figure 2. Synchronisations are summarized in the following vectors: (think,givet), (use,gives), and (end,end).

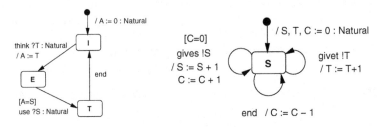

Fig. 2. STS descriptions: process (left) and server (right)

This system is unbounded since variables S, T, and A can store arbitrary large values. We split the variables into {} and {A} for the process, and {C} and {T,S} for the server. With these subsets we can easily check the decomposition of definition 6. Then, this decomposition produces a partial configuration graph on the C counter, on which boundedness is checked.

From such a finite system, safety properties like mutual exclusion can be checked. Mutual exclusion appears as the absence of the situation with more than one process in state T or as the fact that $C \leq 1$. Our prototype succeeds in generating the global system, checking the boundedness, computing the config-uration graph and then checking mutual exclusion for up to 8 processes within about three minutes. The resulting product (for 8 processes and the server) is made up of 6561 states and 52488 transitions; the configuration graph contains 1280 states and 6656 transitions. However CADP and SPIN, with the default configuration values and bounded data types, *e.g.*, natural numbers bounded to 256, do not pass 6 processes.

4.3   Application: A Resource Allocator (V2)

This section illustrates the use of bounded decomposition on a more elaborated variant (Fig. 3) of the Section 3 resource allocator. In this version client iden-tities are communicated to the allocator which hence knows the client (who) and the requested quantity. The allocated (GIVEN) and the requested (QUOTA) amounts are natural number constants (not necessary equal). The constraint M$\geq$QUOTA$\geq$GIVEN$\geq$1 is assumed. The allocator communicates with the client sys-tem on the **delete** event when there are not enough free resources. Whenever this occurs, the client system releases the allocated resources owned by a client. Variable **num** stores the current quantity acquired by a client, while **total** ac-cumulates the acquired resources for all clients. Variable **id** is used to store the client identities and **acq** the allocated quantities.

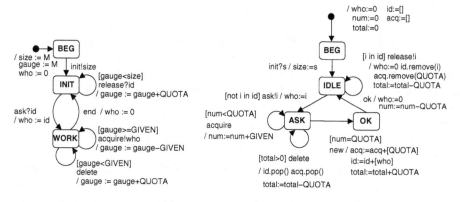

Fig. 3. Revisited resource allocator system (left: allocator, right: client system)

The global system is not bounded, and furthermore none of the components is bounded. A possible decomposition is to separate actions on identities from actions on quantities as allowed by Proposition 5. Hence, one has on the one hand variables {size, gauge} and on the other hand the who variable. Regarding the client, its decomposition is based on a partition between variables {size, num, total} and variables {who, acq, id}. Figure 4 presents the system decomposition view, which was obtained from the synchronous product of the allocator and the client system. Guards and actions not related to the variables {size, gauge} of the allocator and {size, num, total} of the client system are hidden in the decomposition.

Fixing values for M, QUOTA, and GIVEN, the boundedness is checked to be true for this decomposition. We have carried out experiments on the system for

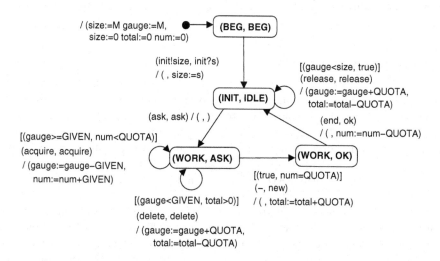

Fig. 4. The system decomposition view for {size, gauge} and {size, num, total}

various values of `size`, `QUOTA`, and `GIVEN`. As an example with M=1000, QUOTA=2, and GIVEN=1, a configuration graph of 2503 states and 3004 transitions is built. Experiments show that if `GIVEN` does not divide `QUOTA` the system deadlocks. In the state (`WORD`, `ASK`) only three transitions are possible: (`acquire`, `acquire`), (`delete`, `delete`), and (`-`, `new`) (see Fig. 4). Since `GIVEN` does not divide `QUOTA`, the condition `num>QUOTA` will be eventually true and `num=QUOTA` will never be true. Note also that the condition `gauge<GIVEN` which enables `delete` becomes false after triggering this transition (since `QUOTA≥GIVEN`), thus the sequence `delete ; delete` cannot occur. This is an example of a safety property we have checked on the bounded decomposition.

On the other hand, if `GIVEN` divides `QUOTA` then the bounded decomposition has no deadlock. However, this fact is not sufficient to ensure that the global system is deadlock free. A thorough look at the bounded decomposition shows that the guards left to evaluate in the G_2 step are `[(gauge<size, i in id)]` and `[(true, not i in id)]`. At least one of these guards is true since either `[not i in id]` or `[i in id]` is true and an allocation has been done thus `gauge<size` is true. Therefore the global system is not blocking if `GIVEN` divides `QUOTA`.

Resource availability is an important property in such a system. Generally it is a mix of safety and liveness properties. However, as stated in [27], availability properties with bounded waiting time are pure safety properties. Thus, bounded decompositions can be applied to check them. Assuming that each action has a maximum duration, we may be interested in the longest logical time sequence between a client request (`ask`) and its end (`end`). The longest sequence has form: `ask ; acquire`^{p}` ; delete ; acquire`^{r}` ; new ; ok`, where $p + r = ($QUOTA % GIVEN$)$. Therefore the global system satisfies the longest sequence property. However one may expect to prove that: *for any client the longest sequence is* `ask ; acquire`^{p}` ; delete ; acquire`^{r}` ; new ; ok`. This is true but actually it requires an additional analysis observing that the client system freezes the client identity during the allocation and the system is not blocking as discussed above.

5   Related Work

Our model of concurrent components can be related to Architectural Description Languages (ADL). It allows one to describe behavioural interfaces of both atomic and composite components. In addition, components can handle data types within their protocols, and communicate synchronizing on messages. However, our focus in this paper is not to provide a new ADL but to tackle analysis issues. [25] presents a formal ADL for which analysis is possible using techniques presented here.

Enumerative model-checking techniques usually bound all the sources of infinity. Similarly, bounded model-checking [6] searches for counterexamples in executions bounded by some length k. Therefore, let us focus on abstraction techniques and approaches dedicated to the verification of STS or parameterized systems.

Several works use abstraction techniques to verify state-based systems [11, 22, 12, 5]. For instance, in [11], the authors show how to extract abstract finite state machines from finite state programs using techniques similar to abstract interpretation. Our notions of abstraction and simulation are close to this work but our starting point is a state and transition based description of a program. In addition, our goal is to check if a bounded approximation can be built from it. Note that Proposition 2.2 in conjunction with a boundedness procedure gives an automatic way to approximate an infinite system. Most authors try to define abstractions over LTS (obtained from low level specification or code) and then address usual verification techniques on these abstracted LTS. We focus on the use of verification in the design phase and our bounded decomposition automatically builds an abstraction mapping. Components are specified directly with STS, then we try to unfold them partially to use usual verification techniques.

Many approaches have been proposed for symbolic model-checking of various kinds of infinite state systems, such as [14, 13, 3, 7]. A formalism similar to our symbolic system is described in [13]. The authors define a general and concurrent system with a translation preserving semantics into Constraint Logic Programming. They also present a method for verifying safety properties which is relevant to infinite state systems. While the formalism is different, our data types with positive conditional axioms are known to be equivalent to constraints written as Horn clauses. Compared to this work, our objectives are slightly different since rather than replacing model-checking approaches we propose to complement them for some specific systems (decomposable and bounded). We also emphasize [3] which computes reachability sets of counter automata. These sets, defined by Presburger formulae, are represented by automata and the authors propose an algorithm to increase convergence computation. Boundedness is equivalent to the property of finite reachability set. A counter automata is a counter STS allowing $c \leq M$ guards and this provides a general semi-algorithm for reachability.

6   Concluding Remarks

Behavioural interfaces are required in component based software engineering to perform analysis and relate efficiently models and implementations. Most proposals in this area deal with LTS models. However, more expressive models such as STS are needed to take data encapsulation and value passing into account. A major weakness of such models is the lack of dedicated analysis techniques. Direct mapping into standard model-checkers results in state explosion problems in the presence of unbounded data types and hence is not directly applicable.

In this paper we proposed an analysis framework for STS based on configuration graphs and LTS interpretations. This enables one to use the usual verification techniques on these LTS. In addition, we have also presented specific analysis techniques, namely bounded analysis and bounded decomposition, and demonstrated how they may complement model-checking. We have developed a prototype in Python (about 4000 lines) which supports STS description, configuration graph computation, product computation and the boundedness checking. We have already applied successfully our approach (boundedness, decomposition and model-checking) to several examples: a flight reservation system, several variants of the bakery protocols, the slip protocol, several variants of a resource allocator, and a cash point service.

Future work aims at extending our techniques on boundedness checking and boundedness decomposition. For instance, the selection of counter variables guiding the decomposition should be assisted by slicing techniques [9]. They can be applied to focus on a property one wants to check (which depends on variables), and then obtain the set of variables with a direct effect on this formula. Another perspective is to link our prototype with the verification tools CADP or SPIN.

Acknowledgments. We would like to thank the reviewers for their useful comments and suggestions.

References

1. R. Allen and D. Garlan. A Formal Basis for Architectural Connection. *ACM Transactions on Software Engineering and Methodology*, 6(3):213–249, 1997.
2. A. Arnold. *Finite Transition Systems*. International Series in Computer Science. Prentice-Hall, 1994.
3. S. Bardin, A. Finkel, and J. Leroux. FASTer Acceleration of Counter Automata in Practice. In *Proc. of TACAS'04*, volume 2988 of *LNCS*, pages 576–590. Springer, 2004.
4. T. Barros, L. Henrio, and E. Madelaine. Behavioural Models for Hierarchical Components. In *Proc. of SPIN'05*, volume 3639 of *LNCS*, pages 154–168. Springer-Verlag, 2005.
5. S. Bensalem, Y. Lakhnech, and S. Owre. Computing Abstractions of Infinite State Systems Compositionally and Automatically. In *Proc. of CAV '98*, volume 1427 of *LNCS*, pages 319–331. Springer-Verlag, 1998.
6. A. Biere, A. Cimatti, E. M. Clarke, and Y. Zhu. Symbolic Model Checking without BDDs. In *Proc. of TACAS'99*, volume 1579 of *LNCS*, pages 193–207. Springer-Verlag, 1999.
7. A. Bouajjani, P. Habermehl, and T. Vojnar. Abstract Regular Model Checking. In *Proc. of CAV'04*, volume 3114 of *LNCS*, pages 372–386. Springer-Verlag, 2004.
8. A. Bracciali, A. Brogi, and C. Canal. A Formal Approach to Component Adaptation. *Journal of Systems and Software*, 74(1), 2005.
9. I. Brückner and H. Wehrheim. Slicing an Integrated Formal Method for Verification. In *Proc. of ICFEM'05*, volume 3785 of *LNCS*, pages 360–374. Springer-Verlag, 2005.
10. M. Calder, S. Maharaj, and C. Shankland. A Modal Logic for Full LOTOS Based on Symbolic Transition Systems. *The Computer Journal*, 45(1):55–61, 2002.
11. E. M. Clarke, O. Grumberg, and D. E. Long. Model-Checking and Abstraction. *ACM Transactions on Programming Languages and Systems*, 16(5):1512–1542, 1994.
12. D. Dams, R. Gerth, and O. Grumberg. Abstract Interpretation of Reactive Systems. *ACM Transactions on Programming Languages and Systems*, 19(2):253–291, 1997.

13. G. Delzanno. An Overview of MSR(C): A CLP-based Framework for the Symbolic Verification of Parameterized Concurrent Systems. In *Proc. of WFLP'02*, volume 76 of *ENTCS*. Elsevier, 2002.

14. J. Esparza, D. Hansel, P. Rossmanith, and S. Schwoon. Efficient Algorithms for Model Checking Pushdown Systems. In *Proc. of CAV'00*, volume 1855 of *LNCS*, pages 232–247. Springer-Verlag, 2000.

15. A. Finkel, P. McKenzie, and C. Picaronny. A Well-Structured Framework for Analysing Petri Nets Extensions. *Information and Computation*, 195(1-2):1–29, 2004.

16. H. Garavel, F. Lang, and R. Mateescu. An Overview of CADP 2001. *EASST Newsletter*, 4:13–24, 2001.

17. G. J. Holzmann. *The Spin Model Checker, Primer and Reference Manual*. Addison-Wesley, Reading, Massachusetts, 2003.

18. A. Ingólfsdóttir and H. Lin. *A Symbolic Approach to Value-passing Processes*, chapter 7 of Handbook of Process Algebra. Elsevier, 2001.

19. B. Jeannet, T. Jéron, V. Rusu, and E. Zinovieva. Symbolic Test Selection Based on Approximate Analysis. In *Proc. of TACAS'05*, volume 3440 of *LNCS*, pages 349–364. Springer Verlag, 2005.

20. J. Kramer, J. Magee, and S. Uchitel. Software Architecture Modeling and Analysis: A Rigorous Approach. In *Proc. of SFM'03*, volume 2804 of *LNCS*, pages 44–51. Springer-Verlag, 2003.

21. S. Leue, R. Mayr, and W. Wei. A Scalable Incomplete Test for the Boundedness of UML RT Models. In *Proc. of TACAS'04*, volume 2988 of *LNCS*, pages 327–341. Springer-Verlag, 2004.

22. C. Loiseaux, S. Graf, J. Sifakis, A. Bouajjani, and S. Bensalem. Property Preserving Abstractions for the Verification of Concurrent Systems. *Formal Methods in System Design*, 6(1):11–44, 1995.

23. R. Mateescu. A Generic On-the-Fly Solver for Alternation-Free Boolean Equation Systems. In *Proc. of TACAS'03*, volume 2619 of *LNCS*, pages 81–96. Springer Verlag, 2003.

24. S. Moschoyiannis, M. W. Shields, and P. J. Krause. Modelling Component Behaviour with Concurrent Automata. In *Proc. of FESCA'05*, volume 114(3) of *ENTCS*, pages 199–220, 2005.

25. P. Poizat and J.-C. Royer. Korrigan: a Formal ADL with Full Data Types and a Temporal Glue. Technical Report 88-2003, LaMI, CNRS et Université d'Evry Val d'Essonne, September 2003.

26. P. Poizat, J.-C. Royer, and G. Salaün. Symbolic Bounded Analysis for Component Behavioural Protocols. Technical report, Écoles des Mines de Nantes, 2005. Available at http://www.emn.fr/x-info/jroyer/rrBounded.pdf.

27. F. B. Schneider. Enforceable Security Policies. *ACM Transactions on Information and System Security*, 3(1):30–50, 2000.

Modeling and Validation of a Software Architecture for the Ariane-5 Launcher*

Iulian Ober[1], Susanne Graf[2], and David Lesens[3]

[1] Toulouse University, GRIMM/ISYCOM laboratory**
IUT-B 1 pl. Brassens BP 73, 31703 Blagnac, France
iulian.ober@imag.fr
[2] VERIMAG
2, av. de Vignate, 38610 Gières, France
susanne.graf@imag.fr
[3] EADS SPACE Transportation
66, route de Verneuil - BP 3002, 78133 Les Mureaux Cedex - France
david.lesens@space.eads.net

Abstract. We present the modeling and validation experiments performed with the IFx validation toolset and with the UML profile developed within the IST Omega project, on a representative space vehicle control system: a model of the Ariane-5 flight software obtained by manual reverse engineering. The goal of the study is to verify functional and scheduling-related requirements under different task architecture assumptions. The study is also a proof of concept for the UML-based validation technique proposed in IFx.

1 Introduction

Model-driven engineering is making its way through the habits of software designers and developers, pushed forward by the increasing maturity of modeling languages and tools. This paradigm promotes a complete re-foundation of software engineering activities on the basis of *models*, as well as the use of automatic tools for most post-design activities. In this context, the *software model* is the central artifact which gathers different aspects ranging from the requirements to software architecture, to component behavior, etc.

More recently, the trend is extending beyond software development activities, to *system* design. For this activity, which traditionally employed rather ad-hoc models, the community is currently seeking new formalisms, like SysML [19] or architecture description languages (ADLs). In the end, this adds new aspects (environment, hardware architecture, process and thread mappings, etc.) to the central artifact which becomes the *system model*.

The use of such heterogeneous models is justified by the complexity of current systems which have to satisfy tightly interwoven functional and non-functional requirements.

---

* This work has been partially financed by the OMEGA IST project.
** Work performed while at VERIMAG.

R. Gorrieri and H. Wehrheim (Eds.): FMOODS 2006, LNCS 4037, pp. 48–62, 2006.

In this paper we discuss the case of such a complex system, the control software of the Ariane-5 launcher, which is typical for the space vehicle control domain. Applications in this field typically involve a time driven part which implements the attitude and orbit control loop, and an asynchronous, event driven part, which performs mission management tasks. The different sub-systems share resources like busses and other spacecraft equipment.

The current practice, which consists in using cyclic sampling of asynchronous events and a Rate Monotonic Scheduling (RMS) policy [17], offers static criteria for deciding schedulability, and can offer correctness by construction (under some additional hypotheses) for other properties like exclusive access to shared resources. However, this policy proves to be very inflexible under demanding reactivity constraints or under processor overloads.

Consequently, more dynamic solutions are sought by system designers, like using fixed priority preemptive scheduling outside the sufficient (but not necessary) schedulability conditions of RMS. Such solutions rely on automatic verification methods, which have to take into account some functional aspects of the system.

In this paper, we describe a study in which the Omega UML profile [5, 10] (defined within the IST Omega project[1]) is used for modeling both functional and architectural aspects of a representative subset of the Ariane-5 system. We discuss the verification of both functional and scheduling-related requirements with the IFx toolset [18] which implements the profile.

1.1 A Short Introduction to Omega UML and the IFx Tool

Omega UML is a profile targeting the design of real-time systems. The profile supports a large subset of the operational concepts of UML: classes, with most of their relationships (associations, composition, generalization), features (attributes, operations) and behavior descriptions (state machines). Actions, which are used to describe the effect of operations and of state machine transitions, are written in a syntax compliant with the UML action semantics. The language contains imperative constructs like assignments, operation calls, object creation, signal exchange, etc.

The description of concurrent systems is supported by means of *active* classes. Instances of active classes define a partition of the object space into *activity groups*, each group having its own thread of control, and functioning in run-to-completion steps. Communication is possible inside or between groups, by exchanging asynchronous signals and by calling operations. The execution model is an extension of the semantics implemented by the Rhapsody UML tool.

Detailed descriptions of Omega UML execution model can be found in [5]. On top of the concepts mentioned above, the Omega profile also defines a set of time-related constructs [10].

IFx[2] [18] is a toolset providing simulation and model-checking functionalities for Omega UML models. It is built on top of the IF environment [4], and provides

---

[1] http://www-omega.imag.fr
[2] http://www-if.imag.fr/IFx

a compiler of UML models to IF specifications. Models may be edited with any XMI-compatible editor[3].

Model checking is based on efficient forward state-space exploration methods for timed automata. Timed safety properties may be expressed as observers, which are described in the sequel. Generated diagnostic traces can be analyzed by simulation. In order to scale to complex models, IF supports optimization and abstraction in several ways: by "exact" static optimizations (like dead variable factorization and dead code elimination), by partial-order reduction, by data abstraction (static slicing). More details can be found in [18].

2   The Ariane-5 Software

The Ariane-5 flight software controls the launcher's mission from lift-off to payload release. It operates in a completely autonomous mode and has to handle both external disturbances (e.g. wind) and different hardware failures that may occur during the flight.

This case study takes into account the most relevant points required for such an embedded application and focuses on the real time critical behavior by abstracting from complex functionality (like control algorithms) and implementation details, such as specific hardware and operating system dependencies. Nevertheless, it is fully representative of an operational space system. The typical characteristic of such systems is that they implement two kinds of behavior:

- *Cyclic synchronous algorithms.* These are principally the control/command algorithms (in the sequel they are called GNC for Guidance, Navigation and Control). The algorithms and their reactivity constraints are defined by the control engineers based on discretization of continuous physical laws.
- *Aperiodic, event driven algorithms.* These algorithms manage the mission phases and perform particular tasks when the spacecraft changes from one permanent mode to another (engine ignition and stop, stage release, etc.), or when hardware failures occur (alternative or abortion manoeuvres).

The software components implementing this functionality are physically deployed on a single processor[4] and share a common bus for acquiring sensor data and sending commands to the equipment.

The proof of correctness of the mission management components can be made by (almost completely) abstracting from the control algorithms. In an earlier experiment, we have used an SDL model of the mission management in order to verify this kind of properties [3].

The correctness of control algorithms concerns two issues: their numerical computation, and their concurrency behavior. The numerical correctness is not considered here. For the concurrency, the proof of correctness is usually done using the synchrony hypothesis. The synchronous approach makes verification

---

[3] Rational Rose and I-Logix Rhapsody have been tested used in the OMEGA project.
[4] In fact, a set of replicated processors, but this is out of the scope of our case study.

using a non-timed semantics much simpler. The non-timed semantics just assumes that all entries are available when the computation cycle starts and the results of the computation are made available at the end of each cycle. There exist results stating sufficient conditions under which such a synchronous design can be implemented in a distributed and/or multi-threaded environment [20]. However, in this case study the sufficient conditions do not hold in all cases, and the satisfaction of the synchrony hypothesis must be verified.

Therefore, in this case study we have considered more particularly the problem of verifying that a low-level software architecture (a task model), together with a set of other non-functional assumptions (worst case execution times, arrival model), satisfy the reactivity constraints imposed on the software and ensure the synchrony hypothesis for the cyclic algorithms.

The current practice for ensuring such non-functional constraints consists in using an RMS-based scheduler. Asynchronous events are sampled with the frequency of the smallest cycle. The schedulability of this architecture can be decided statically, under the assumption that relevant values for WCET of tasks can be provided. Moreover, in the current solution, the exchange of data between the different tasks or between a functional task and the bus are allowed only in predefined time slots at the beginning and at the end of each task's cycle (even if the computation finishes earlier in the cycle). Consequently, mutual exclusion between writes in the exchange memory is satisfied by construction, and with no possibility for priority inversion.

On the other hand, this architecture is very inflexible in the following circumstances:

- when some acyclic events need shorter reaction time than the basic cycle (which is in fact the case for the Ariane-5 system),
- when some cyclic algorithm needs more recent measurement data, that has to be acquired during the cycle (also the case in the Ariane-5 system),
- when an algorithm needs a longer time than the pre-assigned slot, for instance in case of high CPU load (this feature, not required today, will become mandatory for future highly autonomous space systems).

In the case of Ariane-5, the software designers have used a more flexible architecture, which is still based on fixed priority preemptive scheduling, but which violates some of the RMS assumptions mentioned above in order to ensure better reactivity (reads and writes during the cycle, triggering of asynchronous code during a cycle). Nevertheless, such an architecture has to be formally validated with respect to the non-functional requirements concerning timing, scheduling and mutual exclusion. This is the main objective of our case study.

3   The Verification Model

The UML model used for verification has been built manually from the existing software code, by a team from EADS Space Transportation. Its functional decomposition is independent of the task architecture; it is structured around 6 objects implementing the main categories of functionality, each defined by a singleton active class. They are:

- *Acyclic*: the main mission management object, which handles the start of the flight sequence and the switching from one phase to another. Its behavior is described by a state machine reacting to event receptions from the GNC algorithms (e.g., end of thrust detection) or from the environment, and to time conditions (e.g., time window protections ensuring that the treatment associated to an external event is performed within a predefined time window even in case of failure of the event detection mechanism).
- A set of specific objects which handle the acyclic management activities related to a particular launcher stage. They react to events received from *Acyclic* or to internal time constraints. In the study, we considered only two stages: *EAP* (lateral booster) and *EPC* (main stage of the Ariane 5 launcher).
- *Cyclics*: This object manages the activation of the cyclic control/command algorithms (GNC). The algorithms are executed in a predefined order, depending on the current state of the launcher, which is tracked by the *Acyclic* class. Its state machine appears in an example later on in Fig. 3. We consider in more detail two of the algorithms activated by *Cyclics*, each implemented by a separate object: *Thrust_Monitor*, responsible for the monitoring of the *EAP* thrust, and *Guidance_Task*, which has the particularity that its activation frequency is lower than that of the other GNC algorithms.

In order to validate the software, a part of the environment needs to be modeled. In our case, it includes two kinds of spacecraft equipment – *Valves* and *Pyrotechnic commands* (the model includes possible hardware failures), the external environment – namely the ground control centre, as well as abstractions of parts of the software which are not described in the model (such as: a numerical algorithm or the 1553MIL bus allowing the communication between the main software and the equipment).

3.1   Capturing Functional and Timing Requirements

Using Omega UML, requirements can be formalized by means of *observers*, and verified against the design model. In this section, we discuss briefly the concepts and we give an example of how they are put to work in the Ariane-5 model. More detail on observers can be found in [18].

Observers are special objects which monitor the execution of the model and give verdicts when a requirement is satisfied or violated. Observers may have their own local memory (attributes), and their behavior is described by a state machine, in which some states are labeled with the stereotypes <<success>> or <<error>> providing verdicts. The monitoring of model execution is done by observing events like signal outputs, operation calls or returns, state changes, etc., or by observing the state of the system, like attribute values, contents of queues, states of the state machines, etc. [5]

We take for example the following property:

Property P1. *The launcher shall not lift-off if an anomaly is detected during the Vulcain engine ignition. In case of lift-off abort, the valves shall all be closed within 2 seconds and the pyrotechnic commands shall not be ignited.*

An anomaly on the Vulcain ignition corresponds, in our modeling of the environment, to a *Valve* object entering the *Failed_Open* state. This failure shall be detected by the software, which shall then abort the lift-off and secure the launcher. Thus, this property is expressed more precisely as follows:

If any instance of the *Valve* class enters one of the states *Failed_Open* or *Failed_Close*, then:

- All the instances of the *Pyro* class shall never enter the state *Ignition_done*.
- 2 seconds after the valve failure, all instances of the *Valve* class shall be in state *Close* or *Failed_Close*, and then remain in this state forever.

This property is based on a pure black-box view of the software. Nevertheless, since several components are involved in aborting the lift-off, the designers have completed the property with the requirement that the internal events *Request_EAP_Preparation* and *Request_EAP_Release* are never emitted.

Fig. 1 shows how this property can be expressed using a timed observer: each time an *Open* command is received by some valve *v*, the observer tests whether *v* reaches the state *Failed_Open*.

If this premise holds, the observer enters state *aborted*, in which *Pyro* objects entering state *Ignition_done*, as well as emissions of the signals *Request_EAP_Preparation* and *Request_EAP_Release* are prohibited. After 2 seconds from entering state *aborting*, the observer goes to the inner state *aborted* in which, additionally, *Valves* entering the state *Open* or *Failed_Open* are also prohibited.

Note that the testing of the premise done by the observer corresponds to the universal quantification appearing textually in the premise of the property *P1* ("any instance of the *Valve* class"). Such a universal quantification would also have to be used in a state logic formula, had we used a temporal logic for formalizing the properties. However, to the best of our knowledge, no major model checking tool based on LTL or CTL supports directly this kind of first order logic in the specification of state formulas. For example, in UPPAAL [14], the same property could be expressed either by using a helper (observer) automaton which synchronizes with any *Valve* entering *Ignition_done*, or by using quantifier elimination (that only works under the restriction that the set of objects is known in advance – which is generally not true in Omega UML or IF

---

[5] A formal discussion of the expressivity of observers is out of scope. We note that: (1) observers are used to express linear timed *safety* properties, which may combine state or event-based atomic propositions, and (2) observers embed general algorithms, therefore their termination (hence also their satisfaction) is undecidable in general. For practical applications, we do not view this as a limitation.

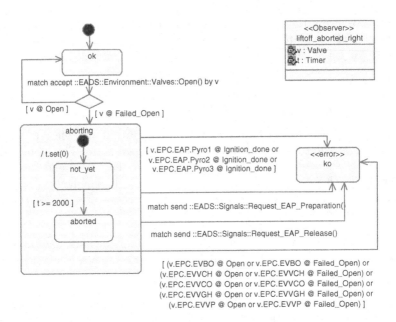

Fig. 1. Property p1

specifications). This supports our claim that observers are a flexible formalism for expressing common event or state-related timed safety properties.

Consider another property, required by electrical constraints on the hardware:

Property P2. *The software shall not send two Open commands to the same valve at less than 50ms of interval.*

P2 constrains the distance between pairs of events concerning a same instance of class *Valve*. The particularity of this property is that it concerns any consecutive pair in the series of commands sent by the software to a (any) *Valve*. This kind of property is typically easier to specify with a temporal logic.

Nevertheless, we show in Fig. 2 an observer which uses non-determinism to pick each particular occurrence of an event pair at a time and either verify the time distance, or skip to the next one (as the model checker explores all alternatives, all pairs are eventually verified)[6]. In state *initial*, the observer waits for a command to be sent to any *Valve*, stores the reference of the concerned *Valve* in v1 and proceeds to state *nondet*. (This behavior ensures universal quantification over the set of valves, in the same way as in *P1*). In state *nondet*, it chooses non-deterministically whether to proceed by verifying the timing of the next command sent to the same valve, or to return to *initial* and wait for another command to (any) *Valve*.

The rest of the observer tests a simple timed safety condition: the next command sent to the *Valve* v1 does not come before 50ms. The clock *t* is used to

---

[6] The observer presented here is not optimal in the required verification time/memory.

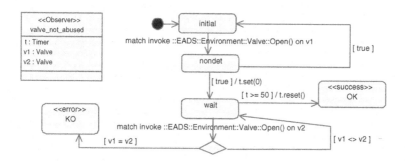

Fig. 2. Property p2

measure 50ms. In state *wait*, other commands may come, but they cause an *error* only if they concern the valve *v1*. If more than 50ms elapse without error, the observer reaches a success state and considers the property verified for this particular events occurrence pair.

Stereotyping the *OK* state with <<**success**>> allows also to make model checking more efficient: after the observer has reached *OK*, the execution of the (system, observer) pair cannot lead to *KO* anymore, and may safely be ignored.

3.2   Scheduling Constraints and Objectives

As mentioned before, the main focus in this study is on validating a particular task architecture based on fixed priority preemptive scheduling, in order to check that is satisfies several conditions concerning schedulability and mutually exclusive access to the bus.

In the architecture that we consider, the hypotheses of RMS [17] are not satisfied, as asynchronous events need to be handled as soon as they arrive. Another difficulty in using RMS-like schedulability decision criteria is that the execution time of the cyclic tasks varies a lot depending on the current flight phase. Fig. 3 shows the state machine of the control cycle, on which we can see that the worst case execution time of this cycle is around 64ms, while the best case is 37ms and the average measured by simulation is around 42ms. One cannot simply consider at each cycle the worst case execution time (of sporadic and cyclic tasks), as this would lead to a huge over-approximation of resource occupation and to the conclusion that the system is non schedulable. We also relax in some cases the requirement that reads and writes are done only in the beginning and in the end of each task's cycle. Therefore, the access to the bus is not mutually exclusive by construction.

The technique we adopt for proving these constraints is to take into account the functional behavior of the system and its impact on resource consumption.

Assigning priority levels to activities. The priorities were assigned just as in the RMS solution from which we started, according to the relative responsiveness required from an activity. Three levels of priority are used:

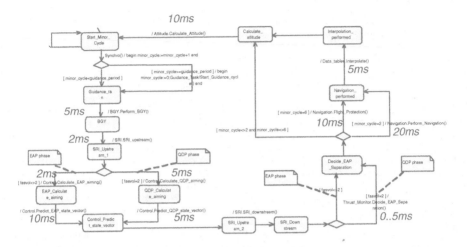

Fig. 3. Statechart of the Control cycle with unitary execution times

- Functions of the Regulation components have highest priority. They are sporadic and take about 2 to 5 ms each time a command is executed (open a valve, ignite a pyrotechnic command, etc.)
- Functions of the Navigation-Control components have medium priority. They are periodic, with a period of 72ms and take 37 to 64ms to execute depending on the current phase of the flight and other parameters.
- Functions of the Guidance components have lowest priority. They execute every 576ms. One of the goals of scheduling analysis was to determine how much processor time they can take in each cycle in order for the system to remain schedulable.

Activities that are on the same priority level are handled by the same runtime task, that is without overlapping.

Modeling the task architecture in Omega UML. Scheduling policies and resource consumption can be modeled using the lower level constructs of the Omega profile: objects which manipulate clocks and do the resource bookkeeping. In parallel with the Ariane-5 study, we developed a reusable model library for the IFx tool, which provides support for different types of schedulers.

The *Scheduling* library contains basically two kinds of classes organized in two hierarchies:

- *Task* classes used to annotate the user model with requests for execution time. Requests are parameterized with a *duration*, and depending on the scheduling policy, with information like *priority*, *deadline*, etc. Instances of *Task* classes can be shared by several objects.
- *Scheduler* classes are used to model the different scheduling policies. Each created *Task* has to be associated with a *Scheduler*. Subsequently, every time a *Task* requires processing time, it will communicate with its *Scheduler* in order to determine the actual time of finish, based on the task duration and

on the state of the *Scheduler* (i.e. the scheduling policy and the charge at that moment).

For modeling the behavior of the fixed priority preemptive scheduler in timed automata constructs, we use the scheme proposed in [9].

Scheduling objectives are modeled by observers. They are:

– The Navigation-Control (NC) functions must terminate within the 72ms cycle and the Guidance functions within the 576ms cycle.
  For the NC functions, this property is formalized in the observer in Fig. 4, by the fact that the *Cyclics* component receives the signal *Synchro*, which signi-fies the beginning of a cycle, only in the states *Start_Minor_Cycle*, *Wait_Start* or *Abort*. If a cycle does not finish in time, the *Cyclics* component is in an intermediate computation state when the next *Synchro* is received and this property is violated.
  The observer expressing the analogous property for the Guidance function is similar.
– The application uses a 1553 MIL bus. In this protocol, all data transfers are performed under the supervision of a bus controller (the main on-board computer in the case of the Ariane 5 case study). The software components read and write data in an exchange memory which is transferred via the bus to the equipment (also called remote terminal) at specific time frames (this process is called low-level transfer). The consistency condition for bus reads and writes is that the software components do not read or write the bus during the low-level transfer time frames. (calls to *read* and *write* operations do not occur while the *Bus* is in *Transfer* state).

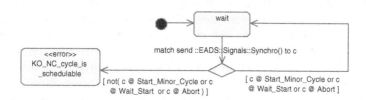

Fig. 4. Scheduling objective: the control cycle finishes in time

4 Ariane-5 Verification Results

4.1 Validation Methodology

In the context of the IFx toolset, the validation of UML models means performing several activities, which range from simple syntactic and static semantic checking to dynamic property verification, with the goal of improving the model and its conformance to its requirements. These activities are supported by different tools. The standard workflow used also in this case study is summarized below[7].

---

[7] A more detailed description can be found in [4].

1. The *translation phase* consists in invoking the *uml2if* compiler. Standard static checks are performed (name and type checks, checking of well formedness constraints).
2. The *simplification phase* consists in the application of static analysis and abstraction methods implemented in IF:
   - in the early validation phases we use mainly methods fully preserving verification results (such as dead variable / dead code analysis and clock reduction)
   - in the later phases (verification), we use in addition methods leading to over approximations such as abstractions of variables or clocks, or relaxation of *urgency* constraints.
3. The *simulation phase* consists in exploring the model by a mixture of interactive, guided and random simulation which allows usual debugging tasks like saving and reloading a played scenario, stepping back and forward through it, inspecting the system state, inserting conditional breakpoints, etc.
4. The *model-checking phase* is the main validation phase, in which the product space of the relevant part of the model and of a set of observers is searched for absence of *error* states, while avoiding the parts of the graph reachable only via *success* states.

   In this phase, there are 2 possibilities for handling time: discrete or symbolic. With discrete time, time progress is represented by a *tick* transition common to all processes, and this representation allows the use of more expressive time constraints. In case of the symbolic representation of time, a DBM is associated with each system state, like in the timed-automata based tools Kronos [22] and Uppaal [14]. The symbolic representation leads in most examples to much smaller state spaces.
5. the IF toolset implements a number of other verification techniques. The most interesting ones are comparison of models and minimization of models with respect to simulations and bisimulations. Minimization has been used in our case study to extract most general properties with respect to an observation criterion, given by a set of observable events (see in [3, 4]).

4.2   State Explosion and Use of Abstractions in Ariane-5

The duration of a basic cycle of the cyclic behavior of the Ariane-5 flight software is 72 ms. Each basic cycle contains several hundreds of steps. As the acyclic behavior uses some timers also to measure long durations, when composed with the cyclic behavior, every state reached through these steps is a new global system state. This quickly leads to an explosion, especially in the case of Ariane-5, where the footprint of a system state is quite large (see also §4.3).

In order to cope with the complexity of the model, we had to apply more evolved abstraction and reduction techniques which need a good understanding of both the functioning of the system and the verification and abstraction technology.

Compositional Abstraction. We have applied this well known technique which consists in the verification of properties of a subsystem, by replacing the other parts of the system — which play here the role of an environment — by a simpler descriptions representing an abstraction. The variable abstractions implemented in IF were not sufficient for the Ariane-5 model and we have built manual abstractions, which were still relatively simple, by using the existing decomposition of the system into a cyclic and an acyclic part and the clear interface between them.

To illustrate this, we take the example of the safety properties related only to the acyclic part (flight program and error handling). To prove their correctness, the cyclic GNC part has been abstracted by eliminating all the internal behavior and by sending messages (flight phase change commands) at arbitrary moments rather than at the precise time points computed by the concrete GNC. This represents clearly an abstraction and it was sufficient to show the satisfaction of all the properties of the asynchronous part (see [18, 3] for an older experience concerning this part). Note also that such an abstraction can in principle be constructed automatically.

Reduction of the duration of the flight phases. In order to validate the properties related to schedulability and concurrent bus access, we have used an alternative reduction without behavioral abstraction. As mentioned before, a huge source of state explosion is the difference of the time scale between the asynchronous and the cyclic behavior.

Asynchronous events are *rare*, and the system is working without occurrence of any asynchronous events during a large number of basic cycles (called *stable phases*). Moreover, most of the output of the cyclic part is irrelevant for the timing properties to be verified. Thus, it is sufficient to perform the proof on a functional abstraction of the cyclic part with a mission duration much greater than the basic cycle, but much shorter than the real mission duration.

In stable phases, all executions of the basic cycle in the cyclic part are identical with respect to the properties to be verified, in particular to the schedulability of all tasks in all relevant cycles, and to the observation of a certain time window for the commands sent from the synchronous to the asynchronous part (stable phases are outside this time window).

This suggests that it is sufficient to verify a reduced model, obtained by a drastic reduction of the overall flight duration, being careful to make sure that only stable phases are shortened, whereas all the critical transition phases are fully explored. The transition phases are defined by the flight phases defined in the acyclic part and by the occurrence of exception events. Exception events can occur at any time, but the correctness of the software must only be guaranteed for 2 exceptions for the entire flight, which means that it is enough to make the stable phases long enough to allow the occurrence of 2 exceptions with subsequent stabilization.

Using such a reduction of the real duration of the mission, the reachable state space for the entire flight could be explored, and all the properties could be finally validated.

4.3   Results and Figures

In this section, we show the efficiency of the applied reductions. The table in Fig. 5 shows the verification time and the cardinality of the state space, using dead variable and partial order reductions, while using different mission durations (but always respecting the required stabilization times).

Mission duration	Nr of states	Nr of transitions	Verif. time (min)
7 s	51 324	54 697	03:30
15 s	161 956	171 734	12:06
22 s	303 496	321 206	11:33
30 s	463 932	490 901	22:58
37 s	658 981	696 031	34:53

Fig. 5. Complexity for different mission durations (all properties combined)

For the comparison, we have used a model with all the properties (observers) enabled simultaneously. There is no state explosion caused by the parallel composition of all properties, since properties are not completely independent.

A discussion is necessary as the figures presented here may seem low compared to other known examples in explicit state or symbolic model checking, which range beyond 10^7 states. One must consider the following:

- The Ariane-5 model (after UML translation) consists of 77 types of IF processes, each having (many) variables of complex types, and sometimes having dynamically created instances. The footprint of the system state is slightly variable, with an average of 10KB.
  In our view, one cannot compare the 10^6 order of magnitude of Ariane-5 (for the largest exploration, shown in Fig. 5), with results obtained on other systems, which may have higher combinatorics but smaller footprints. It is unfortunately impossible to propose this model as a basis for benchmarking, due to confidentiality reasons related to its industrial nature.
- Given that the (approximately) 6GB of Ariane's 658981 states have been explored on a machine with only 1GB of RAM, we see this as evidence of the efficiency of the sharing algorithms [4] of the IF exploration platform.
- Another characteristics of the state spaces obtained here is that they are very narrow and deep (almost a vertical string). This is not because the example is sequential by nature: concurrency is present in this model and the combinatorics is potentially very big. The linear form of the state spaces indicates the efficiency of the partial order reduction of the IF platform.

5   Comparison to Other Approaches, Discussion and Future Work

Discussion of related work. There exist already a number of tools proposed for the validation of UML models by translating a subset of UML into the input language of some existing validation tool [16, 15, 13, 7, 21, 6, 2, 1] to mention only a some of the relevant work in the context of real-time and embedded systems.

Like IFx, most of these tools are based on existing model-checkers such as SPIN [12] (in [16, 15]) or COSPAN [11] (in [21] for non-timed systems, and Kronos [22] (in [2]) or Uppaal [14] (in [13, 6]) for the verification of systems with timing constraints. Also the translation into proof-based frameworks, such as PVS (e.g. in [1]) or B, has been proposed.

With respect to the *expressivity of the UML profile* accepted, the IFx framework goes beyond other existing ones, as it handles a rich subset of UML, including inheritance and dynamic object creation and powerful timing features. Most of the cited UML validation tools are restricted to static systems, fitting exactly the model of the underlying model-checker. Also, they usually handle properties written in the property language proposed by the underlying model-checker. The Omega UML profile proposes *observers* for this purpose.

The IFx tool does not push forward the *theoretical* boundaries of existing verification technology. However, the tool presents a unique combination of features which prove to be very efficient in fighting scalability problems encountered in practice. It includes and combines the on-the-fly exploration of SPIN, the symbolic representation of time constraints of Kronos and Uppaal, the bisimulation based reduction techniques of Aldebaran [8], and adds verification-targeted optimizations based on static analysis, as well as support for industry-backed standards like SDL and UML.

Experience showed that the combination of these techniques allows to obtain feedback very rapidly on most models without much remodeling and adaptation effort by the user. Positive verification results required, for the bigger examples, some effort to find an appropriate property preserving abstraction and to apply it manually – which is a common limitation of major model-checking tools.

The model structuring concepts present in IF allow to limit the overhead induced by the translation a rich user level formalism like UML, and also make the translation more flexible. Consequently, we plan on moving towards UML 2.0 and to system-oriented formalisms like AADL, which are better suited for modeling architectural and non-functional problems in the space vehicle control domain.

References

[1] T. Arons, J. Hooman, H. Kugler, A. Pnueli, and M. van der Zwaag. Deductive verification of UML models in TLPVS. In *Proceedings UML 2004*, pages 335–349. LNCS 3273, 2004.

[2] Vieri Del Bianco, Luigi Lavazza, and Marco Mauri. Model checking UML specifications of real time software. In *Proceedings of 8th International Conference on Engineering of Complex Computer Systems*. IEEE, 2002.

[3] M. Bozga, D. Lesens, and L. Mounier. Model-Checking Ariane-5 Flight Program. In *Proceedings of FMICS'01 (Paris, France)*, pages 211–227. INRIA, 2001.

[4] M. Bozga, S. Graf, I. Ober, I. Ober, and J. Sifakis. The IF toolset. In *SFM-04:RT 4th Int. School on Formal Methods for the Design of Computer, Communication and Software Systems: Real Time*, LNCS, June 2004.

[5] W. Damm, B. Josko, A. Pnueli, and A. Votintseva. Understanding UML: A formal semantics of concurrency and communication in real-time UML. In *Proc. of the 1st Symposium on Formal Methods for Components and Objects (FMCO 2002)*, volume 2852 of *LNCS Tutorials*

[6] A. David, O. Möller, and W. Yi. Formal verification UML statecharts with real time extensions. In *Proceedings of FASE 2002 (ETAPS 2002)*, vol. 2306 of *LNCS*. Springer-Verlag, April 2002.

[7] M. del Mar Gallardo, P. Merino, and E. Pimentel. Debugging UML designs with model checking. *Journal of Object Technology*, 1(2):101–117, August 2002.

[8] J.-C. Fernandez, H. Garavel, A. Kerbrat, L. Mounier, R. Mateescu, and M. Sighireanu. CADP - a protocol validation and verification toolbox. In *Computer Aided Verification, 8th Int. Conf. CAV '96*, vol. 1102 of *LNCS*, 1996.

[9] E. Fersman, L. Mokrushin, P. Pettersson, and W. Yi. Schedulability analysis using two clocks. In *9th International Conference on Tools and Algorithms for the Construction and Analysis of Systems (TACAS)*, volume 2619 of *LNCS*, 2003.

[10] S. Graf, I. Ober, and I. Ober. Timed annotations in UML. *Int. Journal on Software Tools for Technology Transfer*, Springer Verlag, 2006. (In print. Available on Springer On-line at http://dx.doi.org/10.1007/s10009-005-0219-x).

[11] Z. Har'El and R. P. Kurshan. Software for Analysis of Coordination. In *Conference on System Science Engineering*. Pergamon Press, 1988.

[12] G. J. Holzmann. The model-checker SPIN. *IEEE Trans. on Software Engineering*, 23(5), 1999.

[13] A. Knapp, S. Merz, and C. Rauh. Model checking timed UML state machines and collaborations. In *7th Intl. Symp. Formal Techniques in Real-Time and Fault Tolerant Systems (FTRTFT 2002)*, volume 2469 of *LNCS*, September 2002.

[14] K.G. Larsen, P. Petterson, and W. Yi. UPPAAL: Status & Developments. In O. Grumberg, editor, *Proceedings of CAV'97 (Haifa, Israel)*, volume 1254 of *LNCS*, pages 456–459. Springer, June 1997.

[15] D. Latella, I. Majzik, and M. Massink. Automatic verification of a behavioral subset of UML statechart diagrams using the SPiN model-checker. *Formal Aspects of Computing*, (11), 1999.

[16] J. Lilius and I.P. Paltor. Formalizing UML state machines for model checking. In Rumpe France, editor, *Proceedings of UML'1999*, volume 1723 of *Lecture Notes in Computer Science*. Springer-Verlag, 1999.

[17] C. L. Liu and J. W. Leyland. Scheduling algorithms for multiprogramming in a hard real-time environment,. *JACM*, 20(1):46–61, 1973.

[18] Iulian Ober, Susanne Graf, and Ileana Ober. Validating timed UML models by simulation and verification. *Int. Journal on Software Tools for Technology Transfer*, Springer Verlag, 2006. (In print. Available on Springer On-line at http://dx.doi.org/10.1007/s10009-005-0205-x).

[19] SysML Partners. SysML specification v. 0.9 draft (10 jan. 2005). Available at http://www.sysml.org/artifacts.htm.

[20] D. Potop-Butucaru, B. Caillaud, and A. Benveniste. Concurrency in synchronous systems. In *Formal Methods in System Design 2005*, LNCS. Springer Verlag, 2005.

[21] Fei Xie, Vladimir Levin, and James C. Browne. Model checking for an executable subset of UML. In *Proceedings of 16th IEEE International Conference on Automated Software Engineering (ASE'01)*. IEEE, 2001.

[22] S. Yovine. KRONOS: A verification tool for real-time systems. *Springer International Journal of Software Tools for Technology Transfer*, 1(1-2), December 1997.

Synchronizing Behavioural Mismatch in Software Composition*

Carlos Canal[1], Pascal Poizat[2], and Gwen Salaün[3]

[1] University of Málaga, Department of Computer Science
Campus de Teatinos, 29071 Málaga, Spain
canal@lcc.uma.es
[2] IBISC FRE 2873 CNRS – University of Évry Val d'Essonne, Genopole
Tour Évry 2, 523 place des terrasses de l'Agora, 91000 Évry, France
Pascal.Poizat@ibisc.univ-evry.fr
[3] VASY project, INRIA Rhône-Alpes, France
655 avenue de l'Europe, 38330 Montbonnot Saint-Martin, France
Gwen.Salaun@inrialpes.fr

Abstract. Software Adaptation is a crucial issue for the development of a real market of components promoting software reuse. Recent work in this field has addressed several problems related to interface and behavioural mismatch. In this paper, we present our proposal for software adaptation, which builds on previous work overcoming some of its limitations, and makes a significant advance to solve pending issues. Our approach is based on the use of synchronous vectors and regular expressions for governing adaptation rules, and is supported by dedicated algorithms and tools.

1 Introduction

Component-Based Software Engineering (CBSE) focuses on composition and reuse, aiming to develop a market of software components, in which customers select the most appropriate software piece depending on its technical specification [6]. The development of such a market has always been one of the major concerns of Software Engineering, but it has never become a reality. The reason is that we cannot expect that any given software component perfectly matches the needs of a system where it is trying to be integrated. Software is never reused "as it is", especially in case of legacy code, and a certain degree of adaptation is always required [16].

To deal with these problems a new discipline, *Software Adaptation*, which is emerging, is concerned with providing techniques to arrange already developed pieces of software, in order to reuse them in new systems [7]. Software Adaptation promotes the use of *adaptors* —specific computational entities guaranteeing that components will interact in the right way.

---

* This work has been partly funded by the European Network of Excellence on AOSD, AOSD-Europe IST-2-004349-NOE.

R. Gorrieri and H. Wehrheim (Eds.): FMOODS 2006, LNCS 4037, pp. 63–77, 2006.

CBSE postulates that a component must be reusable from its interface [20], which in fact constitutes its full technical specification. Hence, we have to provide components with a specification that helps in the process of adapting and reusing them. The intended adaptation will then take the form of a mapping among the interface descriptions of the components involved.

The characteristics and expressiveness of the language used for interface description determines the degree of interoperability we can achieve using it, and the kind of problems that can be solved. We can distinguish between several levels of interoperability, and accordingly of interface description [8]: signature level (service names and types), behavioural level (interaction protocols), semantic level (functional specification of what the component actually *does*) and service level (non functional properties such as quality of service). At each one, mismatch can occur [8] and would have to be corrected. Currently, industrial component models only tackle the signature level, with Interface Description Languages (IDLs). Although (automatic) adaptation in the semantic and service levels still remains uncertain, several approaches have been presented for extending component interfaces with behaviour, thus resulting in what we may call a Behavioural IDL (BIDL) (*e.g.*, WSBPEL [1] for web services).

In this paper, we focus on mismatch appearing at the behavioural level. Intuitively, it means that two (or more) components cannot —as they are— interact till they reach correct termination states. To compensate such behavioural incompatibilities, we propose first to use synchronous vectors as the mapping language to make explicit communications on different message names. Second, we extend our notation to enable writing regular expressions of vectors. Such a mapping notation is convenient to describe in an abstract way more advanced adaptation scenarios such as reordering of messages. Figure 1 gives a graphical overview of our method for adaptation.

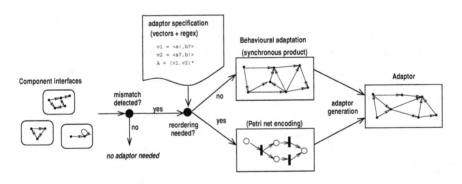

Fig. 1. Overview of our approach for adaptation of incompatible components

The remainder of the paper is organized as follows. Section 2 formally introduces our component interface model, and defines interface mismatch by means of synchronous products. Section 3 presents our approach to component adaptation, which combines the points in favour of different adaptation approaches, while trying to overcome their limitations. Our proposals for behavioural adaptation with or without message reordering are supported by dedicated algorithms, and in both cases the adaptation mappings rely on synchronous vectors. Next, Section 4 extends our initial mapping notation with regular expressions, enabling complex policies for applying the adaptation vectors. In Section 5, we survey the more advanced proposals for software adaptation, and compare ours to them. Finally, Section 6 draws up the main conclusions of this work and sketches some future tasks that will be accomplished to extend its results.

2 Interfaces and Mismatch

2.1 Component Interfaces

Component interfaces are given using a signature and a behavioural interface.

Definition 1 (Signature). *A signature Σ is a set of operation profiles. This set is a disjoint union of* provided *operations and* required *operations. An operation profile is simply the name of an operation, together with its argument types, its return type and the exceptions it raises.*

This definition naturally corresponds to the signature definitions in component based models such as CCM or J2EE. Such signatures are defined using an IDL. For the sake of simplicity in the presentation, in this paper we do not deal with operation arguments, return values or exceptions.

We also take into account behavioural interfaces through the use of Labelled Transition Systems (LTSs).

Definition 2 (LTS). *A Labelled Transition System is a tuple (A, S, I, F, T) where: A is an alphabet (set of events), S is a set of states, $I \in S$ is the initial state, $F \subseteq S$ are final states, and $T \subseteq S \times A \times S$ is the transition function.*

The alphabet of the LTS is built on the signature. This means that for each provided operation p in the signature, there is an element $p?$ in the alphabet, and for each required operation r, an element $r!$. As in CCS, $(a, \bar{a})$ denote complementary actions —*i.e.*, if a is $p?$ (respectively $r!$), then $\bar{a}$ is $p!$ (respectively $r?$).

LTSs are adequate as far as user-friendliness and development of formal algorithms are concerned. However, higher-level behavioural languages such as process algebras can be used to define behavioural interfaces in a more concise way. In this paper, we use as a BIDL the part of the CCS notation restricted to sequential processes which can be translated into LTS models: P ::= 0 | a?.P | a!.P | P1+P2 | A, where 0 denotes a do-nothing process, a?.P a process which receives a and then behaves as P, a!.P a process which sends a and then behaves as P, P1+P2 a process which may act either as P1 or P2, and A denotes the call to a process defined by an agent definition equation A = P.

As process algebras do not enable to define initial and final states, we extend this CCS notation to tag processes with initial (i) and final (f) attributes. Finally, 0 is often omitted in processes (*e.g.*, a!.b![f] is used for a!.b!.0[f]).

Example 1. Consider a client that repetitively sends a query and its argument, and then waits for an acknowledgement, quitting with an **end!**, and a server repetitively waiting for a query and a value, then returning a given service:

```
Client[i] = query!.arg!.ack?.Client + end![f]
Server[i,f] = query?.value?.service!.Server
```

The LTSs for these two components are given below with initial and final states respectively marked by input arrows and black circles.

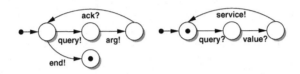

Fig. 2. A simple client/server system

2.2   Behavioural Mismatch

Various definition of behavioural mismatch have been proposed in the field of software adaptation and software architecture analysis [8]. We build on the most commonly accepted one, namely deadlock-freedom. The first step is to define the semantics of a system made up of several identified components. This semantics can be given, following work by Arnold [2] using synchronous product.

Definition 3 (Synchronous Product). *The* synchronous product *of n LTSs $L_i = (A_i, S_i, I_i, F_i, T_i)$, $i \in 1..n$, is the LTS (A, S, I, F, T) such that:*

- $A \subseteq \Pi_{i \in 1..n} A_i$, $S \subseteq \Pi_{i \in 1..n} S_i$, $I = (I_1, \ldots, I_n)$,
- $F \subseteq \{(s_1, \ldots, s_n) \in S \mid \bigwedge_{i \in 1..n} s_i \in F_i\}$,
- T *is defined using the following rule:*
  $\forall (s_1, \ldots, s_n) \in S$, $\forall i, j \in 1..n, i < j$ *such that*
  $\exists (s_i, a, s_i') \in T_i$, $\exists (s_j, \bar{a}, s_j') \in T_j$, *then*
  $(x_1, \ldots, x_n) \in S$ *and* $((s_1, \ldots, s_n), (l_1, \ldots, l_n), (x_1, \ldots, x_n)) \in T$, *where*
  $\forall k \in 1..n, l_k = \{$ a *if* $k = i$, $\bar{a}$ *if* $k = j$, ε *otherwise* $\}$
  $x_k = \{$ s_i' *if* $k = i$, s_j' *if* $k = j$, s_k *otherwise* $\}$

We are now able to characterize behavioural mismatch by means of deadlock.

Definition 4 (Deadlock State). *Let $L = (A, S, I, F, T)$ be an LTS. A state s is a deadlock state for L, noted $dead(s)$, iff it is in S, not in F and has no outgoing transitions: $s \in S \land s \notin F \land \nexists l \in A, s' \in S . (s, l, s') \in T$.*

Definition 5 (Deadlock Mismatch). *An LTS $L = (A, S, I, F, T)$ presents a deadlock mismatch if there is a state s in S such that $dead(s)$.*

To check if a system made up of several components presents behavioural mismatch, its synchronous product is computed and then Definition 5 is used.

Fig. 3. Synchronous product for the client/server system in Figure 2

Example 2. Taking Example 1, we obtain the following synchronous product:

Note that the deadlock is caused by (i) the client required service **end!** which has no counterpart in the server, and (ii) name mismatching between the client required service **arg!** and the server provided service **value?**.

We may now define what is a correct adaptor for a system. An adaptor is given by an LTS which, put into a non-deadlock-free system yields a deadlock-free one. For this to work, the adaptor has to preempt all the component communications. Therefore, prior to the adaptation process, component service names may have to be renamed prefixing them by the component name, *e.g.*, **c:service!**.

The product we have defined here is common in the community and hence is supported by tools such as the CADP toolbox [9]. Our deadlock definition however is slightly different from the one used in these tools, since it has to distinguish between success (deadlock in a final state), and failure (deadlock in a non-final state). Mismatch detection can be automatically checked by CADP up to the adding within component interfaces of specific loop transitions labelled with **accept** over final states. Then the EXP.OPEN tool [13] of CADP is used to perform a full matching product between the component interfaces.

3   Adaptation Based on Synchronous Vectors

3.1   Synchronizing with Vectors

The first thing to solve in adaptation is impossible communication due to different event/message names. Our idea is to use synchronous vectors as a way to denote a morphism between event names in different components.

Vectors generalize synchronous product by expressing not only synchronization between processes on the same event names (a and $\bar{a}$ in Definition 3), but more general correspondences between the events of the process involved.

Definition 6 (Vector). *A synchronous vector (or vector for short) for a set of Id indexed components $L_i = (A_i, S_i, I_i, F_i, T_i)$, $i \in Id$, is a tuple (e_i) with $e_i \in A_i \cup \{\varepsilon\}$, ε meaning that a component does not participate in a synchronization.*

Note that vectors are simple correspondences between events. Extensions can be easily defined to consider relations between events with data.

Definition 7 (Synchronous Vector Product). *The synchronous vector product of n LTSs $L_i = (A_i, S_i, I_i, F_i, T_i)$, $i \in 1..n$ with a set of vectors V, is the LTS (A, S, I, F, T), denoted by $\Pi(L_i, V)$, such that:*

- $A \subseteq \Pi_{i \in 1..n} A_i$, $S \subseteq \Pi_{i \in 1..n} S_i$, $I = (I_1, \ldots, I_n)$,
- $F \subseteq \{(s_1, \ldots, s_n) \in S \mid \bigwedge_{i \in 1..n} s_i \in F_i\}$,

- T is defined using the following rule:
  $((s_1, \ldots, s_n), (l_1, \ldots, l_n), (s'_1, \ldots, s'_n)) \in T$ and $(s'_1, \ldots, s'_n) \in S$ if
  $\exists(s_1, \ldots, s_n) \in S$ and $\exists v = (l_1, \ldots, l_n) \in V$ such that,
  $\forall l_i \in v \ s'_i = s_i$ if $l_i = \varepsilon$ and $\exists(s_i, l_i, s'_i) \in T_i$ otherwise.

3.2   Behavioural Adaptation Without Reordering

We first address adaptation where only event names mismatch is taken into account, that is impossible communications due to different message names. Our algorithm takes as input the Id indexed set of components LTSs L_i of the systems and a mapping which is a synchronous vector V.

1. compute the product $P = (A_P, S_P, I_P, F_P, T_P) = \Pi(L_i, V)$
2. obtain $P_{\text{restr}} = (A_{P_{\text{restr}}}, S_{P_{\text{restr}}}, I_{P_{\text{restr}}}, F_{P_{\text{restr}}}, T_{P_{\text{restr}}})$ from P recursively removing transitions and states yielding deadlocks: find a state s such that $\textbf{dead}(s)$, remove s and any transition t with target s, and do this until there is no more such s in the LTS.
3. from P_{restr}, build the adaptor $A = (A_{P_{\text{restr}}}, S_{P_{\text{restr}}} \cup S_{\text{add}}, I_{P_{\text{restr}}}, F_{P_{\text{restr}}}, T_A)$ where S_{add} and T_A are defined as follows.
   For each $t = (s = (s_1, \ldots, s_n), (l_1, \ldots, l_n), s' = (s'_1, \ldots, s'_n))$ in $T_{P_{\text{restr}}}$, let $L_{\text{rec}} = \{l? \mid l! \in (l_1, \ldots, l_n)\}$ and $L_{\text{em}} = \{l! \mid l? \in (l_1, \ldots, l_n)\}$. Let then Seq_{rec} be the set of all permutations over L_{rec} and Seq_{em} be the set of all permutations over L_{em}. For each couple (R, E) in $\text{Seq}_{\text{rec}} \times \text{Seq}_{\text{em}}$, $R = (r_1, \ldots, r_{nr})$ and $E = (e_1, \ldots, e_{ne})$, $\text{seq} = (r_1, \ldots, r_{nr}, e_1, \ldots, e_{ne})$, construct the transaction

$$s = q_0 \overset{\text{seq}[1]}{\to} q_1 \ldots q_k \overset{\text{seq}[k+1]}{\to} q_{k+1} \ldots q_{n-1} \overset{\text{seq}[n]}{\to} s' = q_n$$

adding each $q_{k \in 1..n-1}$ in S_{add} and each $q_k \overset{\text{seq}[k+1]}{\to} q_{k+1}$ ($k \in 0..n$) in T_A.

This algorithm builds the most general adaptor in the sense that it simulates any other adaptor for the mismatching system. Its complexity lies mainly in the synchronous product construction $\mathbf{O}(|S|^n)$ where S is the largest set of states.

3.3   Behavioural Adaptation with Reordering

Let us now extend the domain of adaptation problems we deal with. The goal is to also address behavioural mismatch with reordering, that is, the incompatible ordering of the events exchanged. Indeed, our behavioural adaptation proposal above would yield an empty adaptor in presence of such behavioural mismatch, concluding that adaptation is not possible. In this case, the adaptation process may try to reorder protocol events in-between the components. To this purpose, we present a second approach which complements the first one. However, it does not replace it as the process may not agree on message reordering.

This behavioural adaptation approach is based on previous works dedicated to the analysis of component queue boundedness [14]. In order to accommodate behavioural mismatch, the events received by the adaptor are de-synchronized from their emission. Our algorithm can be simulated by a translation of the problem into Petri nets [15]. The main advantage of such an approach is that it is equipped with efficient tools.

We first proceed by constructing a Petri net representation of the assumptions the components make on their environment (by mirroring their behavioural interfaces), and then build causal dependences between the events received and sent by the adaptor accordingly to the mapping, given under the form of synchronous vectors. This allows us to build an adaptor which accommodates both behavioural mismatch (with or without reordering).

1. for each component i with LTS L_i, for each state $s_j \in S_i$, add a place `Control-i-s_j`
2. for each component i with initial state I_i, put a token in `Control-i-I_i`
3. for each $a!$ in $\bigcup_i A_i$, add a place `Rec-a`
4. for each $a?$ in $\bigcup_i A_i$, add a place `Em-a`
5. for each component i with LTS L_i, for each $(s, l, s') \in T_i$:
   - add a transition with label l, one arc from place `Control-i-s` to the transition and one arc from the transition to place `Control-i-s'`
   - if l has the form $a!$ then add one arc from the transition to place `Rec-a`
   - if l has the form $a?$ then add one arc from place `Em-a` to the transition
6. for each vector $v = (l_1, \ldots, l_n)$ in V:
   - add a transition with label `tau`
   - for each l_i with form $a!$, add one arc from place `Rec-a` to the transition
   - for each l_i with form $a?$, add one arc from the transition to place `Em-a`
7. for each tuple $(f_1, \ldots, f_n)$, $f_i \in F_i$, of final states, add a (loop) `accept` transition with arcs from and to each of the tuple f_i

Once this Petri net encoding has been performed, we compute its marking graph. If it is finite (*e.g.*, for non recursive adaptors) then it gives a behavioural description of the adaptor. If not (it cannot be computed in finite time), then we compute the coverability graph of the net. Note that due to the overapproximation of such a graph, we add a guard `[#Em-a>1]` (`#Em-a` meaning the number of tokens in place `Em-a`) on any $a!$ transition in this graph leaving a state where `#Em-a` is ω. In both cases (marking or coverability graph), step 2 of the algorithm in Section 3.2 has to be performed on the adaptor obtained. The complexity of this algorithm lies mainly in the marking or coverability graph construction which is exponential [17].

This algorithm is supported by tools. We have made successful experiments with the TINA tool [3] to generate marking and coverability graphs. Our approach yields graphs which can be too large for a human reader. We simplify the adaptor LTS passing the resulting output file to CADP and performing a $\tau * a$ reduction on it to remove the meaningless `tau` transitions it contains.

3.4 Application

We here present an example following the behavioural adaptation technique above.

Example 3. Suppose we have a client `Client[i]=req!.arg!.ack?[f]` and a server `Server[i]=value?.query?.service![f]` with vectors `<req!,query?>`, `<arg!,value?>` and `<ack?,service!>`. Such an example is typical of clients and servers which follow different standards for the order of sending subservice elements. The Petri net encoding (see Section 3.3) of the system is:

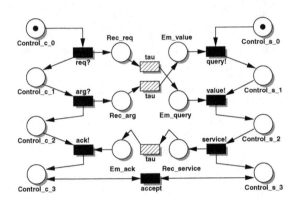

Fig. 4. Petri net encoding of a simple client/server system

Computing the marking graph, we obtain an LTS with 13 states and 16 transitions (Fig. 5, left), which once reduced yields the correct adaptor (Fig. 5, right)[1].

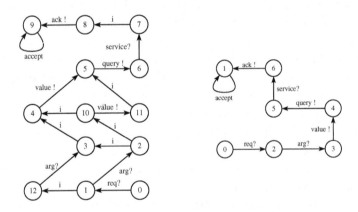

Fig. 5. Initial and reduced adaptor for the client/server system

We want to stress that our adaptation proposal is an *automatic* process. For the sake of the presentation, we have shown here a simple example for which the adaptor could be obtained manually. However, using slightly more complex

---

[1] Note the **i** which stands in CADP for **tau** transitions, and the **accept** loop transitions which enable the detection of correct final states.

component protocols, the adaptor becomes too large to be obtained by hand. Moreover, the use of regular expressions in the next section will increase the complexity of the adapting process and the need for such automatic techniques.

4 Adaptation Patterns

In this section, we tackle the problem of adaptation mappings which may change over time. In the following, we present a way to express such mappings using regular expressions (regex), and then update our algorithms to deal with them.

4.1 Regular Expressions (Regex) of Vectors

First, we introduce the syntax for regex. These will be used in place of the basic vector mappings we presented in Section 3.

Definition 8 (Vector Regex). *Given n LTSs* $L_i = (A_i, S_i, I_i, F_i, T_i)$*, and a set of vectors* $V = \{(e_{ij})\}_j$ *for their adaptation, with* $e_{ij} \in A_i \cup \{\varepsilon\}$*, a (vector) regex for these LTSs can be generated by the following syntax: R ::= v (VECTOR) | R1.R2 (SEQUENCE) | R1+R2 (CHOICE) | R* (ITERATION), where R, R1, R2 are regex, and v is a vector in V.*

A graphical description such as LTS labelled with vectors might be used instead of regular expressions to favour readability and user-friendliness of the notation.

Example 4 (Alternating use client). Suppose we have a system formed by one client C and two servers, S and A:

```
C[i] = end![f] + req!.arg!.ack?.C,
S[i,f] = value?.query?.service!.S, and
A[i,f] = value?.query?.service!.A.
```

One may want to express in the adaptation mapping that the client accesses the two servers alternatively, and not always the same one. For this, we use the following regex: $(v_{s1} . v_{s2} . v_{s3} . v_{a1} . v_{a2} . v_{a3}) * . v_{end}$ with

$v_{s1} =$<req!,query?,ε>, $v_{a1} =$<req!,ε,query?>, $v_{end} =$<end!,ε,ε>,
$v_{s2} =$<arg!,value?,ε>, $v_{a2} =$<arg!,ε,value?>,
$v_{s3} =$<ack?,service!,ε>, $v_{a3} =$<ack?,ε,service!>.

Example 5 (Connected vs non connected modes). Suppose a client/server system where the client C sends its *id* only once at login time, while the server S requires an identification every time the client does a request. Here we have:

```
C[i]=log!.Logged, with
Logged[f]=req!.ack?.Logged, and
S[i,f]=log?.req?.ack!.S
```

The regex describing the adaptation required is now $v_0 . v_2 . v_3 . (v_1 . v_2 . v_3) *$ with
$v_0 =$<log!,log?>, $v_1 =$< ε,log?>, $v_2 =$<req!,req?>, $v_3 =$<ack?,ack!>.

4.2   Behavioural Adaptation Without Reordering

To be able to update our algorithms for using our new regex mappings[2], we first define how to obtain an LTS from them. This corresponds to the well-known problem of obtaining an automaton which recognizes the language of a regex [10]. The only difference is that the atoms of our regex are vectors and not elements of basic alphabets. Instead of using a regex, one may also use directly the LTS that derives from such regex, (*i.e.*, an LTS where the alphabet corresponds to vectors).

We then modify the synchronous vector product to take a regex LTS in place of the vector argument.

Definition 9 (Synchronous Vector Product (with regex LTS)). *The synchronous vector product (with regex LTS) of n LTS $L_i = (A_i, S_i, I_i, F_i, T_i)$, $i \in 1..n$ with a regex LTS $L_R = (A_R, S_R, I_R, F_R, T_R)$, is the LTS (A, S, I, F, T) such that:*

- $A \subseteq A_R \times \Pi_{i \in 1..n} A_i$, $S \subseteq S_R \times \Pi_{i \in 1..n} S_i$, $I = (I_R, I_1, \ldots, I_n)$,
- $F \subseteq \{(s_r, s_1, \ldots, s_n) \in S \mid s_r \in F_R \wedge \bigwedge_{i \in 1..n} s_i \in F_i\}$,
- T *is defined using the following rule:*
  $((s_r, s_1, \ldots, s_n), (l_r, l_1, \ldots, l_n), (s'_r, s'_1, \ldots, s'_n)) \in T$ *and* $(s'_r, s'_1, \ldots, s'_n) \in S$
  if
  $\exists (s_r, s_1, \ldots, s_n) \in S$ *and* $\exists v = (s_r, (l_{r_1}, \ldots, l_{r_n}), s'_r) \in T_R$ *with,*
  $\forall l_{r_i} \ s'_i = s_i$ *if* $l_{r_i} = \varepsilon$ *and* $\exists (s_i, l_{r_i}, s'_i) \in T_i$ *otherwise.*

To apply the Section 3.2 algorithm we just have now to *discard* the first element of the product components, that is, from the LTS $L = (A, S, I, F, T)$ obtain the LTS $L' = \mathtt{proj}(L) = (A', S', I', F', T')$ such that $\forall X \in \{A, S, I, F\}$ $X' = \{\mathtt{cdr}(x) \mid x \in X\}$ and $T' = \{(\mathtt{cdr}(s), \mathtt{cdr}(l), \mathtt{cdr}(s')) \mid (s, l, s') \in T\}$ with $\mathtt{cdr}((x_0, x_1, \ldots, x_n)) = (x_1, \ldots, x_n)$.

We may now modify the algorithm for behavioural mismatching without reodering as presented in Section 3.2. The new algorithm takes as input the *Id* indexed set of components LTSs L_i of the system and a mapping which is a regex R (for the set of LTSs). We just have to replace step 1 in this algorithm by:

1. compute the LTS L_R for the regex R
2. compute the product $P_R = (A_{P_R}, S_{P_R}, I_{P_R}, F_{P_R}, T_{P_R}) = \Pi(L_R, L_i)$
3. compute $P = \mathtt{proj}(P_R)$

Its complexity is $\mathbf{O}(|S|^{n+1})$ where S is the largest set of states.

4.3   Behavioural Adaptation with Reordering

Our algorithm for behavioural adaptation with reordering can also be adapted to deal with regex.

---

[2] Note that our new algorithms would apply to the vector mappings we have defined in the previous section, just taking the set $V = \{v_i\}$ of vectors as the regex $(v_1 + v_2 + \ldots + v_n)*$.

1. compute the LTS $L_R = (A_R, S_R, I_R, F_R, T_R)$ for the regex R.
2. build the Petri net encoding for the problem as presented in section 3.3, replacing part 6 with:
   - for each state s_R in S_R, add a place `ControlR-s_R`
   - put a token in place `ControlR-I_R`
   - for each transition $t_R = (s_R, (l_1, \ldots, l_n), s'_R)$ in T_R:
     - add a transition with label `tau`, one arc from place `ControlR-s_R` to the transition and one arc from the transition to place `ControlR-s'_R`
     - for each l_i which has the form $a!$, add one arc from place `Rec-a` to the transition
     - for each l_i which has the form $a?$, add one arc from the transition to place `Em-a`
3. in the building of `accept` transitions, add F_R to the F_i taken into account (final states now correspond to acceptance states of the regex LTS).

The rest of the algorithm (computing marking or coverability graph, and reducing them) is the same. Similarly to Section 3.3, this algorithm is exponential.

4.4 Application

We here develop Example 4 above, following our behavioural adaptation technique.

Example 6 (Example 4 developed). First note that, as explained before, we rename arguments to avoid name clash. We have:

```
C[i]   = c:end![f] + c:req!.c:arg!.c:ack?.C,
S[i,f] = s:value?.s:query?.s:service!.S, and
A[i,f] = a:value?.a:query?.a:service!.A.
```

To express that the client alternatively uses the two servers we may use the following regex: $R_1 = (v_{s1} \cdot v_{s2} \cdot v_{s3} \cdot v_{a1} \cdot v_{a2} \cdot v_{a3}) * \cdot v_{end}$ with:

$v_{s1} =$ <c:req!,s:query?,ε>, $v_{a1} =$ <c:req!,ε,a:query?>,
$v_{s2} =$ <c:arg!,s:value?,ε>, $v_{a2} =$ <c:arg!,ε,a:value?>,
$v_{s3} =$ <c:ack?,s:service!,ε>, $v_{a3} =$ <c:ack?,ε,a:service!>,
$v_{end} =$ <c:end!,ε,ε>

Note that this mapping is probably overspecified, since it imposes a strict alternation between servers. Instead, one may choose to authorize the client to access any server it wants. Then, the mapping becomes:

$$R_2 = (v_{s1} \cdot v_{s2} \cdot v_{s3} + v_{a1} \cdot v_{a2} \cdot v_{a3}) * \cdot v_{end}$$

We have run both examples and obtained (after reduction) the adaptors in Fig. 6 (left for R_1, and right for R_2.) Note that applying step 2 of the algorithm presented in Section 3.2, the state 1 and the corresponding transition are removed for R_1. Both adapters solve the existing mismatch, making the system deadlock-free.

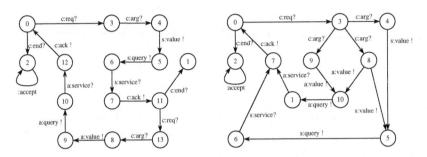

Fig. 6. Adaptors obtained for the alternating client/server system

5   Related Work

For a thorough review of the state of the art in Software Adaptation, we refer to [8]. Here, we will mention only a few works, those more closely related to our proposal.

As said in the introduction, the need for adaptation may occur at any of the levels of interoperability described, while currently available component platforms address software adaptation only at the signature level. Hence, most of the recent proposals for adaptation of software have jumped from the signature level to the specification and analysis of behavioural interfaces, promoting the use of BIDLs for describing component protocols.

The foundation for behavioural adaptation was set by Yellin and Strom. In their seminal paper [21], they introduced formally the notion of *adaptor* as a software entity capable of enabling the interoperation of two components with mismatching behaviour. They used finite state machines to specify component interactive behaviour, to define a relation of compatibility, and to address the task of (semi-)automatic adaptor generation.

More recently, in [18], the authors present an adaptation approach as a solution to particular synchronization problems between concurrent components, for instance one component uses or is accessed by two other components. This approach is based on algorithms close to the synchronous products we use in this paper. Moreover, they can solve protocol incompatibilities enabling one of the involved component to perform several actions before or after several synchronizations with its partners. In comparison, our proposal is more general and based on a rich notation to deal with possibly complex adaptation scenarios, whereas their approach works out only precise situations in which mismatch may happen, without using any mapping language for adaptor specification.

Taking Yellin and Strom's proposal [21] as a starting point, the work of Brogi and collaborators (BBCP) [4, 5] presents a methodology for behavioural adaptation. In their proposal, component behaviour is specified using a process algebra —a subset of the π-calculus—, where service offering/invocation is represented by input/output actions in the calculus, respectively. The starting point of the adaptation process is a mapping that states correspondences between services of the components being adapted. This mapping can be considered as an abstract specification of the required adaptor. Then, an adaptor generation algorithm refines the specification given by the mapping into a concrete adaptor implementation, taking also into account the behavioural interfaces of the components, which ensures correct interaction between them according to the mapping. The adaptor is able to accommodate not only syntactical mismatch between service names, but also the interaction protocols that the components follow (*i.e.*, the partial ordering in which services are offered/invoked).

Another interesting proposal in this field is that of Inverardi and Tivoli (IT) [11]. Starting from the specification with MSCs of the components to be assembled and of the properties that the resulting system should verify (liveness and safety properties expressed as specific processes), they automatically derive the adaptor glue code for the set of components in order to obtain a property-satisfying system. The IT proposal has been extended in [12] with the use of temporal logic; coordination policies are expressed as LTL properties, and then translated into Büchi automata.

Our approach addresses system-wide adaptation (*i.e.*, differently from BBCP, it may involve more than two components). It is based on LTS descriptions of component behaviour, instead of process algebra as in BBCP. However, we may also describe behaviours by means of a simple process algebra, and use its operational semantics to derivate LTSs from it. Differently from IT, we use synchronous vectors for adaptor specification, playing a similar function than the mappings rules in BBCP. With that, we are able to perform adaptation of incompatible events.

With respect to behavioural adaptation, our approach can be considered as both generative and restrictive [8], since we address behavioural adaptation by enabling message reordering (as in BBCP), while we also remove incorrect behaviour (as in IT). Similarly to both approaches, our main goal is to ensure deadlock freedom. However, more complex adaptation policies and properties can be specified by means of regular expressions. Indeed, the most relevant achievement of our proposal is this use of regular expressions for imposing additional properties over mappings. In fact, the semantics of BBCP mappings can be expressed by combining their different rules (in our case, vectors) in a regular expression by

Table 1. Comparison of Adaptation approaches

criteria	IT	BBCP	our proposal
behavioural descriptions	automata	proc. algebra	LTS or proc. algebra
properties	no deadlock, LTL properties	no deadlock —	no deadlock regular expressions
mappings/adaptor abstraction	yes	yes	yes
name mismatch	no	yes	yes
data types	no	yes	no
message reordering	no	yes	yes
system-wide adaptation	yes	no	yes

means of the choice (+) operator. On the contrary, our regex are much more expressive, solving the problem of BBCP underspecified mappings [4], and allowing to take into account a new class of adaptation problems.

In Table 1 we give a synthesis of the features of our approach compared to IT and BBCP.

6   Conclusion

Software Adaptation has become a crucial issue for the development of a real market of components enhancing software reuse, especially when dealing with legacy systems. Recent research work in this field —in particular that of BBCP and IT [4, 5, 11, 12]— has addressed several problems related to signature and behavioural mismatch. In this paper, we have shown our proposal for software adaptation based on a notation, namely regular expressions of synchronous vectors, and equipped with algorithms and tools. It builds on BBCP and IT previous works, overcoming some of their limitations, and making a significant advance to solve some of the pending issues.

There are still some open issues in our proposal, deserving future work. First, and differently from BBCP, we do not deal with data types, nor with one-to-many correspondences between services. Taking data into account would require more expressive models than LTSs, such as Symbolic Transition Systems (STSs) [14]. This is a perspective for our work, since it allows the description of the data involved in the operations within the protocol without suffering from the state explosion problem that usually occurs in process algebraic approaches.

With respect to one-to-many correspondences between services (one of the strong points in favour of the BBCP proposal), we intend to explore how regular expressions can be used for that purpose. More expressive models for mappings, such as non-regular protocols [19], could also be extended to vectors in order to get a bigger class of properties expressible at the adaptor level (*e.g.*, load-balancing adaptation of the access of clients to servers).

Finally, we intend to implement our adaptation algorithms in ETS, an Eclipse plug-in that we have developed for the experimentation over LTS and STS.

Acknowledgements. The authors thank Bernard Berthomieu, Frédéric Lang, and Massimo Tivoli for their interesting comments and fruitful discussions.

References

1. T. Andrews et al. *Business Process Execution Language for Web Services (WS-BPEL)*. BEA Systems, IBM, Microsoft, SAP AG, and Siebel Systems, Feb. 2005.
2. A. Arnold. *Finite Transition Systems*. International Series in Computer Science. Prentice-Hall, 1994.
3. B. Berthomieu, P.-O. Ribet, and F. Vernadat. The Tool TINA – Construction of Abstract State Spaces for Petri Nets and Time Petri Nets. *International Journal of Production Research*, 42(14), 2004.

4. A. Bracciali, A. Brogi, and C. Canal. A Formal Approach to Component Adaptation. *Journal of Systems and Software*, 74(1):45–54, 2005.
5. A. Brogi, C. Canal, and E. Pimentel. Component Adaptation Through Flexible Subservicing. *Science of Computer Programming*, 2006. To appear. A previous version of this work was published as *Soft Component Adaptation*, ENTCS 85(3), Elsevier, 2004.
6. A. W. Brown and K. C. Wallnau. The Current State of CBSE. *IEEE Software*, 15(5):37–47, 1998.
7. C. Canal, J. M. Murillo, and P. Poizat. Coordination and Adaptation Techniques for Software Entities. In *ECOOP 2004 Workshop Reader*, volume 3344 of *Lecture Notes in Computer Science*, pages 133–147. Springer, 2004.
8. C. Canal, J. M. Murillo, and P. Poizat. Software Adaptation. *L'Objet. Special Issue on Coordination and Adaptation Techniques*, 12(1):9–31, 2006.
9. H. Garavel, F. Lang, and R. Mateescu. An Overview of CADP 2001. *EASST Newsletter*, 4:13–24, 2002.
10. J. E. Hopcroft and J. D. Ullman. *Introduction to Automata Theory, Languages and Computation*. Addison Wesley, 1979.
11. P. Inverardi and M. Tivoli. Deadlock Free Software Architectures for COM/DCOM Applications. *Journal of Systems and Software*, 65(3):173–183, 2003.
12. P. Inverardi and M. Tivoli. Software Architecture for Correct Components Assembly. In *Formal Methods for Software Architectures*, volume 2804 of *Lecture Notes in Computer Science*, pages 92–121. Springer, 2003.
13. F. Lang. Exp.Open 2.0: A Flexible Tool Integrating Partial Order, Compositional, and On-The-Fly Verification Methods. In *Integrated Formal Methods (IFM'2005)*, volume 3771 of *Lecture Notes in Computer Science*, pages 70–88. Springer, 2005.
14. O. Maréchal, P. Poizat, and J.-C. Royer. Checking Asynchronously Communicating Components using Symbolic Transition Systems. In *Proc. of the International Symposium on Distributed Objects and Applications (DOA'2004)*, volume 3291 of *Lecture Notes in Computer Science*, pages 1502–1519. Springer, 2004.
15. T. Murata. Petri Nets: Properties, Analysis and Applications. *Proceedings of the IEEE*, 77(4):541–580, 1989.
16. O. Nierstrasz and T. D. Meijler. Research Directions in Software Composition. *ACM Computing Surveys*, 27(2):262–264, 1995.
17. C. Rackoff. The Covering and Boundedness Problems for Vector Addition Systems. *Theoretical Computer Science*, 6:223–231, 1978.
18. H. W. Schmidt and R. H. Reussner. Generating Adapters for Concurrent Component Protocol Synchronization. In *Proc. of the 5th Int. Conf. on Formal Methods for Open Object-Based Distributed Systems (FMOODS'02)*, pages 213–229. Kluwer Academic Publishers, 2002.
19. M. Südholt. A Model of Components with Non-regular Protocols. In *Proc. of Software Composition (SC'05)*, volume 3628 of *Lecture Notes in Computer Science*, pages 99–113. Springer, 2005.
20. C. Szyperski. *Component Software: Beyond Object-Oriented Programming*. Addison-Wesley, 1998.
21. D. M. Yellin and R. E. Strom. Protocol Specifications and Components Adaptors. *ACM Transactions on Programming Languages and Systems*, 19(2):292–333, 1997.

Static Safety for an Actor Dedicated Process Calculus by Abstract Interpretation

Pierre-Loïc Garoche, Marc Pantel, and Xavier Thirioux

IRIT, Toulouse
{garoche, pantel, thirioux}@enseeiht.fr

Abstract. The actor model eases the definition of concurrent programs with non uniform behaviors. Static analysis of such a model was previously done in a data-flow oriented way, with type systems. This approach was based on constraint set resolution and was not able to deal with precise properties for communications of behaviors. We present here a new approach, control-flow oriented, based on the abstract interpretation framework, able to deal with communication of behaviors. Within our new analyses, we are able to verify most of the previous properties we observed as well as new ones, principally based on occurrence counting.

1 Introduction

1.1 Context – Motivation

The development of the telecommunication industry and the generalization of network use bring concurrent and distributed programming in the limelight. In that context, programming is a hard task and, generally, the resulting applications contain much more *bugs* than usual centralized software. As sequential object oriented programming is commonly accepted as a *good* way to build software, concurrent object oriented programming seems to be well-suited for programming distributed systems. Since non-determinism resulting from network communications makes it difficult to validate any distributed functionality using informal approaches, our work is focused on applying formal methods to improve concurrent object oriented programming.

To obtain widely usable tools, we have chosen to use the actor model proposed by HEWITT [19] and developed by AGHA [1]. This model is based on a network of autonomous and cooperative agents (called actors), which encapsulate data and programs, communicating using an asynchronous point to point protocol. An actor stores each received message in a queue and when idle, processes the first message it can handle in this queue. Besides those conventions (which are also true for concurrent objects), an actor can dynamically change its interface. This property allows to increase or decrease the set of messages an actor may handle, yielding a more accurate programming model. This model, also known as concurrent objects with non uniform behavior (or interface), has been adopted by the telecommunication industry for the development of distributed and concurrent applications for the Open Distributed Computing framework (ITU X901-X904) and the Object Description Language (TINA-C extension of OMG IDL with multiple interfaces). Until now, we have been designing several analyses for an actor model, all of which based on typing systems. Our main objective was, and still

R. Gorrieri and H. Wehrheim (Eds.): FMOODS 2006, LNCS 4037, pp. 78–92, 2006.
© IFIP International Federation for Information Processing 2006

is, to detect in a most accurate way typical flaws of distributed applications, like for instance communication deadlock or non linearity (i.e. the fact that several distributed actors have the same address). Due to limitations of our previous attempts, which we could somehow overcome but at the price of a much greater complexity unmatched with only a small gain in precision, we decided to move to the framework of abstract interpretation, whose tools and ideas have now significantly grown in maturity and are being widely used in industrial contexts, or are on the verge of being so. We now investigate these techniques in order to capture our long standing properties of interest (detection of orphan messages, that is messages sent to an actor which will not handled them) as well as new ones, especially dedicated to control of resources' usage.

In a first section, we define our actor calculus. Then in the second part, we introduce our non standard semantics upon which we define, in the third part, an abstraction. Finally, in the last part, we explain how to use the abstraction to observe properties about an analyzed term.

1.2   Related Works

Concerning concurrent objects and actors with uniform or non-uniform behaviors, and more generally process calculi, typing systems (usually related to data-flow like analysis) have been the subject of active research. Two opposite approaches have been followed: type declaration and type inference. In the first case, most proposals make use of types as processes of a simple algebra, for instance CCS (Calculus of Communicating Systems) processes. This allows a form of subtyping through simulation relations or language containment. The works of KOBAYASHI et al. [20, 22], RAVARA et al. [28], NAJM et al. [4, 23], PUNTIGAM [26], and HENNESSY et al. [18] follow this line of thought, to which we can add the works of RAJAMANI et al. [5, 27], bringing model-checking issues for those processes-as-types in the scope. The second case is again twofold: on one side we have unification based typing algorithms focusing on resources' usage control witnessed by the works of FOURNET et al. [16] and BOUDOL et al. [3], whereas on the other side we have flow based algorithms, related to behavior and communication patterns reconstruction, advocated by the works of NIELSON et al. [2] and PANTEL et al. [6, 8, 9]. Explicit typing may provide more precise information but are sometimes very hard to write for the programmer (they might be much more complex than the program itself). Implicit typing requires less user supplied information but lead to less precise results.

One drawback of type-based analyses is that they are mainly concerned with data-flow analyses (as types basically represent sets of possible values for variables). In this context, control flow analyses can be mimicked with sophisticated encodings [24] but abstract interpretation seems to be more adequate in this respect. It has been recently applied with success to concurrent and distributed programming by the work of VENET [29] and later FERET [14, 15].

2   CAP: A Primitive Actor Calculus

In order to ease the definition of static analysis for actor based programming, we proposed, in 96, the CAP primitive actor calculus [7], which merge asynchronous π-calculus and CARDELLI's Primitive Object Calculus. The following example illustrates both replication and behavior passing mechanisms of CAP. The ν operator defines two addresses, a and b, then two actors denoted by program points 1 and 7 are defined on those addresses with the behavior set respectively denoted by 2 and 4 for a and 8 for b.

At this point the actor 1 can handle messages called m or $send$ when b can only handle beh messages.

$$
\begin{aligned}
\nu a^\alpha, b^\beta, \; a \rhd^1 \, [m^2() &= \zeta(e,s)(a \rhd^3 s), \\
send^4(x) &= \zeta(e,s)(x \lhd^5 beh(s))] \\
\| \; a \lhd^6 \, send(b) \\
\| \; b \rhd^7 \, [beh^8(x) &= \zeta(e,s)(e \rhd^9 x)] \\
\| \; b \lhd^{10} \, m()
\end{aligned}
$$

There are also two messages in the initial configuration. One is labeled $send$ and is sent to a, the other one is labeled m and is sent to b. In the initial configuration, there is only one possible interaction, in which the actor a handles the message $send$. The message m is an orphan one: it is in the configuration but cannot be handled for the moment. After one interaction between a and the message $send$, the message beh which argument is the behavior's set of a is sent to b. Thus b can handle that message. In its continuation, the actor b assumes the behavior's set of a. Thus b can now handle the message m. This example shows how to send a behavior to another actor. Such a mechanism increases the difficulty of statically inferring properties. Stuck-freeness, *i.e.* the detection of the set of permanent orphans messages, or linearity, *i.e.* verifying that at most one actor is associated to a particular address at the same time, are harder to statically infer when we allow behavior passing. This point was one of the constraints which led us to switch from type based analysis to abstract interpretation.

2.1 Syntax and Semantics

Let $\mathcal{N}$ be an infinite set of actor names, $\mathcal{V}$ be an infinite set of variables. Let $\mathcal{L}_m$ be a set of message labels, $\mathcal{L}_p$ be the set of program point labels and $\mathcal{L}_n$ be the set of name labels. In the following, we denote $\mathcal{L}_p \cup \mathcal{L}_n$ by $\mathcal{L}$. The syntax of configurations is described as follows:

$$
\begin{aligned}
C &::= 0 \mid \nu a^\alpha \, C \mid C \| C \mid a \rhd^l P \mid a \lhd^l m(\widetilde{P}) \\
P &::= x \quad \mid \quad [m_i^{l_i}(\widetilde{Var}) = \zeta(e,s)C_i^{\,i=1\ldots n}]
\end{aligned}
$$

Configurations can be an empty process, a creation of actor's address, parallel execution, an actor on address a with behavior defined by P and, finally, a message sent to an address a with arguments $\widetilde{P}$. Program points define messages, behaviors' installation or external choices between some actors' behaviors. They will be used to build traces of the execution control flow. Name restriction, in the configuration $(\nu a^\alpha)C$, acts as a name binder, so does the ζ operator and the message label for variables in the behavior description of an actor, *i.e.* in the behavior $[m_i^{l_i}(\widetilde{x_i}) = \zeta(e_i, s_i)C_i^{\,i=1\ldots n}]$, therefore the occurrences of a in C, $\widetilde{x_i}$ in $\zeta(e_i, s_i)C_i$ and e_i and s_i in C_i are bound. The ζ operator is our reflexivity operator, it catches both address and behavior of its actor and allows to re-use them in the behavior. We denote by $\mathcal{FN}(C)$ the set of free names in C and by

$$T = [m_i^{l_i}(\tilde{x}_i) = \zeta(e_i, s_i)C_i^{i=1,\ldots,n}] \quad \begin{cases} m = m_k, \\ length(\tilde{T}_l) = length(\tilde{x}_k), \\ k \in [1,\ldots,n] \end{cases}$$

$$a \rhd T \parallel a \lhd^l m(\tilde{T}_l) \xrightarrow{comm(l,l_k)} C_k[e_k \leftarrow a, s_k \leftarrow T, \tilde{x}_k \leftarrow \tilde{T}_l]$$

In order to distinguish transitions, we label the interacting parts of terms. Here the message has label l and the matching behavior label l_k.

Fig. 1. Transition rule of CAP standard semantics

$$\begin{array}{rcll} C & \equiv & D & C\ \alpha\text{-convertible to D}\ (\alpha - conversion) \\ C\|0 & \equiv & C & (inaction) \\ C\|D & \equiv & D\|C & (commutativity) \\ (C\|D)\|E & \equiv & C\|(D\|E) & (associativity) \\ (va)\varnothing & \equiv & \varnothing & (garbage\ collecting) \\ T \rhd T_1 & \equiv & T \rhd T_2 & \text{if}\ T_1 \equiv T_2\ (behavior\ equivalence) \\ (va)(vb)C & \equiv & (vb)(va)C & \text{if}\ a \neq b\ (swapping) \\ (va)C\|D & \equiv & (va)(C\|D) & \text{if}\ a \notin \mathcal{FN}(D)\ (extrusion) \end{array}$$

Fig. 2. Congruence relation of CAP standard semantics

$\mathcal{FV}(C)$ the set of free variables. The standard semantics of CAP was defined, la Milner, by both the usual transition rule (*cf.* Fig. 1) and the congruence relation (*cf.* Fig. 2).

3   Non Standard Semantics

In order to ease the definition of abstract interpretations, we need to define define, in this section, another semantics for CAP and prove it bisimilar to standard CAP semantics. The non standard semantics allows us to label each process with the history of transitions which led to both its creation and the creation of its values. Our work is based on a generic non standard semantics which has been defined by FERET [14, 15] to model first order process calculi as π-calculus, spi-calculus, Ambients, Bio-ambients calculus. We also describe in this section how we adapt this general framework to express the CAP language which has a notion of higher order due to its behavior passing and reflexivity mechanism (ζ operator). We then briefly describe the operational semantics of the generic non standard semantics.

A configuration of a system, in this semantics, is a set of threads. Each thread t is a triple defined as $t = (p, id, E) \in \mathscr{L}_p \times \mathscr{M} \times (\mathscr{V} \mapsto (\mathscr{L} \times \mathscr{M}))$ where p is the program point representing the thread in the CAP term, id is the history marker, also called its identity, and E its environment. This environment is a partial map from a variable to a pair $(value, marker)$. Each marker is a word on program points representing the history of transitions which led to the creation of values or threads. It is required in order to differentiate recursive instances of a value or thread. All threads with the same program point have an environment defined on the same domain, called the program point interface.

We will describe some primitives that allow us to define the non standard semantics, then, briefly, we show how to compute transitions in this semantics.

3.1   Partial Interactions

We associate to each program point a partial interaction which defines how threads related to this program point can interact with others. We also define the set of variables associated to each thread, constituting its environment, according to its program point. Here, in CAP, partial interactions can represent a syntactically defined actor, a dynamic one (an actor whose behavior is defined by a variable) and a particular behavior of an actor or a sent message.

We thus define the set of partial interactions names $\mathscr{A} = \{static\_actor_n, behavior_n, message_n \mid n \in \mathbb{N}\} \cup \{dynamic\_actor\}$ and their arities as follows:

$$Ari = \{static\_actor_n \mapsto (2,n), dynamic\_actor \mapsto (2,0), behavior_n \mapsto (1,n+2),$$
$$message_n \mapsto (n+2,0)\}$$

Partial interaction arities define the number of parameters and the number of bound variables.

The partial interaction $dynamic\_actor$ denotes a thread representing an actor. It is consumed when interacting. It has only two parameters: its name and set of behaviors. It binds no variables.

Both partial interaction $static\_actor_n$ and $behavior_n$ denote a particular behavior of an actor. The first one is associated to an address when the second one is alone and can be used with a dynamic actor. The second one acts as a definition and stays in the configuration when used, whereas the first one is deleted. They are parametrized by their message labels and binds $n+2$ variables, the variables under the ζ operator expressing reflexivity as well as the parameters of the message it can handle. The first one is also parametrized by its actor's name.

Finally the partial interaction $message_n$ represents the message that is sent to a particular address (actor). So it has $n+2$ parameters: one for the address, one for the message name and n for the variables of this message. It is consumed when interacting.

We associate to each partial interaction a type denoting whether such a partial interaction is consumed or not when interacting.

3.2   Abstract Syntax Extraction

We now define the syntax extraction function that takes a CAP term describing the initial state of an agents' system in the standard syntax and extracts its abstract syntax.

We map each program point labeled $l \in \mathscr{L}_p$ to a set of partial interaction and to an interface.

A partial interaction pi is given by a tuple $(s, (parameter_i), (bound_i), constraints, continuation)$ where $s \in \mathscr{A}$ is a partial interaction name, $(m,n) = Ari(s)$ its arity, $(parameter_i) \in \mathcal{V}^m$ its finite sequence of variables (X_i), $(bound_i) \in \mathcal{V}^n$ its finite sequence of distinct variables (Y_i), $constraints \subseteq \{v \diamond v' \mid (v,v') \in \mathcal{V}^2, \diamond \in \{=,\neq\}\}$ its synchronization constraints and finally $continuation \in \wp(\mathscr{L}_p \times (\mathcal{V} \to \mathscr{L}))$ its syntactic continuation. We will check constraints defined in the set $constrains$ about thread environment with the use of the sequence $(parameter_i)$, then we will use both sequences

($parameter_i$) and ($bound_i$) to compute value passing, finally we will deal with the set *continuation* to determine which threads have to be inserted in the system.

- the label of a program point $a \rhd^l [m_i^{l_i}(\tilde{x}_i) = \zeta(e_i, s_i)C_i^{1 \leq i \leq m}]$ is associated to the interface $\{a\}$ and to the following set of partial interactions:

$$
\left\{
\begin{array}{l}
\left\{(static\_actor_n, [a, m_1], [e_1, s_1, \tilde{x}_1], \beta(C_1, \emptyset))\right\} \\
\left\{(static\_actor_n, [a, m_2], [e_2, s_2, \tilde{x}_2], \beta(C_2, \emptyset))\right\} \\
\cdots \\
\left\{(static\_actor_n, [a, m_m], [e_m, s_m, \widetilde{x_m}], \beta(C_m, \emptyset))\right\}
\end{array}
\right\}
$$

- the label of a program point $a \rhd^l x$ is associated to the interface $\{a, x\}$ and to the following set of partial interactions: $\left\{(dynamic\_actor, [a, x], \emptyset, \emptyset)\right\}$
- the label of a program point $a \lhd^l m(\tilde{P})$ is associated to the interface $\{a\} \cup \mathcal{FV}(\tilde{P})$ and to the following set of partial interactions: $\left\{(message_n, [a; m; \tilde{P}], \emptyset, \emptyset)\right\}$
- the label of a program point l_i corresponding to a particular behavior of an actor i.e. $m_i^{l_i}(\tilde{x}) = \zeta(e_i, s_i)C_i$ is associated to the interface $\mathcal{FV}(C_i) \setminus \{e_i, s_i\}$ and to the following set of partial interactions: $\left\{(behavior_n, [m_i], [e_i, s_i, \tilde{x}], \beta(C_i, \emptyset))\right\}$

Finally, the syntax extraction function β is defined inductively over the standard syntax of the syntactic continuation, as follows:

$$
\begin{aligned}
\beta((va^\alpha)C, E_s) &= \beta(C, E_s[a \mapsto \alpha]) \\
\beta(\emptyset, E_s) &= \{\emptyset\} \\
\beta(C_1 || C_2, E_s) &= \beta(C_1, E_s) \cup \beta(C_2, E_s) \\
\beta(a \rhd^l [m_i^{l_i}(\tilde{x}_i) = \zeta(e_i, s_i)C_i^{i=1,\dots,n}], E_s) &= \{(l, E_s)\} \cup \bigcup_{i=1,\dots,n} \{(l_i, E_s)\} \\
\beta(a \rhd^l B, E_s) &= \{\{(l, E_s)\}\} \\
\beta(a \lhd^l m(\tilde{P}), E_s) &= \{\{(l, E_s)\}\}
\end{aligned}
$$

The initial state for a term $\mathscr{S}$ is described by $init_s$, a set of potential continuations in $\wp(\wp(\mathscr{L}_p \times (\mathscr{V} \to \mathscr{L})))$ defined as $\beta(\mathscr{S}, \emptyset)$.

3.3 Formal Rules

We now define the formal rules that drive the interaction between threads. In the case of CAP, we have two rules that describe an actor handling a message, depending on the kind of actor we have, a static or a dynamic one.

In the following, the i-th parameter, the j-th bounded variable, and the identity of the k-th partial interaction are respectively denoted by X_i^k, Y_j^k and I^k. We define the endomorphism *behavior_set* on the set $\mathscr{L}_p \times \mathscr{M}$ as follows: $(p, m) \mapsto (p', m)$ where p is a behavior program point and p' is the program point where p has been syntactically defined. As an example, in the term $v^\alpha a, a \rhd^1 [m^2() = \zeta(e, s)C]$, we have *behavior_set*$(2, m) = (1, m)$.

Communication with a syntactic defined actor. The first rule needs two threads, the first one must denote a partial interaction *static_actor* when the second one must denote a partial interaction *message$_n$*. We both check that the actor's address (X_1^1) is equal to the message's receiver (X_1^2) and that the actor behavior label (X_2^1) is equal to the message label (X_2^2).

We then define *v_passing* that describe the value passing due to both the ζ operator and message handling.

$$static\_trans_n = (2, components, compatibility, v\_passing)$$

where

1. $components = \begin{cases} 1 \mapsto static\_actor_n, \\ 2 \mapsto message_n \end{cases}$ 2. $compatibility = \begin{cases} X_1^1 = X_1^2; \\ X_2^1 = X_2^2; \end{cases}$

3. $v\_passing = \begin{cases} Y_1^1 \leftarrow X_1^1; \\ Y_2^1 \leftarrow I^1; \\ Y_{i+2}^1 \leftarrow X_{i+2}^2, \forall i \in [\![1;n]\!]; \end{cases}$

Communication with a dynamic actor. The second rule needs three threads: the first one must denote a partial interaction *behavior$_n$*, the second one a partial interaction *dynamic_actor* and the third one a message *message$_n$*. We check the equality between actor's address (X_1^2) and receiver (X_1^3), behavior label (X_1^1) and message label (X_2^3). With the *behavior_set* function we check the link between the behavior and the actor. The value passing is defined in the same way as in the first rule.

$$dynamic\_trans_n = (3, components, compatibility, v\_passing)$$

where

1. $components = \begin{cases} 1 \mapsto behavior_n, \\ 2 \mapsto dynamic\_actor, \\ 3 \mapsto message_n \end{cases}$ 2. $compatibility = \begin{cases} X_1^2 = X_1^3; \\ behavior\_set(I^1) = X_2^3; \\ X_1^1 = X_2^3; \end{cases}$

3. $v\_passing = \begin{cases} Y_1^1 \leftarrow X_1^2; \\ Y_2^1 \leftarrow X_2^2; \\ Y_{i+2}^1 \leftarrow X_{i+2}^3, \forall i \in [\![1;n]\!]; \end{cases}$

3.4   Operational Semantics

We now briefly describe how to use the preceding definitions to express in the non standard syntax both an initial term and the computation of a transition according to a formal rule.

Initial configurations are obtained by launching a continuation in *init$_s$* with an empty marker and an empty environment. That means inserting in an empty configuration, one thread for each pair (p, E_s) in $\beta(init_s)$ where each value in E_s is associated with an empty marker. We focus now on the interaction computation according to one of the two rules. First of all, we have to find some correct interaction. It means that we have to find some threads in the current configuration that can be associated to the right partial interaction according to the matching formal rule. Then we check that their interface satisfies the synchronization constraints. Thus we can compute the interaction:

- we remove interacting threads according to the type of their exhibited partial interaction;
- we choose a syntactic continuation for each thread;
- we compute dynamic data for each of these continuations:
  - we compute the marker;
  - we take into account name passing;
  - we create fresh variables and associate them with the correct values;
  - we restrict the environment according to the interface associated with the program point.

3.5   Correspondence

Theorem 1 (correspondence). *CAP standard semantics and its non standard semantics are in strong bisimulation*

Proof. The proof can be found at the first author's web page, www.enseeiht.fr/ garoche.

3.6   Example

To illustrate the use of the non standard semantics, we will compute the first transition of the example given in section 2.

The initial configuration[1] is:

$$(1,\varepsilon,[a \mapsto \alpha,\varepsilon]) \quad (2,\varepsilon,[a \mapsto \alpha,\varepsilon]) \quad (4,\varepsilon,[]) \quad (6,\varepsilon, \begin{bmatrix} a \mapsto \alpha,\varepsilon \\ b \mapsto \beta,\varepsilon \end{bmatrix})$$
$$(7,\varepsilon,[b \mapsto \beta,\varepsilon]) \quad (8,\varepsilon,[]) \quad (10,\varepsilon,[b \mapsto \beta,\varepsilon])$$

At this point, the only possible transition is labeled by 1,6 and corresponds to the $static\_trans_n$ rule. Program point 1 is able to exhibit the two following partial inter-

actions: $\left\{ \begin{array}{l} \{(static\_actor_n,[a,m],[e,s],\beta(a \triangleright^3 s,\emptyset))\}, \\ \{(static\_actor_n,[a,send],[e,s,x],\beta(x \triangleleft^5 beh(s),\emptyset))\} \end{array} \right\}$ when the program

point 6 exhibits the only partial interaction:

$$\left\{ (message_n,[a,send,b],\emptyset,\emptyset) \right\}$$

We choose the first partial interaction for 1. We first check synchronization constraints. We need that $X_1^1 = X_1^2$ and $X_2^1 = X_2^2$. So $(\alpha,\varepsilon) = (\alpha,\varepsilon)$ and both message share the same label *send*. We can now compute value passing, thread launching and removing. We have to remove interacting threads and to add threads in $\beta(x \triangleleft^5 beh(s),\emptyset)$ with their environment updated by value passing. Value passing gives the value of e, s and x, we have respectively, (α,ε), $(1,\varepsilon)$ and (β,ε). Thus the launched thread is $(5,\varepsilon, \begin{bmatrix} x \mapsto \beta,\varepsilon \\ s \mapsto 1,\varepsilon \end{bmatrix})$.

---

[1] We can notice the absence of threads at program points 3, 5 and 9 which correspond to subterms. There are not present in the initial configuration.

We obtain the new configuration:

$$(2,\varepsilon,[a \mapsto \alpha,\varepsilon])\ (4,\varepsilon,[])\ (5,\varepsilon,\begin{bmatrix} x \mapsto \beta,\varepsilon \\ s \mapsto 1,\varepsilon \end{bmatrix})$$

$$(7,\varepsilon,[b \mapsto \beta,\varepsilon])\ (8,\varepsilon,[])\ (10,\varepsilon,[b \mapsto \beta,\varepsilon])$$

We recall that when computing a transition using the *dynamic_trans_n* rule, new launched threads are associated to a new marker.

4   Abstract Semantics

In order to ensure properties on all the possible execution of the non standard semantics, we rely on the abstract interpretation approach which combines in a single one all the possible executions.

4.1   Abstract Interpretation

Abstract interpretation [10] is a theory of discrete approximation of semantics. A fundamental aspect of this theory is that every semantics can be expressed as fixed points of monotonic operators on complete partial orders. A concrete semantics is defined by a tuple $(S, \subseteq, \bot, \cup, \top, \cap)$. Following [11], an abstract semantics is defined by a pre-ordered set $(S^{\#}, \sqsubseteq)$, an abstract iteration basis $\bot^{\#}$, a concretization function $\gamma: S^{\#} \to S$ and an abstract semantics function $\mathbb{F}^{\#}$.

Abstract Interpretation of Mobile Systems. We approximate here the mobile systems' semantics as described in [15, 29]. The collecting semantics of a configuration $\mathscr{C}_0$ is defined as the least fixed point of the complete join morphism $\mathbb{F}$:

$$\mathbb{F}(X) = (\{\varepsilon\} \times \mathscr{C}_0) \cup \left\{ (u.\lambda, C') \middle| \exists C \in \mathscr{S}, (u,C) \in X \text{ and } C \xrightarrow{\lambda} C' \right\}$$

An abstraction $(\mathscr{C}^{\#}, \sqsubseteq^{\#}, \sqcup^{\#}, \bot^{\#}, \gamma^{\#}, C_0^{\#}, \leadsto, \nabla)$ in this framework must define as usual a pre-order, a join operator, a bottom element, a widening operator (when abstract domains are infinite) as well as:

- the initial abstract configuration $C_0^{\#} \in \mathscr{C}^{\#}$ with $\{\varepsilon\} \times \mathscr{C}_0 \subseteq \gamma(C_0^{\#})$
- the abstract transition relation $\leadsto\ \in \wp(\mathscr{C}^{\#} \times \Sigma \times \mathscr{C}^{\#})$ such that:
  $\forall C^{\#} \in \mathscr{C}^{\#}, \forall (u,C) \in \gamma(C^{\#}), \forall \lambda \in \Sigma, \forall C' \in \mathscr{C},$

$$C \xrightarrow{\lambda} C' \implies \exists C'^{\#} \in \mathscr{C}^{\#}, (C^{\#} \overset{\lambda}{\leadsto} C'^{\#}) \text{ and } (u.\lambda, C') \in \gamma(C'^{\#})$$

Such an abstract transition computes all the concrete transitions labeled λ from all possible C represented by $C^{\#}$.

The abstract counterpart of the $\mathbb{F}$ function is the abstract function $\mathbb{F}^{\#}$ defined as:

$$\mathbb{F}^{\#}(C^{\#}) = \bigsqcup^{\#} \left(\{C'^{\#} \mid \exists \lambda \in \Sigma, C^{\#} \leadsto^{\lambda} C'^{\#}\} \sqcup \{C_0^{\#}; C^{\#}\} \right)$$

4.2   Abstract Domains

An element of an abstract domain expresses the set of invariant properties of a set of terms. We project the initial term into an abstract element to describe its properties. Then we use an abstract counterpart of the transition rules to obtain the set of valid properties when applying the transition rule to all elements of the initial set. Then we compute the union of both abstract elements, to only keep the set of properties which are valid before and after the transition. We repeat these steps until a fixed point is reached. The use of the union and the widening functions guarantees the monotony of the transition and thus the existence of the fixed point. Finally, we obtain an abstract element describing the set of valid properties in all possible evolutions of the initial term. It is a post fixed point of the collecting semantics' least fixed point. Our abstractions are sound counterparts of the non standard semantics.

In order to avoid a too coarse approximation of the collecting semantics, we need, at least, to use a good abstraction of the control flow. We associate to each program point an abstract element describing its set of values and markers. But, most of our properties can be expressed in terms of occurrence counting. We also need to approximate configurations globally. Therefore, we use, as an abstract domain, the cartesian product of an abstract domain to approximate non uniform control flow information in conjunction with a domain to approximate the occurrence of threads in configurations.

Generic Abstractions. In this section, we will briefly describe the two abstract domains defined, by FERET, respectively in [13] and [12] that are used to approximate the non standard semantics of CAP. Their operational semantics is then given in Figs. 3(a) and 3(b).

Control Flow Abstract Domain. This abstract domain approximates variable values of thread environments as well as their marker for a given configuration. It is parametrized by an abstract domain called an Atom Domain. We associate to each program point an atom which describes the values of both variables and markers of the threads that can be associated with this program point. When computing an interaction, we merge the interacting atoms associated to the interacting threads (primitive $reagents^{\#}$) and add synchronization constraints (primitive $sync^{\#}$). If they are satisfiable, the interaction is possible. We then compute the value passing and the marker computation (function $marker\_value$). Finally, we launch new threads (primitive $launch^{\#}$) and update the atom of each program point by computing its union with the appropriate resulting atom.

In this domain, we only focus on values, so we completely abstract away occurrences of threads and thus deletion of interacting threads.

The Atom Domain we use is a reduced product of four domains. The first two represent equality and disequality among values and marker using graphs, the third one approximates the shape of markers and values with an automaton and the fourth one approximates the relationship between occurrences of letters in Parikh's vectors [25] associated to each value and marker.

Occurrence Counting Abstract Domain. In this domain, we count both threads associated to a particular program point and transition label, the set of which is denoted by

Let $C^{\#}$ be an abstract configuration, let $(p_k)_{1 \leq k \leq n} \in \mathcal{L}_p$ be a tuple of program points label and $(pi_k)_{1 \leq k \leq n} = (s_k, (parameter_k), (bd_k), constraints_k, continuation_k)$ be a tuple of partial interactions.

We define mol by $reagents^{\#}((p_k), (parameter_{k,l}), (constraints_k), C^{\#})$.

When

$\forall k \in [\![1;n]\!], pi_k \in interaction(p_k)$;

$mol \neq \bot_{(I(p_k))_k}$

Then

$$C \xrightarrow{(p_k)_k}_{\#} \bigsqcup \{C; mol; new\_threads\}$$

Where

1. $mol' = marker\_value((p_k)_k, mol, (bd_{k,l})_{k,l}, (parameter_{k,l})_{k,l}, v\_passing)$
2. $new\_threads = launch^{\#}((p_k, continuations_k)_k, mol')$.

(a) Abstract semantics for control flow approximation

We define the tuple $t \in \mathbb{N}^{\mathcal{V}_c}$ so that t_v be the occurrence of v in $(p_k)_{1 \leq k \leq n}$.

When

$\forall k \in [\![1;n]\!], pi_k \in interaction(p_k)$; $SYNC_{\mathcal{N}_{\mathcal{V}_c}}(t, C^{\#}) \neq \bot_{\mathcal{N}_{\mathcal{V}_c}}$

Then

$$C \xrightarrow{(p_k)_k}_{\#} SYNC_{\mathcal{N}_{\mathcal{V}_c}}(t, C^{\#}) +^{\#} Transition +^{\#} Launched -^{\#} Consumed$$

Where

1. $Transition = 1_{\mathcal{N}_{\mathcal{V}_c}}(p_1)$;
2. $Launched = \Sigma^{\#}((\beta^{\#}(continuation^k))_k)$;
3. $Consumed = \Sigma^{\#}(1_{\mathcal{N}_{\mathcal{V}_c}}(p_k))_{k \in \{k' | 1 \leq k' \leq n, type(s_{k'}) \neq replication\}}$

(b) Abstract semantics for occurrence counting

Fig. 3. Abstract operational semantics

$\mathcal{V}_c$. We first approximate the non standard semantics by the domain $\mathbb{N}^{\mathcal{V}_c}$ associating to each program point its threads occurrence in the configuration and to each transition label, its occurrence in the word that leads to the configuration. At the level of the collecting semantics, we obtain an element in $\wp(\mathbb{N}^{\mathcal{V}_c})$. We then abstract such a domain by a domain $\mathcal{N}_{\mathcal{V}_c}$ which is a reduced product between the domain of intervals indexed by $\mathcal{V}_c$ and the domain of affine equalities [21] constructed over $\mathcal{V}_c$. When computing a transition, we check that the occurrences of interacting threads are sufficient to allow it (primitive $SYNC_{\mathcal{N}_{\mathcal{V}_c}}$). If we do not obtain the bottom element of our abstract domain, *i.e.* the synchronization constraint is satisfiable, we add (primitive $+^{\#}$) the new transition label, the launched threads (primitives $\beta^{\#}$ and $\Sigma^{\#}$) and remove (primitive $-^{\#}$) consumed threads.

5 Properties

The abstract semantics computes an approximation of all the execution in the non standard one. Its result can then be used in order to check many different properties. In this section, we describe interesting properties and how to observe them in the fixed point of the analysis.

5.1   Linearity

Linearity is a property that expresses the fact that all actors in each possible configuration are bound to different addresses. It can be expressed as in π-calculus when each process listens to at most one channel. It is a useful property to map addresses to resources.

Our analysis is able to prove that a term, without recursive name definitions, *i.e.* without a ν operator inside a behavior continuation, will be linear in all the possible configurations it will take. We can observe such a property with both the control flow domain and the occurrence counting domain. We first determine with the control flow the upper set of program points representing actors that can be associated with each address. Then we check in the occurrence counting domain that each of those program points is mapped to at most one thread in each configuration (within the interval domain) and, moreover, that program points that can be associated with the same address are in mutual exclusion (with the global numerical domain). The mutual exclusion property is observed by exhibiting a constraint from the global numerical domain. Such a constraint must be a linear combination $\Sigma x_i + \Sigma k_j * y_j = 1$ with $\{x_i\}$ the set of program points in mutual exclusion and $\{k_j\}$ a set of positive or null coefficients. Whether such a constraint can be generated by the set of constraints describing the affine space of the global numerical domain then the $\{x_i\}$ program points are in mutual exclusion but they do not have to be present in every configuration of the system.

In the following example, we can automatically determine that the following term satisfies the linearity property.

$$\nu a^{\alpha}, b^{\beta}, a \triangleright^{1:[\![0;1]\!]} [m()^{2:[\![0;1]\!]}() = \zeta(e,s)(e \triangleright^{3:[\![0;1]\!]} s),$$
$$send^{4:[\![0;1]\!]}(x) = \zeta(e,s)(x \triangleleft^{5:[\![0;1]\!]} beh(s))]$$
$$\| \quad b \triangleright^{6:[\![0;1]\!]} [beh^{7:[\![0;1]\!]}(x) = \zeta(e,s)(e \triangleright^{8:[\![0;1]\!]} x)]$$
$$\| \quad a \triangleleft^{9:[\![0;1]\!]} send(b) \| b \triangleleft^{10:[\![0;1]\!]} m()$$

All the actors are associated with the interval $[\![0;1]\!]$. The only actor that can be associated to address a is 1 and others (3, 6 and 8) can be associated with address b. Then the constraint $p_3 + p_6 + p_8 = 1$ can be observed in the global numerical part of the post fixed point of the analysis. We can notice that we have a stronger property: there is exactly one actor on the address b in every configuration of this term.

5.2   Bounded Resources

As CAP is an asynchronous calculus, when a message is sent we cannot ensure that it will be handled. With this property, we want to determine if the system grows infinitely; if the system creates more messages than it can handle. Our analysis is able to infer such a property. We first check which message can have an unbounded number of occurrences. Then we check in the global numerical invariants of the system a constraint between the number of occurrences of this message and the number of occurrences of a transition labeled with the same message label. When such a constraint can be found, we can say that this message will be in the system an unbounded number of times, but it will be handled the same number of times. The system size is constant, it does not diverge.

In the following example, our analysis is able to find that at most one message is present in the system: program points 3, 7 and 9 associated with interval $[\![0;1]\!]$. The system described by this term is bounded. Furthermore, we have the constraint $p_3 + p_7 + p_9 = 1$.

$$\nu a^\alpha, \nu b^\beta, a \rhd^{1:[\![0;1]\!]} [ping^{2:[\![1;1]\!]}() = \zeta(e,s)(b \lhd^{3:[\![0;1]\!]} pong() \;||\; e \rhd^{4:[\![0;1]\!]} s)]$$
$$||\; b \rhd^{5:[\![0;1]\!]} [pong^{6:[\![1;1]\!]}() = \zeta(e,s)(a \lhd^{7:[\![0;1]\!]} ping() \;||\; e \rhd^{8:[\![0;1]\!]} s)]$$
$$||\; a \lhd^{9:[\![0;1]\!]} ping()$$

In addition, we can also detect whether a system does not generate an unbounded number of actor present at the same time in a given configuration.

$$\nu a^\alpha a \rhd^{1:[\![0;1]\!]} [m^{2:[\![1;1]\!]}() = \zeta(e,s)(\nu b^\beta b \rhd^{3:[\![0;1]\!]} s \;||\; b \lhd^{4:[\![0;1]\!]} m())] \;||\; a \lhd^{5:[\![0;1]\!]} m()$$

In the preceding example, we automatically detect that the number of threads associated to program point 3 lies in $[\![0;1]\!]$.

5.3   Unreachable Behaviors

We are interested in determining the subset of behaviors that are really used for each set of behaviors. Due to its high-order capability, CAP allows to send the set of behaviors syntactically associated to an actor to other actors. Therefore the use of the behavior's set depends highly on the messages exchanged.

In the following example, all the behavior branches of the behavior syntactically defined at program point 1 are used. We check such a property by checking that each label of transition is present at least once or its continuation has been launched. *I.e.* $\forall t \in \mathcal{V}_c, Inter(t) \neq [\![0;0]\!]$ where *Inter* is the function that maps each element of $\mathcal{V}_c$ to its image in interval part of the analysis post fixed point.

$$\nu a^\alpha, b^\beta, c^\gamma, a \rhd^1 [m_0^2() = \zeta(e,s)(b \lhd^3 n_1(s) \;||\; b \lhd^4 m_1(c)),$$
$$m_1^5(dest) = \zeta(e,s)(dest \lhd^6 m_2()),$$
$$m_2^7() = \zeta(e,s)(\emptyset)]$$
$$||\; b \rhd^8 [n_1^9(self) = \zeta(e,s)(e \rhd^{10} self \;||\; c \lhd^{11} n_2(self))]$$
$$||\; c \rhd^{12} [n_2^{13}(self) = \zeta(e,s)(e \rhd^{14} self)]$$
$$||\; a \lhd^{15} m_0()$$

We can use such an analysis to clean the term with garbage collecting like mechanisms.

6   Conclusion

We have adapted the framework of FERET [15] to deal with a higher order process calculus modeling actor languages. With such a framework, we are able to analyze CAP terms without any restriction about the kind of values sent within messages: we can now handle behavior passing, which was not able with our previous type based analysis. In contrary to our aforementioned analyses about actor's calculus, we are able to easily count occurrences of both actors and messages. Therefore, most of the properties we obtain are related to occurrence counting. We can detect whether the number of actors and messages is finite, whether there is dead code and whether the message queues are bounded. We also have the linearity property under certain restrictions.

To go further, we need another abstraction which will split thread's information into computation units representing the recursive instances of the same thread. Such an abstract domain will allow us to deal with linearity in the general case as well as handling more properties. In fact the most interesting property with an asynchronous process calculus with non uniform behavior, is the detection of orphan messages, *i.e.* stuck-freeness. An orphan is a message which may not be handled by its target in some execution path. We distinguish two kinds of orphan: safety ones and liveness ones. Safety orphans occur when all future behaviors of the target on a given execution path cannot handle such a message. On the contrary, liveness orphans occur when one of the target behaviors in each execution paths knows how to handle such a message but the target is deadlocked and will never assume the corresponding behavior. We advocate that with this new abstract domain we will be able to detect both kinds of orphans. We also want to define a generic abstract domain dedicated to the data-flow like analyses provided by type systems. Such an abstract domain can be useful to automatically build domains to observe properties for which we already have a type system.

Acknowledgement

We deeply thank Jérôme Feret for fruitful discussions and careful proof reading of the first author's Master's thesis [17].

References

1. G. Agha. *Actors: A model of concurrent computation in distributed systems.* MIT Press, Cambridge, Mass., 1986.
2. T. Amtoft, F. Nielson, and H. R. Nielson. Type and behaviour reconstruction for higher-order concurrent programs. *Journal of Functional Programming*, 7(3):321–347, 1997.
3. G. Boudol. Typing the use of resources in a concurrent calculus. In *Proc. of ASIAN'97*, volume 1345 of *LNCS*, 1997.
4. C. Carrez, A. Fantechi, and E. Najm. Behavioural contracts for a sound composition of components. In *Proc. of FORTE 2003*, volume 2767 of *LNCS*. Springer, 2003.
5. S. Chaki, S. Rajamani, and J. Rehof. Types as models: model checking message-passing programs. In *Proc. of POPL'02*. ACM Press, 2002.
6. J.-L. Colaço, M. Pantel, F. Dagnat, and P. Sallé. Static safety analysis for non-uniform service availability in Actors . In *Proc. of FMOODS'99*, volume 139, pages 371–386. Kluwer, B.V., 1999.
7. J.-L. Colaço, M. Pantel, and P. Sallé. An actor dedicated process calculus. In *Proc. of the ECOOP'96 Workshop on Proof Theory of Concurrent Object-Oriented Programming*, 1996.
8. J.-L. Colaço, M. Pantel, and P. Sallé. Static analysis of behavior changes in Actor languages. In *Object-Oriented Parallel and Distributed Programming*, pages 53–72. Hermès Science, 8, quai du Marché-Neuf, 75004 Paris, France, 2000.
9. M. Colin, X. Thirioux, and M. Pantel. Temporal logic based static analysis for non uniform behaviors. In *Proc. of FMOODS'03*. Springer, 2003.

10. P. Cousot and R. Cousot. Abstract interpretation: a unified lattice model for static analysis of programs by construction or approximation of fixpoints. In *Proc. of POPL'77*, pages 238–252. ACM Press, 1977.
11. P. Cousot and R. Cousot. Abstract interpretation frameworks. *Journal of Logic and Computation*, 2(4):511–547, 1992.
12. J. Feret. Occurrence counting analysis for the pi-calculus. In *Proc. of the 1st Workshop on GEometry and Topology in COncurrency Theory*, volume 39.2 of *ENTCS*. Elsevier, 2001.
13. J. Feret. Dependency analysis of mobile systems. In *Proc. of ESOP'02*, number 2305 in LNCS. Springer, 2002.
14. J. Feret. Abstract interpretation of mobile systems. *Journal of Logic and Algebraic Programming*, 63.1, 2005. special issue on pi-calculus, 2005.
15. J. Feret. *Analysis of Mobile Systems by Abstract Interpretation*. PhD thesis, École polytechnique, Paris, France, february 2005.
16. C. Fournet, C. Lavene, L. Maranget, and D. Rémy. Implicit typing à la ml for the join-calculus. In *Proc. of CONCUR'97*, volume 1283 of *LNCS*. Springer, 1997.
17. P.-L. Garoche. Static analysis of actors by abstract interpretation. Master's thesis, École Normale Suprieure de Cachan, 2005.
18. M. Hennessy, J. Rathke, and N. Yoshida. Safedpi: a language for controlling mobile code. In *Proc. of FoSSaCS'04*, LNCS, pages 241–256. Springer, 2004.
19. C. Hewitt, P. Bishop, and R. Steiger. A universal modular actor formalism for artificial intelligence. In *Proc. of IJCAI'73*, 1973.
20. A. Igarashi and N. Kobayashi. A generic type system for the pi-calculus. *Theoretical Computer Science*, 311(1-3):121–163, January 2004.
21. M. Karr. Affine relationships among variables of a program. *Acta Informatica*, 6:133 – 151, 1976.
22. N. Kobayashi. A type system for lock-free processes. *Information and Computation*, 177(2):122–159, 2002.
23. E. Najm, A. Nimour, and J.-B. Stefani. Infinite types for distributed object interfaces. In *Proc. of FMOODS'99*, volume 139. Kluwer, B.V., 1999.
24. J. Palsberg and P. O'Keefe. A type system equivalent to flow analysis. In *Proc. of POPL'95*, pages 367–378, 1995.
25. R. Parikh. On context-free languages. *Journal of the ACM*, 13(4):570–581, 1966.
26. F. Puntigam. Types for Active Objects based on Trace Semantics. In Elie Najm et al., editor, *Proc. of FMOODS'96*, Paris, France, 1996. Chapman & Hall.
27. S. Rajamani and J. Rehof. A behavioral module system for the pi-calculus. In *Proc. of SAS'01*, volume 2126 of *LNCS*, pages 375–394. Springer, 2001.
28. A. Ravara and V. Vasconcelos. Typing non-uniform concurrent objects. In *Proc. of CONCUR'00*, volume 1877 of *LNCS*. Springer, 2000.
29. A. Venet. *Static Analysis of Dynamic Graph Strutures in Untyped Languages*. PhD thesis, École polytechnique, Paris, France, december 1998.

Temporal Superimposition of Aspects for Dynamic Software Architecture

Carlos E. Cuesta[1], María del Pilar Romay[2],
Pablo de la Fuente[3], and Manuel Barrio-Solórzano[3],*

[1] Kybele, Departamento de Lenguajes y Sistemas Informáticos
ESCET, Universidad Rey Juan Carlos, Madrid (Spain)
`carlos.cuesta@urjc.es`
[2] Departamento de Sistemas Informáticos
Escuela Politécnica Superior, Universidad Europea de Madrid (Spain)
`pilar.romay@uem.es`
[3] Depto. de Informática (Arquitectura, C. Computación y Lenguajes)
E.T.S. Ingeniería Informática, Universidad de Valladolid (Spain)
`{pfuente, mbarrio}@infor.uva.es`

Abstract. The well-known Separation of Concerns Principle has been revisited by recent research, suggesting to go beyond the limits of traditional modularization. This has led to the definition of an orthogonal, *invasive* composition relationship, which can be used all along the software development process, taking several different forms. The object-like entity known as *aspect* is the best known among them, but in the most general case it can be defined as a new kind of structure. Software Architecture must be able to describe such a structure. Moreover, as most ADLs have a formal foundation, this can be used to provide an adequate formalization for the aspectual composition relationship, which is still under discussion. In this paper, we propose to base this architecture-level definition in the concept of *superimposition*, integrating the resulting framework into the process-algebraic, dynamic ADL named $\mathcal{PiLar}$. This language has a reflective design, which allows us to define that extension without redefining the semantics; in addition, the extended syntax can be used to avoid the use of reflective notions. Nevertheless, the language must provide the means to define general patterns to guide the weaving. Such patterns must not only identify locations in the architecture, but also the adequate states of the corresponding process structure. Therefore, we suggest to use *temporal logic*, specifically the μ-calculus, as the quantification mechanism. To illustrate this approach, we expose a case study in which all these ideas are used, and conclude by discussing how the combination of temporal logic and aspect superimposition, in this context, provides also an alternative way to describe architectural dynamism.

1 Introduction

From the very beginning, one of the basic guidelines of Software Engineering has been the *Separation of Concerns* Principle [20]. This is yet another translation of the classic strategy known as *divide et impera*, commonly attributed to Julius Caesar, to the

* This research has been partially financed by the Spanish Ministry of Education and Science under Projects MCYT-TIC2003-07804-C05-01 (DYNAMICA) and MCYT-TIC2003-09268.

R. Gorrieri and H. Wehrheim (Eds.): FMOODS 2006, LNCS 4037, pp. 93–107, 2006.

computing field. The principle itself is at the core of every conceptual division within the Software Engineering body of knowledge, and its purpose is to separately deal with every detail in the development process, thus obtaining both simplicity and cohesion. It is also the deep reason behind the traditional practice of *modularization*, which causes the definition of structures within software; and also the motivation to create a specific discipline to study them, namely Software Architecture.

In recent years, this principle has been revisited and given birth to the approach known as Advanced Separation of Concerns, within which the so-called Aspect-Oriented Software Development [12] is the best known incarnation. Considered as a whole, it is basically an approach to software development in which those different *concerns* –or *aspects*– within a system are conceived and designed as separate entities. The result of this process is a set of overlapping functional elements or modules, maintaining mutual dependencies and crosscutting relationships. Traditional modular barriers are crossed; structural schemas, typically compositional and thus hierarchy-based, are no longer valid. An orthogonal, *invasive* composition [2] relationship is used instead.

This new kind of element, often known as *aspect*, was initially conceived within the boundaries of programming, at the implementation phase; but this origin has been superseded long ago. Nowadays, the principles of Aspect Orientation are applied all along the software lifecycle; in fact, there's even a specific term, namely *early aspects*, to refer to their influence in early stages of the development process, such as requirements specification and architectural design itself.

Therefore, to study the concept of aspect from an architectural point of view is not only reasonable, but even relevant. Moreover, as already exposed in [10], aspects are related to the notion of *architectural viewpoint* [24], still one of the more important and less studied in the field. However, existing Architecture Description Languages (ADLs) are conceived around the dimensions of composition and interaction, and designed to describe their structures. However, *aspectual* structures are not strictly compositional, as they have a different nature; so they are not easily specified using current ADLs. To adapt them to this sort of description, some specific *extension* must be defined.

In this paper we outline such an aspect-oriented extension for an existing ADL namely $\mathcal{P}i\mathcal{L}ar$ [9]. This language has a reflective basis, which has made us able to design this extension without affecting the semantics. But at the same time, the impact of the new syntax on the whole of the language has been greater than at first expected. On the one hand, the *aspectual* perspective can be used to avoid the complex reflective interpretation of the original; on the other hand, the new setting provides a whole new approach to describe *dynamic architecture*.

2   On the Notion of Superimposition

The concept of *superimposition*, also known as *superposition*, was first proposed in Concurrency Theory, both in the context of process algebras and action systems [3, 6]. It was originally conceived as a notion of refinement, relating different versions of a specification as variations from the original. The same approach was later used as an isomorphic notion of extension, composing a basic description with additional details. Consequently, superimposition is now conceived as a privileged relationship between two concurrent entities, such that the first one is able to access the internal details of the second one. This relationship has essentially a *compositional* nature.

Superimposition has also been approached from a different perspective, recently. In the search for an adequate formal foundation for the novel concepts identified in the context of Advanced Separation of Concerns, and particularly in Aspect Orientation, it has been regarded as a suitable candidate. The alternative composition offered by superimposition could possibly be assimilated to the *invasive* composition implicit in those concepts. In fact there are already several proposals relating this formal concept to the notion of aspect [14, 17, 21, 22], though most of them are located at a programming level. The only exception are Katara and Katz [15], who have also studied those concepts at the architectural level, but still using an informal approach.

There are several different definitions of superimposition in the literature. Though similar, they are not actually equivalent. Fiadeiro and Maibaum studied them from a categorical perspective [11], finding out that there are really three different flavours of the concept, which are respectively named *invasive*, *regulative* and *spectative* superimposition. The first one is the simplest as it is unrestricted; the third one is the most complex as it bears several restrictions to achieve better extensional properties.

In the architectural context, the most interesting among all the definitions of superimposition is probably Katz's [16], as it describes not a relationship, but an structure. The traditional strategy is to define the formal semantics for the superimposition relationship and then summarize it in a single compositional operator or morphism. Instead, Katz uses a different approach. He defines superimposition as a high-level concurrent *control structure* which implicitly uses the concept, and then provides the semantics for this construct. Therefore the relationship itself, a well-behaved form or spectative superimposition [11], is only indirectly defined.

This approach seems to be very adequate for the architectural domain, as the construct has a significant resemblance to certain presentations of the concept of connector, particularly higher-order connectors. Moreover, the resulting structure is also somewhat similar to *aspectual collaborations* [19], the most recent result of the work by Lieberherr *et al* on aspect orientation. This coincidence suggests that Katzian superimposition provides indeed a good starting point to explore aspectual composition at the architectural level, and therefore this is the definition to be used in the rest of this document.

2.1 Katzian Superimposition

In the following, the term *superimposition* will be generally used in the most general sense, but assuming Katz's definition [16] when necessary. Therefore, the expression *Katzian Superimposition* will be used to explicitly refer to this restricted meaning, and to concrete features in it which differ from some other approaches.

Structurally, every superimposition relationship has two parts: a superimposed element, and another(s) base element(s) where it is superimposed to. The complete structure receives the name of *superimposure* or *combination*. In the original conception, this is just *spectative superimposition*, in which the superimposed process refines or extends the original. It is able to inhibit the external interaction of the superimposee and also to *observe* its internal behaviour, but it cannot modify the latter [3, 16]. In summary, it doesn't have full control over it, and acts like a monitor.

The frequent use of such terms as *superimposed* or *superimposee* is rather confusing. To avoid complex periphrasis, we have decided to use a prefix-based notation, which states clearly the relative position of involved elements. Then, the superimposed component will be designated as σ-*component*, and it is conceived to be situated "over" some superimposee component, here known as β-*component*.

In Katzian superimposition, the relationship is defined as a structure which could simultaneously comprise several β-processes, such that the set of their σ-processes defines an algorithm –a behaviour– which is globally superimposed over a significant subsystem. The basic idea is that different σ-components may play different roles in this algorithm, thus providing us with the means to modularize the specification, while at the same time grouping these modules in a single construction.

Each one of those roles are defined as subprocesses in a Katzian superimposition, where they receive the name of *roletypes*. The same roletype could have several instances: that is to say, several elements could be playing the same role in the algorithm, and share the same description. In this case, several σ-processes, defined as the same roletype, are superimposed over several β-processes.

Thus the notion of *roletype* is very useful from an architectural perspective, and it would be used in the following sections. However, this could cause some confusion with the concept of *role* in a connector, which is somehow similar. To avoid this, we would use the name *role-component* to refer to the same notion in the architectural domain, as it has features in common to both ideas.

3   Aspect-Oriented Architecture in $\mathcal{P}i\mathcal{L}ar$

The $\mathcal{P}i\mathcal{L}ar$ [7, 8, 9] language is a dynamic, process-algebraic ADL, based on the notion of abstract process [8] and the concept of reflection, and with semantics founded on relation theory and the polymorphic π-calculus. The use of reflection is its distinguishing feature: as a consequence of that, a $\mathcal{P}i\mathcal{L}ar$ description could be stratified in multiple meta-levels, components are implicitly divided in three categories (base component, meta-component and meta-level component) and have a dual nature, and the definition of first-class connectors is not strictly necessary.

Our previous work [10] shows that the existing language, with the associated reflective support, was powerful enough to simulate the superimposition structure and the combination schema in an aspect-oriented architectural description. There, the foundation of our approach was the process-algebraic strategy of Andrews' definition [1]. But at the same time this approach was rather complex, and we suggested ourselves that an specific syntax for the new set of concepts would be rather convenient.

In the next sections we describe a proposal for an aspect-oriented extension of $\mathcal{P}i\mathcal{L}ar$, now using Katzian definition as a foundation. By doing so, we expose the real expressiveness of such an approach, and simultaneously provide a completely different perspective for the ADL, as the syntax acquires an alternative nature.

Of course this new vision does not exclude the previous one, though it can be used to *hide* it. Using it, we're able to describe the language without any mention of the concept of reflection or the meta-level hierarchy, but at the same time we retain most of the expressive power of the reflective vision.

Table 1. Rough Conceptual Analogies in/to both $\mathcal{P}i\mathcal{L}ar$ Models

New Concept	Analogous Aspectual Notion	Former Reflective Concept
Viewpoint	Concern	Reification Category
Architectural View	Crosscut	Meta-Level (subset)
Multi-dimensional Component	Hypermodule	(Extended) Metaspace
Architectural Fragment	Aspectual Component	Composite Meta-level Component
Partial Component	Aspect, Hyperslice	Metaspace (subset)
Exterface	Aspect Interface	Metaface (Meta-Interface)
Bond Assertion	Pointcut Designator (Aspect) Connector	—
Superimposition (target)	Pointcut	Reification (target)
Role-Component	Pointcut (subject)	Reification (origin)
Superimposition (relationship)	Dynamic Weaving	Reification (relationship)
Combination (Superimposure)	Weaved *system*	Reification (set)
β-Component	Base *Module*	Base Component, Avatar
σ-Component	Aspect (part of)	Meta-Component, Rohatar
σ-Constraint	Advice	Meta-Constraint
Component in-a-Fragment	(Aspect) Wrapper	Meta-level Component, Niyatar
Bound β-Action	Join Point	Synchronization with Avatar

However, these *aspectual* and reflective perspectives of the same language are not conflicting at all; on the contrary, they naturally complement each other. So we're not rejecting the reflective interpretation, which is still more powerful; we're just providing an alternative explanation for the language, which allows us to initially avoid some of the most complex notions in the language.

3.1 PiLar Revisited: A New Vision for the Language

We have already exposed the reasons why we consider the description of *aspect-oriented* architectures to be relevant. An explicit aspect-oriented syntax is not strictly required, as we can use the reflective syntax to provide this description indirectly, as already exposed in [10]. However, this approach could allegedly be considered too complex. For this reason, we found it convenient to extend the language's syntax, such that relevant concepts can be directly managed.

This syntax extension would be based in Katzian superimposition, as this construct's shape provides an almost direct mapping to the architectural level. Specifically, the following concepts are introduced:

Architectural Fragment or **Partial Component.** This name designates the analogue of an aspect at the architectural level. Such an aspect is a new kind of module, similar to a component, but which was not designed to work on isolation; that's why it has a partial description. It is syntactically identical to a composite component, which unfolds as a Katzian superimposition.

Superimposition. Relationship which is implicitly introduced in the new model. It has the form of a Katzian construction, where the main structure is a fragment, the elements are plain components and role-components, instantiating as σ-components, and the resulting architecture defines a combination.

Role-Component. Each of the roles we can superimpose over a β-component when defining a Katzian structure. They are the "holes" in the architectural fragment, and they are filled by σ-components when the superimposition is made effective.

σ-**Component.** Every instance of a role-component, which is superimposed over a β-component. It can define also "external", non-superimposed behaviour.

β-**Component.** Every one of the base components where a σ-component is being superimposed, filling a gap in the fragment.

Combination. The set of all the elements involved in a Katzian superimposition, once it has been applied.

This version of the superimposition structure extends Katz's one merely by adding compositional details. Therefore, the fragment could have its own external interface, which is not projected into β-components; it could define its own constraints, which would be combined to those of its internal elements; and of course, a fragment definition can use additional components which are *not* going to be superimposed, that is, which would never act as role-components.

The new conceptual structure of the language is completely based on the implicit mapping between two structural relationships: the already existing, reflective notion of *reification*, and the concurrent concept of *superimposition*, introduced by the aspectual extension. Curiously enough, this idea is supported by the original semantics of the language, as there reflection is unfolded as a π-calculus structure of concurrent processes which is inspired [8] in another definition of superimposition [3].

The syntax is inspired in Katzian superimposition, and this means that this conceptual mapping would not be direct at the linguistic level. This means that some of the more complex aspectual notions are built over a set of several reflective elements; and also that some basic reflective concepts lack a peer in the aspectual view.

However in general terms, the mapping between the more important aspectual and reflective notions is rather intuitive. Every β-component is a base-component, and its σ-component is a meta-component. So, the notion of role-component is just a way to explicitly declare the meta-components in a fragment, and superimposition is just a reification relationship which is reflected over an already existing base component. Consequently, an architectural fragment is a composite meta-component, composed of one or several meta-components and (possibly) some additional meta-level components. Only the notion of combination lacks a reflective equivalent, as it combines elements which are situated in two different meta-levels.

There's no space here to provide a more detailed mapping between the reflective and aspectual concepts in $\mathcal{P}i\mathcal{L}ar$, as this is not our main concern here. Similarly, a detailed explanation of their similarities and differences which analogous notions in the specific field of Aspect Orientation would also require a rather long exposition, particularly to explain those analogues. This comparison is interesting anyway, so we provide a brief and compact summary both mappings in the Table 1.

3.2   A New Extended Syntax for the $\mathcal{P}i\mathcal{L}ar$ Language

Table 2 contains an enumeration of the new syntactic elements added to the language, which are based in the notions we have described in the previous section. Here we

Table 2. Aspect-Oriented Extension for $\mathcal{P}i\mathcal{L}ar$: Syntax

Keyword	Notion	Basic Structure
\fragment	Architectural Fragment	Analogous to a composite component including role-components.
rolecomp	Role-Component	Declaration of a component instance which acts as a σ-component. A "hole" in a fragment.
\exterface	Exterface (External Interface)	Non-superimposed interface, reserved for the private use of the σ-component itself.
bcomp	β-Component	Prefix to designate elements of a β-component.
scomp	σ-Component	Prefix to designate non-superimposed elements.
impose	Superimposition	Dynamic operator to superimpose a fragment over several β-components (see Figure 4).
del	Unweaving	Deletion (destruction) of a superimposition.
\bond assertion	Bond Asssertion	Syntax to select relevant join points.

will not try to describe the minor details of this syntax, as they are rather intuitive, and anyway most of them will be used later for the case study included in section 4.

The only notion we have not mentioned before is that of *bond assertion*. This is the incarnation of the quantification mechanism which is necessary in every aspect-oriented language [13, 10]. As we expose in the next section, this mechanism is based on *temporal logic*, and it provides the syntax to select join points at any place *or moment* in the architecture, resulting in a truly dynamic weaving mechanism.

Of course, already existing introspective (reflective) operands in the language can still be used. In fact, some of them are even essential to outline a good aspect-oriented description, as they fill the role of so-called *aspectual reflection* [18] abstractions. For example, the language already included a reflective operator, **bound**, to obtain the set of links bound to a given port (or the set of ports pount by a given link). This operator happens to be also particularly useful in an aspectual context.

Most of this "extended" syntax is actually just *syntactic sugar* for aspect-oriented abstractions. Not a single element in the language semantics has required to be adapted to the new conception of the ADL. This is in accordance to our initial purpose, in which this new version of $\mathcal{P}i\mathcal{L}ar$ is conceived just as a different presentation of the same language, which tries to avoid the use of reflective notions.

However there is an exception to this rule: the definition of assertions and the use of temporal logic *is* actually a new addition to the language. But this addition has not been an arbitrary decision; as explained next, there are several reasons to use it.

3.3   The Syntax of Temporal Assertions

The existence of some quantification mechanism is strictly necessary for a sensible Aspect Orientation definition [13]. Without it, every join point between two structures has to be individually designated. Though this would still be useful [10], it is not flexible enough; an architectural description is supposed to describe structural *patterns*, and therefore the lack of a general expression to refer to patterns of superimposition would be considered as a severe limitation.

Moreover, in the context of dynamic architectures, the choice of a particular join point to superimpose an architectural aspect does not only depends on the system's structure, but frequently also on the concrete *situation* or state in which an element (or set of elements) is. Superimposition happens not only at a *place* in the architecture, but also at a particular *moment* in the system's evolution.

Existing aspect-oriented languages, at the programming level, use quantification mechanisms based just on name structure; this would be a very inadequate approach at the architectural level. Some other proposals provide a better mechanism by suggesting the use of some variant of predicate logic. While this is much more flexible, it is still not enough, particularly in the presence of time. Besides, classical logic is probably not the best choice to combine with the semantics of a process-algebraic ADL, which would usually consist of transition systems.

Then our proposal tries to be a solution to both problems, and it is based on the addition of *temporal logic* to the language, using the form of assertions or laws. In the context of $\mathcal{P}i\mathcal{L}ar$, which is founded on a process algebra and the notion of bisimulation, the obvious choice is the modal μ-calculus [4], a branching-time temporal logic, which is also considered as the most general among them.

Therefore, the syntax for temporal assertions would be based in that of $\mathcal{P}i\mathcal{L}ar$'s dynamic language and the μ-calculus. There are several different but equivalent notations for the latter; here we follow Stirling's [4, 23], probably the best known among them. Currently we would only use the basic syntax; but this is just a first approach to the problem, so it should not be taken as a final decision. We could consider further additions, like pure temporal operators in the CTL style, which are usually considered easier to understand by the average software engineer. Those would be syntactic sugar anyway, as their semantics are already expressible in the μ-calculus syntax.

The basic extension is just a notion of *law* or *assertion*. With this addition, the language acquires a new quality, as it gets transformed into some sort of *Law-Governed* $\mathcal{P}i\mathcal{L}ar$, which is even capable of describing architectural styles. However, subject to this notion there's a set of new concepts, which are summarized in the following.

Assertion. Following Lamport, we use the term *assertion* to refer to any temporal formula defined over the architecture. The purpose of this term is to easily separate them from behavioural constraints, which in $\mathcal{P}i\mathcal{L}ar$ are defined as processes. The **assertion** structure of the syntax is defined to contain these formulae.

Bond Assertion. The only difference between this and a conventional assertion is that this is *active*. This means that when the formula requires an action to happen, and this action is not observed, the assertion itself is in charge of doing it, *but only if this action is related to a superimposition*. Expressed otherwise, if an assertion states that an **impose** action must happen, the assertion itself is the one which creates a superimposition. Apart from being prefixed with a **bond** qualifier, the syntax is identical to that of a conventional assertion.

Action. Any valid action in a $\mathcal{P}i\mathcal{L}ar$ specification, in particular message inputs and outputs through some port. They are the set of observable events from the assertion's point of view. The syntax allows to specify a single action or an enumeration of several ones. When it is prefixed by a minus (–) sign, this refers to the set of each action *except for* this. Conversely, the asterisk (∗) refers to every of them.

Bound Name. This is not a μ-calculus notion, as it comes from aspect orientation. As noted above, assertions are used as a quantification mechanism, and they observe actions happening in *any port* of the namespace. Then such a port is a join point within a component, and thus we would often need to refer to it again. To be able to do that, we provide a mechanism to *bind* the name of these elements within a special variable defined for this purpose. The binding process must comply with the Scope Inversion Rule, stated below.

Possibility Modality. When referencing an action, this means that if the action happens, the expression which follows in the assertion *may* be true. The purpose is to state that the system is able to do something in this point of its evolution. It is expressed by enclosing the action $\langle a \rangle$ in angles.

Necessity Modality. The second alternative. When referencing an action, this means that if it happens, the expression which follows *must* be true. The purpose is to *forbid any other* possibility to happen in the system, indicating an inhibition. It is expressed by enclosing the action $[a]$ in brackets.

Minimal Fixpoint. It has a complex semantics; but we can summarize it [4] by saying that it specifies a repetition of undefined, but *finite* length. In the μ-calculus, it is often expressed as μ (or min); in $\mathcal{P}i\mathcal{L}ar$, we shall use the keyword **nrec**.

Maximal Fixpoint. It is equally complex; we can summarize it by saying that it specifies a repetition of *infinite* length. In the μ-calculus, it is often expressed as ν (or max); in $\mathcal{P}i\mathcal{L}ar$, we shall use the keyword **xrec**.

This construction has the same semantics as the equivalent notions in the μ-calculus, and therefore it has been already formally defined [4, 23]. There's only one difference from their usual application to a process algebra: here we don't have a flat namespace, but a hierarchy of names. This results in two consequences. First, any assertion must be defined over a concrete namespace, provided by a component; this is designated by using the **over** clause. Second, it is often necessary to bind the name of the components in which actions are observed. As stated above, this binding process must comply with the rule which follows:

Rule 1 (Scope Inversion). *Every action on a port which is observed in an assertion binds the name of the innermost component where this port belongs in the composition hierarchy, using the conventional syntax to qualify those names.*

Next we will expose an example to show how an assertion works. To ease the explanation, and also to show the differences in the notation, we would use the same one which is later provided in $\mathcal{P}i\mathcal{L}ar$ syntax in Figure 4. Moreover, the actions to be observed (acc_1 and acc_2) have been abstracted, so that we just focus on the temporal aspects of the formulae and not on the concrete behaviour.

This assertion[1] uses the conventional notation of the μ-calculus [4]. The mapping to the syntax in $\mathcal{P}i\mathcal{L}ar$ should be apparent by comparison to the descripiton in the Figure 4, taking into account that the actions (acc_1 and acc_2) are themselves $\mathcal{P}i\mathcal{L}ar$ actions, expressed in the syntax of the dynamic language.

---

[1] This is of course just a single assertion (*Always_Do_Tunnel*), but it has been divided in three parts to ease its explanation. The specification in a single formula can use a much more compact notation, which is: $\nu X. ([acc_1]([-acc_2]\textbf{false} \wedge \langle-\rangle\textbf{true}) \wedge [-]X)$.

$$\text{Must\_Tunnel} ::= [-acc_2]\,\textbf{false} \wedge \langle-\rangle\textbf{true} \tag{1}$$

$$\text{Do\_Tunnel} ::= [acc_1]\,\text{Must\_Tunnel} \tag{2}$$

$$\text{Always\_Do\_Tunnel} ::= \nu\,X.\,(\text{Do\_Tunnel} \wedge [-]\,X) \tag{3}$$

The assertion has been separated in three formulae, such that each one of them is contained in the following. So we begin with the most internal one (1). It describes the conjuction of two terms: the second states that it's possible for any action to happen; the first states that when something happens which is *not* the acc_2 action, the formula gets false. This means that the conjunction only gets true if the acc_2 action actually happens. This is the μ-calculus way to indicate that something is mandatory.

The second equation (2) is trivial; it just states that after an acc_1 action happens, the previous one (1) is *necessarily* true; in summary, acc_2 must happen.

The last equation (3) encloses the former one in another conjunction, inside the scope of a maximal fixpoint ($\nu\,X$). The other part of the conjunction is enabling any action to happen, assuming that the fixpoint X (that is, any possible future) gets true. For this to be consistent, if the acc_1 action happens at some point in time, the other equation (2) must be true, and so this forces us to "trigger" acc_2. This is a maximal fixpoint, therefore this sequence can happen as many times as required ("always").

In summary: the assertion states that an acc_1 action may happen at any moment, but in the case the next action is necessarily acc_2; and this is always true, meaning that this happens *every time* the action acc_1 is observed.

4   Case Study: P/S Architecture with Secure C/S Connection

In this section we provide a case study outlining the use of the new aspectual framework, to show how it can be applied for the purposes of architectural description. To simplify things, we use an augmentative (asymmetric) model, which *grows* from an initial basis; a compositive model, though symmetric, would have been much more complex. The general idea is that we begin with a base architecture, and then we superimpose a *security aspect* over it, defining the weaving as a bond assertion. Besides, this superimposition indirectly modifies the system's structure; therefore, this is also an example of a new way to describe *architectural dynamism*, a very interesting side-effect of the aspectual framework.

The case study describes a hybrid architecture, blending the Publisher/Subscriber[2] and the Client/Server architectural styles [5]. The global conception is that of a distributed system composed of a number of *subscribers* which contract the services of a *publisher*; for instance, a news service. As soon as new contents are made available, the publisher notifies subscribers by triggering an event. When a subscriber observes this event, it must decide whether it is interested in those contents or not. If this is the case, the subscriber starts to behave like a *client*, which tries to communicate to a *server*; but the connection to this server has yet to be created. In this particular moment, a *secure connection* among them is created, applying a *tunneling* protocol which ensures that every interaction between them is encrypted in advance. Using this connection, the client receives the selected contents. This process may happen as many times as required.

---

[2] This architectural pattern has also been described in the literature as the *Implicit Invocation* architectural style, and even the *Observer* design pattern. The structure is fairly identical.

```
\component Publisher (                          \constraint (
  \interface ( port notify | port server )         Observe def= rep ( receive?(msg);
  \constraint (                                        tau (msg,ask,req);
    Provide def= ( Publish | Serve )                   if (ask) ( Request(req) ) )

    Publish def= rep ( tau (msg);                  Request(req) def= ( client !( req);
       loopSet ( bound(notify) )                        client ?(data); tau (data ) ) ) )
          ( notify !(msg) ) )
                                                \component System (
    Serve def= rep ( server?(req);              \config (
       tau (req,data); server!(data ) ) ) )       PS: Publisher | S1, S2, S3: Subscriber |
                                                   \bind (
\component Subscriber (                              PS.notify = S1.receive |
  \interface (                                       PS.notify = S2.receive |
    port receive | port client )                     PS.notify = S3.receive ) ) )
```

Fig. 1. Hybrid Publish/Subscribe and Client/Server Architecture (w/o connection)

Many details of this example which are not strictly related to this paper's subject have been left out, as we try to briefly expose an averagely complex system. Therefore, there are details on the final system which don't try to be realistic. Then, the specification shows how new private connections are created, but they are never destroyed; the only reason to omit this step is to keep the example short and simple enough.

The case study is described in Figures 1 to 4. The first one provides the base Publish/Subscribe architecture, and also the Client/Server infrastructure. The second one describes an architectural fragment, which provides the secure connection by using the tunneling protocol. In the last one we provide the bond assertion, which dynamically "triggers" the superimposition of this fragment to the base architecture.

The specification in Figure 1 is therefore fairly standard. The *Publisher* component has two ports, enabling it to act as publisher or server, as required; and two constraints, *Publish* and *Serve*, which control any interaction in these ports. The first process starts when some new content –expressed as an internal **tau** action– is created; then this is notified to every subscriber connected to the *notify* port. The second process describes how the server waits to receive some request; when this happens, it locates the requested data, and sends them to the requesting client.

On the other hand, the *Subscriber* component can similarly behave either as a subscriber or a client. However in this case the two relevant constraints are related. The first process, *Observe*, waits to receive a notification event, which is internally evaluated. If an affirmative decision is taken, the component begins to behave as a client by starting the *Request* process. This just sends a request for the new content, waits to receive the result, and then processes the information.

The *System* component is just a composite to define the whole of the system. Let us note that initially, only the publisher and its subscribers are connected.

Figure 2 describes an architectural fragment defining the superimposition of a secure connection, supported by a tunneling protocol, over the previous base architecture. So it is the equivalent of a *security aspect*. As this is conceived in an augmentative model, a high degree of connascence with the β-architecture is allowed, something that could be less adequate in a symmetric model.

The *Tunnel* fragment is defined as a Katzian superimposition, built as the composition of two role-components connected by a basic link. These components define a

```
\component TBegin (                        \constraint (
  \interface ( port send )                   lock ( bcomp.server );
  \constraint (                              rep   ( recv?(req); shift server(req);
    lock ( bcomp.client );                           catch server(x);
    rep   ( catch client(req); send!(req);            tau (x,ex); recv!(ex ) ) ) )
            send?(ex); tau (ex,x);
            shift  client (x ) ) ) )       \fragment Tunnel (
                                             \config (
\component TEnd (                              rolecomp TB: TBegin I
\interface (                                   rolecomp TE: TEnd I
      port recv )                             \bind ( TS.send = TR.recv ) ) )
```

Fig. 2. Architectural Fragment to Superimpose a Secure Connection

tunnel using this link: every message to be sent is encrypted in advance on origin, and only the legitimate receiver would know how to decrypt it. This way a *secure channel* is created over a conventional connection.

The tunnel has been designed to be asymmetric: only the sending of data is encrypted, while the requests are not, as they are not considered as sensible information. This implies that interaction is always initiated by the same part of the interaction. As a result, the tunnel is conceived as having an explicit beginning and an end, as indicated by the archtypes *TBegin* and *TEnd*, which respectively describe the behaviour to be superimposed over every client and the server.

The former has then been designed to be combined with a *Subscriber*. First, it locks the *client* β-port, thus inhibiting any further uncontrolled interaction. Then it captures (*catch*) any message sent through this port, which must be a request. This request is sent to the server unaltered, using the superimposed connection. Eventually, some *encrypted* response is received, and it must be decrypted; this is made by an internal process (*tau*). The requested data are then obtained, and then they are inserted (*shift*) into the β-port. All this process is transparent to the oblivious client; it just requests some data, and later receives those data in the same port.

The *TEnd* archtype is similar, but it gets superimposed to a *Publisher*. Equivalently, it locks the β-port *server*, but now it waits for a request on the superimposed connection. When this is received, it is inserted into the server component, which "believes" this to be a conventional reception, and answers by providing the relevant data. Those data are captured by the σ-component, which encrypts them in an internal process, and sends the result through the σ-connection.

Figure 3 depicts and summarizes the architecture of the augmented system. Two long arrows represent the superimposition relationship, which imposes *TBegin* and *TEnd* to *Subscriber* and *Publisher*, respectively. Small arrows represent the flow of information within the woven architecture.

Finally, Figure 4 describes the bond assertion which blends the fragment with the β-architecture. Once we're aware of the meaning of the temporal formula, which was described in section 3.3, the explanation is immediate.

First, the assertion is declared: it is a bond assertion, defined over the namespace of the *System* component, and the name of the main formula is *Always_Do_Tunnel*; the rest are subformulae. The temporal expression is now evaluated; it means that any action may indefinitely (*xrec*) happen; but if this action is some kind of sending through a port named *client*, the name of the sending component is bound in a *Sub* variable;

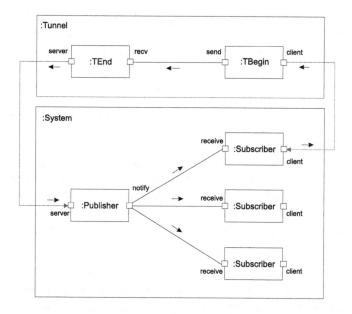

Fig. 3. Publisher/Subscriber System with a superimposed Client/Server Tunnel

\bond assertion Always_Do_Tunnel **over** System (
    Must_Tunnel(s)   **is=**   [– **impose** Tunnel (s | PS)] **false and** <∗> **true**
    Do_Tunnel   **is=**   (**name** Sub) [Sub.client!(_)] Must_Tunnel(Sub)
    Always_Do_Tunnel **is=**   **xrec** X (Do_Tunnel **and** [∗] X))

Fig. 4. Bond Assertion: Superimposing the *Tunneling* Aspect

data themselves are ignored. Now the next step is mandatory, as the formula requires: the *Tunnel* fragment is superimposed over the bounded client and the standalone server. This is a bond assertion, so it is the one which creates the superimposition; this way, the fragment is *woven* into the architecture.

In summary, every time (*always*) a client sends a data request, a *secure connection* between it and the server is transparently created.

Though simple, this example has yet another reason to be notorious; it shows how the dynamic weaving (combination) of architectural aspects, based on the temporal logic support, causes in fact a *dynamic evolution* of the architecture. Temporal logic has been used before in the context of Architecture, but always for analyzing purposes, never to describe a system, or a dynamic effect within it. As far as we know, this is the first time that it is used to cause an effect on the system's structure.

5   Conclusions and Future Work

An ADL must be first conceived as a formal description language. This means that it is used to describe the structure and properties of an architecture, and this can be done just for specification purposes. From this point of view, the existing temporal logic support is adequate for our purposes, as long as it can be used to capture the system's behaviour. But, an ADL can also be used to simulate (or even generate) the system itself; in that case, the existing temporal support would not be enough. Some kind of *timeout* mechanism would be required to limit the timeframe and ensure that a particular superimposition indeed happens; a minimal fixpoint ("eventually") formula would not suffice to provide the required behaviour.

This paper introduces superimposition as "the" third architectural dimension, a role which has previously been played by reflection. This is orthogonal to the traditional dimensions of composition and interaction. The expressiveness of this approach is provided by combining elements located at different places in those three dimensions, even indirectly. Though not as expressive as reflection, it provides still a very high degree of flexibility, and a new approach to tackle the problem of architectural dynamism.

However, this implies *aspect composition*, something that at present has only been tackled by using heuristic techniques. The only notorious exception is a work by Sihman [21, 22], which is also based on Katzian superimposition; so their results could be considered in the context of $\mathcal{P}i\mathcal{L}ar$. A detailed study is scheduled as future work. This work will also include several related questions, such as the management of priorities and dependencies between aspects. These problems are still open questions in research within Aspect Orientation, and therefore any results at the architectural level would be of general interest to the whole field.

On the other hand, the introduction of assertions in the language has been as generic as possible, as it does not only provide the support to bind and weave aspects, but also to define architectural styles. This is obviously a feature we have not exploited in this paper; though very promising, it has yet to be carefully evaluated.

In summary, the introduction of the notion of "aspects" in Software Architecture does not only provide the means to describe several new abstractions, but at the same time simplifies the presentation of previous approaches, and outlines a whole new range of applications, namely the specification of dynamism, the definition of multiple architectural views, the separate description of concrete concerns, such as security or coordination, or the study of new composition schemes.

References

1. James H. Andrews. Process-Algebraic Foundations of Aspect-Oriented Programming. In Akinori Yonezawa and Satoshi Matsuoka, editors, *Reflection 2001: Third International Conference on Metalevel Architectures and Separation of Crosscutting Concerns*, volume 2192 of *Lecture Notes in Computer Science*, Kyoto, Japan, September 2001.
2. Uwe Aßmann. *Invasive Software Composition*. Springer Verlag, 2003.
3. Luc Bougé and Nissim Francez. A Compositional Approach to Superimposition. In *15th Annual ACM Symposium on Principles of Programming Languages, POPL'88*, pages 240–249, San Diego, 1988. ACM Press.
4. Julian C. Bradfield and Colin P. Stirling. Modal Logics and mu-Calculi: An Introduction. In Jan A. Bergstra, Alban Ponse, and Scott A. Smolka, editors, *Handbook of Process Algebra*, chapter 4, pages 293–330. Elsevier Science B.V., 2001.
5. Frank Buschmann, Regine Meunier, Hans Rohnert, Peter Sommerlad, and Michael Stal. *Pattern-Oriented Software Architecture: A System of Patterns*. John Wiley & Sons, 1996.

6. K. Mani Chandy and Jayadev Misra. *Parallel Program Design: A Foundation*. Addison-Wesley, 1988.
7. Carlos E. Cuesta. *Reflection-based Dynamic Software Architecture*. ProQuest Information & Learning, Madrid, May 2003.
8. Carlos E. Cuesta, Pablo de la Fuente, Manuel Barrio-Solórzano, and Encarnación Beato. An "Abstract Process" Approach to Algebraic Dynamic Architecture Description. *Journal of Logic and Algebraic Programming*, 63(2):177–214, May 2005.
9. Carlos E. Cuesta, Pablo de la Fuente, Manuel Barrio Solórzano, and M. Encarnación Beato. Introducing Reflection in Architecture Description Languages. In J. Bosch, M. Gentleman, C. Hofmeister, and J. Kuusela, editors, *Software Architecture: System Design, Development and Maintenance*, chapter 9, pages 143–156. Kluwer, August 2002.
10. Carlos E. Cuesta, M. Pilar Romay, Pablo de la Fuente, and Manuel Barrio-Solórzano. Reflection-based, Aspect-oriented Software Architecture. In Flavio Oquendo, Brian Warboys, and Ron Morrison, editors, *Software Architecture*, volume 3047 of *Lecture Notes in Computer Science*, pages 43–56, May 2004.
11. José Luiz Fiadeiro and Tom S.E. Maibaum. Categorical Semantics of Parallel Program Design. *Science of Computer Programming*, 28(2–3):111–138, 1997.
12. Robert E. Filman, Tzilla Elrad, Siobhán Clarke, and Mehmet Aksit, editors. *Aspect-Oriented Software Development*. The Object Technology Series. Addison-Wesley, October 2004.
13. Robert E. Filman and Daniel P. Friedman. Aspect-Oriented Programming is Quantification and Obliviousness. In *OOPSLA 2000 Workshop on Advanced Separation of Concerns (ASoC'2000)*, October 2000.
14. Mika Katara. Superposing UML class diagrams. In *AOSD'02 First Workshop on Aspect-Oriented Modeling with UML (AOM1)*, Enschede, The Netherlands, April 2002.
15. Mika Katara and Shmuel Katz. Architectural Views of Aspects. In *Proceedings of the Second International Conference on Aspect-Oriented Software Development (AOSD'03)*, pages 1–10. ACM Press, March 2003.
16. Shmuel Katz. A Superimposition Control Construct for Distributed Systems. *ACM Transactions on Programming Languages and Systems*, 15(2):337–356, April 1993.
17. Pertti Kellomäki. A Formal Basis for Aspect-Oriented Specification with Superposition. In Gary T. Leavens and Ron Cytron, editors, *FOAL 2002 Proceedings: Foundations of Aspect-Oriented Languages*, pages 27–32, April 2002. ISU-TR02-06.
18. Sergei Kojarski, Karl Lieberherr, David H. Lorenz, and Robert Hirschfeld. Aspectual Reflection. In *Proceedings of SPLAT'03*, March 2003.
19. Karl Lieberherr, David H. Lorenz, and Johan Ovlinger. Aspectual Collaborations: Combining Modules and Aspects. *The Computer Journal*, 46(5):542–565, September 2003.
20. David Lorge Parnas. On the Criteria to Be Used in Decomposing Systems into Modules. *Communications of the ACM*, 15(12):1053–1058, December 1972.
21. Marcelo Sihman and Shmuel Katz. A Calculus of Superimpositions for Distributed Systems. In *Proceedings of the First International Conference on Aspect-Oriented Software Development (AOSD'02)*, pages 28–40. ACM Press, April 2002.
22. Marcelo Sihman and Shmuel Katz. Superimpositions and Aspect-Oriented Programming. *The Computer Journal*, 46(5):529–541, September 2003.
23. Colin Stirling. Modal and Temporal Logics. In Samson Abramsky, Dov Gabbay, and Tom S.E. Maibaum, editors, *Handbook of Logic in Computer Science*, volume 2, pages 477–563. Oxford University Press, 1991.
24. Eóin Woods. Experiences Using Viewpoints for Information Systems Architecture: an Industrial Experience Report. In Flavio Oquendo, Brian Warboys, and Ron Morrison, editors, *Software Architecture*, volume 3047 of *Lecture Notes in Computer Science*, pages 182–193, St. Andrews, UK, May 2004. Springer Verlag.

Modeling Long–Running Transactions with Communicating Hierarchical Timed Automata

Ruggero Lanotte[1], Andrea Maggiolo-Schettini[2],
Paolo Milazzo[2], and Angelo Troina[2]

[1] Dip. di Scienze della Cultura, Politiche e dell'Informazione, Università dell'Insubria
[2] Dip. di Informatica, Università di Pisa

Abstract. Long-running transactions consist of tasks which may be executed sequentially and in parallel, may contain sub-tasks, and may require to be completed before a deadline. These transactions are not atomic and, in case of executions which cannot be completed, a compensation mechanism must be provided.

In this paper we develop a model of Hierarchical Timed Automata suitable to describe the aspects mentioned. The automaton-theoretic approach allows the verification of properties by model checking. As a case study, we model and analyze an example of long–running transaction.

1 Introduction

The term *transaction* is commonly used in database systems to denote a logical unit of work designed for short-lived activities, usually lasting under a few seconds. These transactions are performed either completely or not at all: this means that if something goes wrong during the execution of the transaction, a roll–back activity is performed, which re–establishes the state of the system exactly as it was before the beginning of the transaction.

In order to permit the system to perform the roll–back activity, locks are acquired on the necessary resources at the beginning of a transaction and are released only at its end (in both the cases of completion and roll–back). The use of locks, which forbids others to access the resources, is justified by the short duration of the transaction. These transactions are called *ACID transactions*, because they satisfy the properties of Atomicity, Consistency, Isolation and Durability. Recent developments in distributed systems have created the need of a new notion of transaction, in which remote entities (possibly of different companies) may interact by performing complex activities (which may require also a human–interaction) that may take minutes, days or weeks. This increased length of time with respect to ACID transactions, forbids the use of locks on resources, and hence makes roll–back activities impossible. The alternative to roll-back activities in this kind of transactions is the use of compensations, which are activities explicitly programmed to remove the effects of the actions performed, and may require, for instance, the payment of some kind of penalty. This new kind of transactions are usually called *long–running transactions*, but they are also known as Sagas [7], web transactions [10], and extended

R. Gorrieri and H. Wehrheim (Eds.): FMOODS 2006, LNCS 4037, pp. 108–122, 2006.

transactions [9]. Although there is an interest for their support in distributed object–based middlewares [9], they are studied in particular in the context of orchestration languages for Web Services (such as BPEL4WS [8] and WSCI [12]).

Web Services are technologies that allow the distribution and the interoperability of heterogeneous software components (providing services) over the Internet. Orchestration languages allow the definition of complex services in terms of interactions among simpler services. Most orchestration languages offer several primitives for composing and handling services. Since the specifications of these languages mainly consist in informal textual description of their constructors, there is a strong interest in the formalization of their semantics (see [4, 5, 6, 10, 13]). Among these papers, [6, 10] give theoretical foundations to the fragments of orchestration languages describing long–running transactions. In particular, [6] identifies three main composition patterns for transactional activities with compensations, namely sequential composition, parallel composition, and nesting, and provides a formal semantics for them.

Communicating Hierarchical Machines (CHMs) [2], which are finite state machines endowed with the ability of refining states and of composing machines in parallel, seem to be a formalisms suitable to describe transactional activities and their composition patterns. Time is an important factor in the functioning of distributed systems, where communication may take time and deadlines may be used to counteract failure of remote components. Besides, transactions may have deadlines imposed by the requested QoS. Hence, to describe transactions a formalism is needed that also allows the representation of time constraints. After the seminal paper by Alur and Dill [1] many models of Timed Automata have been proposed and used to describe systems in which time cannot be abstracted. Furthermore, automata based formalisms are amenable to formal analysis, such as model checking.

In this paper we define the model of Communicating Hierarchical Transaction-based Timed Automata (CHTTAs). CHTTAs take from CHMs [2] the abilities of composing machines in parallel and hierarchically, but differ from CHMs insofar as they have two different terminal states (to describe different terminations of transactions) and provide different communication mechanisms. Moreover, CHTTAs have a notion of explicit time. We give a flattening procedure in order to obtain a timed automaton from a CHTTA, and prove the decidability of the reachability problem for CHTTAs. The class of flattened CHTTAs is a subclass of Timed Automata, hence our flattening procedure may be used in order to verify properties of CHTTAs with model checkers defined for timed automata (e.g. Kronos [14] and UPPAAL [3]).

We propose CHTTAs to describe transactional activities and define operations for composing CHTTAs which correspond to compositional patterns of transactional activities. In particular, among the patterns identified in [6], we focus on the sequential and parallel composition patterns for transactional activities. We give formal representations of these patterns in terms of CHTTAs and prove their correctness. As a case study, we model with CHTTAs a typical long–running transaction and verify some properties with the UPPAAL model checker [3].

2   Communicating Hierarchical Timed Automata

Let us assume a finite set of communication channels $\mathcal{C}$ with a subset $C_{Pub} \subseteq \mathcal{C}$. As usual, we denote with $a!$ the action of sending a signal on channel a and with $a?$ the action of receiving a signal on a.

Let us assume a finite set X of positive real variables called *clocks*. A *valuation* over X is a mapping $v : X \to \mathbb{R}^{\geq 0}$ assigning real values to clocks. Let V_X denote the set of all valuations over X. For a valuation v and a time value $t \in \mathbb{R}^{\geq 0}$, let $v + t$ denote the valuation such that $(v + t)(x) = v(x) + t$, for each clock $x \in X$.

The set of *constraints* over X, denoted $\Phi(X)$, is defined by the following grammar, where ϕ ranges over $\Phi(X)$, $x \in X$, $c \in \mathbb{Q}$ and $\sim \in \{<, \leq, =, \neq, >, \geq\}$:

$$\phi ::= x \sim c \mid \phi \wedge \phi \mid \neg\phi \mid \phi \vee \phi \mid true$$

We write $v \models \phi$ when *the valuation v satisfies the constraint ϕ*. Formally, $v \models x \sim c$ iff $v(x) \sim c$, $v \models \phi_1 \wedge \phi_2$ iff $v \models \phi_1$ and $v \models \phi_2$, $v \models \neg\phi$ iff $v \not\models \phi$, $v \models \phi_1 \vee \phi_2$ iff $v \models \phi_1$ or $v \models \phi_2$, and $v \models true$.

Let $B \subseteq X$; with $v[B]$ we denote the valuation resulting after resetting all clocks in B. More precisely, $v[B](x) = 0$ if $x \in B$, $v[B](x) = v(x)$, otherwise. Finally, with $\mathbf{0}$ we denote the valuation with all clocks reset to 0, namely $\mathbf{0}(x) = 0$ for all $x \in X$.

Definition 1. *A Transaction-based Timed Automaton (TTA) is a tuple $A = (\Sigma, X, S, Q, q_0, \delta)$, where:*

- $\Sigma \subseteq \{a!, a? \mid a \in \mathcal{C}\}$ *is a finite set of labels;*
- X *is a finite set of clocks;*
- S *is a finite set of superstates;*
- $Q = L \cup S \cup \{\odot, \otimes\}$, *where L is a finite set of basic states and $\odot$ and $\otimes$ represent the special states commit and abort, respectively;*
- $q_0 \in L$ *is the initial state;*
- $\delta \subseteq (L \times \Sigma \cup \{\tau\} \times \Phi(X) \times 2^X \times Q) \cup (S \times \{\Box, \boxtimes\} \times Q)$ *is the set of transitions.*

Superstates are states that can be refined to automata (*hierarchical composition*). Note that from superstates in S only transitions with labels in $\{\Box, \boxtimes\}$ can be taken. We assume that $\odot$ and $\otimes$ are the final states of a TTA.

A TTA is said to be flat when it has no refinable states.

Definition 2 (Flat TTAs). *A TTA $A = (\Sigma, X, S, Q, q_0, \delta)$ is flat if $S = \emptyset$.*

Inspired by the definition of CHMs (see [2]) we now introduce CHTTAs as an extension of TTAs allowing superstate refinement and parallelism.

Definition 3. *Let $\Sigma_{Pub} = \{a!, a? \mid a \in C_{Pub}\}$ and $\mathcal{A} = \{A^1, \dots, A^n\}$ be a finite set of TTAs, with $A^i = (\Sigma^i, X^i, S^i, Q^i, q_0^i, \delta^i)$ and such that there exists m $(m < n)$ such that A^j is flat if and only if $j \geq m$. A Communicating Hierarchical Transaction-based Timed Automaton ($CHTTA_{\mathcal{A}}^{\Sigma_{Pub}}$) is given by the following grammar:*

$$CHTTA_{\mathcal{A}}^{\Sigma_{Pub}} ::= \langle A^i, \mu \rangle \quad \mid \quad CHTTA_{\mathcal{A}}^{\Sigma_{Pub}} \| CHTTA_{\mathcal{A}}^{\Sigma_{Pub}}$$

where μ is a hierarchical composition function $\mu : S^i \to CHTTA_{\{A^{i+1}, \dots, A^n\}}^{\Sigma_{Pub}}$.

Parallelism allows concurrent execution of automata. Hierarchical composition allows refining superstates. Automata executed in parallel may communicate by synchronizing transitions labeled with a sending and a receiving action on the same channel. Communication performed using non public channels are only allowed between components inside the same superstate or at top–level. Communication performed by using public channels have no restrictions.

Note that, by definition of $\mathcal{A}$ and μ, cyclic nesting is avoided. In the following, if it does not give rise to ambiguity, we may write CHTTA instead of $CHTTA_{\mathcal{A}}^{\Sigma^{Pub}}$. Finally, if A is a flat TTA, in $\langle A, \mu \rangle$ μ is an empty function.

Example 1. In Figure 1 we show an example of CHTTA. Superstates of the CHTTA are depicted as boxes and basic states as circles; initial states are represented as vertical segments. Transitions are labeled arrows in which labels τ and constraints *true* are omitted. Containment into boxes represents hierarchical composition, while parallel composition is represented by juxtapositions. The CHTTA in the figure is formally defined as $\langle (\emptyset, \emptyset, \{s_1\}, \{q_0, s_1, \odot, \otimes\}, q_0, \delta), \mu \rangle$ where $\delta = \{(q_0, \tau, true, \emptyset, s_1), (s_1, \Box, \odot), (s_1, \boxtimes, \otimes)\}$, and $\mu(s_1) = A_1 \| A_2$. A_1 and A_2 are defined as $A_1 = \langle (\{a!, b?\}, \{x\}, \emptyset, \{q_0, q_1, \odot, \otimes\}, q_0, \delta_1)$ and $A_2 = \langle (\{a?, b!\}, \emptyset, \emptyset, \{q_0, q_2, \odot, \otimes\}, q_0, \delta_2)$, where $\delta_1 = \{(q_0, a!, true, \{x\}, q_1), (q_1, b?, x < 5, \emptyset, \odot), (q_1, \tau, x \geq 5, \emptyset, \otimes)\}$ and $\delta_2 = \{(q_0, a?, true, \emptyset, q_2), (q_2, b!, true, \emptyset, \odot)\}$.

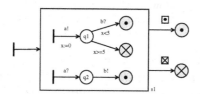

Fig. 1. Example of CHTTA

2.1   Semantics of CHTTAs

Configurations of CHTTAs are pairs $tc = (c, \nu)$ where c, the *untimed configuration*, represents the currently active states, and ν, the *composed valuation*, represents the current clock valuations.

The configuration of a CHTTA without parallel components, when the currently active state is a basic state, is a pair (q, v) with q the currently active state, and v the automaton clock valuation. We represent with $q.c$ the configuration where q is a superstate and c is the untimed configuration of $\mu(q)$, and with $v.\nu$ the composed valuation where v is the clock valuation of the automaton having q as superstate and ν is the composed valuation of the clocks of $\mu(q)$. We denote with $c_1; c_2$ the untimed configuration of the parallel composition of two CHTTAs having c_1 and c_2 as untimed configurations. Analogously, we denote with $\nu_1; \nu_2$ the composed valuation of the parallel composition of two CHTTAs having ν_1 and ν_2 as composed valuations.

Formally, the set of configurations $Conf(A)$ of a CHTTA A is inductively defined as follows:

- if $A = \langle(\Sigma, X, S, Q, q_0, \delta), \mu\rangle$, then $Conf(A) = \{(Q \setminus S) \times V_X\} \cup \{(q.c, v.\nu) \mid q \in S \land v \in V_x \land (c, \nu) \in Conf(\mu(q))\}$;
- if $A = A_1 \| A_2$ then $Conf(A) = \{(c_1; c_2, \nu_1; \nu_2) \mid (c_1, \nu_1) \in Conf(A_1) \land (c_2, \nu_2) \in Conf(A_2)\}$.

For a composed valuation ν and a time value $t \in \mathbb{R}^{\geq 0}$, let $\nu + t$ denote the composed valuation such that $(v+t)(x) = v(x) + t$, for each valuation v occurring in ν.

The initial configuration of A, denoted $Init(A) \in Conf(A)$, is the configuration (c, ν) such that each state occurring in c is an initial state and each valuation occurring in ν is $\mathbf{0}$.

We give a semantics of CHTTAs in SOS style as a labeled transition system where states are pairs (A, tc) with $A \in \text{CHTTA}_A^{\Sigma_{Pub}}$ and $tc \in Conf(A)$, and labels are in $\mathbb{R}^{>0} \cup \bigcup_i \Sigma^i \cup \{\tau\}$.

In order to simplify the SOS semantics for CHTTAs we introduce a notion of structural equivalence for pairs (A, tc), accounting for commutativity and associativity of parallelism. The relation $\approx$ is the least equivalence relation satisfying $(A_1 \| A_2, tc_1; tc_2) \approx (A_2 \| A_1, tc_2; tc_1)$ and $(A_1 \| (A_2 \| A_3), tc_1; (tc_2; tc_3)) \approx ((A_1 \| A_2) \| A_3, (tc_1; tc_2); tc_3)$. Moreover, given an untimed parallel configuration $c = c_1; \ldots; c_n$ we use the following notations: $c \approx \odot$ if for $\forall i. c_i = \odot$, and $c \approx \otimes$ if for $\exists i. c_i = \otimes \land \forall i \neq j. c_j \in \{\odot, \otimes\}$.

Definition 4 (Semantics of CHTTAs). *Given $A \in \text{CHTTA}_A^{\Sigma_{Pub}}$, the semantics of a A is the least labeled transition relation $\xrightarrow{\alpha}$ over $\{A\} \times Conf(A)$ closed with respect to structural equivalence and satisfying the rules in Figure 2.*

Rule (T) allows the elapsing of time for a generic CHTTA A. We note that the time t is the same for any TTA composing A.

Rules (C1) and (C2) describe the behavior of a flat TTA. From a configuration (q, v), the step is performed due to a transition (q, α, ϕ, B, q') such that the condition ϕ is satisfied by v. After the step, the flat TTA is in the configuration composed by state q' and where clocks in B are reset. If q' is a superstate (rule (C2)), then the CHTTA $\mu(q')$ becomes active inside q'.

The synchronization step is described by rule (P2). By definition of the relation $\approx$ also CHTTAs that are not neighborhood in the parallel composition can communicate.

Rules (C3) and (P1) allow expanding the step of a TTA which is a component of a CHTTA. Rule (C3) deals with the hierarchical composition and rule (P1) deals with the parallel composition. The label of the step is either τ or a public channel. Hence, thanks to rule (P2), communication between TTAs in parallel is allowed both for private and public channels, while for TTAs in different superstates the communication is allowed only if the channel is public. Moreover, we note that the step we are expanding cannot be a time step. Hence, time steps

$$\frac{t \in \mathbb{R}^{>0}}{(A, (c, \nu)) \xrightarrow{t} (A, (c, \nu + t))} \tag{T}$$

$$\frac{(q, \alpha, \phi, B, q') \in \delta \quad v \models \phi \quad q' \notin S}{(\langle A, \mu \rangle, (q, v)) \xrightarrow{\alpha} (\langle A, \mu \rangle, (q', v[B]))} \tag{C1}$$

$$\frac{(q, \alpha, \phi, B, q') \in \delta \quad v \models \phi \quad q' \in S \quad Init(\mu(q')) = (c, \nu)}{(\langle A, \mu \rangle, (q, v)) \xrightarrow{\alpha} (\langle A, \mu \rangle, (q'.c, v[B].\nu))} \tag{C2}$$

$$\frac{(\mu(q), (c, \nu)) \xrightarrow{\alpha} (\mu(q), (c', \nu')) \quad \alpha \in \Sigma_{Pub} \cup \{\tau\}}{(\langle A, \mu \rangle, (q.c, v.\nu)) \xrightarrow{\alpha} (\langle A, \mu \rangle, (q.c', v.\nu'))} \tag{C3}$$

$$\frac{(A_1, (c_1, v)) \xrightarrow{\alpha} (A_1, (c_1', v')) \quad \alpha \in \Sigma_{Pub} \cup \{\tau\}}{(A_1 || A_2, (c_1; c_2, v)) \xrightarrow{\alpha} (A_1 || A_2, (c_1'; c_2, v'))} \tag{P1}$$

$$\frac{(A_1, (c_1, v)) \xrightarrow{a!} (A_1, (c_1', v')) \quad (A_2, (c_2, v')) \xrightarrow{a?} (A_2, (c_2', v''))}{(A_1 || A_2, (c_1; c_2, v)) \xrightarrow{\tau} (A_1 || A_2, (c_1'; c_2', v''))} \tag{P2}$$

$$\frac{c \approx \odot \quad (q, \square, q') \in \delta \quad q' \notin S}{(\langle A, \mu \rangle, (q.c, v.\nu)) \xrightarrow{\tau} (\langle A, \mu \rangle, (q', v))} \tag{Com1}$$

$$\frac{c \approx \odot \quad (q, \square, q') \in \delta \quad q' \in S \quad Init(\mu(q')) = (c', \nu')}{(\langle A, \mu \rangle, (q.c, v.\nu)) \xrightarrow{\tau} (\langle A, \mu \rangle, (q'.c', v.\nu'))} \tag{Com2}$$

$$\frac{c \approx \otimes \quad (q, \boxtimes, q') \in \delta \quad q' \notin S}{(\langle A, \mu \rangle, (q.c, v.\nu)) \xrightarrow{\tau} (\langle A, \mu \rangle, (q', v))} \tag{Ab1}$$

$$\frac{c \approx \otimes \quad (q, \boxtimes, q') \in \delta \quad q' \in S \quad Init(\mu(q')) = (c', \nu')}{(\langle A, \mu \rangle, (q.c, v.\nu)) \xrightarrow{\tau} (\langle A, \mu \rangle, (q'.c', v.\nu'))} \tag{Ab2}$$

Where we assume $A = (\Sigma, X, S, Q, q_0, \delta)$ except for rule (T) where A is a generic CHTTA.

Fig. 2. SOS semantics for CHTTAs

can be performed only by the root, implying that the time elapsed is the same for each TTA composing the CHTTA we are considering.

Each execution of a superstate terminates with either a commit or an abort state. Rules (Com1) and (Com2) deal with the case in which the commit of the superstate takes the TTA to a basic state or to a superstate, respectively, and rules (Ab1) and (Ab2) deal with the case in which the abort of the superstate takes the TTA to a basic state or to a superstate, respectively.

Given a string $w = \alpha_1 \ldots \alpha_m$, we will write $(A, (c, \nu)) \xRightarrow{w} (A, (c', \nu'))$ to denote the existence of a sequence of steps $(A, (c, \nu)) \xrightarrow{\alpha_1} \ldots \xrightarrow{\alpha_m} (A, (c', \nu'))$. We denote with $|w| = m$ the length of w and with $w[i] = \alpha_i$ the i–th label.

With $\mathcal{L}(A, \Sigma_V)$ we denote *the language accepted by a CHTTA A w.r.t. a set of visible actions* $\Sigma_V \subseteq \Sigma_{Pub}$. Namely, $\mathcal{L}(A, \Sigma_V) = \{w \in (\{\tau\} \cup \Sigma_V \cup \mathbb{R}^{>0})^* \mid (A, Init(A)) \xRightarrow{w} (A, (\odot, \nu'))$ or $(A, Init(A)) \xRightarrow{w} (A, (\otimes, \nu'))\}$.

The following proposition holds.

Proposition 1. *The class of flat TTAs is equivalent to the class of Timed Automata.*

3   Deciding Reachability for CHTTAs

Reachability is interesting for proving properties. For timed Automata the reachability problem is PSPACE-COMPLETE. In our case the problem is still decidable, but becomes EXPSPACE-COMPLETE.

Firstly, we give an algorithm for flattening a generic CHTTA, hence the reachability problem can be checked on the Timed Automaton resulting by the flattening. Due to the complexity of the flattening, the reachability problem for CHTTAs is EXPSPACE-COMPLETE. The increase of complexity is caused by the communication between different superstates, but it is not caused by the number of clocks.

3.1   Flattening CHTTAs

Let $X = \{x_1, \ldots, x_n\}$ and $Y = \{y_1, \ldots, y_n\}$ and ϕ be a formula in $\Phi(X)$. With $\phi[Y := X]$ we denote the formula where each clock y_i is replaced with x_i. Moreover, with $X_{i,j}$ we denote the renaming of clocks x in X with clocks $x^{i,j}$, more precisely $X_{i,j} = \{x_1^{i,j}, \ldots, x_n^{i,j}\}$.

Given a $CHTTA$ A with $w(A)$ we denote the maximum width of the CHTTAs composing A. Namely:

$$w(\langle A_1, \mu_1 \rangle \| \ldots \| \langle A_m, \mu_m \rangle) = max\{m, w(\langle A_1, \mu_1 \rangle), \ldots, w(\langle A_m, \mu_m \rangle)\},$$

where $w(\langle A, \mu \rangle) = max\{w(\mu(q)) \mid q \in S\}$.

Moreover, $d(A)$ denotes the maximum depth of A. Namely:

$$d(\langle A_1, \mu_1 \rangle \| \ldots \| \langle A_m, \mu_m \rangle) = max\{d(\langle A_1, \mu_1 \rangle), \ldots, d(\langle A_m, \mu_m \rangle)\},$$

where $d(\langle A, \mu \rangle) = 1 + max\{d(\mu(q)) \mid q \in S\}$.

Definition 5. *Let* $\mathcal{A} = \{A^1, \ldots, A^n\}$, *with* $A^i = (\Sigma^i, X^i, S^i, Q^i, q_0^i, \delta^i)$, *be a set of TTAs, and* $A \in CHTTA_{\mathcal{A}}^{\Sigma_{Pub}}$. *Given* $\Sigma_V \subseteq \Sigma_{Pub}$, *with* $Flat(A, \Sigma_V)$ *we denote the flat TTA* $(\Sigma, X, \emptyset, Q, q_0, \delta)$ *such that:*

- $\Sigma = \Sigma_V$;
- $X = \bigcup_{i \in [1, d(A)]} \bigcup_{j \in [1, w(A)]} X_{i,j}$;
- $Q = \{c \mid (c, \nu) \in Conf(A)\}$;
- $q_0 = c_0$ *such that* $Init(A) = (c_0, \nu)$ *is the initial configuration of* A;
- δ *is such that:*
  - $(c, \tau, true, \emptyset, c')$ *is in* δ *if there exists a step* $(A, (c, \nu)) \xrightarrow{\tau} (A, (c', \nu'))$ *triggered by either a commit or an abort transition;*
  - (c, α, ϕ, B, c') *is in* δ *if there exists a step* $(A, (c, \nu)) \xrightarrow{\alpha} (A, (c', \nu'))$, *with* $\alpha \in \Sigma_V$ *triggered by the transition* (q, α, ϕ, B, q') *of a TTA* A^i;
  - (c, τ, ϕ, B, c') *is in* δ *if there exists a step* $(A, (c, \nu)) \xrightarrow{\tau} (A, (c', \nu'))$ *triggered by the transition* $(q^1, a!, \phi^1, B^1, p^1)$ *of the TTA* A^i *at position* i_1, j_1 *and by the transition* $(q^2, a?, \phi^2, B^2, p^2)$ *of the TTA* A^j *at position* i_2, j_2 *such that* $\phi = (\phi_1[X^i := (X^i)_{i_1,j_1}]) \wedge (\phi_2[X^j := (X^j)_{i_2,j_2}])$ *and* $B = (B^1)_{i_1,j_1} \cup (B^2)_{i_2,j_2}$.

Proposition 2. *Let* $\mathcal{A} = \{A^1, \ldots, A^n\}$ *and* $A \in CHTTA_{\mathcal{A}}^{\Sigma_{Pub}}$ *where each* A^i *has at most* h *states and* k *clocks. The reachability problem for* A *can be computed in* $O(h^{w(A)^{d(A)}} \cdot 2^{k \cdot d(A) \cdot w(A)})$.

Hence, the reachability problem for a CHTTA A is EXPSPACE-COMPLETE w.r.t. m, $w(A)$ and $d(A)$. As it happens for the reachability problem for Timed Automata (see [1]), the number of clocks does not influence the complexity.

Proposition 3. *Let* $\mathcal{A} = \{A^1, \ldots, A^n\}$ *and* $A \in CHTTA_{\mathcal{A}}^{\Sigma_{Pub}}$ *where each* A^i *has at most* m *states. The reachability problem for* A *is EXPSPACE-COMPLETE w.r.t.* m, $w(A)$ *and* $d(A)$.

4   Compositional Patterns for Long–Running Transactions

A *long–running transaction* is composed by atomic activities (called *subtransactions* or simply *activities*) that should be executed completely. Atomicity for activities means that they are either successfully executed (*committed*) or no effect is observed if their execution fails (*aborted*). Activities may be composed by other subtransactions.

Partial executions of a long–running transaction are not desirable, and, if they occur, they must be compensated for. Therefore, all the activities A_i in a long–running transaction have a compensating activity B_i that can be invoked to repair from the effects of a successful execution of A_i if some failure occurs later. Compensations are assumed to be transactions that always complete their execution successfully (they always commit and can never abort).

We assume that both activities and compensations are described as CHTTAs, and we denote with $A \!\restriction\! B$ the association of compensation B with activity A.

Following the approach in [6], we identify some composition patterns for transactional activities with compensations. In particular, we focus on the sequential composition pattern and on the parallel composition one.

We denote with $A_1 \!\restriction\! B_1 \cdot A_2 \!\restriction\! B_2$ the sequential composition of two transactional activities with compensations, and we use the standard parallel composition of CHTTAs also to describe parallel composition of transactional activities with compensations. We show that the compositional patterns on transactional activities can be formulated as compositions of CHTTAs.

4.1   Sequential Transactions

Activities $A_1, \ldots, A_n$ composing a *sequential transaction* are assumed to be executed sequentially, namely, when activity A_i is committed, activity A_{i+1} starts its execution. Compensation activities $B_1, \ldots, B_n$ are associated with each activity A_i. Transactions of this kind must be guaranteed that either the entire sequence $A_1, \ldots, A_n$ is executed or the compensated sequence $A_1, \ldots, A_i, B_i, \ldots, B_1$ is executed for some $i < n$. The first case means that all activities in the sequence completed successfully, thus representing a successful commit of the whole transaction. The second case stands for the abort of activity A_{i+1}; hence, all the activities already completed $(A_1, \ldots, A_i)$ are recovered by executing the compensating activities $(B_i, \ldots, B_1)$.

In Figure 3 (a) we show the CHTTA $A = [\![A_1 \mathord{\restriction} B_1 \cdot A_2 \mathord{\restriction} B_2]\!]^S$ modeling the pattern of sequential transactions. We consider just two activities A_1, A_2 and compensations B_1, B_2. Note that, since the transaction is composed by only two activities, the compensation B_2 is not executed. This is because compensations are invoked only for activities that complete successfully, however, if activity A_2 commits, then the whole transaction successfully commits and no compensation needs to be invoked. The compensation B of the whole transactional activity A is defined as the sequential execution of the compensations B_2 and B_1 (see Figure 3 (b)).

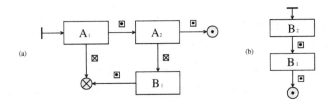

(a)

(b)

Fig. 3. Pattern for Sequential Transactions

Definition 6. *Given* $A_1, A_2, B_1, B_2 \in CHTTA_{\mathcal{A}}^{\Sigma_{Pub}}$ *we define the sequential composition of activities* A_1, A_2 *with compensations* B_1, B_2 *as the* $CHTTA_{\mathcal{A}}^{\Sigma_{Pub}}$ $A = [\![A_1 \mathord{\restriction} B_1 \cdot A_2 \mathord{\restriction} B_2]\!]^S = \langle (\emptyset, \emptyset, \{s_1, s_2, s_3\}, \{s_1, s_2, s_3, q_0\odot, \otimes\}, q_0, \delta), \mu \rangle$ *where* $\delta = \{(q_0, \tau, true, \emptyset, s_1), (s_1, \square, s_2), (s_1, \boxtimes, \otimes), (s_2, \square, \odot), (s_2, \boxtimes, s_3), (s_3, \square, \otimes)\}$ *and* $\mu = \{(s_1, A_1), (s_2, A_2), (s_3, B_1)\}$. *The compound compensation of* A *is defined as the* $CHTTA_{\mathcal{A}}^{\Sigma_{Pub}}$ $B = [\![B_1 \cdot B_2]\!]_C^S = \langle (\emptyset, \emptyset, \{s_1, s_2\}, \{s_1, s_2, q_0, \odot, \otimes\}, q_0, \delta'), \mu' \rangle$ *with* $\delta' = \{(q_0, \tau, true, \emptyset, s_2), (s_2, \square, s_1), (s_1, \square, \odot)\}$ *and* $\mu' = \{(s_1, B_1), (s_2, B_2)\}$.

Considering only two activities in the sequential pattern is not a real limitation, since the case of n activities may be reduced by iteratively grouping the activities in pairs. Intuitively, $A = [\![A_1 \mathord{\restriction} B_1 \cdot A_2 \mathord{\restriction} B_2 \cdot A_3 \mathord{\restriction} B_3]\!]^S = [\![A' \mathord{\restriction} B \cdot A_3 \mathord{\restriction} B_3]\!]^S$ where $A' = [\![A_1 \mathord{\restriction} B_1 \cdot A_2 \mathord{\restriction} B_2]\!]^S$ and B is the compensation for the whole sequential subtransaction A' (see Figure 4).

In order to prove the correctness of our definitions of compositional patterns, we introduce the notion of *wrapped* CHTTAs. Intuitively, for a CHTTA A, we call *wrapper* the automaton A^M which performs the special action $commit_A!$ before reaching the final commit state.

Given a CHTTA A, $A^M = \langle (\{commit_A!\}, \emptyset, \{s\}, Q, q_0, \delta), \mu \rangle$ is the *wrapped* CHTTA of A with set of states $Q = \{s, q_0, q_1, \odot, \otimes\}$, set of transitions $\delta = \{(q_0, \tau, true, \emptyset, s), (s, \square, q_1), (s, \boxtimes, \otimes), (q_1, commit_A!, true, \emptyset, \odot)\}$ and $\mu(s) = A$. In Figure 5 we show the CHTTA A^M.

The next lemma derives immediately from the definition of A^M.

Lemma 1. *Given a CHTTA* A, $(A, (c, \nu)) \overset{w}{\Longrightarrow} (A, (c', \nu'))$, *with* $c \not\approx \odot$ *and* $c \not\approx \otimes$ *and either* $c' \approx \odot$ *or* $c' \approx \otimes$ *if and only if* $(A^M, (s \cdot c, \epsilon \cdot \nu)) \overset{w'}{\Longrightarrow} (A^M, (s \cdot \hat{c}, \epsilon \cdot \hat{\nu}))$, *where (given* $\tilde{z} \in \{\mathbb{R}^{>0}\}^*$):

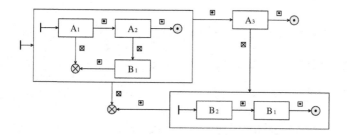

Fig. 4. Composing Sequential Transactions

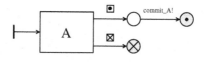

Fig. 5. A^M

$$\begin{cases} w' = \tilde{z} \cdot \tau \cdot w \cdot \tau \cdot commit_A! \ \ and \ \ \hat{c} = \odot & if \ c' \approx \odot \\ w' = \tilde{z} \cdot \tau \cdot w \cdot \tau \ \ and \ \ \hat{c} = \otimes & if \ c' \approx \otimes \end{cases}$$

Let us assume $\Sigma_V = \{commit_{A_1}!, commit_{B_1}!, \ldots, commit_{A_n}!, commit_{B_n}!\}$.

Theorem 1 (Correct Completion). *Given* $A = [\![A_1^M \upharpoonright B_1^M \cdot \ldots \cdot A_n^M \upharpoonright B_n^M]\!]^S$, $(A, Init(A)) \overset{w}{\Longrightarrow} (A, (\odot, \nu))$ *if and only if* $w \in \mathcal{L}(A, \Sigma_V)$ *and* $w = \tilde{x}_1 \cdot commit_{A_1}! \cdot \ldots \cdot \tilde{x}_n \cdot commit_{A_n}! \cdot \tilde{x}_{n+1}$ *where* $\tilde{x}_i \in (\{\tau\} \cup \mathbb{R}^{>0})^*$.

Theorem 2 (Correct Compensation). *Given* $A = [\![A_1^M \upharpoonright B_1^M \cdot \ldots \cdot A_n^M \upharpoonright B_n^M]\!]^S$, $(A, Init(A)) \overset{w}{\Longrightarrow} (A, (\otimes, \nu))$ *if and only if,* $w \in \mathcal{L}(A, \Sigma_V)$ *and, for some* $k \in [1, n]$, $w = \tilde{x}_1 \cdot commit_{A_1}! \cdot \ldots \cdot \tilde{x}_{k-1} \cdot commit_{A_{k-1}}! \cdot \tilde{x}'_{k-1} \cdot commit_{B_{k-1}}! \cdot \ldots \cdot \tilde{x}'_1 \cdot commit_{B_1}! \cdot \tilde{x}'$ *where* $\tilde{x}_i, \tilde{x}'_i \in (\{\tau\} \cup \mathbb{R}^{>0})^*$.

4.2 Parallel Transactions

If activities $A_1, \ldots, A_n$ composing a *parallel transaction* are executed concurrently, the whole transaction terminates when all the activities A_i complete their execution. Again, we assume compensation activities $B_1, \ldots B_n$. If all the activities terminate successfully then the whole transaction reaches a commit state. If some A_i aborts, then compensation activities should be invoked for the activities that completed successfully. In this latter case, the result of the whole transaction is "abort".

The pattern for parallel transactions is shown in Figure 6. As for sequential transactions, we consider only two activities A_1, A_2 with compensations B_1, B_2 composed in parallel, thus resulting in the CHTTA $A = [\![A_1 \upharpoonright B_1 || A_2 \upharpoonright B_2]\!]^P$ of Figure 6. We remark that, by the semantics of CHTTAs, the parallel operator $||$ is assumed to be commutative and associative. In such a pattern, activities A_1 and A_2 are executed concurrently together with a *controller* that invokes compensations when one of the two activities commits and the other aborts.

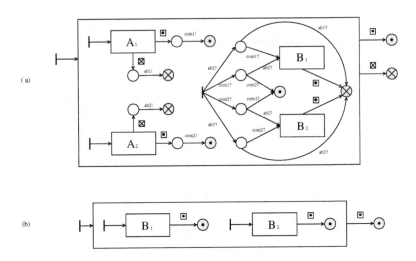

Fig. 6. Pattern for Parallel Transactions

Definition 7. *Given $A_1, A_2, B_1, B_2 \in CHTTA_{\mathcal{A}}^{\Sigma_{Pub}}$ we define the parallel compo-sition of activities A_1 and A_2 with compensations B_1 and B_2 as the $CHTTA_{\mathcal{A}}^{\Sigma_{Pub}}$ $A = [\![A_1 \upharpoonright B_1 || A_2 \upharpoonright B_2]\!]^P = \langle (\emptyset, \emptyset, \{s\}, \{s, q_0\odot, \otimes\}, q_0, \delta), \mu \rangle$ with transitions $\delta = \{(q_0, \tau, true, \emptyset, s), (s, \boxdot, \odot), (s, \boxtimes, \otimes)\}$, and $\mu(s) = A'||A''||C$, where A' and A'' are the two CHTTAs depicted in Figure 6 (a) contained in the superstate and referring to activities A_1 and A_2, and C is the compensation controller shown on the right part of the superstate. The compound compensation of A is defined as the $CHTTA_{\mathcal{A}}^{\Sigma_{Pub}}$ $B = [\![B_1||B_2]\!]_C^P = \langle (\emptyset, \emptyset, \{s\}, \{s, q_0, \odot, \otimes\}, q_0, \delta'), \mu' \rangle$ with $\delta' = \{(q_0, \tau, true, \emptyset, s), (s, \boxdot, \odot)\}$ and $\mu'(s) = B'||B''$, where B' and B'' are the two CHTTAs in Figure 6 (b) referring to B_1 and B_2 respectively.*

As for sequential transactions, considering only two activities in the parallel pattern is not a limitation, since the case of n activities may be reduced by iteratively grouping the activities in pairs. For instance, $A = [\![A_1 \upharpoonright B_1 || A_2 \upharpoonright B_2 || A_3 \upharpoonright B_3]\!]^P = [\![A' \upharpoonright B || A_3 \upharpoonright B_3]\!]^P$ where $A' = [\![A_1 \upharpoonright B_1 || A_2 \upharpoonright B_2]\!]^P$ and B is the compensation for the whole parallel subtransaction A'. Given B_1 and B_2, we define the compensation B of A' as the concurrent execution of the compensations B_1 and B_2 (see Figure 6 (b)).

Theorem 3 (Correct Completion). *Given $A = [\![A_1^M \upharpoonright B_1^M || \ldots || A_n^M \upharpoonright B_n^M]\!]^P$, $(A, Init(A)) \overset{w}{\Longrightarrow} (A, (\odot, \nu))$ if and only if, $w \in \mathcal{L}(A, \Sigma_V)$ and $\forall i \in [1, n].\exists! j \in [1, |w|]. \ w[j] = commit_{A_i}!$.*

Theorem 4 (Correct Compensation). *Given $A = [\![A_1^M \upharpoonright B_1^M || \ldots || A_n^M \upharpoonright B_n^M]\!]^P$, $(A, Init(A)) \overset{w}{\Longrightarrow} (A, (\otimes, v))$ if and only if $w \in \mathcal{L}(A)$ and, there exists Commited \subset \{A_1, \ldots, A_n\} such that $\forall A_i \notin Committed \ w[j] \neq commit_{A_i}!$ and $\forall A_i \in Committed \ \exists! \ j \in [1, |w|[$ such that $w[j] = commit_{A_i}! \land \exists! \ k \in]j, |w|]$ such that $w[k] = commit_{B_i}!$.*

4.3   Long–Running Transactions

Sequential and parallel transactions may be composed in order to define complex transactions. Hence, resorting to the patterns of sequential and parallel transactions, we give the definition of long–running transactions.

Definition 8 (Long–running Transaction). *Given activities* $A_1, \ldots, A_n \in CHTTA_{\mathcal{A}}^{\Sigma_{Pub}}$ *and compensations* $B_1, \ldots, B_n \in CHTTA_{\mathcal{A}}^{\Sigma_{Pub}}$, *a* long–running transaction *is given by the following grammar:*

$$T ::= A_i \wp B_i \quad | \quad T \cdot T \quad | \quad T \| T.$$

Now, we need to introduce an *encoding* function $[\![\cdot]\!] \to A \wp B$ that takes in input a long–running transaction and returns the CHTTAs A and B where A is the compound CHTTA modeling the transaction and B its compensation. We define $[\![\cdot]\!]$ recursively as follows:

- $[\![A_i \wp B_i]\!] = A_i \wp B_i$,
- $[\![T_1 \cdot T_2]\!] = [\![A_1 \wp B_1 \cdot A_2 \wp B_2]\!]^S \wp [\![B_1 \cdot B_2]\!]^S_C$, where $A_i \wp B_i = [\![T_i]\!]$ for $i \in [1, 2]$,
- $[\![T_1 \| T_2]\!] = [\![A_1 \wp B_1 \| A_2 \wp B_2]\!]^P \wp [\![B_1 \| B_2]\!]^P_C$, where $A_i \wp B_i = [\![T_i]\!]$ for $i \in [1, 2]$.

Since the building blocks of the encoding function are the patterns of sequential and parallel transactions, the correctness of $[\![\cdot]\!]$ is given by Theorems 1– 4.

Given a long–running transaction T, we define the *top–level* of T (denoted $top(T)$) as the CHTTA A such that $[\![T]\!] = A \wp B$.

Modeling long–running transactions with CHTTAs allows verifying properties by model checking. In fact, given a long–running transaction T obtained as in Definition 8, and a set of visible actions Σ_V, we may flatten the CHTTA $top(T)$ according to Definition 5, and then verify properties of the transaction by model checking on the timed automaton $Flat(top(T), \Sigma_V)$.

5   Case Study: A Double Request

We model a typical all–or–nothing scenario in which a client performs two concurrent requests to two different servers, waits for replies, and sends back acknowledgements either to both servers (if it receives both replies) or to none of them (if it receives at most one reply). A similar scenario in a realistic context is given in [11], where a typical e–commerce application is described in which a customer of an on–line shop orders two products which are provided by two different stores. In that case, acknowledgements are sent (and products are bought) only if both products are available, instead, in our case, acknowledgements are sent only if replies are received before given times.

A single request/reply activity performed by the client is described by the transaction given in Figure 7 (a). We denote such a transaction with $A_i \wp B_i$. The client sends the request to the server by synchronizing on channel req_i and waits for the reply as a synchronization on channel rep_i. The time deadline for the reply is T_i. This is expressed as a constraint on the value of clock x_i which is set

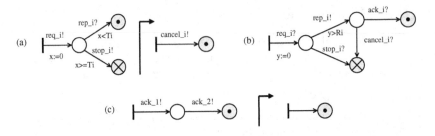

Fig. 7. A Double Request

to zero when the request is sent. If the reply is received in time, the transaction commits, otherwise a stop message is sent to the server as a synchronization on channel $stop\_i$, and the transaction is aborted. The compensation of this transaction consists in a synchronization on channel $cancel\_i$, which corresponds to sending an undo message to the server.

A server is modeled by the automaton given in Figure 7 (b). We denote such an automaton with S_i. The server receives a request and sends the reply by synchronizing on the proper channels, and it spends a time between these two synchronizations which is greater than R_i. This amount of time models the time spent by the server to satisfy the request of the client. Then, the server reaches a state in which it waits for either an acknowledge or an undo message from the client. These two communications are modeled as synchronizations on channels ack_i and $cancel\_i$, respectively, and lead to commit and abort of the server activity, respectively.

The activity of sending acknowledgments to two servers S_1 and S_2 is modeled by the transaction given in Figure 7 (c). We denote such a transaction with $A_{ack} \rceil B_{ack}$. Finally, the whole client transaction in which two requests are sent to two different servers and the corresponding acknowledgments are sent if both requests are satisfied, is modeled by the long–running transaction $T = (A_1 \rceil B_1 \| A_2 \rceil B_2) \cdot A_{ack} \rceil B_{ack}$ and the whole system in which both the client and the two servers are modeled is $SYSTEM = T \| S_1 \| S_2$.

To verify properties of this system, we consider the CHTTA $top(T)$, and then we compute the flat TTA $T' = Flat(top(T), \Sigma_V)$, where $\Sigma_V = \{a!, a? \mid a \in \{req_i, rep_i, stop_i, cancel_i, ack_i\}\}$. Now, since S_1 and S_2 are both flat, we have that $T' \| S_1 \| S_2$ can be used as an input for the UPPAAL model checker. In order to reduce the size of the model we remove unnecessary τ transactions, and in order to avoid the execution of paths containing an infinite sequence of timed transitions we include time invariants in the states of the automaton modeling the client.

In Table 1 we show the results of the model checking. We have verified eight properties, and each property has been verified three times: once by setting both timeouts T_1 and T_2 greater than R_1 and R_2, respectively, once by setting $T_1 < R_1$ and $T_2 > R_2$, and once by setting both T_1 and T_2 smaller than R_1 and R_2, respectively.

Properties are expressed as logical formulas using the operators accepted by the UPPAAL model checker. A logical formula may have one of the following

Table 1. Results of the model checking

	$T_1 > R_1$ $T_2 > R_2$	$T_1 < R_1$ $T_2 > R_2$	$T_1 < R_1$ $T_2 < R_2$
1. $\quad A\Diamond(T.\odot \vee T.\otimes)$	true	true	true
2. $\quad (A_1.\otimes \vee A_2.\otimes) \leadsto T.\otimes$	true	true	true
3. $\quad (A_1.\odot \wedge A_2.\odot) \leadsto T.\odot$	true	true	true
4. $\quad T.\odot \leadsto (S_1.\odot \wedge S_1.\odot)$	true	true	true
5. $\quad x_1 \geq T_1 \leadsto T.\otimes$	true	true	true
6. $\quad x_2 \geq T_2 \leadsto T.\otimes$	true	true	true
7. $\quad E\Diamond T.\odot$	true	false	false
8. $\quad E\Diamond T.\otimes$	true	true	true

forms: $E\Diamond\phi, E\Box\phi, A\Diamond\phi, A\Box\phi$ and $\phi \leadsto \psi$, where ϕ and ψ are state formulas, namely conditions which could be satisfied by a state. In particular: $E\Diamond\phi$ represents reachability: it asks whether ϕ is satisfied by some reachable state; $E\Box\phi$ says that there should exists a maximal path such that ϕ is always true; $A\Diamond\phi$ says that ϕ is eventually satisfied in all paths; $A\Box\phi$ expresses that ϕ should be true in all reachable states; finally, $\phi \leadsto \psi$ means that whenever ϕ is satisfied, then eventually (in the continuation of the path) ψ will be satisfied.

Properties 1–3 express the correctness of the encoding of long–running transactions into automata. These properties must be satisfied for any setting of the parameters. In particular, property 1 says that either the commit or the abort states of the transaction (denoted $T.\odot$ and $T.\otimes$, respectively) must be eventually reached. Property 2 requires that if at least one of the abort states of the parallel activities A_1 and A_2 is reached, then the whole transaction must reach its abort state, and property 3 requires that if both parallel activities A_1 and A_2 reach their commit states, then the whole transaction must reach its commit state.

Properties 4–7 express the correctness of the modeling of the scenario. As before, these properties must be satisfied for any setting of the parameters. Property 4 says that if the transaction reaches a commit state, then eventually both servers must reach their commit states. Properties 5 and 6, instead, say that if one of the two clocks of the parallel activities A_1 and A_2 becomes greater than its deadline, then the whole transaction must reach its abort state.

Finally, properties 8 and 9 express that the commit and abort states of the transaction can be reached, for different settings of the parameters. In particular, the commit state can be reached only if both the timeouts T_1 and T_2 are greater than the times R_1 and R_2 spent by the two servers. The abort state, instead, can be reached with any setting of the parameters. This is true because R_1 and R_2 are lower bounds, hence a server may spend more time than its minimum time, and may exceed the corresponding deadline in the transaction.

6   Conclusions

We studied some pattern for the composition of activities in long–running transactions. In particular we focused our attention on the sequential and parallel pattern. In [6] another pattern is identified allowing to deal with *nested transactions*. Intuitively, a nested transaction is composed by a hierarchy of subtransactions as activities. In the nested pattern, the top–level transaction completes its activity when all its sub–transactions terminate. When a transaction aborts, all its sub–transactions should abort, and the committed subtransactions should be compensated. Nevertheless, a top–level transaction can commit even though some of its subtransactions have aborted. In [6] the compensation pattern for nested transactions is defined by resorting to a stack where the compensations of each subtransactions are stored when the related activities commit. If, at some point, the supertransactions needs to be compensated, compensations of the subtransactions are invoked from the stack.

With the model of CHTTAs given in this paper, we may represent the pattern of nested transaction by defining a compensation controller which should be put in parallel with the top–level transaction. While the patterns for sequential and parallel transactions are expressed in a rather natural way by CHTTAs, it is not so for the latter mechanism. Hence, we plan to enrich the model of CHTTAs with a notion of memory to store compensations of committed subtransactions.

For a version of this paper with complete proofs see [15].

References

1. R. Alur and D. L. Dill. "A Theory of Timed Automata". Theoretical Computer Science, volume 126, pages 183–235, 1994.
2. R. Alur, S. Kannan, and M. Yannakakis. "Communicating Hierarchical State Machines". ICALP'99, LNCS 1644, pages 169–178, 1999.
3. T. Amnell, G. Behrmann, J. Bengtsson, P. R. D'Argenio, A. David, A. Fehnker, T. Hune, B. Jeannet, K. G. Larsen, M. O. Moeller, P. Pettersson, C. Weise, and W. Yi. "Uppaal-now, next and future". LNCS 2067, pages 99–124, 2000.
4. B. Benatallah and R. Himadi. "A Petri Net–Based Model for Web Service Composition". ADC'03, Australian Computer Society, pages 191–200, 2003.
5. A. Brogi, C. Canal, E. Pimentel, and A. Vallecillo. "Formalizing Web Services Choreographies". WS–FM'04, ENTCS 105, pages 73-94, 2004.
6. R. Bruni, H. Melgratti, and U. Montanari. "Theoretical Foundations for Compensations in Flow Composition Languages". POPL'05, ACM Press, pages 209–220, 2005.
7. H. Garcia–Molina and K. Salem. "Sagas". SIGMOD'87, ACM Press, pages 249–259, 1987.
8. BPEL Specifications: www-128.ibm.com/developerworks/library/ws-bpel/.
9. I. Houston, M.C. Little, I. Robinson, S. K. Shrivastava, and S. M. Wheater. "The CORBA Activity Service Framework for Supporting Extended Transactions". Software — Practice and Experience, volume 33, number 4, pp. 351–373, 2003.
10. C. Laneve and G. Zavattaro. "Foundations of Web Transactions". FOSSACS'05, LNCS 3441, pp. 282–298, 2005.
11. M. Mazzara and S. Govoni. "A Case Study of Web Services Orchestration.". CO-ORDINATION'05, LNCS 3454, pp. 1–16, 2005.
12. WSCI Specification. Version 1.0. Available at http://www.w3.org/TR/wsci/.
13. M. Viroli. "Towards a Formal Foundation to Orchestration Languages". WS–FM'04, ENTCS 105, pages 51–71, 2004.
14. S. Yovine. "Kronos: A verification tool for real-time systems". International Journal on Software Tools for Technology Transfer, volume 1, pages 123–133, 1997.
15. http://www.di.unipi.it/~troina/fmoods06.pdf.

Transformation Laws for UML-RT

Rodrigo Ramos, Augusto Sampaio, and Alexandre Mota

Centre for Informatics, Federal University of Pernambuco
P.O.Box 7851, CEP 50740-540, Recife-PE, Brazil
{rtr, acas, acm}@cin.ufpe.br

Abstract. With model-driven development being on the verge of becoming an industrial standard, the need for systematic development strategies based on safe model transformations is a demand. Transformations must take into account changes in both behavioural and structural diagrams. In this paper, we present a set of transformation laws that aims to systematise the evolution of semantically well-defined UML-RT models, with preservation of both static and dynamic aspects. The proposed laws support the transformation of initial abstract analysis models into concrete design models. Furthermore, we show the seamless application of the laws through design activities of the Rational Unified Process in the development of a case study. Soundness and completeness of the laws are briefly addressed.

1 Introduction

In Model Driven software Engineering (MDE) [1], the central artifacts, and the driving force, of a software development are models, rather than code in a programming language. As a departure from the general idea that the usefulness of models are only for documentation or to capture interesting design aspects during development, the main objective in MDE is that the development process is driven by the activity of modelling.

The purpose of MDE is combining an architecture of the model roles with other process activities. In this framework, transformations help to overcome the challenges of model evolution, allowing restructure of the software with preservation of behaviour; the idea is similar to well-known code transformation techniques like refactorings [2] and refinements [3].

Models are widely expressed using the Unified Modeling Language (UML) [4], as well as its extensions. In particular, we emphasise the use of UML-RT [5], an UML profile, which has a clear definition for reactive components and component protocols, and is useful to describe concurrent and distributed domains. In previous work [6] we defined a formal semantics for UML-RT, and illustrated how model transformations can be verified. We have also explored refinement notions for UML-RT, together with some large grain transformation rules [7], which seemed useful to support the evolution and restructure of architectural UML-RT models.

Here we concentrate on an algebraic presentation of UML-RT. We propose a set of algebraic laws for the language, focusing on the new elements that it adds

R. Gorrieri and H. Wehrheim (Eds.): FMOODS 2006, LNCS 4037, pp. 123–137, 2006.
© IFIP International Federation for Information Processing 2006

to UML: active classes (capsules), protocols, ports and connections. The proposed laws express both basic properties of each individual construct, as well as relationships among them. For instance, the laws permit justifying transformations of initial abstract models into concrete design models, using consistent steps with preservation of both static and dynamic model aspects (taking into account structural and behavioural properties together); this is illustrated through the development of a case study: a simple manufacturing system. We also address a notion of completeness, briefly presenting a strategy to reduce an arbitrary UML-RT model to a extended UML model, entirely based on the laws.

Our work can be considered complementary to others that focus on laws for UML design elements [8, 9], as well as on component transformations [10]. A more detailed account of related work is left for the concluding section.

We briefly present an overview of UML-RT, including part of a formal semantics, in the next section. In Section 3, we present a selection of our set of laws, and address completeness. In Section 4, we show how these laws can be used to capture and formalise some design guidelines adopted, for example, by the Rational Unified Process (RUP) [11], through the development of our case study. Our conclusions and related work are presented in Section 5.

2   UML-RT Semantics Overview

The specification of reactive systems is a complex task, involving data, control behaviour, communication and architectural modelling aspects. In order to incorporate support for all these facets into a widely used language, like UML, several ROOM concepts have been added to the UML-RT. Although some of these concepts have also influenced the component model of the recent UML 2.0 [12] version, here we use the UML-RT profile because we consider that its proposed model for active objects is more consolidated than that proposed for UML 2.0. A detailed comparison between UML-RT and UML 2.0 is out of the scope of this paper; the work reported in [13] presents some problems on the statechart specification of UML 2.0. Furthermore, there is commercially established tool support for UML-RT.

UML-RT, like other Architectural Description Languages, models reactive systems with active architectural components working concurrently and communicating among themselves. Communication is modelled by means of input and output message exchanges, which can be synchronous or asynchronous; here we assume synchronous communication. These concepts have been introduced to UML-RT via four new design elements: capsule, protocol, port and connector. Capsules (active classes) describe architectural components whose points of interaction are called ports, which are assembled by connectors and realise communication signals previously declared in a protocol.

Despite the expressiveness of UML-RT, the rigorous development of nontrivial applications does not seem feasible without an assigned formal semantics. In previous work [6] we defined a semantics for UML-RT via mapping into the formal notation *Circus* [14], which combines CSP, Z and specification statements.

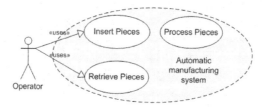

Fig. 1. Use Case Diagram

The semantics of *Circus* is defined in the setting of the Unifying Theories of Programming [15]; this relational model has proved convenient for reasoning. Another advantage is that *Circus* includes the main design concepts of UML-RT and provides a refinement calculus [3]. Both the semantics and the laws of *Circus* have been inspiring to prove laws that we propose for UML-RT.

Throughout this section, an example of a simplified manufacturing system is used to illustrate the UML-RT notation and semantics. In this system, the entire application is responsible for processing a number of workpieces, which are inserted by an operator and made available for retrieving after processed. These functionalities are presented by the use case diagram in Figure 1. Processing pieces is an autonomous process that does not require any operator intervention.

In Figure 2, an abstract model of this system is presented. The model is formed by a set of diagrams and system properties, using diagrams that mainly represent the following architectural views: static data, dynamic behaviour, and instance relationships; these are expressed, respectively, by class, state and structure diagrams. We directly express the system properties by invariants, pre- and post-conditions in *Circus*; they could alternatively be expressed in OCL, but an OCL to *Circus* mapping is out of the scope of this work.

In the class diagram (top left rectangle) of Figure 2, capsules and protocols are graphically represented by stereotyped classes with labels Capsule and Protocol. The diagram emphasises the relationships between the capsules ProdSys and Storage. The capsule Storage is a bounded reactive buffer that is used to store objects of class Piece, and ProdSys is used to process these objects. These capsules have an association to the protocols STO and STI, which are used to govern their communications: STO declares the input signal req and the output signal output (used to communicate the request and the delivery of a work piece, respectively), while STI declares a signal input to store a piece.

By their own nature, capsules provide a high degree of information hiding. As the communication mechanism is via message passing, all capsule elements are hidden, including not only attributes, but also methods. The only visible elements in the capsule are ports, which can be connected to other capsule ports to establish communication. This decoupling makes capsules highly reusable. In addition, a capsule can also be defined hierarchically.

A structure diagram describes a capsule structural decomposition in sub-capsules, showing the capsule interaction through connections among its ports. We assume that a configuration of the manufacturing system, given by the

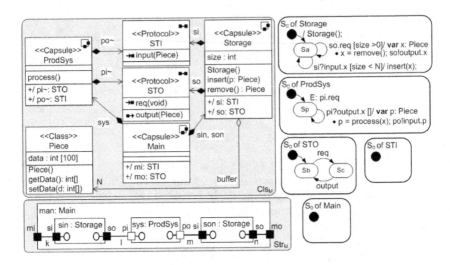

Fig. 2. Abstract Analysis Model

structure diagram in Figure 2 (bottom rectangle), is represented by an instance (man) of capsule Main, which is structurally decomposed into the sub-capsules sin, son and sys; these sub-capsule instances are created as a consequence of the association of Main with Storage and ProdSys in the class diagram. Black filled squares in the capsule instances represent their ports, which are used for communication (*end ports*) or just to convey signals to other sub-capsules (*relay ports*). Each end port can be connected only to another *conjugated* port of the same protocol; conjugated ports are represented by (unfilled) squares and have the directions of their input and output signals inverted in order to fully assemble with other ordinary ports. For instance, in the structure diagram, the ports pi and po are public end ports of ProdSys, while mi and mo are public relay ports of Main used only to connect ports of sub-capsules to the environment.

The capsule behaviour is described in terms of UML-RT statecharts, which differ from the standard UML statecharts [16] by including some adaptations to better describe active objects. A statechart is composed by transitions and states; in general, a transition has the form p.e[g]/a, where e is an input signal, p is the port through which the signal arrives, g is a guard and a is an action. Input signals and a true guard trigger the transition. As a result, the corresponding action is executed.

We assume that events, guards and actions are expressed using the *Circus* notation. For example, in the statechart of Storage, there are two transitions from state Sa. The one on the right triggers if the req signal arrives through port so and the buffer is non-empty. The corresponding action declares a variable x to capture the result of the method remove. This is the way it is done in *Circus*, since remove is actually interpreted as a Z Schema. The value of x is then sent through port so. The syntax for writing these actions related to communication are also as in CSP. In this work we do not consider capsule inheritance, mainly because its semantics in UML-RT is not yet well-defined.

The formal counterpart of the UML-RT concepts are also found in *Circus*, since, in this language, concurrent components are represented by processes that interact via channels. Therefore, capsules and protocols, classifiers with an associated behaviour, are semantically mapped into processes, ports into channels, and classes into Z paragraphs, which act as passive data registers. Furthermore, connections are represented by means of using common channels. As an example, consider the following mapping of the capsule Storage into *Circus*.

$| N : \mathbb{N}$
$T_{\mathsf{STI}} ::= \mathsf{input} \ll \mathsf{Piece} \gg$
$T_{\mathsf{STO}} ::= \mathsf{req} \mid \mathsf{output} \ll \mathsf{Piece} \gg$
channel si : T_{STI}, so : T_{STO}
process Storage $\widehat{=}$ **begin**
    state *StorageState* $\widehat{=}$ [buffer : seq Piece; size : $0..N$ | size = #buffer $\leq N$]
    initial *StorageInit* $\widehat{=}$ [*StorageState′* | buffer′ = $\langle\rangle$ $\wedge$ size′ = 0]
    insert $\widehat{=}$ [Δ*StorageState*; $x?$: Piece | size $< N$ $\wedge$
        buffer′ = buffer $^\frown$ $\langle x?\rangle$ $\wedge$ size′ = size + 1]
    remove $\widehat{=}$ [Δ*StorageState*; $x!$: Piece | size > 0 $\wedge$ $x!$ = *head* buffer $\wedge$
        buffer′ = *tail* buffer $\wedge$ size′ = size $- 1$]
    Sa $\widehat{=}$ (size $< N$ & si?input.x $\rightarrow$ insert; Sa)
        $\square$ (size > 0 & so.req $\rightarrow$ (**var** x : Piece • remove; so!output.x); Sa)
  • *StorageInit*; *Sa*
end

In *Circus*, a process declaration body (delimited by the **begin** and **end** keywords) is composed of a Z state schema, action paragraphs and a main action (delimited after the • symbol), which defines the process behaviour; action paragraphs are used to structure the behaviour of a main action and to express data operations. In this specification, the maximum size of the buffer is a positive constant N. The Storage process takes its inputs and supplies its outputs through the channels si and so, respectively. The free types T_{STI} and T_{STO} categorise the values communicated by these channels. In our example, the process Storage encapsulates two state components in the Z schema *StorageState*: an ordered list buffer of contents and the size of this list. Initially, buffer is empty and, therefore, its size is zero; this is specified as a state initialisation action *StorageInit*. Pre- and postconditions of methods, and state invariants play a corresponding role as annotations in the model; they have not been included in Figure 2 for conciseness. The main action initialises the buffer and then acts like the action Sa, repeatedly offering the choice of input and req, like Sa in the statechart of Storage (Figure 2). The main action represents the topmost state (S_0) of Storage; this contains all other states in the statechart, and each of these enclosing states is also mapped to another action paragraph. In the following we present a semantic mapping for protocols and capsules.

A protocol declaration in UML-RT encapsulates both the communication elements (signals) and the allowed flow of these elements (statechart). In *Circus*, this gives rise to two major elements: a process that captures this behaviour and a channel to represent the communication elements. This single channel communicates values of a free type, with each constructor representing a signal.

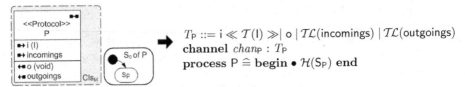

$T_P ::= i \ll T(I) \gg | o | \mathcal{TL}(\text{incomings}) | \mathcal{TL}(\text{outgoings})$
channel $chan_P : T_P$
process $P \cong$ **begin** $\bullet \; \mathcal{H}(S_P)$ **end**

In names like $chan_P$ above, we assume that P is a placeholder for the actual protocol name. The channel $chan_P$ communicates values of the free type T_P; each value represents a signal. Parameterless and parameterised signals are mapped into constants and data constructors, like the signals o and i above. The type of the parameter is translated into a corresponding *Circus* type by the function $T()$. The remaining signals (incomings and outgoings) are mapped by the meta function $\mathcal{TL}()$ that translates this remaining lists such as the elements that was singled out. The main action is represented by $\mathcal{H}(S_P)$, where S_P stands for the topmost composite state of P and the function $\mathcal{H}()$ translates a statechart into a *Circus* action.

Capsules are also defined as processes, with methods and attributes defined as Z operation and state schemas. Each port generates a channel with the same type of the corresponding channel of the protocol, and has its behaviour described by the process obtained from the mapping of its protocol synchronised with that obtained from the capsule statechart. Observe that in UML-RT the type of a port is the protocol itself. In *Circus*, the type of the channel originated from the port is the free type that represents the protocol signals.

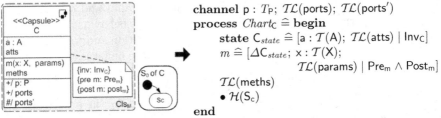

channel $p : T_P; \; \mathcal{TL}(\text{ports}); \; \mathcal{TL}(\text{ports}')$
process $Chart_C \cong$ **begin**
    state $C_{state} \cong [a : T(A); \; \mathcal{TL}(\text{atts}) | \text{Inv}_C]$
    $m \cong [\Delta C_{state}; \; x : T(X);$
                       $\mathcal{TL}(\text{params}) | \text{Pre}_m \wedge \text{Post}_m]$
    $\mathcal{TL}(\text{meths})$
    $\bullet \; \mathcal{H}(S_c)$
end

In the above mapping, the process $Chart_C$ deals with the views represented by class and state diagrams. It encapsulates all actions that manipulate the private attributes of the capsule C. In the capsule C above, the compartments correspond to attributes, methods and ports. Therefore, a, m and p are those that we single out, and remaining lists in these compartments are mapped by the function $\mathcal{TL}()$. The attribute a is mapped to an attribute in the state of $Chart_C$ with its corresponding type in *Circus* given by $T(A)$. The method m() is mapped to an operator that could change any state attribute and whose parameters are mapped into schema attributes, just like a has been included in the state schema. The invariant Inv_C, preconditions Pre_m and postconditions Post_m come from the UML-RT note element on the left, and it is assumed to be already described in *Circus*. The port p is mapped to a channel with the same type T_P of the channel $Chan_P$ used by the protocol P. The main action of $Chart_C$ is expressed by $\mathcal{H}(S_C)$, which represents the mapping of the statechart of capsule C.

In *Circus* the semantics of the dynamic behaviour of a capsule C, including its internal structure diagram, is captured by the parallelism of its internal behaviour (*Chart$_C$*), its connected sub-capsules and its ports. The dynamic behaviour considers restrictions imposed by its ports to the corresponding communication channels and the interaction with its sub-capsules in a hierarchical and compositional way. This is expressed in *Circus* by means of a parallel composition of these processes. Further details about our semantics for UML-RT is presented in [6].

3   Transformation Laws

Based on the formal semantics briefly presented in the previous section, we propose some transformation laws for UML-RT. As with the formal semantics, we concentrate on the elements that UML-RT adds to UML, and the relationships of these with UML elements, especially classes. The laws deal with static and dynamic model aspects represented by the three most important diagrams of UML-RT: statechart, class and structure diagrams. The proof of the laws can be found in [17, 6], using both semantics and the refinement laws of *Circus* [14].

Each law is defined by an equivalence relation on models (filled arrow) with a subscript M that stands for the context in which the equality holds; the soundness of this equivalence relation is based on the formal semantics: the models on the two sides of each law are semantically equivalent, when mapped into *Circus* specifications. Our laws do not modify the context M, but impose side conditions on some of its views: Cls$_M$ represents the class diagrams of M, and Str$_M$ denotes the architecture configuration of M, expressed by structure diagrams. State diagrams of protocols and capsules are explicitly expressed in the law. Diagrams and notes describing properties (invariants, pre- and postconditions) are presented only as the need arises. On each side of the law we use a dotted line box to single out the relevant part of the model affected by the transformation.

The first law establishes when it is possible to introduce a new capsule into the model.

Law 1. *Declare Capsule*

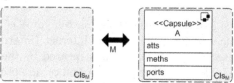

provided

($\rightarrow$) Cls$_M$ *does not declare any element named* A.
($\leftarrow$) *No capsule in M has a relationship with capsule* A *in any diagram.*

The left-hand side of Law 1 displays an empty box, meaning that the new capsule can be included anywhere in the model, provided the side conditions are satisfied; the subscript M fixes the context for the law application. We write ($\rightarrow$) before the proviso of a law to indicate that it is required only for applications of this law from left to right. Similarly, we use ($\leftarrow$) to indicate that it is only for applying the law from right to left, and we use ($\leftrightarrow$) to indicate that the proviso is necessary in both directions.

A proviso to remove a capsule A (application from right to left) is that no other capsule extends, is associated to or connected with it. Since UML (and UML-RT) does not allow two elements with the same name, then there is a proviso stating that the name of the new element is fresh. We assume that atts, meths and ports always represent the set of attributes, methods and ports of a capsule. As the capsule is assumed not to be associated with any other in M, the structure diagram or a statechart can have any form that obeys our provisos, and their presentation is immaterial. We have similar laws to add or remove other basic elements (for instance, protocols, ports and connections).

The next law captures a more elaborate transformation; it decomposes a capsule A into parallel component capsules (B and C) in order to tackle design complexity and to potentially improve reuse. The side condition requires that A be partitioned, a concept that is explained next. Note that protocols X and Z are not illustrated because any deterministic machines can be used.

Law 2. *Capsule Decomposition*

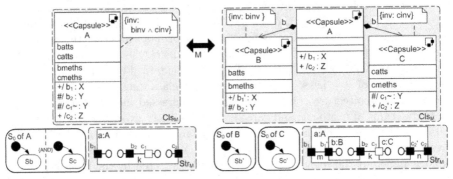

provided

($\rightarrow$) $\langle$batts, binv, bmeths, (b_1, b_2), Sb$\rangle$ and $\langle$catts, cinv, cmeths, (c_1, c_2), Sc$\rangle$ partition A.

($\leftrightarrow$) *The statecharts of the protocols* X *and* Z *are deterministic.*

On the left-hand side of Law 2 the state machine of A is an And-State composed of two states (Sb and Sc), which may interact (internal communication) through the conjugated ports b_2 and c_1 (as captured by the structure diagram on the left-hand side). The two other ports (b_1 and c_2) are used for external communication by states Sb and Sc, respectively. Furthermore, in transitions on Sb, only the attributes batts and the methods bmeths (that may reference only the attributes batts) are used; analogously, transitions of Sc use only the attributes catts and the methods cmeths (that may reference only the attributes catts). Finally, the invariant of A is the conjunction binv $\wedge$ cinv, where binv involves only batts as free variables, and cinv only catts. When a capsule obeys such conditions, we say that it is partitioned. In this case, there are two partitions: one is $\langle$batts, binv, bmeths, (b_1, b_2), Sb$\rangle$ and the other is $\langle$catts, cinv, cmeths, (c_1, c_2), Sc$\rangle$.

The effect of the decomposition is to create two new component capsules, B and C, one for each partition, and redesign the original capsule A to act as a mediator. In general, the new behaviour of A might depend on the particular form of decomposition. Law 2 captures a parallel decomposition. On the right-hand side of the law, A has no state machine. It completely delegates its original behaviour to B and C through the structure diagram.

Concerning the structure diagram on the right-hand side of the law, it shows how A encapsulates B and C. When A is created, it automatically creates the instances of B and C, which execute concurrently. The public ports b_1 and c_2 are preserved in A. Capsule B has as its public port an image of b_1, called b'_1. Although this port is public in B, it is only visible inside the structure diagram of A. The role of this port is to allow B to receive the external signals received from A through port b_1, as captured by the connection between b'_1 and b_1 in the structure diagram of A. Analogously, c_2 and b'_2 have the same relationship, concerning capsules A and C. The internal ports b_2 and c_1 are moved to capsules B and C, respectively, and play the same role as before.

Motivated by existing development practices, we propose a law that replaces a capsule by a class, or vice-versa. This establishes an interesting connection between passive and active classes.

Law 3. *Replace a Class by a Capsule*

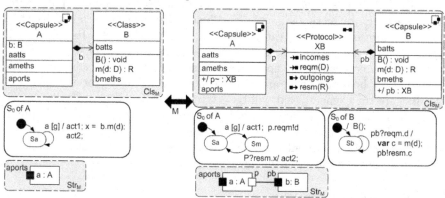

provided

($\rightarrow$) *All attributes within* batts *are private.*
($\leftrightarrow$) *No capsule, except A, has a relationship with* B.

Law 3 transforms a class B (left-side) into a capsule, also named B, on the right-hand side. The behaviour of method calls is preserved by a statechart that simulates a synchronised communication with the client protocol. Now, all services (public methods) of the class are exposed in a new protocol XB. The constructor of class B becomes an action in its statechart's initial transition.

The following law promotes a hidden abstraction inside a capsule into an independent passive class. This simple transformation seems recurrent during several design steps. It is particularly helpful in the context where the system is initially modelled as components, since it allows the extraction of relevant classes from these components. Concerning side conditions, we need to consider the effect on the state machine of the capsule, whose behaviour must be preserved by the transformations. A simplified version of this law allows extracting a class from another class.

Law 4. *Extract Class*

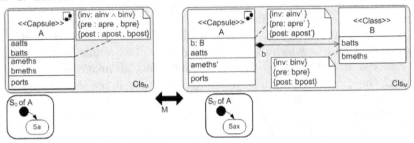

provided

($\rightarrow$) bmeths, binv, bpre and bpost *refer only to methods and attributes within* bmeths *and* batts; B *is a fresh identifier.*

($\leftarrow$) *No element, except* A, *refers to* B; *there is an equivalence relationship between* Sax *and* Sa, *and also between* ameths *and* ameths'.

On the left-hand side of law 4, capsule A is composed by the set of attributes aatts and batts, of methods ameths and bmeths, and of ports ports. Its state machine, represented by Sa, can access any of these elements. Its invariant is represented by the conjunction ainv $\land$ binv, and the pre- and postconditions of its methods are captured by apre, bpre, apost and bpost. The elements inside batts, bmeths, bpre and bpost are assumed not to refer to any other element of A. These are the elements that will be extracted into a new class.

On the right-hand side, any action in Sax, methods within ameths' or predicates (ainv', apre' or apost') of A, which on the left-hand side accessed attributes of batts or methods of bmeths, will now access these elements via a qualifier b, which represents an object of the new class B.

3.1 A Word on Completeness

One way of showing that a set of laws is comprehensive is to define a reduction strategy based on the laws, whose target is a normal form described in terms of a restricted subset of the language being discussed. This shows that the laws are sufficiently powerful to reduce any program to this normal form, and moreover any pair of equivalent programs to the same normal form. This is what we briefly discuss here, for a normal form that extends a UML model with a single capsule responsible for all the interactions with the environment; this capsule also centralises the entire active behaviour of the modelled system. The reason for keeping one active element as part of the normal form (rather than a pure UML model containing only passive classes) is that the autonomous control flows of the original capsules cannot be simply eliminated; the closest we can get is combining them as a single statechart. Reducing an arbitrary UML-RT model to such a form suggests that our laws are expressive enough to reason about the new design elements that UML-RT adds to UML, which is our major concern.

As it is not possible to present all the equality laws used by our structural reduction strategy, we list some categories of laws below; the laws already presented fall in these categories. We also refer to these categories in the development of our case study.

- *Laws of declaration*: for introducing/removing capsules (Law 1), protocols, ports, signals of a protocol, attributes, methods, and associations.
- *Communication*: for introducing new connections and intermediate capsules.
- *Merging*: combining/decomposing capsules (Law 2), protocols and ports.
- *Delegation*: transferring part of a protocol/capsule behaviour to another capsule, protocol or class (for instance, Law 4).
- *Structuring*: Encapsulate (making it local) or replace a capsule with another capsule or class (for instance Law 3)
- *Statechart*: Adding a new state, rewriting a transition action, partitioning regions, among others.

Laws in these categories are used in the main steps of our reduction strategy, as summarised below.

1. Merge capsule ports. Capsules should have a unique binary connection between them; this is justified by *Laws of Merging*.
2. Eliminate capsule hierarchy in structure diagrams. In this step, sub-capsules are moved out the structure of its enclosing capsule; this is justified by *Laws of Structuring*.
3. Move protocol behaviour to capsules. The entire system behaviour is expressed in its capsules; this is justified by the *Laws of Delegation*.
4. Capsule composition. Every two capsules that communicate should be encapsulated in a topmost capsule, and then composed; this is justified by *Laws of Merging*.
5. Remove unreferenced model elements. All disconnected elements can be removed from the model by the application of *Laws of Declaration*.

As a result of this strategy all the active elements are transformed into a single capsule that centralises the entire autonomous behaviour of the model. The (passive) classes are not affected by the strategy. This model might be reduced even further, by eliminating the classes as well; Law 4 (in its reverse order) is relevant here. However, for a complete elimination of classes, possibly involving inheritance, additional laws would be necessary, as suggested in [18] for a programming language; our focus here is on active rather than on passive classes. Our complete set of laws and more details of the reduction strategy can be found in [17].

Clearly, the objective of such a reduction strategy is merely to study the expressiveness of a set of laws. In a development process, the laws are applied in the reverse direction, supporting the evolution of simple and abstract models into more elaborate design models, as illustrated in the next section.

4   Case Study

The transformation laws we have proposed may be useful to formalise informal analysis and design guidelines widely adopted by development processes such as, for instance, the Rational Unified Process (RUP) [11]. The analysis and design disciplines of RUP include several activities that guide the developer to systematically realise the use case view into the so-called logical view. Broadly, abstractions are identified, an abstract (analysis) model is developed, and this is progressively refined into a concrete design model.

The focus of our approach is to support a formal transition from analysis into design. Complementary approaches, like [19], for example, address the rigorous migration from the use case view to an initial abstract model (Figure 1) with active objects in the logical view. We allow great flexibility concerning the starting point for our development. An extreme could be a centralised model with a single capsule, just like the normal form discussed in the previous section. In the context of our case study, such a model would include a single capsule Main with all the interactions described in the use case diagram in Figure 1.

The proposed laws can then be applied to evolve this monolithic model into a concrete detailed model like the one in Figure 2. For example, Law 2 justifies the decomposition of Main into ProdSys and Storage, and Law 4 justifies the extraction of class Piece from Storage. The remainder of this section further refines this model to a more concrete version, with more than one processor, working in a pipeline, and a transportation agent (Holon) that intermediates the communication.

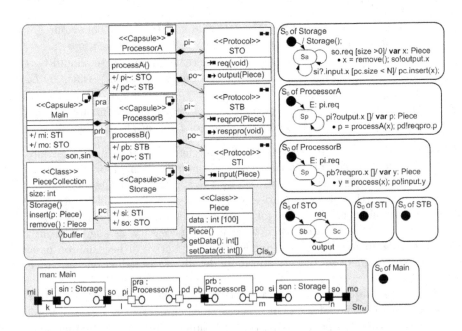

Fig. 3. Extracting PieceCollection and Decomposing the Processor

From the analysis model in Figure 2, we proceed to find a *candidate architecture*. We adopt a simple layered architecture where data manipulation is isolated from the business rules of the control elements. Therefore we use an explicit data collection class PieceCollection to store the workpieces; this class is actually extracted from Storage using Law 4.

The candidate architecture is incrementally enhanced by means of the activity *identify design elements*. In particular, we decompose the processor ProdSys into two other capsules (ProcessorA and ProcessorB), using Law 2 as well as *Laws of Statecharts, Communication* and *Delegation*. With the introduction of ProcessorA and ProcessorB, the statechart of ProdSys is split into the statecharts of these new processors, and it is then represented by the interaction between ProcessorA and ProcessorB. The remaining role of ProdSys is only to mediate communication with these processors through its delay ports, and it is transferred to Main (*Laws of Communication*); then ProdSys becomes useless and can be eliminated (Law 1). The resulting model is presented in Figure 3.

Transportation agents are needed not only to intermediate the communication between physically separated processors, but also to relieve processors from concerns of the global processing plan. To create one transportation agent (Holon), we introduce intermediate capsule instances among the capsules that communicate with the processor (using *Laws of Communication*); these capsules need to be composed pairwise using a variation of Law 2 (*Laws of Merging*). As Holon

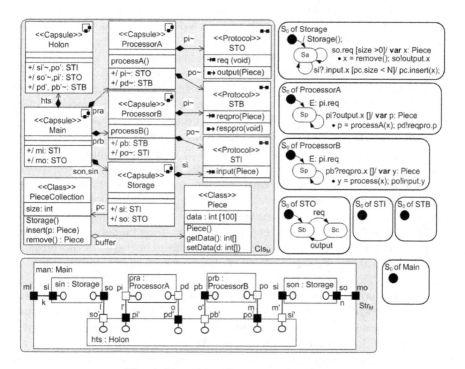

Fig. 4. Identifying Transportation Agents

was created by the composition of proxy capsules, it plays only a delegating role at this moment. The resulting design is depicted in Figure 4.

The result of the entire development is a system with a structure very close to the final architecture described in [20], but with a unique transport agent. A further refinement could extend the design to include some new agents to form a more complex automated transportation system, as well as refining the behaviour and the structure of each agent to a more concrete version. An advantage of our development strategy when contrasted to [20] is the justification of each design decision using transformation laws; no algebraic law has been proposed in [20].

5   Conclusions and Related Works

We have proposed laws for UML-RT that capture both basic properties of individual design elements as well as more elaborate transformations that correspond, for instance, to refactorings [2, 21]. The presentation of the laws makes explicit the transformation effects both on behavioural and on structural diagrams. Considering the elements that UML-RT adds to UML, our set of laws is comprehensive, as discussed in Section 3.1, and can be regarded as an algebraic semantics of these design elements. Another important issue is the connection between classes and capsules, as captured by Law 3. We have also suggested a guide for the law applications based on the RUP analysis and design discipline, as illustrated through the case study developed in Section 4. Soundness has been previously addressed through mapping into *Circus* [6], which acts as a hidden formalism, useful to define a sound interface for software engineering practice. The proof of the laws presented here, as well as the complete set of laws, can be found in [17].

Regarding laws for UML models, there are several works [21, 8, 9] that consider only transformations on structural or on behavioural diagrams in isolation. They neglect possible interferences between static and dynamic aspects, unlike our approach that takes into account these effects simultaneously. In [21], an important relationship between code refactoring concepts and model transformations is presented. Other approaches [8, 22, 9] define a formal semantics for UML using, respectively, Z, Alloy and Real-time Action Logic.

Regarding transformations for UML-RT, the work reported in [23] discusses a stepwise development process using UML-RT, incorporating notions of refinement, based on principles of *behavioural interface refinement* and *incorporating time*. In [24] the *locality principle* is explored, formalising model evolution using some local transformations; it also analyses the effects of these transformations on various consistency properties. None of these works, however, makes side conditions of laws explicit, presents a comprehensive set of laws for UML-RT, or systematises a strategy for algebraic-based model transformations, as we have done here. The work [10] also proposes an elaborated set of refactorings similar to ours, but the semantics used does not allow usage of an algebraic strategy.

As future work we intend to investigate the formalisation of design and architectural patterns based on our laws, and build tool support for automated transformations related to component based development.

References

1. Kent, S.: Model driven engineering. In: Proc. of the IFM Conference. Volume 2335 of LNCS., Springer (2002) 286–298
2. Fowler, M.: Refactoring-Improving the Design of Existing Code. Addison Wesley (1999)
3. Morgan, C.: Programming From Specifications. second edn. Prentice Hall (1994)
4. Booch, G., Jacobson, I., Rumbaugh, J.: The Unified Modeling Language User Guide. Addison-Wesley (1999)
5. Selic, B., Rumbaugh, J.: Using UML For Modeling Complex RealTime Systems. Rational Software Corporation (1998) available at http://www. rational.com.
6. Ramos, R., Sampaio, A., Mota, A.: A Semantics for UML-RT Active Classes via Mapping into *Circus*. In: Proc. of the FMOODS Conference. Volume 3535 of LNCS., Springer (2005) 99–114
7. Sampaio, A., Mota, A., Ramos, R.: Class and Capsule Refinement in UML For Real Time. In: Proc. WMF'03. Volume 95 of ENTCS., Elsevier (2004) 23–51
8. Evans, A., France, R., Lano, K., Rumpe, B.: The UML as a Formal Modeling Notation. In: Proc. of the UML Conference. LNCS, Springer (1999)
9. Lano, K., Bicarregui, J.: Semantics and Transformations For UML Models. In: Proc. of the UML'99. Volume 1618 of LNCS., Springer (1999) 107–119
10. Meng, S., B.L., Naixiao, Z.: On refinement of software architectures. In: Proc. of the ICTAC Conference. Volume 3722 of LNCS., Springer (2005) 482–497
11. Kruchten, P.: Rational Unified Process: An Introduction, The. 2 edn. Addison-Wesley (2000)
12. OMG: UML 2.0 Superstructure Specification (2003) OMG Adopted Specification.
13. Fecher, H., Schönborn, J., Kyas, M., de Roever, W.P.: 29 New Unclarities in the Semantics of UML 2.0 State Machines. In: Proc. of the ICFEM Conference. Volume 3785 of LNCS., Springer (2005) 52–65
14. Sampaio, A., Woodcock, J., Cavalcanti, A.: Refinement in *Circus*. In: Proc. of the FME Symposium. Volume 2391 of LNCS., Springer (2002) 451–470
15. Hoare, C.A.R., He, J.: Unifying Theories of Programming. Prentice-Hall (1998)
16. OMG: Unified Modeling Language Specification, Version 1.4. Object Management Group. (2001) Available at http://www.omg.org/uml.
17. Ramos, R.: Desenvolvimento Rigoroso com UML-RT. Master's thesis, Federal University of Pernambuco, Recife, Brazil (2005)
18. Borba, P., Sampaio, A., Cavalcanti, A., Cornélio, M.: Algebraic Reasoning for Object-Oriented Programming. Science of Computer Programming 52 (2004)
19. Zhang, L., Xie, D., Zou, W.: Viewing Use Cases As Active Objects. ACM SIGSOFT Software Engineering Notes 26 (2001) 44–48
20. Wehrheim, H.: Specification of an Automatic Manufacturing System: A Case Study in Using Integrated Formal Methods. In: Proc. of the FASE Conference. Volume 1783 of LNCS., Springer (2000) 334–348
21. Sunyé, G., Pollet, D., Traon, Y.L., Jézéquel, J.M.: Refactoring UML Models. In: Proc. of the UML'01. Volume 2185 of LNCS., Springer (2001) 134–148
22. Gheyi, R., Borba, P.: Refactoring Alloy Specifications. In: Proc. WMF'03. Volume 95 of ENTCS., Elsevier (2004) 227–243
23. Sandner, R.: Developing Distributed Systems Step By Step With UML-RT. In: Proc. of the VVVNS Workshop, Universität Münster (2000)
24. Engels, G., Heckel, R., Küster, J.M., Groenewegen, L.: Consistency-Preserving Model Evolution Through Transformations. In: Proc. of the UML Conference. Volume 2460 of LNCS., Springer (2002) 212–226

Underspecification, Inherent Nondeterminism and Probability in Sequence Diagrams

Atle Refsdal[1,2], Ragnhild Kobro Runde[1], and Ketil Stølen[1,2]

[1] Department of Informatics, University of Oslo, Norway
[2] SINTEF ICT, Norway

Abstract. Nondeterminism in specifications may be used for at least two different purposes. One is to express underspecification, which means that the specifier for the same environment behavior allows several alternative behaviors of the specified component and leaves the choice between these to those responsible for implementing the specification. In this case a valid implementation will need to implement at least one, but not necessarily all, alternatives. The other purpose is to express inherent nondeterminism, which means that a valid implementation needs to reflect all alternatives. STAIRS is an approach to the compositional and incremental development of sequence diagrams supporting underspecification as well as inherent nondeterminism. Probabilistic STAIRS builds on STAIRS and allows probabilities to be included in the specifications. Underspecification with respect to probabilities is also allowed. This paper investigates the use of underspecification, inherent nondeterminism and probability in sequence diagrams, the relationships between these concepts, and how these are expressed in STAIRS and probabilistic STAIRS.

1 Introduction

Nondeterminism in specifications may be used for expressing underspecification as well as inherent nondeterminism. Underspecification means that the specifier leaves some freedom of choice to those who will implement or further refine the specification. This is useful when different design alternatives fulfill a function equally well from the specifier's point of view. For example, when specifying an automatic teller machine we need to ensure that money is delivered and the card is returned at the end of the transaction. But whether the card is returned before or after the money is not important, and we may leave the choice to those responsible for making the teller machine.

Inherent nondeterminism, on the other hand, means that all alternatives must be reflected also in the final implementation. For example, when specifying a program to simulate a coin flip it is essential that both heads and tails are possible outcomes. An inherently nondeterministic choice can be seen as an abstraction of a probabilistic choice where the probabilities are greater than 0 but otherwise unknown.

The difference between underspecification and inherent nondeterminism is related to refinement. In an implementation, which is not supposed to be refined and has no underspecification, the distinction is not relevant.

R. Gorrieri and H. Wehrheim (Eds.): FMOODS 2006, LNCS 4037, pp. 138–155, 2006.

STAIRS ([HHRS05b],[RHS05c]) is a method for the compositional development of interactions, such as sequence diagrams and interaction overview diagrams. STAIRS employs two different choice operators to distinguish between underspecification and inherent nondeterminism; alt represents underspecification and xalt represents inherent nondeterminism. Probabilistic STAIRS ([RHS05a]) replaces xalt with the palt operator that also allows specification of probabilities on its operands.

STAIRS includes all the main composition operators of UML 2.0 interactions, such as seq and par for specifying sequential and parallel composition respectively. As these operators are not important for the discussion in this paper, we refer to [HHRS05b] for formal definitions and examples using these operators.

This paper summarizes insights gained during our work with formalization of various forms of nondeterminism in STAIRS and probabilistic STAIRS by investigating the different roles of nondeterminism in interactions. In particular we

- demonstrate the usefulness of underspecification, inherent nondeterminism and probability in specifications,
- show that these concepts are adequately expressed in STAIRS and probabilistic STAIRS by the operators alt, xalt and palt,
- explore the properties of these operators, in particular with respect to refinement,
- provide simple examples that give a thorough understanding of the use of these operators, both separately and combined.

The paper is organized as follows: Section 2 discusses underspecification and its representation in a simplified version of STAIRS. In Section 3 we motivate the need for inherent nondeterminism and show how this is incorporated in full STAIRS. Section 4 introduces probabilistic STAIRS. We discuss related work in Section 5 before concluding in Section 6.

2   Underspecification

2.1   Motivation

Often, it is useful to write specifications where certain aspects of the behavior of the system are left open. This is known as underspecification. In many cases, underspecification will be an implicit consequence of using abstraction when describing the important features of a system. Many specification languages also include some kind of 'or' operator for explicitly specifying the alternatives the implementer may choose between. In STAIRS, this is the alt operator.

In our setting of interactions, the alt operator may be used to describe scenarios that are different, but still seen as alternative means to achieve the same purpose in some sense. The alt operator is also called potential choice, as the alternatives represent choices that the implementation may choose between in order to satisfy the specification. As an everyday example, consider the action of making a u-turn when walking. This may be achieved by turning either 180 degrees left or 180 degrees right. Which alternative you choose is usually insignificant.

2.2 Semantic Representation

In STAIRS the semantics of an interaction is defined by denotational trace semantics, where a trace is a sequence of events representing a system run. We denote the semantics of an interaction d by $[\![\, d \,]\!]$. For the subset of STAIRS presented so far, containing only underspecification (and not inherent nondeterminism) the semantics of an interaction is represented by an *interaction obligation* (p, n). Here, p is a set of positive traces, representing desired or acceptable behavior, while n is a set of negative traces, representing undesired or unacceptable behavior.

An interaction is a partial specification in the sense that it does not in general define all the behavior of the system. Traces that are neither positive nor negative are called inconclusive, meaning that these are traces that the specifier has not yet considered. Letting $\mathcal{H}$ denote the universe of all traces, the traces $\mathcal{H} \setminus (p \cup n)$ are inconclusive in the obligation (p, n).

From an implementation point of view, there is no distinction between inconclusive and positive traces, as they all represent possible behaviors of the system. However, conceptually there is an important difference between behaviors that are explicitly described and behaviors that are not. Also, positive and inconclusive traces are treated differently by composition operators such as seq (sequential composition) and par (parallel composition), see [HHRS05b].

Underspecification by means of alt corresponds to taking the pairwise union of the positive and negative trace-sets of the operands. Formally:

$$[\![\, d_1 \text{ alt } d_2 \,]\!] \stackrel{\text{def}}{=} [\![\, d_1 \,]\!] \uplus [\![\, d_2 \,]\!] \tag{1}$$

where

$$(p_1, n_1) \uplus (p_2, n_2) \stackrel{\text{def}}{=} (p_1 \cup p_2, n_1 \cup n_2) \tag{2}$$

From this definition it is clear that the alt operator can be used not only to introduce underspecification in the form of alternative ways of fulfilling a task (i.e. new positive traces), but also to introduce more restrictions by adding new negative traces. By taking the union also of the negative traces, the alt operator can be used to merge alternatives that are considered to be similar, both at the positive and the negative level. In addition, the above definition ensures monotonicity of refinement with respect to alt, which will be clear from the following sections.

2.3 Refinement

Refinement of a specification means to reduce underspecification by adding information so that the specification becomes closer to an implementation. As in [HHRS05b], we distinguish between two special cases of refinement, called narrowing and supplementing. Narrowing reduces the set of positive traces to capture new design decisions or to match the problem more accurately. Supplementing categorizes (to this point) inconclusive behavior as either positive or negative. Formally, an interaction obligation (p', n') is a refinement of an interaction obligation (p, n), written $(p, n) \rightsquigarrow (p', n')$, iff

$$n \subseteq n' \wedge p \subseteq p' \cup n' \tag{3}$$

Intuitively, supplementing means that it is possible to add new positive or negative traces to those already specified. Specifying more alternative traces is usually achieved by using the alt operator, meaning that we want d_1 alt d_2 to be a valid refinement of d_1 (and of d_2). As negative traces must remain negative in a refinement, this means that d_1 alt d_2 must include the negative traces of both d_1 and of d_2, as in equation 2 above.

2.4   Simple Example

We now give a simple example of underspecification and refinement. Figure 1 specifies the game of tic-tac-toe between a player and the system. Either the player or the system may make the first move, and this is specified using alt. The player and the system then alternate making moves until the game is over. The opt operator is a shorthand for an alt with an empty second operand, while loop(2,3) may be interpreted as an alt between performing the contents of the loop two and three times. For formal definitions of opt and loop, see [RHS05c]. The game is finished after minimum five and maximum eight moves, depending on how many times the loop is executed, and whether the move inside opt is performed or not. (A ninth move is never really necessary, as the result of the game will be given at latest after the eight move.) We have omitted the details describing the exact positions taken in each move.

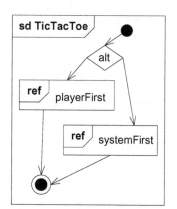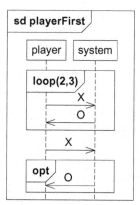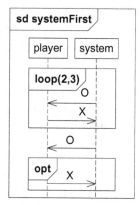

Fig. 1. Playing tic-tac-toe

In TicTacToe, the choice of who gets the first move is an example of underspecification. A possible refinement could be to use narrowing in order to remove this underspecification, as in TicTacToe2 where the player always moves first:

TicTacToe2 = (playerFirst) alt (refuse systemFirst)

where the operator refuse intuitively means that all traces defined by its argument should be considered negative. (For a formal definition of refuse, se Section 3.2.) A further refinement could be to add behavior to the specification by e.g. defining that traces where the system makes a second move before the player gets to do his/her move, are negative. These behaviors were inconclusive in TicTacToe2 (and TicTacToe), making this an example of supplementing.

2.5 Properties of alt and Refinement

As can be expected, the operator alt is

- associative: d_1 alt $(d_2$ alt $d_3) = (d_1$ alt $d_2)$ alt d_3
- commutative: d_1 alt $d_2 = d_2$ alt d_1

This follows trivially from the associativity and commutativity of $\cup$.

As proved in [HHRS05a], we also have that the refinement operator $\rightsquigarrow$ is

- reflexive: $(p, n) \rightsquigarrow (p, n)$
- transitive: $(p, n) \rightsquigarrow (p', n') \wedge (p', n') \rightsquigarrow (p'', n'') \Rightarrow (p, n) \rightsquigarrow (p'', n'')$
- monotonic with respect to alt:
  $[\![\, d_1 \,]\!] \rightsquigarrow [\![\, d_1' \,]\!] \wedge [\![\, d_2 \,]\!] \rightsquigarrow [\![\, d_2' \,]\!] \Rightarrow [\![\, d_1 \text{ alt } d_2 \,]\!] \rightsquigarrow [\![\, d_1' \text{ alt } d_2' \,]\!]$

3 Inherent Nondeterminism

3.1 Motivation

Underspecification gives rise to nondeterminism, as the system behavior is not completely determined by the specification. Still, nondeterminism in the sense of underspecification does not require that the implementation itself should be nondeterministic. Sometimes, however, it is desirable to specify nondeterminism that *must* be present also in the implementation. We call this *inherent nondeterminism*. The throwing of a dice is an example of a process we would specify as inherently nondeterministic. Another example is a password generator, that should select passwords nondeterministically, at least from the perspective of the user (and the attacker). Inherent nondeterminism is in fact also essential in the domain of (information) security, see [Ros95].

As inherent nondeterminism and underspecification impose different requirements on an implementation, they should be described differently both in the syntax and the semantics of interactions. In STAIRS, inherent nondeterminism is specified by the use of the operator xalt. The xalt operator is also called mandatory choice, as the implementation must be able to perform (i.e. choose) any one of the given alternatives.

3.2 Semantic Representation

In Section 2.2 we represented the semantics of a STAIRS specification with underspecification as an interaction obligation (p, n). With this simple semantics, it is not possible to express cases where *all* alternatives need to be present in an implementation, as traces could be moved from positive to negative by means of refinement. For STAIRS specifications with both underspecification and inherent nondeterminism, we therefore extend the semantics to be a *set* of interaction obligations. The interpretation is that for each interaction obligation (p_i, n_i) a valid implementation needs to be able to produce at least one trace allowed by (p_i, n_i). Intuitively, each interaction obligation (p_i, n_i) defines an inherently nondeterministic alternative that needs to be implemented, but exactly how this should be achieved is underspecified, since $\mathcal{H} \setminus n_i$ is a set. This leads us to the following formal definition of xalt:

$$[\![d_1 \text{ xalt } d_2]\!] \stackrel{\text{def}}{=} [\![d_1]\!] \cup [\![d_2]\!] \tag{4}$$

We now define the operator refuse, informally explained in Section 2.4, and generalize the definition of alt to cover operands with several interaction obligations:

$$[\![\text{ refuse } d]\!] \stackrel{\text{def}}{=} \{(\varnothing, p \cup n) \mid (p, n) \in [\![d]\!] \} \tag{5}$$

$$[\![d_1 \text{ alt } d_2]\!] \stackrel{\text{def}}{=} \{(p_1 \cup p_2, n_1 \cup n_2) \mid (p_1, n_1) \in [\![d_1]\!] \wedge (p_2, n_2) \in [\![d_2]\!] \} \tag{6}$$

3.3   Refinement Revisited

The whole point of inherent nondeterminism in a specification is to ensure that the alternatives are preserved during refinement. Since each interaction obligation represents an inherently nondeterministic alternative, we need to ensure that each interaction obligation from the abstract specification will be represented also in the more concrete specification. Formally, a specification d' is a refinement of a specification d, written $d \rightsquigarrow d'$, iff

$$\forall o \in [\![d]\!] : \exists o' \in [\![d']\!] : o \rightsquigarrow o' \tag{7}$$

where $o \rightsquigarrow o'$ is refinement of interaction obligations as given by definition 3.

3.4   Simple Example

As an example, we consider a so-called 'randomizer' that should provide nondeterministic output selected randomly. Figure 2 gives a specification where the randomizer simulates the flipping of a coin, where both heads and tails should be possible outcomes.

Textually, we may write the Coin specification and its semantics as:

Coin   =   (heads alt (refuse tails)) xalt (tails alt (refuse heads))

$[\![$ Coin $]\!]$ = $\{ (\{h\}, \{t\}), (\{t\}, \{h\}) \}$

where h denotes the trace(s) where the outcome is heads and t denotes the trace(s) where the outcome is tails. This semantics is illustrated in the bottom

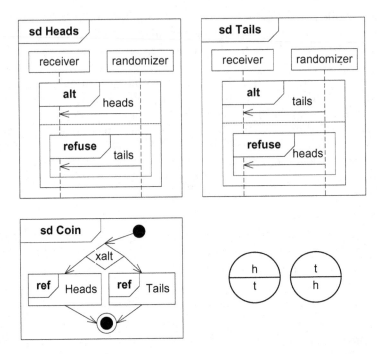

Fig. 2. The coin specification. Semantic representation to the bottom right.

right of Figure 2, where each circle represents an interaction obligation with the positive traces in the upper half and the negative traces in the lower half.

As another example, we specify how throwing a dice may simulate the flipping of a coin. One way of doing this is to let odd numbers represent heads, and even numbers represent tails. This is expressed by the specification

DiceCoin = Throw135 xalt Throw246

where Throw135 specifies a throw resulting in an odd number and Throw246 specifies a throw resulting in an even number:

Throw135 = (1 alt 3 alt 5) alt (refuse (2 alt 4 alt 6))
Throw246 = (2 alt 4 alt 6) alt (refuse (1 alt 3 alt 5))

Using the given definitions of alt and xalt, we thereby get:

$[\![$ DiceCoin $]\!] = \{$ $(\{1,3,5\},\{2,4,6\}), (\{2,4,6\},\{1,3,5\})$ $\}$

As should be expected, this semantics tells us that when using a dice to simulate a coin, the dice should at least be able to produce one of the numbers 1, 3 and 5 (representing heads) and one of the numbers 2, 4 and 6. However, it is not significant that all numbers may be produced, and DiceCoin may be implemented by the unfair dice DiceCoin2 giving only the numbers 1 and 6:

$$[\![\text{DiceCoin2}]\!] = \{\ (\{1\}, \{2, 3, 4, 5, 6\}), (\{6\}, \{1, 2, 3, 4, 5\})\ \}$$

We see that DiceCoin2 is a valid refinement of DiceCoin, as each obligation of DiceCoin is refined into an obligation of DiceCoin2 where some of the positive behaviors have been redefined as negative (i.e. narrowed).

3.5   Relating xalt to alt

It is interesting to investigate what kinds of specifications we get by combining the operators for underspecification (i.e. alt) and inherent nondeterminism (i.e. xalt). We have already seen examples of alt within xalt in DiceCoin and DiceCoin2 in the previous section. It remains to investigate the use of xalt within one or both of the operands of alt.

A possible refinement of the Coin specification in Figure 2, is to strengthen the specification by stating that the coin should never land on the side. As landing on the side is negative both in the heads and the tails alternative, this behavior may be added by using alt as the top-level operator as in Coin2:

$$\begin{array}{rcl}
\text{Coin2} & = & \text{Coin alt (refuse side)} \\
[\![\text{Coin2}]\!] & = & \{\ (\{h\}, \{t, s\}), (\{t\}, \{h, s\})\ \}
\end{array}$$

where s denotes the trace(s) where the coin lands on the side. As the example demonstrates, alt may in general be used to add (i.e. supplement) the same positive and/or negative traces to *all* interaction obligations specified by xalt.

It remains to consider the case where we have xalt in both operands of alt. Consider again the flipping of a coin as given in Figure 2. Another specification where the randomizer simulates the rolling of a three-sided dice is given by:

$$\begin{array}{rcl}
\text{Dice} & = & (1 \text{ alt (refuse (2 alt 3)))) xalt (2 alt (refuse (1 alt 3))) xalt} \\
& & (3 \text{ alt (refuse (1 alt 2)))}
\end{array}$$

In Figure 3 the specifications Coin and Dice are merged by the alt operator. Observe that Coin/Dice is a refinement of both the Coin and the Dice specifications. Each interaction obligation defined by Coin has three refined obligations in Coin/Dice (one would have been sufficient), as the earlier inconclusive traces related to Dice have been supplemented as positive or negative. Similarly, each of the three interaction obligations defined by Dice is refined by two interaction obligations in Coin/Dice. In this sense we may say that the specification of Coin/Dice represents both the Coin and the Dice specifications.

On the other hand, neither Coin nor Dice are valid refinements of Coin/Dice, since the traces $1, 2, 3$ are inconclusive in the interaction obligations of Coin and the traces h and t are inconclusive in the interaction obligations of Dice. However, the specifications (Coin alt (refuse Dice)) and ((refuse Coin) alt Dice) are

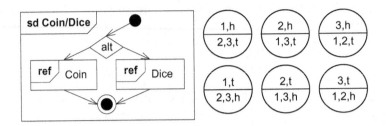

Fig. 3. The Coin and Dice specifications combined by alt. Semantic representation to the right.

both valid refinements of Coin/Dice, since these specifications ensure that none of the traces from the Coin/Dice specification are inconclusive. Intuitively, these specifications mean that traces from the Dice (or Coin) alternative should not be produced, which means that the opposite alternative is chosen. In general, for any specifications d_1 and d_2 the set of valid refinements (and therefore implementations) of d_1 alt d_2 will be both a subset of the valid refinements of d_1 and a subset of the valid refinements of d_2.

A valid refinement of the specification in Figure 3 would be to move the trace h to the negative sets in all interaction obligations, without doing the same with the trace t. The possible outcomes of a single run would then be 1, 2, 3 or t – so we know that if a coin trace is produced, it will be t (assuming 1, 2, 3, h and t are the only relevant traces).

The alt operator should be interpreted as underspecification w.r.t. traces and not w.r.t. interaction obligations. As demonstrated by the examples in this section it is not sufficient for an implementation to consider only one of the alt operands. In general, the alt characterizes the intersection of its operands, meaning that d_1 alt d_2 is a refinement of both d_1 and d_2. If we restrict refinement to narrowing, using alt between two specifications with xalt may be interpreted as 'the implementation must include the inherent nondeterminism specified by at least one of the alternatives'.

3.6   Properties of xalt and Refinement

As for alt, xalt is

- associative: d_1 xalt $(d_2$ xalt $d_3) = (d_1$ xalt $d_2)$ xalt d_3
- commutative: d_1 xalt $d_2 = d_2$ xalt d_1

This follows trivially from the associativity and commutativity of $\cup$.
With respect to xalt, alt is

- right distributive: $(d_1$ xalt $d_2)$ alt $d_3 = (d_1$ alt $d_3)$ xalt $(d_2$ alt $d_3)$
- left distributive: d_1 alt $(d_2$ xalt $d_3) = (d_1$ alt $d_2)$ xalt $(d_1$ alt $d_3)$

meaning that a specification with arbitrary nesting of alt and xalt may always be rewritten as a specification with xalt as the top-level operator. This is proved in [RRS06].

As in the simple case, we have that the refinement operator $\leadsto$ is:

- reflexive: $d \leadsto d$
- transitive: $d \leadsto d' \wedge d' \leadsto d'' \Rightarrow d \leadsto d''$
- monotonic with respect to alt and xalt:
  $$d_1 \leadsto d'_1 \wedge d_2 \leadsto d'_2 \Rightarrow d_1 \text{ alt } d_2 \leadsto d'_1 \text{ alt } d'_2 \wedge d_1 \text{ xalt } d_2 \leadsto d'_1 \text{ xalt } d'_2$$

These results are proved in [HHRS05a].

4 Probability

4.1 Motivation

Being able to specify probabilities add useful expressiveness to the specifications. One typical example is in the specification of a coin or a dice, where the alternatives must occur with the same probability. Another example is a gambling machine, where the winning alternatives should occur, but less often than the losing ones.

Interactions are mainly used for specifying communication scenarios. Probabilities are equally relevant in this setting, for instance to specify the probability that a message will never be received when sent over an unreliable communication channel. Another example is when specifying soft real-time constraints such as 'the user of the system will receive an answer within 10 seconds at least 90% of the time' (for more details, see [RHS05a]). As this example demonstrates, we are not only interested in assigning exact probabilities to all alternatives specified by an xalt, but also to specify a possible range for the probabilities, i.e. to allow underspecification with respect to probabilities as well as behaviors. In STAIRS, this is achieved by generalizing xalt to the palt operator.

4.2 Semantic Representation

Semantically, a probabilistic STAIRS specification is represented by a set of *probability obligations* (also called *p-obligations*). A p-obligation $((p, n), Q)$ consists of an interaction obligation (p, n) and a set of probabilities Q. In any valid implementation the p-obligation $((p, n), Q)$ should be selected with a probability in Q. The fact that Q is a set and not a single probability allows us to represent underspecification w.r.t. probabilities.

If a specification includes the p-obligation $((\{t_1, t_2\}, \mathcal{H} \setminus \{t_1, t_2\}), \{0.6\})$, this does not necessarily mean that the probability of getting either t_1 or t_2 is 0.6; it may be greater if there is another p-obligation $((p, n), Q)$ such that $\{t_1, t_2\} \not\subseteq n$. On the other hand, if a specification contains a p-obligation $((p, n), \{0.6\})$ such that $\{t_3, t_4\} \subseteq n$, then we know that the probability of getting a trace in $\{t_3, t_4\}$ is at most 0.4.

The palt construct expresses probabilistic choice. Use of the palt operator is the only way to assign probabilities different from 1. Before defining the semantics of the palt, we introduce the notion of probability decoration, used to specify the probabilities associated with the operands of a palt. It is defined by

$$\llbracket d;Q' \rrbracket \overset{\text{def}}{=} \{(o, Q * Q') \mid (o, Q) \in \llbracket d \rrbracket\} \tag{8}$$

where multiplication of probability sets is defined by

$$Q_1 * Q_2 \overset{\text{def}}{=} \{q_1 * q_2 \mid q_1 \in Q_1 \wedge q_2 \in Q_2\} \tag{9}$$

We also define the summation of n probability sets:

$$\sum_{i=1}^{n} Q_i \overset{\text{def}}{=} \{\min(\sum_{i=1}^{n} q_i, 1) \mid \forall i \le n : q_i \in Q_i\} \tag{10}$$

The palt operator describes the probabilistic choice between two or more alternative operands whose joint probability should add up to one. Formally, the palt is defined by

$$\llbracket \mathsf{palt}(d_1;Q_1, \ldots, d_n;Q_n) \rrbracket \overset{\text{def}}{=} \tag{11}$$

$$\{(\oplus \bigcup_{i \in N} \{po_i\}, \sum_{i \in N} \pi_2.po_i) \mid$$

$$N \subseteq \{1, \ldots, n\} \wedge N \ne \varnothing \wedge \forall i \in N : po_i \in \llbracket d_i;Q_i \rrbracket\} \tag{a}$$

$$\cup \ \{(\oplus \bigcup_{i=1}^{n} \llbracket d_i;Q_i \rrbracket, \{1\} \cap \sum_{i=1}^{n} Q_i)\} \tag{b}$$

where $\pi_2.po$ returns the probability set of the p-obligation po and $\oplus$ is an operator for combining the interaction obligations of a set S of p-obligations into a single interaction obligation, defined as

$$\oplus S \overset{\text{def}}{=} ((\bigcup_{((p,n),Q) \in S} p) \cap (\bigcap_{((p,n),Q) \in S} p \cup n), \bigcap_{((p,n),Q) \in S} n) \tag{12}$$

We now explain definition 11 in detail. We first look at 11a. If we restricted each N to be a singleton set then this part of the definition could be written equivalently as $\bigcup_{i=1}^{n} \llbracket d_i;Q_i \rrbracket$. This would correspond to the definition of xalt and means simply that each probabilistic alternative should be reflected in a valid implementation.

By including also the cases where N is any non-empty subset of $\{1, \ldots, n\}$ we are able to define the semantics as a set of p-obligations instead of as a multiset. The operator $\oplus$ characterizes the traces allowed by all the p-obligations in its argument set: A trace t is positive if it is positive according to at least one p-obligation and not inconclusive according to any; t is negative only if it is negative according to all p-obligations; traces that are inconclusive according to at least one p-obligation remain inconclusive. So if a p-obligation $((p, n), Q)$ occurs for example in two operands of the palt, then the resulting semantics will contain a p-obligation $((p, n), Q + Q)$.

The single p-obligation in 11b requires the probabilities of the operands to add up to one. If it is impossible to choose one probability from each Q_i so that the sum is 1, then the probability set will be empty and the specification is not implementable.

We also redefine the refuse and alt operators to take probabilities into account. Redefining positive traces as negative does not influence probabilities, so refuse is defined simply by

$$[\![\text{ refuse } d]\!] \overset{\text{def}}{=} \{((\varnothing, p \cup n), Q) \mid ((p, n), Q) \in [\![d]\!]\} \tag{13}$$

The alt construct captures underspecification with respect to traces. Two sets of p-obligations are combined by taking the pairwise combination of p-obligations from each set. As before, interaction obligations are combined by taking the union of the positive traces and the union of the negative traces. In Section 3.5 we showed that the resulting interaction obligation is a refinement of both the original ones, and therefore represents both of these interaction obligations. Since the two p-obligations from the different operands are chosen independently from each other, probabilities are multiplied. Formally:

$$[\![d_1 \text{ alt } d_2]\!] \overset{\text{def}}{=} \{(o_1 \uplus o_2, Q_1 * Q_2) \mid (o_1, Q_1) \in [\![d_1]\!] \wedge (o_2, Q_2) \in [\![d_2]\!]\} \tag{14}$$

4.3   Refinement Revisited

A p-obligation is refined by either refining its interaction obligation, or by reducing its set of probabilities. Formally, a p-obligation $((p', n'), Q')$ is a refinement of a p-obligation $((p, n), Q)$, written $((p, n), Q) \rightsquigarrow ((p', n'), Q')$, iff

$$(p, n) \rightsquigarrow (p', n') \wedge Q' \subseteq Q \tag{15}$$

All abstract p-obligations must be represented by a p-obligation also at the refined level, unless it has 0 as an acceptable probability, which means that it does not need to be implemented. Formally, a specification d' is a refinement of a specification d, written $d \rightsquigarrow d'$, iff

$$\forall po \in [\![d]\!] : (0 \notin \pi_2.po \Rightarrow \exists po' \in [\![d']\!] : po \rightsquigarrow po') \tag{16}$$

We now explain further why also the cases where N is any non-singular subset of $\{1, \ldots, n\}$ is included in definition 11a. Firstly, we want to avoid a situation where two p-obligations (o_1, Q_1) and (o_2, Q_2) coming from different operands of a palt are represented *only* by a single p-obligation (o, Q) that is a refinement of both (o_1, Q_1) and (o_2, Q_2) at the concrete level. We avoid this since also the p-obligation $(\oplus\{(o_1, Q_1), (o_2, Q_2)\}, Q_1 + Q_2)$ is included in the semantics and hence needs to be represented at the concrete level.

Secondly, it should be possible to let a single p-obligation at the abstract level be represented by a combination of p-obligations at the concrete level, as long as each of these p-obligations are valid refinements of the original p-obligation w.r.t. interaction obligations and their probability sets add up to a subset of the original probability set. The inclusion of the combined p-obligations (resulting from N sets with more than one element) in the palt semantics makes this possible.

Our definition of refinement also explains why we have chosen to assign sets of acceptable probabilities to the operands, and not simply lower bounds. Consider the following specifications:

$$d_a = \text{palt}(d_1;[\tfrac{1}{5}\ldots 1], d_2;[\tfrac{1}{5}\ldots 1], d_3;[\tfrac{1}{5}\ldots 1])$$
$$d_b = \text{palt}(d_1;[\tfrac{1}{5}\ldots\tfrac{1}{2}], d_2;[\tfrac{1}{5}\ldots\tfrac{1}{2}], d_3;[\tfrac{1}{5}\ldots\tfrac{1}{2}])$$
$$d_c = \text{palt}(d_1;\{\tfrac{1}{5}\}, d_2;\{\tfrac{1}{5}\}, d_3;\{\tfrac{3}{5}\})$$

Then d_c is a refinement of d_a, but not of d_b. So by using only lower bounds we would have less expressive power.

4.4   Simple Example

We now demonstrate a simple refinement in probabilistic STAIRS, building on the DiceCoin/DiceCoin2 example from Section 3.4. Let pDiceCoin be a probabilistic version of DiceCoin where the probabilities of odd and even numbers are the same, represented syntactically and semantically by

$$\text{pDiceCoin} \quad = \quad \text{palt}(\text{Throw135};\{\tfrac{1}{2}\}, \text{Throw246};\{\tfrac{1}{2}\})$$
$$[\![\,\text{pDiceCoin}\,]\!] \quad = \quad \{\,((\{1,3,5\},\{2,4,6\}),\{\tfrac{1}{2}\}),((\{2,4,6\},\{1,3,5\}),\{\tfrac{1}{2}\}),$$
$$((\{1,2,3,4,5,6\},\varnothing),\{1\})\,\}$$

The semantic representation tells us that the dice should be able to produce at least one number in $\{1,3,5\}$, and the probability for this alternative should be $\tfrac{1}{2}$. Similarly, the dice should be able to produce at least one number in $\{2,4,6\}$, with probability $\tfrac{1}{2}$. Obviously, the probability of producing a number in $\{1,2,3,4,5,6\}$ should then be 1.

Suppose now that we require that the dice should be fair w.r.t. the odd numbers, give equal chances of odd and even number, and not produce any even number different from 6. We first let $[\![\,\text{Throw1}\,]\!] = \{\,((\{1\},\{2,3,4,5,6\}),\{1\})\,\}$ and similarly for the other numbers. We then refine Throw135 by Throw135Fairly:

$$\text{Throw135Fairly} = \text{palt}(\text{Throw1};\{\tfrac{1}{3}\}, \text{Throw3};\{\tfrac{1}{3}\}, \text{Throw5};\{\tfrac{1}{3}\})$$
$$[\![\,\text{Throw135Fairly}\,]\!] = \{\,((\{1\},\{2,3,4,5,6\}),\{\tfrac{1}{3}\})\,,$$
$$((\{3\},\{1,2,4,5,6\}),\{\tfrac{1}{3}\})\,,((\{5\},\{1,2,3,4,6\}),\{\tfrac{1}{3}\})\,,$$
$$((\{1,3\},\{2,4,5,6\}),\{\tfrac{2}{3}\})\,,((\{1,5\},\{2,3,4,6\}),\{\tfrac{2}{3}\})\,,$$
$$((\{3,5\},\{1,2,4,6\}),\{\tfrac{2}{3}\})\,,((\{1,3,5\},\{2,4,6\}),\{1\})\,\}$$

As Throw135 has the semantics $\{((\{1,3,5\},\{2,4,6\}),\{1\})\}$, we see that this is indeed a valid refinement, since the only p-obligation in $[\![\,\text{Throw135}\,]\!]$ is identical to one of the p-obligations in $[\![\,\text{Throw135Fairly}\,]\!]$. A dice that is fair w.r.t. the odd numbers, has equal chances of odd and even numbers, and does not produce any even number different from 6 can now be expressed by pDiceCoin2 = palt(Throw135Fairly;$\{\frac{1}{2}\}$, Throw6;$\{\frac{1}{2}\}$)

$[\![$ pDiceCoin2 $]\!]$ = { $((\{1\}, \{2,3,4,5,6\}), \{\frac{1}{6}\})$,

$\quad ((\{3\}, \{1,2,4,5,6\}), \{\frac{1}{6}\})$, $((\{5\}, \{1,2,3,4,6\}), \{\frac{1}{6}\})$,

$\quad ((\{1,3\}, \{2,4,5,6\}), \{\frac{1}{3}\})$, $((\{1,5\}, \{2,3,4,6\}), \{\frac{1}{3}\})$,

$\quad ((\{3,5\}, \{1,2,4,6\}), \{\frac{1}{3}\})$, $((\{1,6\}, \{2,3,4,5\}), \{\frac{2}{3}\})$,

$\quad ((\{3,6\}, \{1,2,4,5\}), \{\frac{2}{3}\})$, $((\{5,6\}, \{1,2,3,4\}), \{\frac{2}{3}\})$,

$\quad ((\{1,3,6\}, \{2,4,5\}), \{\frac{5}{6}\})$, $((\{1,5,6\}, \{2,3,4\}), \{\frac{5}{6}\})$,

$\quad ((\{3,5,6\}, \{1,2,4\}), \{\frac{5}{6}\})$, $((\{1,3,5\}, \{2,4,6\}), \{\frac{1}{2}\})$,

$\quad ((\{6\}, \{1,2,3,4,5\}), \{\frac{1}{2}\})$, $((\{1,3,5,6\}, \{2,4\}), \{1\})$ }

Each p-obligation in $[\![$ pDiceCoin $]\!]$ has a refining p-obligation in $[\![$ pDiceCoin2 $]\!]$, so pDiceCoin ⤳ pDiceCoin2 holds.

4.5 Relating palt to xalt and alt

In STAIRS, every xalt-operand represents an alternative that must be reflected in the implementation. Its probability should be greater than 0, but is otherwise unknown. In probabilistic STAIRS, a specification $\mathsf{xalt}(d_1, \ldots, d_n)$ is therefore interpreted as $\mathsf{palt}(d_1;Q, \ldots, d_n;Q)$ where $Q = \langle 0, \ldots, 1]$.

We now discuss what it means to have probabilistic STAIRS specifications that combine the use of the alt and palt operators. We hope the meaning of underspecification within probabilistic alternative is intuitively clear, and do not go further into this. Instead we show a probabilistic version of the previous examples. pCoin specifies a coin, while pDice specifies a 3-sided dice:

$$\begin{aligned}
\text{pCoin} \quad &= \quad \mathsf{palt}(\text{Heads};\{\tfrac{1}{2}\}, \text{Tails};\{\tfrac{1}{2}\}) \\
\text{pDice} \quad &= \quad \mathsf{palt}(\text{One};\{\tfrac{1}{3}\}, \text{Two};\{\tfrac{1}{3}\}, \text{Three};\{\tfrac{1}{3}\}) \\
[\![\text{pCoin}]\!] \quad &= \quad \{((\{h\}, \{t\}), \{\tfrac{1}{2}\}), ((\{t\}, \{h\}), \{\tfrac{1}{2}\}), ((\{h,t\}, \varnothing), \{1\})\} \\
[\![\text{pDice}]\!] \quad &= \quad \{((\{1\}, \{2,3\}), \{\tfrac{1}{3}\}), ((\{2\}, \{1,3\}), \{\tfrac{1}{3}\}), ((\{3\}, \{1,2\}), \{\tfrac{1}{3}\}), \\
& \qquad ((\{1,2\}, \{3\}), \{\tfrac{2}{3}\}), ((\{1,3\}, \{2\}), \{\tfrac{2}{3}\}), ((\{2,3\}, \{1\}), \{\tfrac{2}{3}\}), \\
& \qquad ((\{1,2,3\}, \varnothing), \{1\})\}
\end{aligned}$$

These examples use only a single probability in each probability set (there is no underspecification w.r.t. probabilities). Figure 4 shows the semantics of

pCoin/Dice = pCoin alt pDice

We see that the interaction obligation of each p-obligation in pCoin/Dice refines the interaction obligation of a p-obligation for both pCoin and pDice. For example, the interaction obligation of the leftmost, uppermost p-obligation in Figure 4 represent the first p-obligation of both $[\![$ pCoin $]\!]$ and $[\![$ pDice $]\!]$. Since these represent two independent probabilistic choices it is reasonable to multiply their probabilities. This also gives the nice result that if we consider

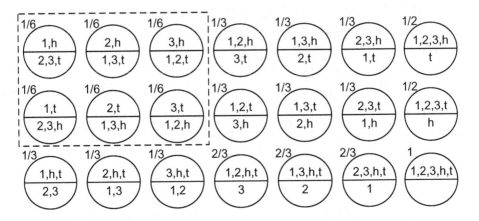

Fig. 4. The semantics of (pCoin alt pDice) in probabilistic STAIRS

only 'pure' p-obligations (those we get from definition 11a in the cases where N is a singleton set), then their probabilities add up to 1. In Figure 4 these 'pure' p-obligations are enclosed by the dotted line.

4.6   Properties of alt, palt and Refinement

For alt, the revised definition 14 is still associative and commutative.

In contrast to xalt, palt is *not* associative. The order in which obligations are combined according to 11b is significant, since this determines which probabilities must add up to 1. Remember that the requirement that probabilities for the operands add up to 1 applies to each occurrence of a palt operator, independently of the nesting level. For similar reasons, alt is not distributive with respect to palt. Consider the following specifications:

$$d_a = (\text{palt}(d_1; Q_1, d_2; Q_2)) \text{ alt } (\text{palt}(d_3; Q_3, d_4; Q_4))$$
$$d_b = \text{palt}((\text{palt}(d_1; Q_1, d_2; Q_2) \text{ alt } d_3); Q_3, (\text{palt}(d_1; Q_1, d_2; Q_2) \text{ alt } d_4); Q_4)$$

In d_b we are free to choose different probabilities from the sets Q_1 and Q_2 in the two operands of the outermost palt. In d_a there is no such freedom, so in this respect d_a is more restrictive than d_b.

However, we do have commutativity of palt:

$$\forall\, i, j \in [1, n] : \text{palt}(\ldots, d_i; Q_i, \ldots, d_j; Q_j, \ldots) = \text{palt}(\ldots, d_j; Q_j, \ldots, d_i; Q_i, \ldots)$$

This follows trivially from the commutativity of ∪.

For probabilistic STAIRS, the refinement operator ⤳ is:

- reflexive, transitive, and monotonic with respect to alt
- restricted monotonic with respect to palt:
  $$(\forall\, i \in [1 : n] : d_i \rightsquigarrow d_i' \wedge Q_i' \subseteq Q_i \wedge \oplus[\![\, d_i \,]\!] \rightsquigarrow \oplus[\![\, d_i' \,]\!]) \Rightarrow$$
  $$\text{palt}(d_1; Q_1, \ldots, d_n; Q_n) \rightsquigarrow \text{palt}(d_1'; Q_1', \ldots, d_n'; Q_n')$$

This is proved in [RHS05b], which also motivates the last requirement in the monotonicity for palt.

The interpretation given for xalt in probabilistic STAIRS is reasonable, as $\mathsf{xalt}(d_1, \ldots, d_n)$ and $\mathsf{palt}(d_1; \langle 0 \ldots 1], \ldots d_n; \langle 0 \ldots 1])$ are refinements of each other when abstracting away the probabilities. This is proved in [RRS06].

5   Related Work

Most specification languages do not distinguish between underspecification and inherent nondeterminism the way it is done in STAIRS. The most well known dialects of interactions are UML [OMG04] and MSC [ITU99]. Neither of these have two different operators corresponding to alt and xalt. In practice, the alt operator of UML is probably used by different groups to describe both inherent nondeterminism and underspecification.

Live Sequence Charts [DH01] and [HM03] is a dialect of MSC where a (part) of an interaction may be designated as either universal (mandatory) or existential (optional). Explicit criteria in the form of precharts decide when the chart applies; whenever the communication behavior described by the prechart occurs, behavior described by the chart *must* follow (in the case of universal locations) or *may* follow (in the case of existential locations). Universal charts specify all allowed traces. This is therefore not the same as inherently nondeterministic alternatives in STAIRS, since the latter only specifies some of the traces that must be present in an implementation.

CSP [Hoa85] defines two different operators for nondeterministic choice. Their difference, however, is explained in terms of internal versus external choice. This is not the same distinction as the one between underspecification and inherent nondeterminism. As an example, let ? denote an input event, ! denote an output event, and seq be the operator for sequential composition in the STAIRS specification $(?a \text{ seq } (!b \text{ xalt } !c)) \text{ alt } ((?b \text{ seq } !d))$. Here, the environment may choose between the two alt-operands, corresponding to external choice in CSP. However, the choice between !b and !c should be inherently nondeterministic, a requirement that may not be expressed using the CSP operators, while replacing xalt with alt, would correspond to internal choice in CSP.

[SBDB97] extends the process algebraic language LOTOS [ISO89] with a disjunction operator for specifying implementation freedom (i.e. underspecification), leaving the LOTOS choice operator to be used for inherent nondeterminism. The disjunction operator is similar to our alt operator, and the choice operator corresponds to xalt. An important difference between disjunction and alt is that an implementation will have to select exactly one of the disjunction operands, while it may include several of the traces specified by alt.

Probabilistic automata [Seg95] includes both nondeterminism and probabilistic choice. Underspecification with respect to probabilities is represented by nondeterministic choices between distributions. As for automata in general, specifications are complete in the sense that there is no notion of inconclusive behavior.

In [MM99] a probabilistic extension of Dijkstra's Guarded Command Language GCL [Dij76] called $pGCL$ is presented. The language includes both an operator ⊓ for 'demonic' choice and an operator $_p\oplus$ for probabilistic choice. The following intuitive explanation is given for the meaning of the construct *this* ⊓ *that*: 'The customer will be happy with either *this* or *that*; and the implementer may choose between them according to his own concerns.' This indicates that the role of the ⊓ operator in a *pGCL* specification is to express underspecification, similar to the role of the alt operator in (probabilistic) STAIRS. By specifying probabilistic choices the role of the $_p\oplus$ operator in *pGCL* corresponds to the role of palt in probabilistic STAIRS. There is no notion of inconclusive behavior in *pGCL*.

[Heh04] shows how probabilistic reasoning can be applied to predicative programs and specifications. Nondeterminism is disjunction, and equivalent to a deterministic choice in which the determining expression is a variable of unknown value (probability). Nondeterminism gives freedom to the implementer; it can be refined by a deterministic or a probabilistic choice. Since the implementer is not forced to produce both alternatives, the nondeterminism in [Heh04] corresponds to underspecification in STAIRS. Cases where both alternatives need to be possible are expressed by a probabilistic choice, as in probabilistic STAIRS.

6   Conclusion

This article has shown the need for underspecification, inherent nondeterminism and probability in specifications. We have demonstrated that these phenomena are adequately expressed in STAIRS and probabilistic STAIRS by the operators alt, xalt and palt. New insight has been gained into the interplay between these operators through studies of simple examples. The focus of this paper has been on the theoretical understanding of how underspecification and inherent nondeterminism is expressed in specifications and represented semantically. The simplicity of the specifications has allowed us to properly explain their semantic representations. For more examples related to communication see [HHRS05b], [RHS05c] and [RHS05a]. We firmly believe that STAIRS and probabilistic STAIRS offer a suitable expressiveness for practical specifications, and intend to show this in the future through studies of real-life specifications.

The research on which this paper reports has been partly carried out within the context of the IKT-2010 project SARDAS (15295/431) and the IKT SOS project ENFORCE (164382/V30), both funded by the Research Council of Norway. We thank Roberto Segala and the other members of the SARDAS project for useful discussions related to this work. We also thank the anonymous reviewers for constructive feedback.

References

[DH01]   W. Damm and D. Harel. LSCs: Breathing life into message sequence charts. *Formal Methods in System Design*, 19(1):45–80, 2001.

[Dij76]   E. W. Dijkstra. *A Discipline of Programming*. Prentice-Hall, 1976.

[Heh04]   E. C. R. Hehner. Probabilistic predicative programming. In Dexter Kozen and Carron Shankland, editors, *Mathematics of Program Construction, 7th International Conference*, number 3125 in Lecture Notes in Computer Science, pages 169–185. Springer, 2004.

[HHRS05a]   Ø. Haugen, K. E. Husa, R. K. Runde, and K. Stølen. Why timed sequence diagrams require three-event semantics. Technical Report 309, Department of Informatics, University of Oslo, 2005.

[HHRS05b]   Ø. Haugen, K.E. Husa, R.K. Runde, and K. Stølen. STAIRS towards formal design with sequence diagrams. *Software and System Modeling*, 4(4):349–458, 2005.

[HM03]   D. Harel and R. Marelly. *Come, Let's Play: Scenario-Based Programming Using LSC's and the Play-Engine*. Springer, 2003.

[Hoa85]   C. A. R. Hoare. *Communicating Sequential Processes* Prentice-Hall, 1985.

[ISO89]   International Standards Organization. *Information Processing Systems – Open Systems Interconnection - Lotos – a Formal Description Technique Based on the Temporal Ordering of Observational Behaviour – ISO 8807*, 1989.

[ITU99]   International Telecommunication Union. *Recommendation Z.120 — Message Sequence Chart (MSC)*, 1999.

[MM99]   C. Morgan and A. McIver. pGCL: Formal reasoning for random algorithms. *South African Computer Journal*, 22:14–27, 1999.

[OMG04]   Object Management Group. *UML 2.0 Superstructure Specification*, ptc/04-10-02 edition, 2004.

[RHS05a]   A. Refsdal, K. E. Husa, and K. Stølen. Specification and refinement of soft real-time requirements using sequence diagrams. In P. Pettersson and W. Yi, editors, *Proc. Formal Modeling and Analysis of Timed Systems: Third International Conference, FORMATS, 2005*, number 3829 in Lecture Notes in Computer Science, pages 32–48. Springer, 2005.

[RHS05b]   A. Refsdal, K. E. Husa, and K. Stølen. Specification and refinement of soft real-time requirements using sequence diagrams. Technical Report 323, Department of Informatics, University of Oslo, 2005.

[RHS05c]   R.K. Runde, Ø. Haugen, and K. Stølen. Refining UML interactions with underspecification and nondeterminism. *Nordic Journal of Computing*, 12(2):157–188, 2005.

[Ros95]   A. W. Roscoe. CSP and determinism in security modelling. In *Proc. IEEE Symposium on Security and Privacy*, pages 114–127. IEEE Press, 1995.

[RRS06]   A. Refsdal, R. K. Runde, and K. Stølen. Underspecification, inherent nondeterminism and probability in sequence diagrams. Technical Report 335, Department of Informatics, University of Oslo, 2006.

[SBDB97]   M.W.A. Steen, H. Bowman, J. Derrick, and E.A. Boiten. Disjunction of LOTOS specifications. In T. Mizuno, N. Shiratori, T. Higashino, and A. Togashi, editors, *Formal Description Techniques and Protocol Specification, Testing and Verification: FORTE X / PSTV XVII '97*, pages 177–192. Chapman & Hall, 1997.

[Seg95]   R. Segala. *Modeling and Verification of Randomized Distributed Real-Time Systems*. PhD thesis, Massachusetts Institute of Technology, 1995.

Generating Instance Models from Meta Models

Karsten Ehrig[1], Jochen M. Küster[2],
Gabriele Taentzer[3], and Jessica Winkelmann[3]

[1] Department of Computer Science, University of Leicester, UK
karsten@mcs.le.ac.uk
[2] IBM Zurich Research Laboratory, CH-8803 Rüschlikon, Switzerland
jku@zurich.ibm.com
[3] Department of Computer Science, Technical University of Berlin, Germany
{gabi, danye}@cs.tu-berlin.de

Abstract. Meta modeling is a wide-spread technique to define visual languages, with the UML being the most prominent one. Despite several advantages of meta modeling such as ease of use, the meta modeling approach has one disadvantage: It is not constructive i. e. it does not offer a direct means of generating instances of the language. This disadvantage poses a severe limitation for certain applications. For example, when developing model transformations, it is desirable to have enough valid instance models available for large-scale testing. Producing such a large set by hand is tedious. In the related problem of compiler testing, a string grammar together with a simple generation algorithm is typically used to produce words of the language automatically. In this paper, we introduce instance-generating graph grammars for creating instances of meta models, thereby overcoming the main deficit of the meta modeling approach for defining languages.

1 Introduction

With models expressed in the Unified Modeling Language (UML) [14] becoming widely used in software engineering, also the meta modeling approach to define the syntax of modeling languages has gained a wide acceptance: Commonly, a meta model is designed which defines the abstract syntax of the language in a declarative way. Instantiation of the meta model then yields a concrete model.

The meta modeling approach has several advantages, one of them being that a visual meta model allows a quick grasp of the concepts being defined. Further, the meta modeling approach is also beneficial when it comes to defining complex modeling languages, consisting of several individual models. Nevertheless, there exists also one disadvantage: Whereas constructing words of a language defined by a string grammar can easily be done by applying grammar derivations, meta model instantiation is hard to operationalize.

In common applications of the UML, this does not pose a problem because the process of instantiation is performed by the software engineer when constructing models. However, there are certain applications when an automatic approach is needed: In compiler testing [4], the generation of a large amount of models from

R. Gorrieri and H. Wehrheim (Eds.): FMOODS 2006, LNCS 4037, pp. 156–170, 2006.
© IFIP International Federation for Information Processing 2006

a context-free grammar is common practice and a key issue in being able to test compilers automatically. Whereas until now such a problem could be neglected in model engineering based on the meta modeling approach, this situation drastically changes with the idea of model driven architecture [13] and the more widespread usage of model transformations. For testing model transformations, a large set of automatically generated instance models must be available in order to ensure the quality of the model transformation developed. Another area requiring an operational description of a language defined by a meta model is automatic editor generation for domain specific languages.

Graph grammars [5] provide a constructive, well-studied approach to language definition with a formal foundation that allows to prove important properties. However, the relationship between meta models and graph grammars has not been studied in depth so far, but started in [3]. Deriving an *instance-generating* graph grammar from an existing meta model is complicated. Here, one has to ensure that every model that is created by a derivation of the graph grammar is a valid instance of the meta model and further it is desirable that for every instance of the meta model there exists a derivation in the graph grammar. This completeness of the instance-generating graph grammar is important for model transformation testing because it allows a complete coverage of all possible inputs. For editor generation, it ensures that the language defined by the meta model is indeed the one supported by the editor.

In this paper, we present our approach for automatic derivation of instance-generating graph grammars from meta models. We first introduce meta models in Section 2 and graph transformation in Section 3. In Section 4, we explain how an instance-generating graph grammar can be derived for a meta model containing all main features. OCL constraints are not yet considered during the generation process, but have to be checked afterwards. Section 5 contains the proof that the derived graph grammar generates exactly those instances induced by the given meta model. As a consequence, the concept of the instance-generating graph grammar allows to formally show the completeness of the generated instances. We conclude by a discussion of related and future work.

2   Metamodels with OCL-Constraints

Visual languages such as the UML [14] are commonly defined using a meta modeling approach. In this approach, a visual language is defined using a meta model to describe the abstract syntax of the language. A meta model can be considered as a class diagram on the metalevel, i. e. it contains meta classes, meta associations and cardinality constraints. Further features include special kinds of associations such as aggregation, composition and inheritance as well as abstract meta classes which cannot be instantiated.

The instance of the meta model must conform to the cardinality constraints. In addition, instances of meta models may be further restricted by the use of additional constraints specified in the Object Constraint Language (OCL) [15].

Figure 1 shows a slightly simplified statechart meta model (based on [14]) which will be used as running example. A state machine has one top CompositeState. A CompositeState contains a set of StateVertices where such a StateVertex can be either an InitialState or a State. Note that StateVertex and State are modeled as abstract classes. A State can be a SimpleState, a CompositeState or a FinalState. A Transition connects a source and a target state. Furthermore, an Event and an Action may be associated to a transition. Aggre-

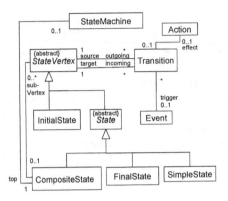

Fig. 1. Meta Model for statecharts

gations and compositions have been simplified to an association in our approach but they could be treated separately as well. For clarity, we hide association names, but show only role names in Figure 1. The association names between classes StateVertex and Transition are called source and target as corresponding role names. The names of all other associations are equal to their corresponding role names. Since we want to concentrate on the main concepts of meta models here, we do not consider attributes in our example. Having an instance at hand, it is straight forward to generate attribute values in a post processing step.

The set of instances of the meta model can be restricted by additional OCL constraints. For the simplified statecharts example at least the following OCL constraints are needed:

1. A final state cannot have any outgoing transitions: context FinalState inv:
   self.outgoing->size()=0
2. A final state has at least one incoming transition: context FinalState inv:
   self.incoming->size()>=1
3. An initial state cannot have any incoming transitions: context InitialState inv:
   self.incoming->size()=0
4. Transitions outgoing InitialStates must always target a State: context Transition inv: self.source.oclIsTypeOf(InitialState) implies self.target.
   oclIsKindOf(State)

The complexity of generating instances of meta models crucially depends on the language elements used within meta models. For simple meta models without any constraints (not even multiplicity constraints) and inheritance, instantiation is rather straightforward by creating instances of metaclasses and associations. However, meta models as commonly used in language specification documents such as [14] make heavily use of multiplicity and OCL constraints as well as inheritance and abstract classes. For instantiation of such meta models, more sophisticated techniques are needed. In particular, there is a need for a systematic derivation of instances of meta models. In the following, we will describe the concepts of graph transformation which will represent the formal basis of our approach (inspired by the use of context-free grammars for deriving textual languages).

3   Graph Transformation

In this section we present the formal theory of *typed graph transformations with inheritance* (see [3]), which will be the basis for the formal background for *Instance Generating Graph Grammars (IGGG)* in Section 5.

In object-oriented modeling, graphs can be used at two levels: the type level (a class diagram) and the instance level (an instance of the class diagram). This typing concept has been described by *typed graphs* [5], where a fixed *type graph* serves as abstract representation of the class diagram. As in object-oriented modelling, types can be attributed and structured by an inheritance relation. Types should be divided into abstract types which cannot have instances and concrete types. Instances of a *type graph with inheritance (TGI)* are object graphs equipped with a structure-preserving mapping to the type graph. A class diagram can thus be represented by a type graph with inheritance plus a set of constraints over this type graph expressing multiplicities. For examples of the following definitions we refer to Section 4.

Definition 1 (type graph with inheritance). *A type graph with inheritance is a triple $TGI = (TG, I, Abs)$ consisting of a type graph $TG = (TG_V, TG_E, src_{TG}, tgt_{TG})$ (with a set TG_V of nodes, a set TG_E of edges, source and target functions $src_{TG}, tgt_{TG} : TG_E \rightarrow TG_V$), an acyclic inheritance relation $I \subseteq TG_V \times TG_V$, and a set $Abs \subseteq TG_V$, called abstract nodes. For each $x \in TG_V$, the inheritance clan is defined by $clan_I(x) = \{y \in TG_V \mid (y, x) \in I^*\}$, where I^* is the reflexive-transitive closure of I.*

A graph can be typed over the type graph with inheritance by a pair of functions, from nodes to node types and from edges to edge types, respectively. This pair of functions does not constitute a graph morphism, but will be called *clan morphism*; it uniquely characterizes the type morphism into the flattened type graph.

Definition 2 (clan morphism). *Let $TGI = (TG, I, Abs)$ with $TG = (TG_V, TG_E, src_{TG}, tgt_{TG})$ be a type graph with inheritance. A clan-morphism $ctp : G \rightarrow TGI$ from a graph $G = (G_V, G_E, src_G, tgt_G)$ to TGI is a pair $ctp = (ctp_V : G_V \rightarrow TG_V, ctp_E : G_E \rightarrow TG_E)$ such that for all $e \in G_E$ the following holds:*

- *$ctp_V \circ src_G(e) \in clan_I(src_{TG} \circ ctp_E(e))$ and*
- *$ctp_V \circ tgt_G(e) \in clan_I(tgt_{TG} \circ ctp_E(e))$.*

(G, ctp) is called a clan-typed graph.

The main ingredients of graph grammars are graph rules which will be defined in Definition 4. Between clan-typed graphs we use type-refining morphisms (see also Def. 5 in [16]) where a node with type t can be mapped to a node with a type in $clan(t)$. In the following, we call a type-refining morphism just morphism. If each node is mapped to a node with the same type, the corresponding morphism is called type-preserving.

For controlling a rule application, simple negative application conditions $NAC(x)$ and atomic application conditions $P(x, \wedge_{i \in I} x_i))$ are defined which are needed in Section 4. Although $NAC(x)$ is a special case of $P(x, \wedge_{i \in I} x_i))$ with $I = \emptyset$, we introduce both kinds of application conditions, due to more clear definition of instance generating rules.

Definition 3 (application condition). *A simple negative application condition is of the form $NAC(x)$, where $x : L \to X$ is an injective morphism. A morphism $m : L \to G$ satisfies $NAC(x)$ if there does not exist an injective morphism $p : X \to G$ with $p \circ x = m$. An atomic application condition is of the form $P(x, \wedge_{i \in I} x_i)$ where $x : L \to X$ and $x_i : X \to C_i$ with $i \in I$ are injective morphisms. A morphism $m : L \to G$ satisfies $P(x, \wedge_{i \in I} x_i)$ if for all injective morphisms $p : X \to G$ with $p \circ x = m$ there does exist an $i \in I$ and an injective morphism $q_i : C_i \to G$ with $q_i \circ x_i = p$.*

Definition 4 (rules). *A rule typed over a type graph $TGI = (TG, I, Abs)$ with inheritance is given by $p = (L \xleftarrow{l} K \xrightarrow{r} R, A_p)$, where L, K, R are clan-typed graphs, l and r are type-preserving injective graph morphisms, $ctp_R^{-1}(Abs) \subseteq r(K_V)$, and A_p is a set of application conditions of the form $NAC(x)$ or $P(x, \wedge_{i \in I} x_i)$ as defined in Def. 3.*

Definition 5 (rule matching and application). *Given a rule p as in Def. 4 and a clan-typed graph (G, ctp_G), then m is a match of p in G if*

- *m is an injective match of the rule $p = (L \xleftarrow{l} K \xrightarrow{r} R, A_p)$ as defined in Def. 4 in the graph G;*
- *$t_K(x_1) = t_K(x_2)$ for $t_K = ctp_G \circ m \circ l$ and $x_1, x_2 \in K_V$ with $r(x_1) = r(x_2)$;*
- *m satisfies all simple negative application conditions and all atomic applications in A_p.*

Given a match m, a direct derivation $(G, ctp_G) \overset{p,m}{\Longrightarrow} (H, ctp_H)$ exists if there is a span of graph morphisms $G \leftarrow D \to H$ and a co-match $m^* : R \to H$ of p in H that give rise to a derivation in the double-pushout approach of untyped graph transformation as defined in [5] where pushouts are used to model the gluing of graphs.

Given a rule set R, $(G, ctp_G) \overset{*}{\Rightarrow}_R (H, ctp_H)$ is a finite sequence of an arbitrary number of direct derivations by rules of R. A derivation $(G, ctp_G) \overset{*}{\Rightarrow}_R (H, ctp_H)$ terminates, if $\nexists r \in R : (H, ctp_H) \Rightarrow_r (H', ctp_{H'})$.

4 Generating Instances by Graph Grammars

In this section, we introduce the idea of an instance-generating graph grammar that allows one to derive instances of an arbitrary meta model in a systematic way. The corresponding graph grammar requires (1) a start graph that will be the empty graph, (2) a type graph that is obtained by converting the meta model class diagram to a type graph and (3) graph grammar rules which are described below.

We use the concept of layered graph grammars [6] to order rule applications. Layer 1 rules create instances of each class. To generate all possible instances we have to allow an arbitrary number of applications of these rules, meaning that Layer 1 does not terminate and has to be interrupted by user interaction or after a random time period. Layer 2 rules deal with generating links corresponding to associations with at least one 1-multiplicity. Those rules have to be applied as long as possible to ensure the multiplicity constraints, requiring that rule application in this layer has to terminate. Layer 3 creates links corresponding to associations with $0..n$-multiplicities. The rules in this layer can be applied arbitrarily often because these links are optional.

We use abstract node types (corresponding to abstract classes) leading to the concept of abstract rules. An abstract rule contains at least one node of abstract type. For each concrete subtype of the abstract type this induces a corresponding rule.

Given a concrete meta model, assembling the rules derived, the type graph created and the empty start graph leads to an instance-generating graph grammar for this meta model. The rules of the instance-generating graph grammar are determined by the occurrence of specific meta model patterns: The idea is to associate to a specific meta model pattern a graph grammar rule that creates an instance of the meta model pattern under certain conditions. In the following, we describe the rules that we derive for common meta model patterns.

Instance-generating rules: Layer 1 of any instance-generating graph grammar (see pattern p_0 in Figure 2) contains rules of the form createE' where E' is replaced by the name of any non-abstract class. The meta model pattern for this rule is simply a class. For a concrete meta model, we will get such a create rule for each non-abstract class within the meta model, allowing us to create an arbitrary number of instances of all non-abstract classes.

We have three meta model patterns for the rules in Layer 2 (corresponding to the three possible multiplicity constraints) (see Fig. 3 and 4). The first rule for each pattern creates a link between existing instances. The NACs ensure, that the created link does not violate the multiplicity constraints (e.g. the two instances are not already connected by such a link, or the instance of A is not already connected to an instance of E).

To ensure the *to one* multiplicity on the specified association ends insertE'_a_ANewObj resp. insertE'_a_ANewObj2 creates a new instance of any concrete E' $\in clan(E)$ resp. A' $\in clan(A)$ if no application condition holds. In case of a 1 to * relation (see pattern p_1) a new instance of E' $\in clan(E)$ is created if no concrete instance of E is present, which is ensured by NAC_1. In case of a 1 to 0..1 or 1 to 1 relation (see pattern p_2 and p_3) the rule can only be applied if any match of an instance of E is already connected to an instance of A, which is ensured by the application condition. NAC_2 of the rules insertE'_a_ANewObj resp. insertE'_a_ANewObj2 requires that the instance of A is not connected to an instance of E yet.

Fig. 2. Rules for graph grammar derivation: Layer 1

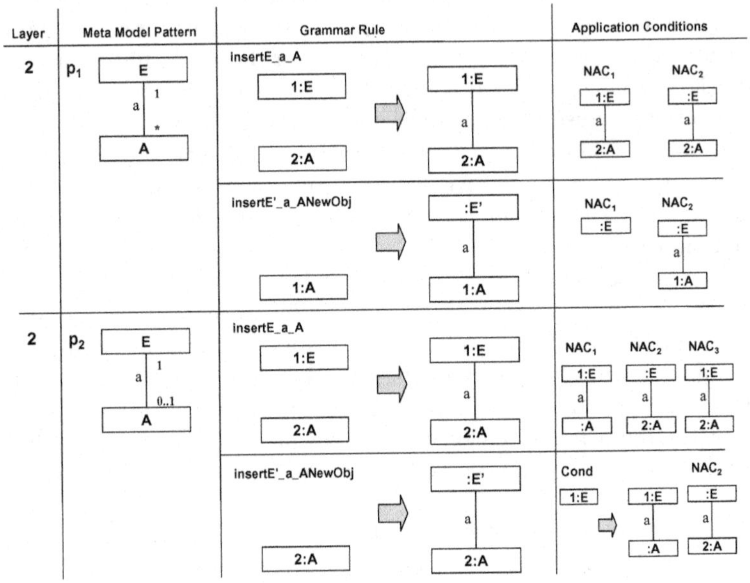

Fig. 3. Rules for graph grammar derivation: Layer 2

We also have three meta model patterns for the rules of Layer 3 (corresponding to the three possible multiplicity constraints) (see Fig. 5). The rules for these patterns create links between existing instances. The NACs ensure, that the created link does not violate the upper multiplicity constraints as in the first rules of the corresponding pattern in Layer 2. The graph grammar derivation rules in layer 3 can be applied *arbitrarily often*, they are terminating as described above.

Generating Statechart Instances: We now discuss an instance-generating graph grammar for the meta model of statecharts (see Figure 1). Due to space limitation we do not show the details of all rules. The example rules shown in Figure 6 - 8 construct a simple instance graph consisting of a state machine with its top CompositeState containing three state vertices and two transitions between them. In the application conditions shown in Figures 6 - 8 the node types are abbreviated (CS for CompositeState etc.).

First, we get Layer 1 rules for all concrete classes occurring in the class diagram. These are createStateMachine, createCompositeState, createSimpleState, createFinalState, createInitialState, createTransition, createEvent, and createAction.

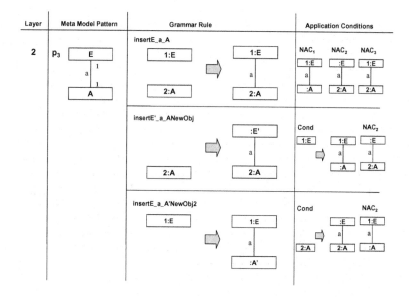

Fig. 4. Rules for graph grammar derivation: Layer 2

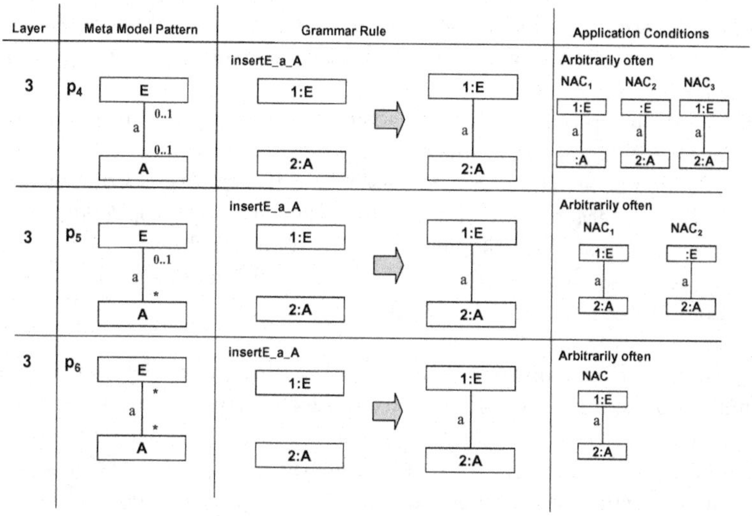

Fig. 5. Rules for graph grammar derivation: Layer 3

For association source between StateVertex and Transition (corresponding to an instance of pattern p_1), we derive four rules: one rule creates a link source between an existing StateVertex and an existing Transition. Further, for each concrete class that inherits from class StateVertex one rule is derived that creates the StateVertex, an InitialState, a CompositeState, SimpleState or a FinalState, and the link source. Note that the abstract class StateVertex could be matched

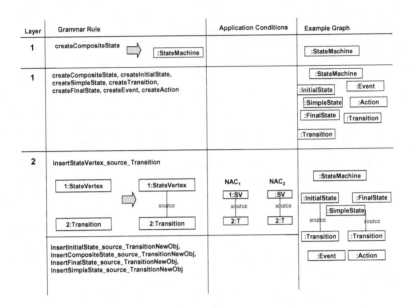

Fig. 6. Example Grammar Rules 1

to any of its concrete subclasses InitialState, CompositeState, FinalState, and SimpleState. For association target between StateVertex and Transition, similar rules are derived.

For association top between StateMachine and CompositeState, an instance of pattern p_2, we derive the corresponding two rules. One of them is shown in Figure 6, creating a CompositeState to a StateMachine if each other CompositeState is bound and the StateMachine is not already connected to a top CompositeState.

We further get instances of pattern p_4 (association between Transition and Action) and p_5 (association between Transition and Event as well as association between CompositeState and StateVertex).

Extensions: So far, we considered a generation of meta model instances that is somewhat simplified: First of all, we have not explicitly dealt with generating attribute values. There are (at least) two possible solutions for this: One possibility is to perform a postprocessing step which generates arbitrary attribute values. A set of predefined values is specified for each attribute, to be used within attribute assignment. Another approach would be to explicitly include attributes in the graph grammar rules and assign attributes already while deriving the instance of the meta model. Also properties of associations like navigation directions, role names, etc. can be included in certain attributes.

Then, associations being loops as well as associations with arbitrary cardinality constraints (i. e. $m..n$) can be achieved by extending the rule set of the instance generating graph grammar. Moreover if the meta model contains singleton classes, the create rule for the corresponding class has to have an additional application condition that ensures that at most one instance of this class is created.

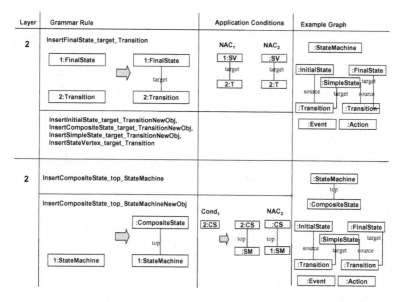

Fig. 7. Example Grammar Rules 2

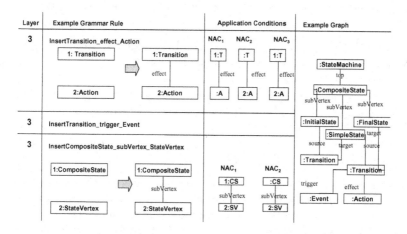

Fig. 8. Example Grammar Rules 3

Ensuring OCL constraints can be done by a constraint checker, once the overall derivation of an instance model has terminated. The instance generation and the translation of simple OCL constraints are described in [7, 8] in more detail.

5   Formal Background for Instance Generating Graph Grammars

In this section we present the formal background for *Instance Generating Graph Grammars (IGGG)* based on the formal theory of typed graph transformations with inheritance (see [3]). As the main result of this paper, we present the equivalence of instance sets generated by an instance-generating graph grammar on the one hand, and induced by a type graph with multiplicities on the other hand.

Definition 6 (multiplicities). *A multiplicity is a pair* $[i, j] \in \mathcal{N} \times (\mathcal{N} \cup \{*\})$ *with* $i \leq j$ *or* $j = *$. *The set of multiplicities is denoted Mult. The special value* $*$ *indicates that the maximum number of nodes or edges is not constrained. For an arbitrary finite set* X *and* $[i, j] \in Mult$, *we write* $|X| \in [i, j]$ *if* $i \leq |X|$ *and either* $j = *$ *or* $|X| \leq j$.

Now we define an induced graph language over a type graph with multiplicities TGI_{mult}. As usual, we use multiplicities to decorate the edges of type graphs. The multiplicities express the number of incoming, respectively outgoing edges for each target, respectively source instance.

Definition 7 (Type graph with multiplicities). *A type graph with multiplicities (see [16]) is a tuple* $TG_{mult} = (TGI, m_{src}, m_{tgt})$ *consisting of a type graph with inheritance TGI and additional functions* $m_{src}, m_{tgt} : TGI_E \rightarrow Mult$, *called* edge multiplicity functions.

Considering the meta model in Figure 1, it can be formalized to a type graph with multiplicities in a straight forward way. The node types are given by classes, the edge types by associations. In contrast to the associations, edge types have to be always directed. For each edge type a direction can be arbitrarily chosen.

Definition 8 (TGI_{mult}-induced graph language). *Given a type graph* TGI_{mult} *with multiplicities as defined in Def. 7, the induced graph language is defined by:*

$$L(TGI_{mult}) = \{(G = (G_V, G_E, src_G, tgt_G), ctp_G : G \rightarrow TGI) \mid \forall e \in TGI_E \land$$
$$\forall v \in ctp_G^{-1}(t) \text{ with } t \in clan(src(e)) : |ctp_G^{-1}(e) \cap src^{-1}(v)| \in m_{tgt}(e)$$
and
$$\forall e \in TGI_E \land \forall v \in ctp_G^{-1}(t) \text{ with } t \in clan(tgt(e)) : |ctp_G^{-1}(e) \cap tgt^{-1}(v)| \in$$
$$m_{src}(e)\}, \text{ where } ctp_G \text{ is a clan morphism.}$$

Example 1. Considering e.g. the example graph in Fig. 8, the multiplicities for edge type subvertex are fulfilled: For the only composite state c $|ctp^{-1}(\text{subvertex}) \cap src^{-1}(c)| = 3 \in [0, *]$ and for all state vertices s $|ctp^{-1}(\text{subvertex}) \cap tgt^{-1}(s)| \leq 1 \in [0, 1]$. The composite state is not subvertex of any vertex and all other state vertices are subvertex of the composite state.

Having formalized a meta model given by a class diagram through a type graph with multiplicities, we are now ready to define the language of an instance-generating graph grammar. Based on a given type graph with multiplicities, we mainly formalize the set of rules needed for instance generation. The rules are already given in Sec. 4. Please note that rules insertE_a_A and insertE'_a_ANewObj differ dependently on the source and target multiplicities of the corresponding patterns.

Since all given rules are intended to be matched injectively, they do not capture the case of patterns with loops as edge types, which would be translated to loops in the type graph. That's why loops are excluded in the following.

Definition 9 (instance-generating graph grammar and language).
Given a type graph TGI_{mult} with multiplicities as in Def. 7 without loops, an instance generating graph grammar is denoted by $IGGG = (TGI, \emptyset, R)$, where R is the union of the following sets of rules. The rules are depicted in Figures 2 - 5 and are formalized in the obvious way according to Def. 4.

- $R_1 = \{createE' \mid \forall E' \in TGI_N \wedge E' \notin Abs\}$ *with rules* createE' *as in Fig. 2*
- $R_2 = R_{21} \cup R_{22} \cup R_{23}$ *with*
  $R_{21} = \{insertE\_a\_A \mid \forall A, E \in TGI_N, a \in TGI_E : with$
  $(m_{src}(a) = [1,1] \vee m_{tgt}(a) = [1,1])\}$
  $R_{22} = \{insertE'\_a\_ANewObj \mid \forall A, E \in TGI_N, a \in TGI_E : with$
  $(m_{src}(a) = [1,1] \vee m_{tgt}(a) = [1,1]) \wedge E' \in clan(E) \wedge E' \notin Abs\}$
  $R_{23} = \{insertE\_a\_A'NewObj2 \mid \forall A, E \in TGI_N, a \in TGI_E : with$
  $(m_{src}(a) = [1,1] \vee m_{tgt}(a) = [1,1]) \vee A' \in clan(A) \wedge A' \notin Abs\}$
  with rules insertE_a_A, insertE'_a_ANewObj, *and* insertE'_a_ANewObj2 *as in Fig. 3 - 4*
- $R_3 = \{insertE\_a\_A \mid \forall A, E \in TGI_N, a \in TGI_E \text{ with } m_{src}(a) \neq [1,1] \wedge m_{tgt}(a) \neq [1,1]\}$ *with rules* insertE_a_A *as in Fig. 5*

R is layered, i.e. there is a function $rl : R \to \mathcal{N}$ with $rl(r) = i$ for all $r \in R_i$ for $i = \{1, 2, 3\}$. Function rl is called rule layer function.
The generated graph language *is defined by the following set of concrete typed graphs: $L(IGGG) = \{(G, ctp_G) \mid \emptyset \overset{*}{\Rightarrow}_{R_1} (H, ctp_H) \overset{*}{\Rightarrow}_{R_2} (K, ctp_K) \overset{*}{\Rightarrow}_{R_3} (G, ctp_G) \wedge \nexists r \in R_2 : (K, ctp_K) \Rightarrow_r (K', ctp_{K'})\}$.*

The following lemma states that the rule application of rules in R_2 to any graph created by rules of R_1 always terminates. This property is needed in the following theorem.

Lemma 1 (termination of rule layer 2). *Given an instance generating graph grammar $IGGG(TGI, \emptyset, R)$ where TGI does not contain any loop as edge type, let $L_1(IGGG) = \{(H, ctp_H) \mid \emptyset \overset{*}{\Rightarrow}_{R_1} (H, ctp_H)\}$. All derivation sequences $(H, ctp_H) \overset{*}{\Rightarrow}_{R_2} (G, ctp_G)$ with $(H, ctp_H) \in L_1(IGGG)$ terminate.*

Proof. See [7].

As one main result the following theorem states that the instance sets generated by an *IGGG* and those induced by a type graph with multiplicities are equal.

Theorem 1 (equality of languages). *Given a type graph TGI_{mult} with multiplicities and without loops and an instance generating graph grammar $IGGG = (TGI, \emptyset, R)$ for TGI_{mult}, we have $L(IGGG) = L(TGI_{mult})$.*

Proofidea. We have to proof that

(1) $(G, ctp_G) \in L(TGI_{mult})$ holds for any derivation $\emptyset \overset{*}{\Rightarrow}_{R_1} (H, ctp_H) \overset{*}{\Rightarrow}_{R_2} (K, ctp_K) \overset{*}{\Rightarrow}_{R_3} (G, ctp_G)$. This is true, since Layer 1 creates nodes of valid types only, the NACs prohibit the exceeding of the upper bound, and the rules in Layer 2 are applied until the lower bounds are fulfilled.

(2) For a given graph $(G, ctp_G) \in L(TGI_{mult})$ there exists a derivation sequence $\emptyset \overset{*}{\Rightarrow} (G, ctp_G)$ over $IGGG$. We create the sequence by first creating all nodes by rules of Layer 1, and then creating the edges for each pattern. For the complete proof see [7].

6   Related Work

One closely related approach is the one by Alanen and Porres [2]: They describe two algorithms, one to derive a context-free grammar from a meta model and another one for deriving a meta model from a context-free grammar. However, their algorithm for grammar derivation can only deal with composite associations between metaclasses, restricting it to tree-like meta models which is a severe limitation for practical usage. Further, the algorithm does not support ordinary associations with arbitrary cardinalities. This limitation is not surprising given the properties of context-free grammars and represents one reason for the approach to use graph grammars instead of context-free grammars.

Another related problem is the one of automated snapshot generation for class diagrams for validation and testing purposes, tackled by Gogolla et al. [10]. In their approach, properties that the snapshot has to fulfill are specified in OCL. For each class and association, object and link generation procedures are specified using the language ASSL. In order to fulfill constraints and invariants, ASSL offers try and select commands which allow the search for an appropriate object and backtracking if constraints are not fulfilled. The overall approach allows snapshot generation taking into account invariants but also requires the explicit encoding of constraints in generation commands. As such, the problem tackled by automatic snapshot generation is different from the meta model to graph grammar translation.

Formal methods such as Alloy [1] can also be used for instance generation: After translating a class diagram to Alloy one can use the instance generation within Alloy to generate an instance or to show that no instances exist. This instance generation relies on the use of SAT solvers and can also enumerate all possible instances. In contrast to such an approach, our approach aims at the construction of a grammar for the metamodel and thus establishes a bridge between metamodel-based and grammar-based definition of visual languages.

In the area of pattern recognition, there have been several approaches to grammatical inference: Given a finite set of sample patterns, a grammar should be deduced such that the language generated by the grammar contains the sample patterns. Originally, this problem has been tackled where patterns are encoded as strings and regular grammars are generated [9]. In the context of graph grammars, Jeltsch and Kreowski [12] describe how a hyperedge replacement grammar can be derived from a finite set of graph samples. Our problem setting is slightly different because we are given a meta model to describe all instances and not only a finite set of samples.

Further (complementary) related work can be seen in the area of model-driven testing [11] where the aim is to use a model of the system to produce suitable test data. The problem of generating those instances from the grammar that provide a suitable coverage for testing can possibly benefit from existing research in this area.

7 Conclusion and Future Work

Currently, the widespread approach of defining visual languages has one main disadvantage: The systematic generation of instances of meta models is difficult to automate which poses limitations for e. g. automated testing of model transformations. In this paper, we have introduced the idea of instance-generating graph grammars which is basically the equivalent to a Chomsky grammar for textual languages.

On the basis of meta model patterns and corresponding derivation rules, our approach allows the construction of an instance-generating graph grammar for meta models without OCL constraints. This construction is based on a type graph with inheritance. As running example, we have constructed an IGGG for a simplified statechart meta model. Using the theory of typed graph transformation with inheritance, we have shown that the instance sets generated by an IGGG and those induced by the corresponding type graph with multiplicities are equal.

Automatic derivation of instances from meta models is a complex task which needs tool support. So far, we have automated the construction of an IGGG by providing a model transformation that automatically derives an IGGG from a meta model. For a complete description of this implementation we refer to the URL http://tfs.cs.tu-berlin.de/agg/MM2GraGra. Although the current model transformation does not support all features of meta models yet, it nevertheless shows the feasibility of our approach.

Future work should extend the automatic instance generation by meta models with OCL constraints. Ensuring OCL constraints can be done in two ways: One is to check constraints once the overall derivation of an instance model has terminated. However, this leads to the generation of a large number of non-valid instances. An approach avoiding the generation of invalid instances is presented in [7, 8].

Further work is needed to apply our approach to testing model transformations: For that, techniques are needed that allow the generation of selected instance models that represent a suitable diversity of all possible models. Furthermore a syntax graph grammar could be generated from a meta model providing the basis for automatically generated visual editing rules.

References

1. *The Alloy Analyzer - 3.0 Beta* http://alloy.mit.edu/, 2000.
2. M. Alanen and I. Porres. A Relation Between Context-Free Grammars and Meta Object Facility Metamodels. Technical Report TUCS No 606, TUCS Turku Center for Computer Science, March 2003.

3. R. Bardohl, H. Ehrig, J. de Lara, and G. Taentzer. Integrating Meta Modelling with Graph Transformation for Efficient Visual Language Definition and Model Manipulation. In M. Wermelinger and T. Margaria-Steffens, editors, *Proc. Fundamental Aspects of Software Engineering 2004*, volume 2984. Springer LNCS, 2004.

4. A. S. Boujarwah and K. Saleh. Compiler test case generation methods: a survey and assessment. *Information and Software Technology*, 39(9):617–625, 1997.

5. A. Corradini, U. Montanari, F. Rossi, H. Ehrig, R. Heckel, and M. Löwe. Algebraic Approaches to Graph Transformation Part I: Basic Concepts and Double Pushout Approach. In G. Rozenberg, editor, *Handbook of Graph Grammars and Computing by Graph transformation, Volume 1: Foundations*, pages 163–246. World Scientific, 1997.

6. H. Ehrig, K. Ehrig, J. de Lara, G. Taentzer, D. Varró, and S. Varró-Gyapay. Termination Criteria for Model Transformation. In M. Wermelinger and T. Margaria-Steffen, editors, *Proc. Fundamental Approaches to Software Engineering (FASE)*, volume 2984 of *Lecture Notes in Computer Science*, pages 214–228. Springer Verlag, 2005.

7. K. Ehrig, J. Küster, G. Taentzer, and J. Winkelmann. Automatically Generating Instances of Meta Models. Technical Report 2005–09, Technical University of Berlin, Dept. of Computer Science, November 2005.

8. K. Ehrig, J. Küster, G. Taentzer, and J. Winkelmann. Translation of Restricted OCL Constraints into Graph Constraints for Generating Meta Model Instances by Graph Grammars. In *Proc. (GT-VMT)*, 2006. To appear. A preliminary version of the proceedings is available at `http://hobbit.inf.mit.bme.hu/GT-VMT2006/ProceedingsGTVMT2006.pdf`.

9. K. S. Fu and T. L. Booth. Grammatical Inference: Introduction and Survey. *IEEE Transcations on Systems, Man, and Cybernetics*, SMC-5:95–111, 409–423, 1975.

10. M. Gogolla, J. Bohling, and M. Richters. Validating UML and OCL Models in USE by Automatic Snapshot Generation. *Software and Systems Modeling*, 2005. To appear.

11. A. Hartman and K. Nagin. Model Driven Testing - AGEDIS Architecture, Interfaces, and Tools. In *Proceedings 1st European Conference on Model-Driven Software Engineering*, 2003.

12. E. Jeltsch and H.-J. Kreowski. Grammatical Inference Based on Hyperedge Replacement. In Hartmut Ehrig, Hans-Jörg Kreowski, and Grzegorz Rozenberg, editors, *Proc. 4th. Int. Workshop on Graph Grammars and their Application to Computer Science*, volume 532 of *Lecture Notes in Computer Science*, pages 461–474. Springer-Verlag, 1991.

13. Object Management Group. *MDA Guide Version 1.0.1*, June 2003.

14. Object Management Group (OMG). *UML 2.0 Superstructure Final Adopted Specification. OMG document pts/03-08-02*, August 2003.

15. Object Management Group (OMG). *OCL 2.0 Specification. OMG document ptc/2005-06-06*, June 2005.

16. A. Rensink and G. Taentzer. Ensuring Structural Constraints in Graph-Based Models with Type Inheritance. In *Proc. Fundamental Approaches to Software Engineering (FASE)*, pages 64–79. LNCS 3442, Springer, 2005.

KM3: A DSL for Metamodel Specification

Frédéric Jouault and Jean Bézivin

ATLAS team, INRIA and LINA
{frederic.jouault, jean.bezivin}@univ-nantes.fr

Abstract. We consider in this paper that a DSL (Domain Specific Language) may be defined by a set of models. A typical DSL is the ATLAS Transformation Language (ATL). An ATL program transforms a source model (conforming to a source metamodel) into a target model (conforming to a target metamodel). Being itself a model, the transformation program conforms to the ATL metamodel. The notion of metamodel is thus used to define the source DSL, the target DSL and the transformation DSL itself. As a consequence we can see that agility to define metamodels and precision of these definitions is of paramount importance in any model engineering activity. In order to fullfill the goals of agility and precision in the definition of our metamodels, we have been using a notation called KM3 (Kernel MetaMetaModel). KM3 may itself be considered as a DSL for describing metamodels. This paper presents the rationale for using KM3, some examples of its use and a precise definition of the language.

1 Introduction

Model engineering is strongly related to language engineering. Considering the important number of problem domains, there is a need for an equally important number of specialized languages. We have been using a language named KM3 (Kernel MetaMetaModel) to help defining these special purpose languages. This paper presents the rationale, semantics and other particularities of this language.

KM3 has its roots in the complex and evolving relations between modeling and visual languages. UML is a general purpose visual modeling language, but not every modeling language is a general purpose visual language. The OMG has proposed a language called MOF 2.0 [1] for the definition of its various metamodels (SPEM, UML, CWM, etc.). The problem was that there was no practical support environment for this language. As a replacement, the solution found was to use UML CASE tools for this purpose. The price to pay for this was an alignment of MOF with a subset of UML (mainly class diagrams). Since this time, the alignment has been more or less maintained through the various versions of UML and MOF. In other words, UML may be considered by certain as a multi-purpose language allowing defining software object-oriented terminal models and allowing also defining MOF metamodels. But this is not without drawbacks. When we need to build a metamodel (e.g. as source or target of a transformation), we have first to start building a UML class diagram, with certain properties. The result is serialized in a first XMI file corresponding to the

R. Gorrieri and H. Wehrheim (Eds.): FMOODS 2006, LNCS 4037, pp. 171–185, 2006.
© IFIP International Federation for Information Processing 2006

terminal model. It is then transformed into another XMI file corresponding to the metamodel. This conversion from a UML model to a MOF metamodel is called a *promotion* and implemented by some widely available tools like UML2MOF available in the NetBeans MDR [2] suite or also by an ATL [3] model transformation program.

We have experimented for some time with this approach. When the number of involved metamodels is limited (i.e. when one mainly deals with OMG fixed and stable metamodels), there are no major problems. But when we need multiple and evolving metamodels, we have found this approach to be very cumbersome. The only alternative has been to define KM3, a specialized textual language for specifying metamodels, including MOF metamodels. After experimenting with this language for two years, we are completely convinced of the practicality of the approach. Public libraries of more than one hundred metamodels expressed in KM3 are now available [4]. ATL, a QVT-like [5] model transformation language, uses KM3 natively to facilitate the handling of metamodels. Many other projects are also based on this format.

What remained to do is to establish a precise semantics for KM3. This is one of the objectives of the present work. Of course we have also to understand clearly the purpose and rationale of metamodel writing languages. In order to do so, we first need to define precisely what a metamodel exactly is. The definitions provided in this paper apply to the OMG MDA framework, but they are more general and may also correspond to several other technical spaces as defined in [6].

This paper is organized as follows. Section 2 provides the basic definitions related to models and DSLs. Section 3 provides an overview of KM3 including some current applications. Section 4 comes back on a more formal conceptual definition of KM3. A related work description is provided in section 5 before the conclusion.

2   Definitions

We consider models as the unifying concept in IT engineering. Models come in various flavors. A UML model, a Java program, an XML or RDF document, a database relational table, an entity-association schema are all examples of models. We call all of these λ-models where λ identifies a technical space [6] associated with a given precise metametamodel. A simple representation of terminal model, metamodel and metametamodel is given in Figure 1.

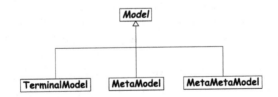

Fig. 1. General organization of a metamodeling stack

We may consider two main definitions of a model corresponding to its internal *organization* and its potential *utilization*. We choose to focus here on the *organization* of models. The study of model *utilization* and of its relations with model *organization* is out of the scope of this work. Then we give a definition of DSL and analyze the relations between DSLs and models.

2.1   Model Organization Definition

From an organization point of view, we propose the following definitions:

Definition 1. *A directed multigraph $G = (N_G, E_G, \Gamma_G)$ consists of a finite set of nodes N_G, a finite set of edges E_G, and a function $\Gamma_G : E_G \to N_G \times N_G$ mapping edges to their source and target nodes.*

Definition 2. *A model $M = (G, \omega, \mu)$ is a triple where:*

- *$G = (N_G, E_G, \Gamma_G)$ is a directed multigraph,*
- *ω is itself a model (called the reference model of M) associated to a graph $G_\omega = (N_\omega, E_\omega, \Gamma_\omega)$,*
- *$\mu : N_G \cup E_G \to N_\omega$ is a function associating elements (nodes and edges) of G to nodes of G_ω.*

Remarks. The relation between a model and its reference model is called conformance and is noted *conformsTo* or abbreviated in *c2* throughout this paper. Elements of ω are called metaelements. μ is neither injective (several model elements may be associated to the same metaelement) nor surjective (not all metaelements need to be associated to a model element).

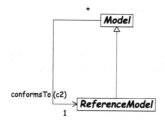

Fig. 2. Definition of *model* and *reference model*

Figure 2 illustrates definition 2. The definition of model given above allows for an indefinite number of upper modeling layers. For practical purpose, we need to stop at some level. We observe that only three levels are used in several technical spaces:

- In *XML*: documents, schemas and the schemas of XML Schema for XML,
- In *EBNF*: programs, grammars and the grammar of EBNF.

We call these levels: M1, M2 and M3. M1 consists of all models that are not metamodels. M2 consists of all metamodels that are not the metametamodel.

M3 consists of a unique metametamodel for each given technical space. We may now proceed to giving additional definitions.

Definition 3. *A metametamodel is a model that is its own reference model (i.e. it conforms to itself).*

Definition 4. *A metamodel is a model such that its reference model is a meta-metamodel.*

Definition 5. *A terminal model is a model such that its reference model is a metamodel.*

Figure 3 shows how to adapt the definition of model to this three-level modeling stack. The structure for models defined in this section is compatible with the OMG view as illustrated in the MDA guide [7].

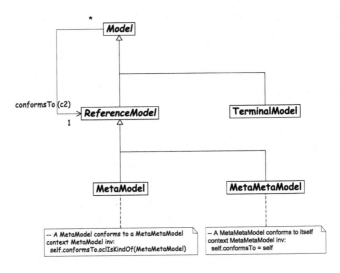

Fig. 3. Metamodeling stack representation with model definition

2.2   Domain Specific Language

Language engineering is at the hearth of computer science. There are a variety of categories of languages. We discuss here only a small facet of language engineering. A distinction is often made between programming languages and modeling languages. Typical examples are PL/1 and UML. The distinction between these categories has mainly to do with canonical executability and is currently much evolving. Another distinction is between General Purpose Languages (GPLs) and Domain Specific Languages (DSLs). PL/1 and UML are two examples of GPLs. R [8], SQL [9] or Excel are examples of DSLs. Java and C# are examples of general purpose programming languages.

We also understand that the distinction between GPLs and DSLs is orthogonal to many other language classifications. For example there are indifferently visual or textual GPLs or DSLs. Similarly DSLs and GPLs may fall under various categories of being object-oriented, event-oriented, rule-oriented, function-oriented, etc. There are examples of imperative and declarative GPLs and DSLs as well.

A DSL is a language designed to be useful for a limited set of tasks, in contrast to general-purpose languages that are supposed to be useful for much more generic tasks, crossing multiple application domains. A typical example of DSL is GraphViz [10], a language used to define directed graphs, which creates a visual representation of that graph as a result. Some GPLs have started as DSLs and have sometimes evolved towards genericity to become GPLs. The reverse process has not been observed in the history of programming languages.

Like many other languages, DSLs have many common properties [11]:

– They have usually a concrete syntax
– They may also have an abstract syntax
– They have a semantics, implicitly or explicitly defined

Of course there are several ways to define these syntax and semantics. The most known are grammar-based systems.

2.3   DSLs and Models

There are strong relations between DSLs and models. We discuss here the possibility of using model-based solutions for defining the syntax and semantics of DSLs.

Definition 6. *A DSL is a set of coordinated models.*

Each model in this set contributes to a part of its definition. A given model may, for instance, specify one of the following aspects:

– **Domain definition metamodel.** One of the defining entities of a DSL is a Domain Definition MetaModel (DDMM). It introduces the basic entities of the domain and their mutual relations. This *base ontology* plays a central role in the definition of the DSL. For example, a DSL for directed graph manipulation will contain the concepts of nodes and edges, and will state that an edge may connect a source node to a target node. Such a DDMM plays the role of the abstract syntax for a DSL.
– **Concrete syntaxes.** A DSL may have different concrete syntaxes. Each one is defined by a transformation model mapping the DDMM onto a *display surface* metamodel. Examples of display surface metamodels may be SVG or DOT [10], but also XML. An example of such a transformation for a Petri

net DSL is the mapping from places to circles, from transitions to rectangles and from arcs to arrows. The display surface metamodel will then have the concepts of Circle, Rectangle and Arrow.

- **Execution semantics.** A DSL may have an execution semantics definition. This semantics definition is also defined by a transformation model mapping the DDMM onto another DSL having itself an execution semantics or even to a GPL. The firing rules of a Petri net may for example be mapped into a Java code model.
- **Other operations on DSLs.** In addition to canonical execution, there are plenty of other possible operations on programs based on a given DSL. Each may be defined by a similar mapping represented by a transformation model. For example if one wishes to query DSL programs, a standard mapping of the DDMM onto Prolog may be useful. The study of these other operations on DSLs is an open research subject.

3   KM3 Overview

3.1   Description

The purpose of KM3 is to give a relatively simple solution to define the Domain Definition MetaModel of a DSL. KM3 is therefore a Domain Specific Language to define metamodels:

- **Domain definition metamodel.** The DDMM of KM3 is a metametamodel, to which other DDMMs conform. This DDMM may be defined in KM3 (see [4]), just like EBNF (a notation to define grammars) may be described in EBNF using only a few lines. It uses concepts like *Class*, *Attribute*, and *Reference*. It is structurally close to eMOF 2.0 [1] and Ecore [12].
- **Concrete syntax.** A default textual concrete syntax has been defined for KM3 (see [4]). This allows straightforward definitions of metamodels with any text editor.
- **Semantics.** The semantics of KM3 enables the specification of metamodels and models according to the definitions given in section 2. A precise conceptual definition of KM3 is presented in section 4. Mappings to and from MOF 1.4 [13] and Ecore have notably been defined in ATL, making KM3 usable with tools like Eclipse EMF [12] and Netbeans MDR.

As a metametamodel, KM3 is simpler than MOF 1.4, MOF 2.0 [1] and Ecore. It contains only 14 classes whereas, for instance, Ecore has 18 classes and MOF 1.4 has 28 classes. Only the core concepts of these other metametamodels are available in KM3.

Figure 4 describes an XML metamodel in the standard visual notation of class diagrams. This XML metamodel corresponds to the following KM3 description:

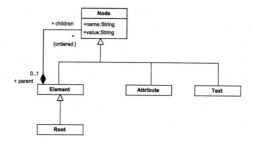

Fig. 4. Visual presentation of an XML metamodel

```
package XML {
    abstract class Node {
        attribute name : String;
        attribute value : String;
        reference parent[0-1] : Element oppositeOf children;
    }

    class Attribute extends Node {}

    class Text extends Node {}

    class Element extends Node {
        reference children[*] ordered container : Node oppositeOf parent;
    }

    class Root extends Element {}
}

package PrimitiveTypes {
    datatype Boolean;
    datatype Integer;
    datatype String;
}
```

3.2   Applications

KM3 has been defined as an answer to frequent requests of users that were defining model transformations in the ATL language. In principle source and target metamodels for QVT-like transformations should be written in XMI. When the transformation is based on standard metamodels like UML metamodels, the XMI serialization of these metamodels may be found on the OMG site and there is no need for any additional formalism.

The practice of model transformation, with a growing community of ATL users, has however obliged to amend this opinion. During the development of these transformations, it became clear that very often the standard metamodels were not sufficient and that many of the transformations needed specific metamodels. Furthermore, the definition of these metamodels is often an iterative process involving a progressive elaboration.

In order to illustrate this, we provide below some examples of transformations written in ATL. The complete code and documentation of these transformations may be found in the open source library of transformation available on [14] and [15].

– *Ant2Maven* and *Make2Ant* are partial transformations between well known software engineering build tools (Make, Ant and Maven).

- *BibTeX2DocBook* is a transformation of a BibTeXML model to a DocBook composed document.
- The *JavaSource2Table* example computes a static call graph of a Java program and presents it in a tabular style. From there, one may use the XHTML or the Excel metamodels to project to other display surfaces, by transformation chaining.
- The *KM32DOT* allows drawing graphical presentations of metamodels. DOT is an automatic graph layout program from GraphViz [10]. The aim of this transformation is to generate a visualization, in the form of a class diagram, of any KM3 metamodel by automatic layout
- The *UMLActivityDiagram2MSProject* example describes a transformation from a loop free UML activity diagram (describing some tasks series) to MS Project. The transformation is based on a simplified subset of the UML State Machine metamodel. This transformation produces a project defined in conformance to a limited subset of the MSProject metamodel.

The following table (Figure 5) gives another sample from the same model transformation library, where the numbers of classes in the source and target metamodels are provided. Without describing in detail all these transformations, it becomes clear that most source and target metamodels have to be defined and even in the case they are standard (like the UML activity diagram), they often correspond to a small subset of the standard metamodel.

Name	Source Classes	Target Classes
BibTeXML to Docbook	21	6
Class to Relational	5	4
Java source to Table	5	3
KM3 to DOT	16	26
KM3 to Problem	16	2
PathExp to PetriNet	5	7
Table to Microsoft Excel	3	15
UML to Amble	11	14
UML to Java	11	8
UML Activity Diagram to MS Project	6	3
UMLDI to SVG	26	38
XSLT to XQuery	13	18

Fig. 5. A sample of transformations from the ATL library

As a consequence, the definition of source and target metamodels in a transformation is an important part of the design of this transformation. We need a notation that will allow easy and precise definition and modification of these metamodels. Even if this seems counter intuitive, users have been asking for textual languages instead of visual languages for performing this task.

The KM3 language has been very useful in supporting rapid and precise definition of metamodels for various situations. When studying the interoperability between several tools (like Bugzilla, Make, MS Project, or Mantis), the data models of these tools are usually captured in a metamodel, and the bridges may be designed as transformations, directly using these metamodels.

We have previously mentioned the initial library of ATL transformations. What is also interesting is that a significant library of the corresponding metamodels has also grown in the same time and may be found at [16]. There are many issues that can be studied on the basis of this initial library. The first one is related to reusability of these metamodels. More important questions may be raised on the various relations that may hold between these metamodels and also to the metadata about them.

4   Conceptual Definition of KM3

Definition 7. *A* KM3-model *is a model defined using KM3 as a metametamodel.*

This section only deals with KM3-models. Therefore, we use model to mean KM3-model. We present here a formal specification of KM3 based on first order logic. Only metamodels, not terminal models, may conform to KM3. However, KM3 semantics also impacts terminal models by constraining them according to their reference models. Two main predicates are used to define KM3-models, including the KM3 metametamodel itself. For a model M (see definition 2), we define:

- $Node(x, y)$. This predicate states that a node $x \in N_G$ is associated to a node $y \in N_\omega$ by the function μ.
- $Edge(x, y, z)$. This predicate states that an edge between node $x \in N_G$ and node $y \in N_G$ is associated to a node $z \in N_\omega$ by the function μ. In KM3, multiple edges between two given nodes may only exist if their associated metaelements are distinct. Therefore, the triple (x, y, z) uniquely identifies an edge.

Formulas are used to express constraints on KM3-models. We start by defining a simplified version of KM3 called *SimpleKM3* with only classes and references. Then we introduce additional concepts: opposite references and inheritance.

4.1   Definition of SimpleKM3

SimpleKM3 is a simplified version of KM3 using only classes and references. A visual representation of *SimpleKM3* is given in Figure 6. Figure 7 gives the formal definition of *SimpleKM3*. There are only two classes: *class* (line 1) and *reference* (line 2). There are two references: *features* (line 3) and *type* (line 4). The *features* reference connects a class to its references (lines 5 and 6). The *type* reference connects a reference to its type (lines 7 and 8).

We define a new predicate $IsKindOf(x, y)$, which is for now equivalent to predicate $Node(x, y)$:

$$\forall xy IsKindOf(x, y) \leftrightarrow Node(x, y) \tag{1}$$

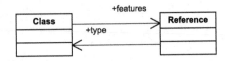

Fig. 6. Class diagram representation of *SimpleKM3*

1. $Node(\text{class}, \text{class})$
2. $Node(\text{reference}, \text{class})$
3. $Node(\text{features}, \text{reference})$
4. $Node(\text{type}, \text{reference})$
5. $Edge(\text{class}, \text{features}, \text{features})$
6. $Edge(\text{features}, \text{reference}, \text{type})$
7. $Edge(\text{reference}, \text{type}, \text{features})$
8. $Edge(\text{type}, \text{class}, \text{type})$

Fig. 7. Formal definition of *SimpleKM3*

It will be redefined in section 4.3 when we introduce class inheritance in *SimpleKM3*. We still use the $Node(x, y)$ predicate to define nodes but use this new predicate in formulas that are also valid for subclasses. This is the case for formulas (5) and (6).

A *SimpleKM3*-model (i.e. model, metamodel or metametamodel) is valid if the following formulas are verified:

- **Metaelement uniqueness.** μ, as a function, can only associate a single metaelement to a given model node.

$$\forall xyz Node(x, y) \wedge Node(x, z) \rightarrow y = z \qquad (2)$$

There is no similar formula for edges because there may be several edges of different types between two given nodes.

- **Node metaelements are classes.** Any node that is used as a metaelement of another node must have node *class* as its metaelement.

$$\forall xy Node(x, y) \rightarrow Node(y, \text{class}) \qquad (3)$$

- **Edge metaelements are references.** An edge can only exists between nodes and must have node *reference* as its type.

$$\forall xyz Edge(x, y, z) \rightarrow (\exists x_t Node(x, x_t)) \wedge (\exists y_t Node(y, y_t)) \qquad (4)$$
$$\wedge Node(z, \text{reference})$$

- **Edge target.** An edge typed by reference z can only target a node typed y_t if the type of z is y_t.

$$\forall xyz Edge(x, y, z) \rightarrow (\exists y_t IsKindOf(y, y_t) \wedge Edge(z, y_t, \text{type})) \qquad (5)$$

- **Edge source.** An edge typed by reference z can only have a node typed x_t as source if z is a feature of x_t.

$$\forall xyz Edge(x, y, z) \rightarrow (\exists x_t IsKindOf(x, x_t) \wedge Edge(x_t, z, \text{features})) \qquad (6)$$

– **Reference type uniqueness.** A reference has a unique type.

$$\forall xyz \, Edge(x, y, \text{type}) \wedge Edge(x, z, \text{type}) \rightarrow y = z \qquad (7)$$

We must specify this constraint in *SimpleKM3* because it does not have the concept of multiplicity.

4.2 Adding Opposite References

Opposite references work in pairs. They are especially convenient to enable bidirectional navigation. For instance, in our first version of *SimpleKM3*, although we can get the features of a class, we cannot get the class owning a given reference. Figure 8 defines the *opposite* reference belonging to and targeting the *reference* class.

9. *Node*(opposite, reference)   11. *Edge*(opposite, reference, type)
   10. *Edge*(reference, opposite, features)

Fig. 8. Addition of opposite reference to *SimpleKM3*

A *SimpleKM3*-model (i.e. model, metamodel or metametamodel) with *opposite* is valid if the following formulas are verified:

– **Opposite uniqueness.** A reference has at most one opposite.

$$\forall xyz \, Edge(x, y, \text{opposite}) \wedge Edge(x, z, \text{opposite}) \rightarrow y = z \qquad (8)$$

– **References work in pairs**

$$\forall xy \, Edge(x, y, \text{opposite}) \rightarrow Edge(y, x, \text{opposite}) \qquad (9)$$

– **Opposite references have opposite extremities**

$$\forall xyz \, Edge(x, y, \text{opposite}) \wedge Edge(z, x, \text{features}) \rightarrow Edge(y, z, \text{type}) \quad (10)$$

We can now extend *SimpleKM3* with an *owner* reference opposite to the *features* reference as shown on Figure 9. The resulting definition of *SimpleKM3* corresponds to the class diagram given in Figure 10. It is now possible to navigate from *reference* to *class*.

12. *Node*(owner, reference)   15. *Edge*(owner, features, opposite)
13. *Edge*(reference, owner, features)   16. *Edge*(features, owner, opposite)
14. *Edge*(owner, class, type)

Fig. 9. Addition of some opposite references to *SimpleKM3*

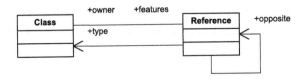

Fig. 10. Class diagram representation of *SimpleKM3* with opposites

4.3   Adding Inheritance

In KM3, inheritance allows reuse of references defined in supertypes. Overriding of inherited features is not allowed. Figure 11 introduces the *supertypes* reference from *class* to *class*. Figure 12 gives the class diagram of *SimpleKM3* with inheritance. In order to be able to use inherited references or to define edges targeting subclasses of a reference type, we redefine $IsKindOf(x)$ (see formula 1) accordingly:

$$\forall xy IsKindOf(x,y) \leftrightarrow Node(x,y) \vee (\exists z Node(x,z) \wedge ConformsTo(z,y)) \quad (11)$$

This new definition makes use of the $ConformsTo(x,y)$ predicate, recursively defined as follows:

$$\forall xy ConformsTo(x,y) \leftrightarrow (x=y)\vee \quad (12)$$
$$(\exists z Edge(x,z,\text{supertypes}) \wedge ConformsTo(z,y))$$

Circular inheritance is forbidden. The $ConformsTo(x,y)$ predicate could not be defined otherwise. With this new definitions, formulas (6) and (5) remain valid.

17. $Node(\text{supertypes}, \text{reference})$ 19. $Edge(\text{supertypes}, \text{class}, \text{type})$
18. $Edge(\text{class}, \text{supertypes}, \text{features})$

Fig. 11. Addition of inheritance to *SimpleKM3*

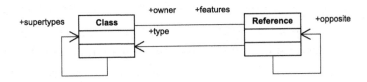

Fig. 12. Class diagram representation of *SimpleKM3* with opposites and inheritance

4.4   Other KM3 Concepts

We defined the formal semantics of the remaining KM3 concepts as well: packages, class abstractness, data types, attributes, enumerations, reference containment, multiplicity, etc. However, they do not fit in this paper because of space limitation. A complete specification of KM3 in Prolog is available on the AM3

GMT website [4]. This program uses the same predicates we defined in this section plus the $Prop(x, y, z)$ predicate where $x \in N_G$, $y \in N_\omega$ is an *attribute*, and z is a value. We do not further detail this predicate, which is used as a shortcut to avoid representing primitive values as nodes explicitly. The set of constraints implemented in the program is illustrative of the characterization of KM3. We do not claim completness here.

5   Related Work

Other modeling frameworks offer capabilities similar to those of KM3:

- **OMG MOF.** MOF is a standard metametamodel from OMG, of which there exist several versions (e.g. MOF 1.4 [13] and MOF 2.0 [1]). All of them are more complex than KM3 (i.e. they contain more classes, see section 3.1). None has a formal semantics. Their standard concrete syntax is XMI, which is based on XML and is, as such, more verbose than KM3. As noted in section 3.1, we have defined ATL transformations from MOF 1.4 to KM3 and from KM3 to MOF 1.4.
- **HUTN.** Human Usable Textual Notation [17] (HUTN) is a standard by OMG to give a default textual notation to each metamodel. Because it is an automatic mapping from MOF to EBNF, it is more verbose than KM3.
- **Eclipse EMF Ecore.** Ecore [12] is a metametamodel close to MOF 2.0 but with a standard textual notation: emfatic. One difference with KM3 is that emfatic provides EMF-specific constructs (e.g. to customize Java code generation). One of our experiments has shown that such additional information may be embedded into KM3 comments. Another difference is that Ecore has no formal semantics. As noted in section 3.1, we have defined ATL transformations from Ecore to KM3 and from KM3 to Ecore.
- **Typed graphs.** Typed Attributed Graphs [18] are the conceptual framework on which graph transformation is based. They have a precise formal semantics. In opposition to KM3 and the definitions given in section 2, there is no explicit metametamodel: type graphs are not themselves typed.
- **sNets.** sNets [19] are one of our past experiments. We have learnt much from them and KM3 is based on this knowledge. One difference with KM3 is that there is an explicit representation of μ in the sNet metametamodel. However this may lead to using hypergraphs to provide a complete general solution, with possible strong constraints on implementation overhead.

6   Conclusions

In this paper we have proposed a metamodel definition language. We have seen other possibilities of DSLs for performing such tasks like XMI or Emfatic. Each DSL has some specificities, some advantages and drawbacks. For Emfatic for example, the projection to Java is an important feature; for XMI, the possibility to take into account terminal models as well as metamodels is an essential property.

The KM3 language is intended to be a lightweight textual metamodel definition language allowing easy creation and modification of metamodels. The metamodels expressed in KM3 have good readibility properties. The formalism is sufficiently rich to support essential information. Additional information can be expressed as metadata pragmas not described here. Metamodels expressed in KM3 may be easily converted to/from other notations like Emfatic or XMI.

Among the properties of KM3 is the possibility to use it for the definition of non-MOF based models. KM3 has also been designed to cross technical spaces.

The contribution of this paper is a clean semantics for a metamodel definition language. To the best of our knowledge, such a definition has not been proposed for such a language. As a side effect of this work, we have been able to give a precise and original definition of a model, in the context of multiple technical spaces. All the tools currently available in the ATLAS Model Management Platform [15] are completely based on this operational definition.

Acknowledgements

This work has been partially supported by ModelWare, IST European project 511731. We thank Ivan Kurtev and all the members of the ATLAS team for their support to this work.

References

1. OMG: Meta Object Facility (MOF) 2.0 Core Specification, OMG Document ptc/03-10-04, http://www.omg.org/docs/ptc/03-10-04.pdf. (2003)
2. netBeans.org: Netbeans Meta Data Repository (MDR), http://mdr.netbeans.org/. (2006)
3. Jouault, F., Kurtev, I.: Transforming models with ATL. In: Satellite Events at the MoDELS 2005 Conference. Volume 3844 of Lecture Notes in Computer Science., Springer-Verlag (2006) 128–138
4. ATLAS team: ATLAS MegaModel Management (AM3) Home page, http://www.eclipse.org/gmt/am3/. (2006)
5. OMG: MOF QVT Final Adopted Specification, OMG Document ptc/2005-11-01, http://www.omg.org/docs/ptc/05-11-01.pdf. (2005)
6. Bézivin, J., Kurtev, I.: Model-based technology integration with the technical space concept. In: Proceedings of the Metainformatics Symposium, Springer-Verlag (2005)
7. Object and Reference Model Subcommittee (ORMSC) of the OMG Architecture Board: A Proposal for an MDA Foundation Model, white paper OMG-ORMSC/05-08-01, http://www.omg.org/cgi-bin/doc?ormsc/05-08-01. (2005)
8. Bates, D., et al.: R Language Definition, http://stat.ethz.ch/R-manual/R-patched/doc/manual/R-lang.html. (2006)
9. McJones, P.R., ed.: The 1995 SQL Reunion: People, Project, and Politics, May 29, 1995. Volume SRC1997-018. (1997)
10. Gansner, E.R., North, S.C.: An open graph visualization system and its applications to software engineering. Software — Practice and Experience **30**(11) (2000) 1203–1233

11. Harel, D., Rumpe, B.: Meaningful modeling: What's the semantics of "semantics"? Computer **37**(10) (2004) 64–72
12. Budinsky, F., Steinberg, D., Ellersick, R., Merks, E., Brodsky, S.A., Grose, T.J.: Eclipse Modeling Framework. Addison Wesley (2003)
13. OMG: Meta Object Facility (MOF) Specification, version 1.4, OMG Document formal/2002-04-03, `http://www.omg.org/technology/documents/formal/mof.htm` . (2002)
14. Eclipse Foundation: Generative Model Transformer (GMT) Home page, `http://www.eclipse.org/gmt/`. (2006)
15. ATLAS team: ATLAS Transformation Language (ATL) Home page, `http://www.eclipse.org/gmt/atl/`. (2006)
16. ATLAS team: Atlantic Metamodel Zoo, `http://www.eclipse.org/gmt/am3/zoos/atlanticZoo/`. (2006)
17. OMG: Human-Usable Textual Notation, v1.0, OMG Document formal/04-08-01, `http://www.omg.org/technology/documents/formal/hutn.htm`. (2004)
18. Ehrig, H., Prange, U., Taentzer, G.: Fundamental theory for typed attributed graph transformation. In: Graph Transformations: Second International Conference, ICGT 2004. Volume 3256 of Lecture Notes in Computer Science., Springer-Verlag (2004) 161–177
19. Bézivin, J.: sNets: A first generation model engineering platform. In: Satellite Events at the MoDELS 2005 Conference. Volume 3844 of Lecture Notes in Computer Science., Springer-Verlag (2006) 169–181

Defining Object-Oriented Execution Semantics Using Graph Transformations

Harmen Kastenberg*, Anneke Kleppe**, and Arend Rensink

University of Twente
Department of Computer Science
Enschede, The Netherlands
{h.kastenberg,rensink,kleppeag}@cs.utwente.nl

Abstract. In this paper we describe an application of the theory of graph transformations to the practise of language design. In particular, we have defined the static and dynamic semantics of a small but realistic object-oriented language (called TAAL) by mapping the language constructs to graphs (the static semantics) and modelling their effect by graph transformation rules (the dynamic semantics). This gives rise to execution models for all TAAL-programs, which can be used as the basis for formal verification.

This work constitutes a first step towards a method for defining all aspects of software languages, besides their concrete syntax, in a consistent and rigorous manner. Such a method facilitates the integration of formal correctness in the software development trajectory.

1 Introduction

A widely recognized proposal for combating the maintenance and evolution problems faced in software engineering is the model driven approach, brought to the world's attention by the OMG's Model Driven Architecture (MDA) framework [17]. In this approach, models and model transformations are central concepts. The models are specified in diverse (modeling and programming) software languages (SLs), and the model transformations define relations between these languages.

Model transformations are intended to be correctness preserving: they should not introduce errors or essential changes. This, however, can be guaranteed only if the meaning of the SLs involved is defined with sufficient precision. Unfortunately, this is often lacking: many SLs have a well-defined syntax but only an informal semantics, e.g. described by text or, in the case of a programming language, by a compiler.

The longer-term goal of our research is to define a way in which all aspects of SLs, besides their concrete syntax, can be defined in a consistent and rigorous

---

* The author is employed in the GROOVE project funded by the Dutch NWO (project number 612.000.314).

** The author is employed in the GRASLAND project funded by the Dutch NWO (project number 612.063.408).

R. Gorrieri and H. Wehrheim (Eds.): FMOODS 2006, LNCS 4037, pp. 186–201, 2006.

manner. As a common formal foundation we use graphs and graph transformations, which we believe to be powerful enough to capture all relevant SL aspects. Furthermore, current research in the field of graph transformations [23] offers us a large knowledge base of theories ready to apply to our topic. Ultimately, we plan to develop a meta-language for designing SLs. This meta-language will enable us to provide semantic definitions of the source and target SLs involved in a given model transformation on a compatible basis; this in turn will enable us to precisely formulate and check the requirement of correctness preservation. We believe these abilities to be essential in realizing the full potential of MDA.

This paper describes the first phase of our research: the formal definition of both the static and the dynamic semantics of a small but realistic object-oriented language, called TAAL, using graph transformations. We have defined our own language because in this way we can avoid dealing with more complex constructs like exception handling and multi-threading. Still TAAL includes common object-oriented features like inheritance. While formal, we do not leave this exercise on a theoretical level only: we have developed a parser/analyzer and used an existing graph transformation tool so as to actually simulate programs. In fact, all graphs shown in this paper are directly taken from the implementation. We are confident that we can extend the approach described here to be applicable to a large category of SLs, including modeling languages and imperative programming languages.

This paper is structured as follows. Sect. 2 gives an overview of our approach and introduces graph transformations and TAAL. In Sect. 3 we discuss how we represent and generate the flow of control of a TAAL-program. Sect. 4 then discusses our main contribution, namely our way of specifying object-oriented dynamic semantics through an operational definition. We conclude in Sect. 5 with a brief description of the tooling used and some remarks on related and further work. All steps described in this paper are explained by using a simple example.

2   Approach

In this work we model object-oriented programs as graphs, and specify their semantics using graph transformations. The approach we have taken is to define a small language that nonetheless contains the most relevant concepts from object-oriented programming languages. This language is called TAAL. We define a series of transformations that will turn any TAAL-program into a simulation of its execution.

The transformations are depicted in Fig. 1. The first transformation, from textual program to Flat Abstract Syntax Graph, actually consists of three transformations. Due to space limitations, we do not discuss the details of these transformations, two of which are similar to the first steps in a compiler [3]. The interested reader is referred to [13]. The more interesting transformations, i.e. the flow graph construction and the simulation, involve the application of

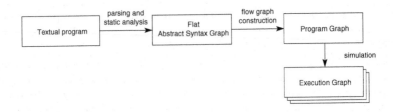

Fig. 1. Overview of the transformation from program to simulation

graph transformations and will therefore be discussed in more detail. The graph transformations are carried out in the Groove Tool Set [20].

During flow graph construction we apply a set of graph transformation rules to transform a plain graph representing the abstract syntax of the textual program, called the Flat Abstract Syntax Graph, into a graph that includes control flow information. The result of this transformation is called the Program Graph. The execution of the TAAL-program is simulated by Execution Graphs which are the result of applying another set of graph transformation rules. These rules define the dynamic (or execution) semantics of our object-oriented language TAAL.

Note that the Program Graph and the corresponding Execution Graphs are at a different level of modelling. This is reflected in Fig. 1 by the use of a vertical arrow instead of a horizontal one. The Program Graph is a single graph representing the static TAAL-program including control flow information, whereas during simulation the dynamics of the program execution are represented by a series of Execution Graphs, each of which represents the system state at a certain point in time.

2.1   The Formalism

After the parsing and static analysis phase, the textual program in Fig. 1 is represented as a plain graph (the Flat Abstract Syntax Graph), and the subsequent transformations are driven by sets of graph transformation rules. Such rules are themselves given as graphs. This will be shown later in this section.

In this paper we use edge-labelled graphs, defined over a global set *Lab* of labels, as follows.

Definition 1. *A graph* $G = \langle V, E \rangle$ *consists of:*
- *a set V of vertices (or nodes), and*
- *a set $E \subseteq V \times Lab \times V$ of edges.*

The following is a definition of a graph transformation rule.

Definition 2. *A graph transformation rule* $p = \langle L, R, \mathcal{N} \rangle$ *consists of:*

- *a graph L being the* left hand side *(LHS) of the rule;*
- *a graph R being the* right hand side *(RHS) of the rule;*
- *a set of graphs $\mathcal{N}$ being the* negative application conditions *(NACs).*

The application of a graph transformation rule transforms a graph G, the *source graph*, into a graph H, the *target graph*, by looking for an occurrence of L in G and then replacing that occurrence of L with R, resulting in H. The role of the NACs [10] is that they can still prevent application of the rule when an occurrence of the LHS has been found, namely if there is an occurrence of some $N \in \mathcal{N}$ in G that *extends* the candidate occurrence of L. A precise technical description of the search for occurrences and the transformation process is given in [22]; for a more theoretical exposition see [23].

It is important to realize that the application of a graph transformation rule to a given graph G is non-deterministic in that there may be more than occurrence of L in G; but for any particular occurrence, the application is deterministic.

Individual graph transformation rules are collected into *graph production systems* (GPSs), which as a whole are used to model transformation or computation processes. The application of a GPS comes down to the unscheduled, non-deterministic application of successive individual rules until a graph is obtained that cannot be transformed any further. Note that this introduces another level of non-determinism, namely in the choice of rule to be applied. A GPSs is *confluent* if it is such that the order of application actually does not make a difference to the end result.

In this paper we use two GPSs, namely to model the flow graph construction and simulation steps of Fig. 1. As we will see, the first of these is confluent whereas the second is deterministic due to the fact that at any stage during the transformation system, at most one rule is applicable, which then has precisely one occurrence.

When visualizing graphs and graph transformation rules, we use a shorthand notation for labelled edges pointing from one node to itself, so called *self-edges*. In this shorthand notation we put the label inside the node.

Example 1. Fig. 2 (i) depicts a graph transformation rule by showing its LHS and its RHS. The LHS consists of three nodes and five labelled edges; the RHS consists of three nodes and six labelled edges. Note that self-edges are also counted. The result of applying this transformation rule is the creation of a **flowNext**-edge and the redirection of the **flowIn**-edge. (To be precise, the **flowIn**-edge in the LHS graph will be removed and a new **flowIn**-edge will be created.)

In this paper we use a shorthand notation for graph transformation rules by displaying them as single graphs. The different roles a graph element can have in the transformation process are distinguished by different coloured shapes:

- thin solid nodes and edges, called *readers*: they are required to be in the source graph in order for the rule to apply, and are unaffected by rule application, i.e. they are still present in the target graph.
- thin dashed nodes and edges (blue in a coloured print-out), called *erasers*: they are required to be in the source graph in order for the rule to apply, and are deleted by rule application.
- fat solid nodes and edges (green), called *creators*: they are not required to be in the source graph, and are created by rule application.

– fat dashed nodes and edges (red), called *embargoes* (or negative application conditions): they are forbidden to occur in a graph in order for the rule to apply.

Fig. 2 (ii) shows the graph transformation rule from Fig. 2 (i) using the described shorthand notation. Note that this rule does not include negative application conditions.

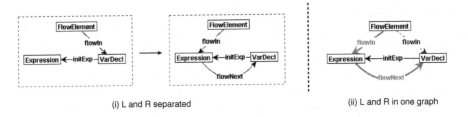

(i) L and R separated   (ii) L and R in one graph

Fig. 2. Example of a graph transformation rule

When using graphs for representing *states* and graph transformations as *state transitions*, applying graph transformations is analogue to creating a *transition system* in which the transitions are labelled with the names of the transformation rules. In Sect. 4 we will show a labelled transition system generated this way representing the simulation of an example program.

2.2   The Mini Language TAAL

In this section we discuss the mini language TAAL, which incorporates the basic aspects of many commonly used object-oriented programming languages. For instance, the notions of class, attribute, operation, inheritance, instantiation and overriding are all present. The meta-model shown in Fig. 3 gives an impression of the abstract syntax of the language. The driving intuition behind the semantics is that a TAAL-program has essentially the same meaning as a corresponding Java-program. An important difference with Java is that the start of the program is represented by a single start expression. Listing 1 contains a TAAL-program that will be used as example throughout this paper. More details on the definition of TAAL can be found in [13]. We emphasize that the developed sets of transformation rules enable simulation of any TAAL-program, not just this example.

Some elements from Fig. 3 that will be referred to later in this paper are Program, ObjectType, OperImpl, and VarDecl. The class Program represents the whole program. The Flat Abstract Syntax Graph of any TAAL-program has exactly one instance of this class. Within a TAAL-program we can declare multiple data-structures, each being an instance of ObjectType. Such a data-structure may contain operations (being instances of OperImpl) and fields (being instances of VarDecl). The classes Statement and Expression are abstract and indicate that the language facilitates different types of both.

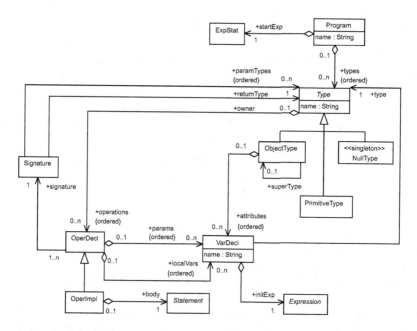

Fig. 3. The types in the abstract syntax graph meta-model

```
 1  program amoebaworld
 2  { new Amoeba().clone() }
 3    class Amoeba
 4    child: Amoeba;
 5    clone() : Amoeba {
 6      child := new Amoeba();
 7      return child;
 8    }
 9    endclass
10  endprogram
```

Listing 1. An example TAAL-program

The result of the parsing and static analysis of a TAAL program (see Fig. 1) is a Flat Abstract Syntax Graph. The Flat Abstract Syntax Graph of the example from Listing 1 is shown in Fig. 4. This graph is an instance of the meta-model from Fig. 3. Some cross-referencing edges have been grayed-out in order to make the graph more readable.

3   Flow Graph Construction

Flow graph construction is the analysis of the flow of control and the construction of flow graph elements which will later on enable the program's simulation. The result of this analysis is the Program Graph (cf. Fig. 1), which consists of the

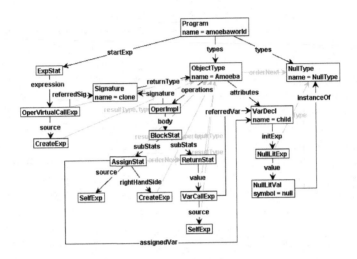

Fig. 4. Flat Abstract Syntax Graph for the example

Flat Abstract Syntax Graph enriched with a number of flow graphs. In this section we will describe the structure of flow graphs and the way we construct them.

Flow Graph Structure. Traditionally (e.g. [9]), flow graphs are directed graphs consisting of four types of nodes (also called flow elements), namely one *start node*, one *end node*, and a number of *procedure* and *predicate nodes* in between, which are connected by *successor*-edges. In our approach we enrich flow graphs with a new node-type, namely the *context node*, and distinct between three types of successor-edges, namely **flowNext**, **flowTrue**, and **flowFalse**. Fig. 5 shows the meta-model of such Flow Graphs.

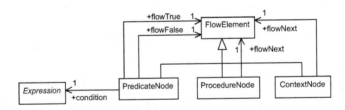

Fig. 5. Flow Graph meta-model

Procedure nodes represent statements or expressions after which it is deterministic which statement to execute next. Predicate nodes represent executable statements and expressions that are related to a boolean condition. The actual value of the condition determines which statement will be executed next. The context nodes represent the start and end node of each Flow Graph. Note that as a result every Flow Graph is cyclic.

The edges in a Flow Graph represent the sequential relation between statements. Fig. 5 shows what kind of edges are allowed between different flow elements. The edges have one of the labels *flowNext*, *flowTrue*, or *flowFalse*.

Flow Graphs, in this paper, appear at three different contexts corresponding to the type of context-node (the types are elements from Fig. 3).

- **Program** context. **Program** Flow Graphs control the startup of the program being modelled. In TAAL, program startup is modelled by the execution of the initial expression of the program (line 2 in Listing 1). A Program Graph always contains exactly one Flow Graph at **Program** context.
- **ObjectType** context. **ObjectType** Flow Graphs are traversed when an object is instantiated. Object creation will be discussed in more detail in Sect. 4. A Program Graph contains an **ObjectType** Flow Graph for each **ObjectType** being specified in the original program.
- **OperImpl** context. **OperImpl** Flow Graphs control the execution of the body of operations. A Program Graph contains an **OperImpl** Flow Graph for each operation that has been implemented in the original program.

Flow Graphs that appear in the Program Graph at any context are not interconnected. The connection between different Flow Graphs is established during simulation. For example, when instantiating a class inside a operation, the Flow Graph of that operation and the Flow Graph of the object to be created are then 'dynamically connected'. This will be discussed in more detail in Sect. 4.

Graph Transformations for Flow Construction. To extract the flow information from the abstract syntax graph, we apply a set of graph transformation rules that traverses the syntax graph in a *top-down* fashion. The general approach is that for every type of statement or expression we specify a graph transformation rule. Each rule contains a node representing the statement type involved. Fig. 2 showed the Flow Graph construction rule for a **VarDecl**-element. These graph transformation rules together form a *confluent* graph production system.

After finishing the phase of Flow Graph construction the part of the Program Graph which models the Flow Graphs (i.e. projected on the flow-edges) is an instance of the meta-model shown in Fig. 5. The Program Graph which is constructed from the Flat Abstract Syntax Graph from Fig. 4 is shown in Fig. 6. Elements in Fig. 6 that are not part of any Flow Graph are grayed-out.

4 Simulation

This section presents the next step from Fig. 1, namely defining the operational semantics of TAAL, in terms of graph transformation. The graphs being transformed are so-called *Execution Graphs*, which represent snapshots of the program state. The transformation rules themselves simulate individual program constructs. The resulting GPS, when applied to a flow graph of the kind

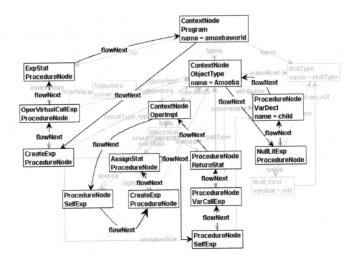

Fig. 6. Program Graph of the example highlighting its Flow Graphs

discussed in the previous section, gives to a transition system, in which the graphs are states and rules applications are transitions. Since program execution is deterministic, so are the transition systems; in other words, at any point in time at most one rule from the GPS is applicable. (In Sect. 5 we briefly discuss the extension of this work to parallel programs, which instead will be non-deterministic, due the independent execution of parallel threads.)

4.1 Execution Graphs

Each Execution Graph combines three kinds of information: a *Program Graph* (see Sect. 3), which provides static context information, a *Value Graph*, which models the data part of the current state, and a *Frame Graph*, which models the process part of the current state. In compiler terms, the Value Graph models the heap and the Frame Graph the stack during program execution.

A Value Graph contains elements representing the objects that will be created and referred to while executing the program. A meta-model for the Value Graph is shown in Fig. 7. The meta-model was inspired by the instance models from [5] and [18]. The new concepts in value graphs are: **Value**, which stands for any data value, be it a primitive value or an object; and **Slot**, which is essentially a container for such a value. **Slots** can either represent program variables (the sub-type **VarSlot**) or holders of auxiliary, intermediate values (**AuxSlot**). For the former there is always an associated variable declaration (**VarDecl**), whereas the latter are bound to **Expressions** in the Program Graph at which the intermediate values occur.

The Frame Graph meta-model is shown in Fig. 8. It essentially introduces only one new type of node: the **Frame**. This stands for the execution of the

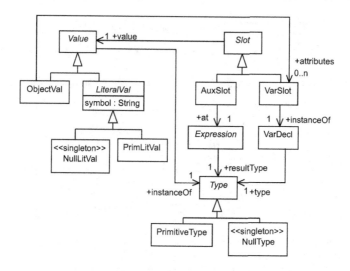

Fig. 7. Value Graph meta-model

program fragment at a **ContextNode** (see Fig. 5), with a pointer (labelled **pc** for *program counter*) to the **FlowElement** in the corresponding Flow Graph at which control currently resides. In fact, for each sub-type of **ContextNode** there is one **Frame** sub-type.

An example (partial) Execution Graph can be found in Fig. 9. This represents the state of our example program (Listing 1) before executing the return-statement in Line 7. At this moment three frames are active: the **ProgramFrame**, the **OperFrame** for the clone method, and the **ConstrFrame** for the creation of the new object.

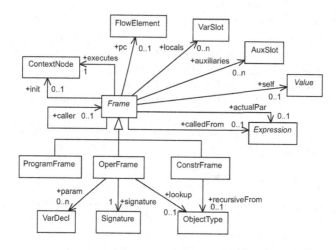

Fig. 8. Frame Graph meta-model

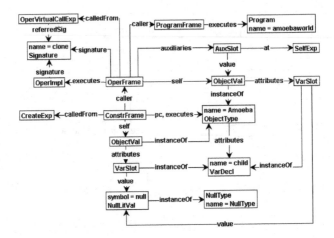

Fig. 9. Fragment of an Execution Graph (at Line 7 of Listing 1)

4.2 Operational Semantics

We now discuss the graph transformation rules that define the dynamic semantics of TAAL. The rules essentially define the effect of the individual statements and expressions of the program in terms of the Value Graph and Frame Graph. For instance, object creation, and assignment to attributes are reflected in the Value Graph, whereas method invocation is reflected mainly in the Frame Graph.

This means that, when we apply the resulting transformation system to the start graph of a given program (being the Program Graph resulting from the Flow Graph construction described in the previous section), each rule application corresponds to the execution of a small step in the program. As an example, Fig. 10 shows the resulting transition system for the example program of Listing 1 in the form of another graph, where the edge labels are rule names. In Sect. 5 we describe the tools used to generate this view.

The complete set of simulation rules for TAAL is too large to include in this paper. They can be found in [13]. Fig. 11 shows a few example rules. The complete set of rules can be divided into three categories: flow element execution rules, object creation rules, and method lookup rules. We believe these three categories to be invariant with respect to the chosen language.

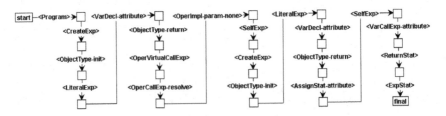

Fig. 10. Transition system of the simulation of Listing 1

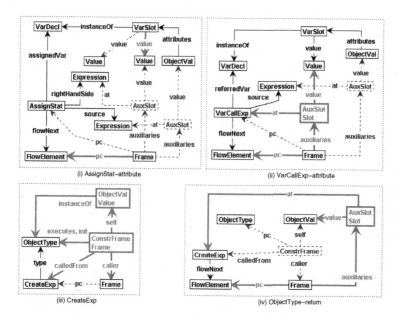

Fig. 11. Example simulation rules

Flow Element Execution. This category consists of a small number of rules (usually one, in some cases two) per kind of FlowElement. These rules describe the essential function of that particular FlowElement. They are always triggered by the fact that the **pc**-edge from a **Frame** node (in the Frame Graph) arrives at an instance of the relevant flow element type (in the Program Graph), and they also always adapt the **pc**-edge to point to a next statement in the Flow Graph. We illustrate this on two examples.

VarCallExp. A VarCallExp is an expression that retrieves the value of a variable. We distinguish two cases: the variable may be an instance variable or attribute (signalled by the fact that the **VarCallExp**-node has a **source**) or a local variable or parameter. The first of these is illustrated in Fig. 11 (ii). In either case the **referredVar** (in the Program Graph) identifies a unique **VarSlot** (in the Value Graph); execution of the **VarCallExp**-rule then consists of creating a fresh **AuxSlot** for the expression and assigning the current value of the **referredVar** to it. Furthermore, the pc-pointer is moved forward.

AssignStat. The effect of an AssignStat is to make a variable (modelled by a VarSlot) point to a pre-computed value - the **rightHandSide** of the assignment. Just as for the VarCallExp-rule, we have to distinguish the cases of instance and local variables; the former is illustrated in Fig. 11 (i). In either case, the **assignedVar** (possibly together with the **AuxSlot** at the **source**-referenced **Expression**) uniquely identifies a **VarSlot**-instance; this receives the value of the **AuxSlot** at the **rightHandSide**. The **AuxSlot**-instances involved are subsequently discarded.

Object Creation. This consists of allocating and initializing nodes for a new object and its instance variables. In most object-oriented languages, allocation and initialization are done in two different passes, of which the first assigns a default initial value to all fields. In TAAL, we have taken a more simplistic approach: all attributes have an initializing expression. This means we can construct locations for the variables and simultaneously assign initial values to those locations, provided we take care that this process starts at the top of the inheritance hierarchy. This results in the following steps:

Allocation: The actual object creation occurs when control reaches a CreateExp-instance. A ConstrFrame and an ObjectVal are created straight away. The ObjectVal is referenced through self from the ConstrFrame. Moreover, the fresh ConstrFrame has an init-pointer to the ObjectType, to indicate the fact that we are initializing an instance of this type. This is shown as rule CreateExp in Fig. 11 (iii).

Initialization: A ConstrFrame-instance with an init-edge to an ObjectType is treated in either of two ways, depending on whether the ObjectType has a super type. If it has a super type, then a new ConstrFrame is created recursively for that, but with the same self. If it has no super type, then execution is started, by replacing the init-edge with a pc-edge pointing to the first FlowElement reachable from the ObjectType. The subsequent simulation rules will compute initial values and assign them to newly instantiated AuxSlot-instances for the ObjectVal.

Termination: A ConstrFrame terminates when the pc-edge has arrived (back) at the ObjectType. The frame is discarded, and a pc-edge is (re)created at the caller frame. Just as for initialization, there is a case distinction, depending on whether the current frame was called recursively from a sub-type or directly from a CreateExp. The latter case is depicted in Fig. 11 (iv): the ConstrFrame is discarded and the underlying object, pointed to by self, is returned to the caller, where it is assigned to an AuxSlot-instance (also created freshly) storing the value at the CreateExp-node.

Method Lookup. This is a phase that occurs each time after a method is called (through an OperCallExp). The call itself creates a new OperFrame (in the Frame Graph). However, the call (in the Program Graph) only references the *signature* of the method to be executed; a matching method implementation (OperImpl) must be looked up in the server object's self-type. When it is found, the arguments (in the Value Graph) are transferred to that OperImpl's formal parameters. Finally, the new OperFrame is started by creating a pc-edge for it, after which the flow element execution rules take over.

5   Conclusion

The work described in this paper shows a complete example of how programming languages can be defined using graphs and graph transformation rules. The language definition of TAAL includes all necessary parts of a language definition: (abstract) syntax and semantics, which have been defined using a single formalism. Although other work has been presented that uses graphs and graph transformation rules (e.g. [6]) for (parts of) language definitions, none of these reaches the same level of completeness. For instance, the semantics specification in [27] merely includes the static semantics, while our work encompasses execution semantics as well as static semantics. Independently, Hausmann and Engels [11, 8] have developed a similar approach to the definition of language semantics. Both their and our work is based on earlier work by the pUML group [15, 5].

The use of graph transformation rules to specify the semantic rules offers a number of advantages. First, the visual representation of the graph transformation rules provides an intuitive understanding of the semantics. Second, the graph transformation rules offer the possibility to include in one mathematical structure, the graph, information on both the run-time system and the program that is being executed. Traditional approaches to operational semantics (e.g. [1, 26, 19, 4, 12, 2, 7]) often need to revert to inclusion of run-time concepts in the syntax definition, e.g. inclusion of the concept of location to indicate a value that may possibly change over time. This seems to be an artificial manner of integrating parts of the language definition, i.e. of the abstract syntax and the semantic domain, that become much more natural in a graph representation. Finally, in graph transformation rules, context information can be included more naturally and uniformly than for example when using SOS-rules [26].

The example language that we have chosen comprises some of the fundamental aspects of object-oriented programming languages, like inheritance, including dynamic method look-up, and object creation. The structure of our solution makes us confident that the approach can be extended to real-life software languages in the object-oriented paradigm:

- All the transformation steps (parsing, static analysis, flow generation and simulation) are structured according to the concepts in the abstract syntax. This lends a modularity to the definitions that is independent of the language being defined.
- The structure of the Flow and Execution Graphs is generic, in the sense that the elements therein are not specific to TAAL; rather, they capture the essential aspects of imperative, object-oriented languages.

Work that is closely related to ours is by Corradini et al. [6]. They use graph transformations to formalize the semantics of a realistic programming language: they address a fairly large fragment of Java. Technically, the difference is that they interpret method invocation *unfolding* — meaning that the *program graph* changes dynamically. This obviates the need for the frame graph, at the price of having program-dependent rules (namely, one per method implementation).

Another difference is that they provide no tool support, and in that sense theirs is a more theoretical exercise. Another, less directly related source of research is on defining dynamic semantics of (UML-type) design models, where also the idea of using graph transformations has been proposed, e.g. in [8, 16, 25]. Furthermore, in Engels et al. [8] ideas are presented on how to use collaboration diagrams, interpreted as graph transformation rules, for defining SL semantics.

A final aspect of the work reported here is that we have not only developed the TAAL language definition but supporting tools as well. This means that we can actually compile and simulate any TAAL-program and store the resulting transition system so, for instance, all the ingredients for verification are there. Both tool sets as well as the full sets of transformation rules defined the flow generation and simulation phases are available for downloading [14, 21].

An area of further research will be to lift the approach outlined here to a more general level, thus creating a meta language to define software languages, including their semantics. A first step has already been reported in [24], in which rules are specified for building a control flow graph for any imperative object-oriented language. This will give rise to a method for defining the semantics of SLs, which fill the gap currently present in MDA, as pointed out in the introduction. We also intend to investigate whether this approach is applicable for non OO-languages as well. Currently we are working on implementing model checking techniques for verifying object-oriented programs where states are represented as graphs and execution steps as graph transformations.

References

1. M. Abadi and L. Cardelli. *A Theory of Objects*. Monographs in Computer Science. Springer, 1996.
2. E. Ábrahám, F. S. de Boer, W.-P. de Roever, and M. Steffen. Inductive proof outlines for monitors in java. In E. Najm, U. Nestmann, and P. Stevens, editors, *Formal Methods for Open Object-based Distributed Systems*, volume 2884 of *Lecture Notes in Computer Science*, pages 155–169. Springer, 2003.
3. A. V. Aho, R. Sethi, and J. D. Ullman. *Compilers: Principles, Techniques, and Tools*. Addison-Wesley, 1986.
4. K. Bruce, J. Crabtree, and G. Kanapathy. An operational semantics for TOOPLE: A statically-typed object-oriented programming language. In S. Brookes, M. Main, A. Melton, M. Mislove, and D. Schmidt, editors, *Mathematical Foundations of Programming Semantics*, volume 802 of *Lecture Notes in Computer Science*, pages 603–626. Springer, 1994.
5. T. Clark, A. Evans, S. Kent, S. Brodsky, and S. Cook. A feasibility study in rearchitecting UML as a family of languages using a precise OO meta-modelling approach, September 2000. Version 1.0 available from www.puml.org.
6. A. Corradini, F. L. Dotti, L. Foss, and L. Ribeiro. Translating Java code to graph transformation systems. In H. Ehrig, G. Engels, F. Parisi-Presicce, and G. Rozenberg, editors, *Proceedings of the 2nd International Conference on Graph Transformations (ICGT'04)*, volume 3256 of *Lecture Notes in Computer Science*, pages 383–398. Springer, 2004.
7. F. S. de Boer and C. Pierik. How to cook a complete hoare logic for your pet OO language. In F. S. de Boer, M. M. Bonsangue, S. Graf, and W.-P. de Roever, editors, *Formal Methods for Components and Objects (FMCO'04)*, volume 3188 of *Lecture Notes in Computer Science*, pages 111–133. Springer, 2004.
8. G. Engels, J. H. Hausmann, R. Heckel, and S. Sauer. Dynamic meta modeling: A graphical approach to the operational semantics of behavioral diagrams in UML. In A. Evans, S. Kent, and B. Selic, editors, *Proceedings of the Third International Conference on the Unified Modelling Language (UML2000)*, volume 1939 of *Lecture Notes in Computer Science*, pages 323–337. Springer, 2000.

9. N. E. Fenton and S. L. Pfleeger. *Software Metrics: A Rigorous & Practical Approach*. International Thomsen Publishing Inc., 2nd edition, 1997.
10. A. Habel, R. Heckel, and G. Taentzer. Graph grammars with negative application conditions. *Fundamenta Informaticae*, 26(3-4):287–313, 1996.
11. J. H. Hausmann. *Dynamic Meta Modeling, A Semantics Description technique for Visual Modeling Languages*. PhD thesis, University of Paderborn, 2006.
12. im B. Bruce, A. Schuett, R. van Gent, and A. Fiech. PolyTOIL: A type-safe polymorphic object-oriented language. *ACM Trans. Program. Lang. Syst.*, 25(2):225–290, 2003.
13. H. Kastenberg, A. Kleppe, and A. Rensink. Engineering object-oriented semantics using graph transformations. CTIT Technical Report 06-12, University of Twente, 2006. Available at http://www.cs.utwente.nl/~kastenbe/papers/taal.pdf.
14. A. Kleppe. Taal eclipse plugin, 2006. Available from http://www.klasse.nl/english/research/taal-install.html.
15. A. Kleppe and J. Warmer. Unification of static and dynamic semantics of UML, a study in redefining the semantics of the UML using the pUML OO meta modelling approach. Technical report, Klasse Objecten, July 2001. Available at http://www.klasse.nl/papers/unification-report.pdf.
16. S. Kuske, M. Gogolla, R. Kollmann, and H.-J. Kreowski. An integrated semantics for UML class, object and state diagrams based on graph transformation. In M. J. Butler, L. Petre, and K. Sere, editors, *Proceedings of the 3rd International Conference on Integrated Formal Methods (IFM'02)*, volume 2335 of *Lecture Notes in Computer Science*, pages 11–28. Springer, 2002.
17. OMG. MDA guide version 1.0.1, June 2003. Available from www.omg.org.
18. OMG. UML 2.0 OCL specification, October 2003. Available from www.omg.org.
19. B. C. Pierce. *Types and Programming Languages*. The MIT Press, 2002.
20. A. Rensink. The GROOVE Simulator: A tool for state space generation. In J. L. Pfaltz, M. Nagl, and B. Böhlen, editors, *Applications of Graph Transformations with Industrial Relevance (AGTIVE'03)*, volume 3062 of *Lecture Notes in Computer Science*, pages 479–485. Springer, 2004.
21. A. Rensink. The Groove Tool Set, 2005. Available from http://groove.sf.net.
22. A. Rensink. The joys of graph transformation. *Nieuwsbrief van de Nederlandse Vereniging voor Theoretische Informatica*, 9, 2005.
23. G. Rozenberg, editor. *Handbook of Graph Grammars and Computing by Graph Transformation*, volume I: Foundations. World Scientific, 1997.
24. R. M. Smelik. Specification and construction of control flow semantics. Master's thesis, University of Twente, January 2006.
25. D. Varró. A formal semantics of UML statecharts by model transition systems. In A. Corradini, H. Ehrig, H.-J. Kreowski, and G. Rozenberg, editors, *Proceedings of the 1st International Conference on Graph Transformation (ICGT'02)*, volume 2505 of *Lecture Notes in Computer Science*, pages 378–392. Springer, 2002.
26. G. Winskel. *The formal semantics of programming languages: an introduction*. MIT Press, 1993.
27. K.-B. Zhang, M. A. Orgun, and K. Zhang. Visual language semantics specification in the vispro system. In J. S. Jin, P. Eades, D. D. Feng, and H. Yan, editors, *VIP*, volume 22 of *CRPIT*. Australian Computer Society, 2002.

Type-Safe Runtime Class Upgrades in Creol

Ingrid Chieh Yu, Einar Broch Johnsen, and Olaf Owe

Department of Informatics, University of Oslo
P.O. Box 1080 Blindern, NO-0316 Oslo, Norway
{ingridcy, einarj, olaf}@ifi.uio.no

Abstract. Modern applications distributed across networks such as the Internet may need to evolve without compromising application availability. Object systems are well suited for runtime update, as encapsulation clearly separates internal structure and external services. This paper considers a type-safe asynchronous mechanism for dynamic class upgrade, allowing class hierarchies to be updated in such a way that the existing objects of the upgraded class and of its subclasses gradually evolve at runtime. New external services may be introduced in classes and old services may be reprogrammed while static type checking ensures that asynchronous class updates maintain type safety. A formalization is shown in the Creol language which, addressing distributed and object-oriented systems, provides a natural framework for dynamic upgrades.

1 Introduction

Long-lived distributed applications with high availability requirements need the ability to adapt to new requirements that arise over time without compromising application availability. These requirements include bugfixes but also new or improved features. Examples of such applications are found in financial transaction processes, aeronautics and space missions, and mobile and Internet applications. In these examples, updates must be applied at runtime. Early approaches to software updates [4, 12, 16] do not address the issue of continuous availability, but runtime reconfiguration and upgrade have recently attracted attention [3,2,9,10,11,19,17,1,5,21]. In large distributed systems runtime updates need to be applied in an asynchronous and modular way, and propagate gradually through the distributed system. An appropriate update system should [1,21]: propagate updates automatically, provide a means to control *when* components may be upgraded, and ensure the availability of system services during the upgrade process.

This paper considers a type-safe mechanism for distributed runtime updates in Creol [13], a formally defined object-oriented language which specifically targets open distributed systems. We consider updates in the form of runtime upgrades of existing classes combined with runtime additions of new interfaces and new classes. Upgrading a class affects all future and existing object instances of the class and its subclasses. As runtime upgrades are handled by asynchronous messages, allowing message overtaking, dependencies between different upgrades could violate type safety. Extending previous work [14], this paper introduces a

R. Gorrieri and H. Wehrheim (Eds.): FMOODS 2006, LNCS 4037, pp. 202–217, 2006.

type system for class upgrades which derives the upgrade dependencies of each upgrade. These dependencies enforce an ordering of the upgrades in the runtime system, formalized in rewriting logic [18], which ensures that the application of the distributed upgrades is type-safe. Consequently, runtime class upgrades will not introduce type errors. The upgrade mechanism proposed in this paper allows new interfaces to be added to classes at runtime. This way upgraded classes may provide new external services. The following simple example illustrates dependencies between several updates.

Motivating example. We adopt a separation of concerns between external service specifications, given as interfaces, and implementation code, organized in classes. Object pointers are typed by interfaces while objects are instances of classes. A type system is used to ensure that methods invoked on object pointers are supported by the objects. Consider a simple scenario with three classes C_1, C_2, and C_3, where C_3 inherits C_2 (the comment *V:1* means version 1 of a class):

```
class C1 --- V:1, U:0       class C2 --- V:1, U:0       class C3 --- V:1, U:0
begin                       begin    end               inherits C2
op run() == n(); run()                                 begin    end
op n() == skip
end
```

The example sketch is given in Creol, *U:0* comments that a class has not (yet) been upgraded. Here, C_1 objects are active as the *run* method is activated at object creation, with a nonterminating behavior consisting of repeated local calls to a method n. The external functionality of each class is given by its interfaces. None are given here, so in this example only internal calls are possible in C_1.

By *dynamically upgrading* the class C_2 with a new method m, this method will become available via objects of classes C_2 and its subclass C_3. However, after the update the new method is only known internally in these classes. In order to *export* the new functionality, we dynamically add a new interface I providing a method m with an appropriate signature, after which m may be invoked on pointers typed by I. If we can type check that C_3 implements I, it is type-safe to bind a pointer typed by I to an instance of C_3 and invoke the new method m on this object. This may be achieved by dynamically redefining method n in class C_1 to create an appropriately typed instance of C_3 and invoke m on this instance, for instance by the code **var** $x : I; x :=$ **new** $C_3(); x.m()$. These dynamic updates may be realized by four update messages added to the running system: introducing I, upgrading C_1 by the redefinition of n, C_2 by a new method m, and C_3 by the new interface I. After successful upgrades (*U:1*), the following classes replace the previous runtime class definitions:

```
class C1 --- V:2, U:1       class C2 --- V:2, U:1       class C3 --- V:3, U:1
begin                       begin                       implements I
op run() == n(); run()      op m() == Body              inherits C2
op n() == var x : I;        end                         begin    end
   x := new C3(); x.m()
end
```

Furthermore, the active behavior of existing instances of C_1 now create instances of C_3 on which the new method m is invoked.

A type-safe introduction of these upgrades in a distributed system requires a combination of type checking and careful timing at runtime. In particular, the redefinition of method n has an immediate effect on any instance of C_1. In order to avoid errors, this upgrade cannot be applied *before* C_3 implements the new interface I. However, the addition of the new interface requires the presence of method m, which in turn requires that the application of the upgrade of C_2 has *already* occurred. In fact, C_3 has been upgraded twice, once directly and once indirectly through the upgrade of C_2. This paper formalizes an asynchronous update mechanism which handles these dependencies, maintaining runtime type safety throughout the upgrade process.

Paper overview. Sect. 2 introduces behavioral interfaces, Sect. 3 summarizes Creol, Sect. 4 presents Creol's type system, and Sect. 5 presents the dynamic class construct. Sect. 6 discusses related work and Sect. 7 concludes the paper.

2   Behavioral Interfaces

An object may assume different roles, depending on the context of interaction, which are captured by specifications of aspects of its externally observable behavior. A *behavioral interface* consists of a set of method names with signatures and semantic constraints on the use of these methods. In this paper we restrict semantic constraints to cointerface requirements, explained as follows: For active objects it may be desirable to restrict access to the methods in an interface to calling objects of a particular *cointerface*. This way the called object may invoke methods of the caller and not only passively complete invocations of its own methods, thus providing support for callback. *Mutual dependency* is specified if two interfaces have each other as cointerface. Let *Any* be the superinterface of all interfaces; *Any* is used as cointerface if no callback knowledge is required.

Object references (pointers) are typed by behavioral interfaces. References typed by different interfaces may refer to the same object identifier. A class *implements* an interface if its object instances provide the behavior described by the interface. A class may implement several interfaces and different classes may implement the same interface. Reasoning control is ensured by interface-level substitutability: *a reference typed by an interface I may be replaced by another reference typed by I or by a subinterface of I.* This substitutability is reflected in the executable language by the fact that late binding applies to all external method calls, as the runtime class of the object need not be statically known.

Let τ_B be a set of basic data type names and τ_I a set of interface names, such that $\tau_B \cap \tau_I = \emptyset$. Let τ denote the set of all types; $\tau_B \subseteq \tau$ and $\tau_I \subseteq \tau$. Let I and J be typical elements of τ_I, and T of τ. We assume that τ_B includes standard types such as Booleans and natural numbers. Type schemes such as parametrized data types may be applied to types in τ to form new types in τ, Set$[T]$ and List$[T]$ are included among the type schemes. To conveniently organize object viewpoints, interfaces may be structured in an inheritance hierarchy.

Definition 1. *An* interface *is denoted by a term* $int(Inh, Mtd)$ *of type* $\mathcal{I}$, *where* Inh *is a list of (inherited) interfaces and* Mtd *is a set of method declarations* $mdecl(Nm, Co, In, Out)$, *where* Nm *is a method name,* Co *is a cointerface, and* In *and* Out *are lists of parameter types.*

Dot notation is used to access the elements of tuples such as methods and interfaces; e.g., $int(Is, M).Mtd = M$. The empty list is denoted ε. The name $Any \in \tau_{\mathcal{I}}$ is reserved for $int(\varepsilon, \emptyset)$, and the name $Internal \in \tau_{\mathcal{I}}$ is reserved for type checking purposes (see Sect. 3). If I inherits J, the methods of both I and J must be available in any class that implements I. We consider a nominal subtype relation [20] for interfaces. Two interfaces with the same set of methods may be part of different subtype relationships.

3   Creol: A Language for Distributed Concurrent Objects

Creol is a high-level object-oriented language targeting open distributed systems by combining interface types and concurrent objects with asynchronous method calls, and by combining active and reactive object behavior [15,13]. In this paper blocking and nonblocking (suspending) method calls are considered, although the results of the paper apply to the full language. An object has its own processor which evaluates local processes. Processes result from method activations. Active behavior is initiated by the special *run* method, activated at object creation, and interleaved with reactive behavior by means of suspension. Due to suspension, the values of object variables may depend on the nondeterministic interleaving of processes, so local process variables supplement the object variables and include the formal parameters. An object may contain several (pending) activations of a method, possibly with different values for local variables.

Objects only interact through asynchronous method calls. Calls can always be emitted, as a receiving object cannot block communication. Method overtaking is allowed: if methods offered by an object are invoked in one order, the object may start execution of the method activations in another order. A *blocking* call $x.m(\text{E}; \text{V})$ immediately blocks the processor while waiting for a reply. A *nonblocking* call **await** $x.m(\text{E}; \text{V})$ releases the processor while waiting for a reply, allowing other processes to execute. When the reply arrives, the suspended process becomes enabled and evaluation may resume. This approach provides flexibility in the distributed setting: suspended processes or new method activations may be evaluated while waiting. If the called object never replies, deadlock is avoided as other activity in the object is possible. However, when the reply arrives, the *continuation* of the process must compete with other pending and enabled processes. After processor release, any enabled pending process may be selected for evaluation. When x evaluates to *self*, the call is said to be local. *Internal* calls are not prefixed by an object identifier and are identified syntactically, otherwise the call is external. All internal calls are here late bound.

The language distinguishes data, typed by data types, and objects, typed by interfaces. We assume given a *strongly typed functional language* of well-typed expressions $e \in$ Expr without side effects, including two subtypes ObjExpr and

$$CL \quad ::= [\textbf{class } C \; [(Vdecl)]^? \; [\textbf{implements } [I]_;^+]^? \; [\textbf{inherits } [C[(\text{E})]^?]_;^+]^?$$
$$\textbf{begin } [\textbf{var } Vdecl]^? \; [[\textbf{with } I]^? \; Methods]^* \; \textbf{end}]^*$$
$$Methods ::= [\textbf{op } m \; ([\textbf{in } Vdecl]^? \; [\textbf{out } Vdecl]^?) == [\textbf{var } Vdecl;]^? \; \text{s}]^+$$
$$Vdecl \quad ::= [v : T]_;^+$$

Fig. 1. An outline of the language syntax for classes, excluding expressions e, expression lists E, and statement lists S. The meta notation $[\ldots]^?$ denotes optional parts, $[\ldots]^*$ repetition zero or more times, and $[\ldots]_d^+$ non-empty repetition with d as delimiter.

BoolExpr whose expressions reduce to object references (typed by interface) and Booleans, respectively. There are no constructors or field access functions for terms in ObjExpr, but variables bound to object references may be compared by an equality function. Let Γ_F be a typing environment which includes all relevant type information for the constants and functions of the functional language, and let Γ extend Γ_F with variable declarations. Then $\Gamma \vdash_F e : T$ denotes that e has type T in Γ. It is assumed that expressions are *type-sound*: well-typed expressions remain well-typed during evaluation. If $\Gamma \vdash_F e : T$ and e reduces to e', then $\Gamma \vdash_F e' : T'$ such that $T' \preceq T$.

Object-oriented features extend the functional language. Class definitions include declarations of persistent state variables and method definitions.

Definition 2. *A* class *is denoted by a term* class(Par, Upg, Imp, Inh, Var, Mtd), *where* Par *is a list of typed program variables,* Upg *the current upgrade number,* Imp *a list of interface names,* Inh *a list of class names, defining class inheritance,* Var *a list of typed program variables (possibly with initial expressions), and* Mtd *a set of methods* mtd(Nm, Co, In, Out, Body) *where* Nm *is a method name,* Co *an interface,* In *and* Out *lists of variable declarations, and* Body *a pair of variable declarations* Vdecl *and statements* s.

The Upg attribute is not a part of the Creol syntax and cannot be altered by programmers. For internal methods, the cointerface field is *Internal*. The field Imp represents interfaces supported by this class. The typing of remote method calls in a class C relies on the fact that the calling object supports the interfaces of C, and these are used to check any cointerface requirements of the calls.

Let τ_C denote the set of class names, with typical element C, and $\mathcal{C}$ the set of class terms. An abstract representation of a class may be given following the BNF syntax of Figure 1. Method declarations in classes consist of local variable declarations and a list of program statements (see Figure 2). Assignment to local and object variables is expressed as V := E for a disjoint list of program variables V and an expression list E, of matching types. In-parameters as well as the pseudo-variables *self*, for self reference, and *caller* are read-only variables.

Due to the interface typing of object variables, the actual class of the receiver of an external call is not statically known. Consequently, external calls are *late bound*. Let the nominal subtype relation $\preceq$ be a reflexive partial ordering on types, including interfaces. The nominal subtype relation restricts a structural subtype relation which ensures substitutability; If $T \preceq T'$ then any value of T may masquerade as a value of T' [20]. For product types R and R', $R \preceq R'$

Syntactic categories.   *Definitions.*
s in Stm v in Var $p ::= m \mid x.m$
m in Mtd p in MtdCall $\textsf{s} ::= s \mid s; s$
e in Expr x in ObjExpr $s ::= \mathbf{skip} \mid \textsc{v} := \textsc{e} \mid v := \mathbf{new}\ C(\textsc{e}) \mid p(\textsc{e}; \textsc{v}) \mid \mathbf{await}\ p(\textsc{e}; \textsc{v})$

Fig. 2. Program statements in method definitions, with typical terms for each category. Capitalized terms such as E denote lists of the given syntactic categories.

is the point-wise extension of the subtype relation. To explain the typing and binding of methods, $\preceq$ is extended to function spaces $A \to B$, where A and B are (possibly empty) product types: $A \to B \preceq A' \to B' \Leftrightarrow A' \preceq A \wedge B \preceq B'$. The static analysis of an internal call $m(\textsc{e}; \textsc{v})$ or **await** $m(\textsc{e}; \textsc{v})$ will assign unique types to the in- and out-parameters depending on the textual context, say $\textsc{e} : T_\textsc{e}$ and $\textsc{v} : T_\textsc{v}$. The call is *type-correct* if there is a method declaration $m : T_1 \to T_2$ in the class C such that $T_1 \to T_2 \preceq T_\textsc{e} \to T_\textsc{v}$. An external call $o.m(\textsc{e}; \textsc{v})$ or **await** $o.m(\textsc{e}; \textsc{v})$ to an object o of interface I is type-correct if it can be bound to a method declaration in I in a similar way. The static analysis of a class will verify that it implements its declared interfaces. Assuming that any object variable typed by I is an instance of a class implementing I, method binding at runtime will succeed regardless of the dynamically identified class of the object.

4   Typing

The typing environment Γ in Creol's nominal type system is a *mapping family*: $\Gamma_\mathcal{I}$ maps interface names to interfaces, $\Gamma_\mathcal{C}$ class names to classes, and $\Gamma_\textsc{v}$ program variable names to types. Without class upgrades, $\Gamma_\mathcal{I}$ and $\Gamma_\mathcal{C}$ correspond to static tables. Declarations may only update $\Gamma_\textsc{v}$, and program statements may not update $\Gamma_\textsc{v}$. For the purposes of dynamic updates, a *dependency mapping* Γ_d captures the dependencies that a class has to different classes in the program.

Definition 3. *The* dependency mapping $\Gamma_d : \tau_C \times \mathsf{Nat} \to \mathsf{Set}[\tau_C \times \mathsf{Nat}]$ *maps pairs of class names and upgrade numbers to sets of such pairs.*

Each upgrade of a class C is uniquely identified by a pair $\langle C, u \rangle$. Thus, elements in $\Gamma_d(\langle C, u \rangle)$ represent classes on which upgrade u of class C depends, and structural requirements to these classes. At runtime Γ_d helps to monitor whether these structural requirements are fulfilled, and to enforce an ordering of local updates obeying the dependency requirements.

The type analysis of a syntactic construct D is formalized by a deductive system for judgments $\Gamma \vdash D \langle \Delta \rangle$, where Γ is the typing environment and Δ the *update* of the typing environment. After analysis of D, the typing environment becomes Γ *overridden by* Δ, denoted $\Gamma + \Delta$. Sequential composition has the rule

$$(\text{SEQ}) \quad \frac{\Gamma \vdash D \langle \Delta \rangle \qquad \Gamma + \Delta \vdash D' \langle \Delta' \rangle}{\Gamma \vdash D; D' \langle \Delta + \Delta' \rangle}$$

where $+$ is an associative operator on mappings with the identity element $\emptyset$. We abbreviate $\Gamma \vdash D \langle \emptyset \rangle$ to $\Gamma \vdash D$. Mapping families are now formally defined.

Definition 4. *Let n be a name, d a declaration, $i \in I$ a mapping index, and $[n \mapsto_i d]$ the binding of n to d indexed by i. A mapping family Γ is built from the empty mapping family $\emptyset$ and indexed bindings by the constructor $+$. The extraction of an indexed mapping Γ_i from Γ and application for the indexed mapping Γ_i, are defined as follows*

$$\emptyset_i \quad\quad\quad\quad = \varepsilon$$
$$(\Gamma + [n \mapsto_{i'} d])_i \quad = \textbf{if } i = i' \textbf{ then } \Gamma_i + [n \mapsto_i d] \textbf{ else } \Gamma_i$$

$$\varepsilon(n) \quad\quad\quad\quad = \bot$$
$$(\Gamma_i + [n \mapsto_i d])(n') = \textbf{if } n = n' \textbf{ then } d \textbf{ else } \Gamma_i(n').$$

A class or interface declaration binds a name to a class or interface term, respectively. Class and interface names need not be distinct. A program consists of a list of interface and class declarations, represented by the mappings $\Gamma_\mathcal{I}$ and $\Gamma_\mathcal{C}$. For type checking a program, each interface and class term is type checked based on these mappings (binding *self* to the class name in the second case). The type rules are given in Figure 3 (omitting the rule for interfaces). To simplify the exposition, some auxiliary functions are used to retrieve information from the typing environment. The predicate *matchpar* verifies that the formal and actual parameters of (inherited) classes match, given a list of classes and a typing environment. The predicate *matchext* checks that an external invocation may be bound through the interface of the callee, based on the types of actual parameter values and the possible cointerfaces of the caller. The function *matchint* returns a list of classes in which an internal invocation may be bound given a method, a list of classes, and a typing environment. This function is used to check that a class provides method bodies for the method declarations of its interfaces, and for type checking internal calls. The function *InhAttr* returns a list of typed variables when given a list of classes and a typing environment, and is used to extend the typing environment with inherited attributes.

The main type rules are now briefly explained. Programs are type checked in the context of Γ_F. Variable declarations extend the context used to type check methods in rule (CLASS). Local variable declarations extend the typing environment used to type check the program statements of a method in rule (METHOD). For object creation, (NEW) ensures that the class must implement an interface which is a subtype of the declared interface of the object pointer. For external calls $x.m$, (EXT) checks that the interface of x offers a method m with a cointerface implemented by the class of the caller. Consequently, *remote calls to self* are allowed when the class implements an interface used as the cointerface of the method in the current class. For internal calls m, (INT) checks that the method has cointerface *Internal*. For a variable occurring in a method body, the pair consisting of the name of the class in which the variable is declared and the upgrade number of this class, are added to the dependency mapping for the method. Similarly, matching classes for internal calls and object creations also extend the mapping. This way, the type system constructs a dependency mapping which captures the dependencies a method has to different classes in the program. This dependency mapping is exploited for system upgrades.

$$(\text{PROG}) \ \frac{\forall I \in \tau_{\mathcal{I}} \cdot \Gamma_{\mathcal{I}} \vdash \Gamma_{\mathcal{I}}(I) \quad \forall C \in \tau_{\mathcal{C}} \cdot \Gamma_F + \Gamma_{\mathcal{I}} + \Gamma_{\mathcal{C}} + [self \mapsto_{\mathsf{v}} C] \vdash \Gamma_{\mathcal{C}}(C)}{\Gamma_F \vdash \Gamma_{\mathcal{I}}, \Gamma_{\mathcal{C}}}$$

$$(\text{CLASS}) \ \frac{\begin{array}{c} \Gamma \vdash Par\langle\Delta\rangle \qquad\qquad \Gamma + \Delta \vdash InhAttr(Inh, \Gamma_{\mathcal{C}}), Var\langle\Delta'\rangle \\ matchpar(\Gamma + \Delta, Inh) \quad \forall m \in Mtd \cdot \Gamma + \Delta + \Delta' \vdash m\langle\Delta^m\rangle \\ \forall I \in Imp \cdot \forall m \in \Gamma_{\mathcal{I}}(I).Mtd \cdot matchint(m, \Gamma_{\mathsf{v}}(self), \Gamma) \neq \varepsilon \end{array}}{\Gamma \vdash class\,(Par, Upg, Imp, Inh, Var, Mtd)\,\langle\Delta + \Delta' + \bigcup_{m \in Mtd} \Delta^m\rangle}$$

$$(\text{METHOD}) \ \frac{\Gamma \vdash (caller : Co); In; Out; Body\,\langle\Delta\rangle}{\Gamma \vdash mtd\,(Nm, Co, In, Out, Body)\,\langle\Delta_d\rangle}$$

$$(\text{SKIP}) \ \Gamma \vdash \mathbf{skip} \qquad (\text{ASSIGN}) \ \frac{\Gamma \vdash_{\mathsf{F}} \mathrm{E} : T' \quad T' \preceq \Gamma_{\mathsf{v}}(\mathrm{V})}{\Gamma \vdash \mathrm{V} := \mathrm{E}\,\langle[\bullet \mapsto_d \Gamma_d(\bullet) \cup [\![\mathrm{V}; \mathrm{E}]\!]]\rangle}$$

$$(\text{VAR}) \ \frac{v \notin \Gamma_{\mathsf{v}} \quad T \preceq \mathsf{Data}}{\Gamma \vdash v : T\,\langle[v \mapsto_{\mathsf{v}} T]\rangle} \qquad (\text{NON-BL}) \ \frac{\Gamma \vdash p(\mathrm{E}; \mathrm{V})\,\langle\Delta\rangle}{\Gamma \vdash \mathbf{await}\ p(\mathrm{E}; \mathrm{V})\,\langle\Delta\rangle}$$

$$(\text{NEW}) \ \frac{\Gamma \vdash_{\mathsf{F}} \mathrm{E} : T \quad T \preceq type(\Gamma_{\mathcal{C}}(C).Par) \quad \exists I \in \Gamma_{\mathcal{C}}(C).Imp \cdot I \preceq \Gamma_{\mathsf{v}}(v)}{\Gamma \vdash v := \mathbf{new}\ C(\mathrm{E})\,\langle[\bullet \mapsto_d \Gamma_d(\bullet) \cup [\![v; \mathrm{E}]\!] \cup \{\langle C, \Gamma_{\mathcal{C}}(C).Upg\rangle\}]\rangle}$$

$$(\text{EXT}) \ \frac{\Gamma \vdash_{\mathsf{F}} e : I \quad \Gamma \vdash_{\mathsf{F}} \mathrm{E} : T \quad matchext(m, T, \mathrm{V}, I, \Gamma_{\mathsf{v}}(self), \Gamma)}{\Gamma \vdash e.m(\mathrm{E}; \mathrm{V})\,\langle[\bullet \mapsto_d \Gamma_d(\bullet) \cup [\![\mathrm{E}; \mathrm{V}]\!]]\rangle}$$

$$(\text{INT}) \ \frac{\Gamma \vdash_{\mathsf{F}} \mathrm{E} : T \quad C' \in matchint(mtd\,(m, Internal, T, \Gamma_{\mathsf{v}}(\mathrm{V}), \varepsilon), \Gamma_{\mathsf{v}}(self), \Gamma)}{\Gamma \vdash m(\mathrm{E}; \mathrm{V})\,\langle[\bullet \mapsto_d \Gamma_d(\bullet) \cup [\![\mathrm{E}; \mathrm{V}]\!] \cup \{\langle C', \Gamma_{\mathcal{C}}(C').Upg\rangle\}]\rangle}$$

Fig. 3. The type system, where $\bullet$ acts as a placeholder for values of type $\langle\tau_{\mathcal{C}} \times \mathsf{Nat}\rangle$, $[\![\mathrm{E}]\!]$ returns a set of class names and upgrade numbers for the classes in which the attributes in an expression list E are declared (relative to $self$ in Γ), and $type$ extracts the types of a declaration list.

5   Dynamic Class Upgrades

New interfaces, new classes, and class upgrades may update the running system. New interfaces and classes extend the system while class upgrades allow method redefinition as well as extending the class with new attributes, methods, interfaces, and superclasses. Modifications should not compromise the type safety of the running program; e.g., a method redefinition must preserve the signature so the class consistently supports its interfaces. In an open distributed setting, upgrades of classes and objects are not sequentialized; rather, upgrades propagate *asynchronously* through the network causing objects of different versions to coexist. Consequently, the order in which upgrades happen at runtime may differ from the order in which they were type checked. For upgrades with no syntactic dependencies, this overtaking does not affect runtime type safety. If there are syntactic dependencies between upgrades, the order of upgrades must respect these dependencies. The following kinds of system updates are considered:

Definition 5. *Systems are updated through the following operations:*

- *An* interface addition *is represented by a term* new-interface(N, R), *where N is an interface name and R is an interface term.*

$$\text{(NEW-INTERFACE)} \quad \frac{N \notin \Gamma_\mathcal{I} \qquad \Gamma + [N \mapsto_I R] \vdash R}{\Gamma \vdash \text{new-interface}\,(N, R)\,\langle N \mapsto_I R\rangle}$$

$$\text{(NEW-CLASS)} \quad \frac{N \notin \Gamma_\mathcal{C} \qquad \Gamma + [self \mapsto_\mathsf{v} N] + [N \mapsto_\mathcal{C} R] \vdash R\,\langle \Delta\rangle}{\Gamma \vdash \text{new-class}\,(N, R)\,\langle [N \mapsto_\mathcal{C} R] + [\langle N, 1\rangle \mapsto_d (\Delta_d(\bullet) \setminus \{\langle N, 0\rangle\})]\rangle}$$

$$\text{(UP)} \quad \frac{\begin{array}{c} \Gamma \vdash self : N; \Gamma_\mathcal{C}(N)\,\langle \Gamma'\rangle \qquad\qquad \forall I \in Imp \cdot I \in \Gamma_\mathcal{I} \\ \Gamma + \Gamma' \vdash InhAttr(Inh, \Gamma_\mathcal{C}); Var\,\langle \Delta\rangle \qquad matchpar(\Gamma + \Gamma', Inh) \\ \forall m \in Mtd \cdot \textbf{if } m.Nm \in \Gamma_\mathcal{C}(N).Mtd \\ \quad \textbf{then } \Gamma + \Gamma' + [N \mapsto_\mathcal{C} upg(\Gamma_\mathcal{C}(N), 0, \epsilon, Inh, \epsilon, Mtd \setminus m)] + \Delta \vdash_r m\,\langle \Delta^m\rangle \\ \quad \textbf{else } \ \ \Gamma + \Gamma' + [N \mapsto_\mathcal{C} upg(\Gamma_\mathcal{C}(N), 0, \epsilon, Inh, \epsilon, Mtd)] + \Delta \vdash m\,\langle \Delta^m\rangle \ \textbf{fi} \\ \forall I \in Imp \cdot \forall m' \in \Gamma_\mathcal{I}(I).Mtd \ \cdot (matchint(m', (N; Inh)), \Gamma) \neq \epsilon \\ \vee (\exists m \in Mtd(m'.Nm) \cdot Sig(m) \preceq Sig(m'))) \end{array}}{\begin{array}{c} \Gamma \vdash upd\,(N, Imp, Inh, Var, Mtd)\,\langle [N \mapsto_\mathcal{C} upg(\Gamma_\mathcal{C}(N), 1, Imp, Inh, Var, Mtd)] \\ + [\langle N, \Gamma_\mathcal{C}(N).Upg + 1\rangle \mapsto_d \bigcup_{m \in Mtd} \Delta_d^m(\bullet) \cup \{\langle N, \Gamma_\mathcal{C}(N).Upg\rangle\}]\rangle \end{array}}$$

$$\text{(MTD-RDEF)} \quad \frac{Sig(mdef) \preceq Sig(\Gamma_\mathcal{C}(\Gamma_\mathsf{v}(self)).Mtd(mdef.Nm))}{\Gamma + [\Gamma_\mathcal{C}(\Gamma_\mathsf{v}(self) \mapsto_\mathcal{C} upg(\Gamma_\mathcal{C}(\Gamma_\mathsf{v}(self), 0, \epsilon, \epsilon, \epsilon, mdef)] \vdash mdef\,\langle \Delta\rangle}{\Gamma \vdash_r mdef\,\langle \Delta_d(\bullet)\rangle}$$

Fig. 4. The type system for class upgrades. Here, $\vdash_r$ is used for type checking of redefined methods, and $Mtd(N)$ denotes the subset of methods in Mtd with name N.

- A class addition *is represented by a term* new-class(N, R), *where N is a class name and R is a class term.*
- A class upgrade *is represented by a term* upd (N, Imp, Inh, Var, Mtd), *where N is the name of the class to be upgraded, Imp a list of interfaces, Inh a list of classes, defining additional superclasses to be inherited, Var a list of typed program variables, and Mtd a set of methods.*

Type checking class upgrades results in dependency conditions which ensure that system modifications do not violate the type safety of the running system. Given an upgrade of a class C in a well-typed program P, an upgrade is type checked based on the current typing environment Γ of P: the mappings in Γ are modified by upgrades. Thus, the upgraded versions of classes as accumulated in the environment resulting from a (successful) type checking, serve as the starting point of future updates.

5.1 Type Checking System Updates

The rules to type check new interfaces and classes, class upgrades, and method redefinitions are given in Figure 4. After type checking new interfaces and classes, the typing environment is extended. Let Γ be the typing environment after type checking a well-typed program P. An upgrade of a class $C \in P$ is then type checked in Γ; i.e., $\Gamma \vdash upd\,(C, Imp, Inh, Var, Mtd)\,\langle \Gamma_d' + \Gamma_\mathcal{C}'\rangle$, where $\Gamma_\mathcal{C}'$ is updates of the class representation in $\Gamma_\mathcal{C}$, computed by the auxiliary function upg, and Γ_d' is dependency requirements to classes in P for the upgrade of C accumulated while type checking. The next update is type checked in $\Gamma + \Gamma_d' + \Gamma_\mathcal{C}'$.

Definition 6. *Let n be a natural number, I a list of interfaces, I' a list of classes, V a list of variables, and M a set of methods. The upgraded version of a class resulting from a class update is defined by the upg function:*

$$upg(class\,(Par, Upg, Imp, Inh, Var, Mtd), n, \mathrm{I}, \mathrm{I}', \mathrm{V}, \mathrm{M})$$
$$= class\,(Par, Upg + n, Imp;\,\mathrm{I}, Inh;\,\mathrm{I}', Var;\,\mathrm{V}, Mtd \oplus \mathrm{M})$$

For class upgrades, the typing environment is reloaded for the upgrading class before type checking the upgrade elements with the rule (UP). By adding new interfaces, the class may provide new external services. For each new interface, the type system requires that the class provides, either by inheritance, by local declarations, or by the current upgrade, at least one type-correct method body for each method in the interface. The function *Sig* takes a method as argument and returns its signature, including the cointerface as an explicit in-parameter. If new superclasses are added, the inheritance list in Γ_C must be extended accordingly before type checking method bodies, as there might be internal calls to methods in the new superclasses. This also applies to methods, due to calls to methods introduced in the same upgrade. The function *matchpar* verifies that the formal and actual parameters of new inherited classes match, and that these classes are contained in the class mapping Γ_C. Inherited attributes, as well as new object variables, will further extend the typing environment. For each method, the effect system of rule (METHOD) computes the dependencies associated with the method body. Finally, after the type analysis of the upgrade term of a class C, the Γ_C mapping is upgraded and the dependency mapping for the $(\Gamma_C(C).Upg + 1)$'th upgrade of class C is constructed, which is a mapping from $\langle C, \Gamma_C(C).Upg + 1 \rangle$ to the dependencies identified by the type analysis of the upgrade term. For method redefinition, the rule (MTD-RDEF) ensures that the redefined method still satisfies the interface requirements implemented by the class. For purely internal methods, the new cointerface must be *Internal*.

At runtime, upgrades are asynchronous and may bypass each other. Hence, well-typed upgrades may give runtime errors if not applied in a type-correct order. We show that Γ_d, provided by the type system, helps to ensure that each upgrade is applied at an appropriate time: If both a class C' and a superclass C are updated, then upgrades will be applied at runtime in the order decided by the static type system, e.g., C is upgraded first if the upgrade of C' depends on the upgrade of C. However, upgrades that do not depend on each other may be applied in parallel. It is therefore necessary that $\Gamma_d(\langle C, u \rangle)$ is included as an argument to the runtime class upgrade $\langle C, u \rangle$. This is achieved by translating the update term $upd\,(C, Imp, Inh, Var, Mtd)$ into the runtime message $upgrade\,(C, Inh, Var, Mtd, \Gamma_d(\langle C, \Gamma_C(C).Upg \rangle))$ where Γ is the environment obtained from type checking the update term. Note that the implements-clause is not needed after type checking.

5.2 Operational Semantics

The operational semantics of Creol is defined in rewriting logic (RL) [18] and is executable on the RL system Maude [6]. A rewrite theory is a 4-tuple (Σ, E, L, R)

where the signature Σ defines the function symbols, E defines equations between terms, L is a set of labels, and R is a set of labeled rewrite rules. Rewrite rules apply to terms of given sorts. Sorts are specified in (membership) equational logic (Σ, E). When modeling computational systems, different system components are typically modeled by terms of the different sorts defined in the equational logic. The global state configuration is defined as a multiset of these terms. RL extends algebraic specification techniques with transition rules: The dynamic behavior of a system is captured by rewrite rules supplementing the equations which define the term language. From a computational viewpoint, a rewrite rule $t \longrightarrow t'$ may be interpreted as a *local transition rule* allowing an instance of the pattern t to evolve into the corresponding instance of the pattern t'. When auxiliary functions are needed in the semantics, these are defined in equational logic, and are evaluated in between the state transitions [18]. If rewrite rules apply to non-overlapping sub-configurations, the transitions may be performed in parallel. Consequently, concurrency is implicit in RL. Conditional rewrite rules $t \longrightarrow t'$ **if** *cond* are allowed, where the condition *cond* can be formulated as a conjunction of rewrites and equations that must hold for the main rule to apply.

A *system configuration* is a multiset combining Creol classes, objects, and messages. A Creol method call is reflected by a pair of messages, and object activity is organized around a *message queue* which contains incoming messages and a *process queue* which contains pending processes, i.e., remaining parts of method activations. The associative list constructor is written as ';', and the associative and commutative constructors for multisets and sets by whitespace. Representing argument positions by "_", terms $\langle$ _ : $Ob \,|\, Cl :$ _, $Pr :$ _, $PrQ :$ _, $Lvar :$ _, $Att :$ _, $Qu :$ _$\rangle$ denote Creol objects, where Ob is the object identifier, Cl the *class identifier* which consists of a class name and *version number*, Pr the active process code, PrQ and Qu are multisets of pending processes and incoming messages with unspecified queue orderings, respectively, and $Lvar$ and Att the local and object state, respectively. Terms $\langle$ _ : $Cl \,|\, Upd :$ _, $Inh :$ _, $Att :$ _, $Mtds :$ _$\rangle$ represent Creol classes, where Cl is the class identifier, Upd the upgrade number, Inh a list of class identifiers, Att a list of attributes, and $Mtds$ a set of methods. The class identifier for version n of class C is denoted $C\#n$. The rules for the static language constructs may be found in [13]. Focus here is on method binding and dynamic class constructs, given in Figure 5.

An *implicit inheritance graph* is used to facilitate dynamic reconfiguration mechanisms. The binding mechanism dynamically inspects the class hierarchy in the system configuration. When an invocation message $invoc(m, Sig, In)$ representing a call to a method m is found in the message queue of an object o of class $C\#n$, where Sig is the method signature as provided by the caller and In is the list of actual in-parameters, a message $bind(o, m, Sig, In)$ **to** $C\#n$ is generated. If m is defined locally in $C\#n$ with a matching signature, a process with the declared method code and local state is returned in a *bound* message. Otherwise, the *bind* message is retransmitted to the superclasses of C. Thus the *bind* message is sent from a class to its superclasses, dynamically unfolding the inheritance graph as far as needed and resulting in a *bound* message

$\langle o\!:\!Ob \mid Cl : C\#n \rangle \; \langle o\!:\!Qu \mid Ev : \mathrm{Q} \; invoc(m, Sig, In) \rangle$
$\longrightarrow \langle o\!:\!Ob \mid Cl : C\#n \rangle \; \langle o\!:\!Qu \mid Ev : \mathrm{Q} \rangle \; (bind(o, m, Sig, In) \text{ to } C\#n)$

$bind(o, m, Sig, In) \text{ to } \varepsilon \longrightarrow bound(none) \text{ to } o$
$bind(o, m, Sig, In) \text{ to } (C\#n); \mathrm{I}' \; \langle C\#n' : Cl \mid Inh : \mathrm{I}, Mtds : \mathrm{M} \rangle$
$\longrightarrow \textbf{if } match(m, Sig, \mathrm{M}) \textbf{ then } (bound(get(m, \mathrm{M}, In)) \text{ to } o)$
$\qquad\qquad\qquad\quad \textbf{else } (bind(o, m, Sig, In) \text{ to } \mathrm{I}; \mathrm{I}') \textbf{ fi}$
$\qquad \langle C\#n : Cl \mid Inh : \mathrm{I}, Mtds : \mathrm{M} \rangle$

$(bound(w) \text{ to } o) \; \langle o\!:\!Ob \mid PrQ : \mathrm{W} \rangle \longrightarrow \langle o\!:\!Ob \mid PrQ : w \; \mathrm{W} \rangle$

$new\text{-}class(C, \mathrm{I}, \mathrm{A}, \mathrm{M}, ((C'\#n) \; \mathrm{R})) \; \langle C'\#n' : Cl \mid Upd : u \rangle$
$\longrightarrow new\text{-}class(C, \mathrm{I}, \mathrm{A}, \mathrm{M}, \mathrm{R}) \; \langle C'\#n' : Cl \mid Upd : u \rangle \textbf{ if } u \geq n$

$new\text{-}class(C, \mathrm{I}, \mathrm{A}, \mathrm{M}, \varepsilon) \longrightarrow \langle C\#1 : Cl \mid Upd : 1, Inh : \mathrm{I}, Att : \mathrm{A}, Mtds : \mathrm{M}, Tok : 1 \rangle$

$upgrade(C, \mathrm{I}, \mathrm{A}, \mathrm{M}, ((C'\#n) \; \mathrm{R})) \; \langle C'\#n' : Cl \mid Upd : u \rangle$
$\longrightarrow upgrade(C, \mathrm{I}, \mathrm{A}, \mathrm{M}, \mathrm{R}) \; \langle C'\#n' : Cl \mid Upd : u \rangle \textbf{ if } u \geq n$

$upgrade(C, \mathrm{I}', \mathrm{A}', \mathrm{M}', \emptyset) \; \langle C\#n : Cl \mid Upd : u, Inh : \mathrm{I}, Att : \mathrm{A}, Mtds : \mathrm{M}, Tok : T \rangle$
$\longrightarrow \langle C\#(n+1) : Cl \mid Upd : u+1, Inh : \mathrm{I}; \mathrm{I}', Att : \mathrm{A}; \mathrm{A}', Mtds : \mathrm{M} \oplus \mathrm{M}', Tok : T \rangle$

$\langle C\#n : Cl \mid Inh : \mathrm{I}; (C'\#n'); \mathrm{I}' \rangle \; \langle C'\#n'' : Cl \mid \; \rangle$
$= \langle C\#(n+1) : Cl \mid Inh : \mathrm{I}; (C'\#n''); \mathrm{I}' \rangle \; \langle C'\#n'' : Cl \mid \; \rangle \textbf{ if } n'' > n'$

$\langle o\!:\!Ob \mid Cl : C\#n, Pr : \varepsilon \rangle \langle C\#n' : Cl \mid Att : \mathrm{A} \rangle$
$= \langle o\!:\!Ob \mid Cl : C\#n', Pr : \varepsilon \rangle \; \langle C\#n' : Cl \mid Att : \mathrm{A} \rangle \; (getAttr(o, \mathrm{A}) \text{ to } C) \textbf{ if } n' > n$

$(gotAttr(\mathrm{A}') \text{ to } o) \; \langle o\!:\!Ob \mid Att : \mathrm{A} \rangle = \langle o\!:\!Ob \mid Att : \mathrm{A}' \rangle$

Fig. 5. A RL specification of method binding and dynamic class upgrades

returned to the object which generated the *bind* message. The auxiliary predicate $match(m, Sig, \mathrm{M})$ is true if m is declared in M with a signature Sig' such that $Sig' \preceq Sig$, and the function get fetches method m in the method set M of the class and returns a process, resulting from the method activation. Values of the actual in-parameters In are stored in the local process state. The process is loaded into the internal process queue of the callee.

Class upgrades may be direct, or indirect through the upgrade of one of the superclasses. In order to control the upgrade propagation, class representations include an *upgrade number* and a *version number*; i.e., counters which record the number of times a class has been directly upgraded and (directly or indirectly) modified, respectively. When a class is upgraded, both its upgrade and version numbers are incremented. When a super-class of a class C is modified, the version number of C is incremented but the upgrade number of C does not change.

A *direct class upgrade* of a class C is realized through the insertion of a message $upgrade(C, \mathrm{I}, \mathrm{A}, \mathrm{M}, \Gamma_d(\langle C, \Gamma_C(C).Upg \rangle))$ in the system configuration at runtime, where I is an inheritance list, A a state, M a set of method definitions, and $\Gamma_d(\langle C, \Gamma_C(C).Upg \rangle)$ the set of upgrade requirements to classes in the runtime system directly derived from Γ, found by type checking. The upgrade of a class may not be applied unless these requirements are fulfilled. As upgrade is asynchronous, several upgrades may be pending in the runtime system, and the current upgrade may need to wait. A message $upgrade(C, \text{I}', \text{A}', \text{M}', \varepsilon)$, with an empty requirement set, does not have unverified dependencies, and the upgrade may be applied to C. The rule for *direct class upgrade* uses an operator $\oplus$ to overwrite the method set M with the new or redefined methods in M'. During the upgrade, the upgrade and version numbers of the class are also incremented.

Indirect class upgrade propagates upgrade information to subclasses by means of an equation, so instances of the subclasses will acquire new state attributes. Note that by using an equation the indirect class upgrade happens in zero rewrite steps, which corresponds to temporarily locking the upgraded class.

The *upgrade of object instances* must ensure that new attributes are acquired before new code which may rely on new class attributes is evaluated. New object instances automatically get the new class attributes. However, the upgrade of existing object instances of the class must be closely controlled. Each time an object needs to evaluate a method, it requests the code associated with this method name. Problems may arise when executing new or redefined methods which rely on new attributes that are not presently available in the object. With recursive or nonterminating processes, objects cannot generally be expected to reach a state without pending processes, even if the loading of processes corresponding to new method calls from the environment is postponed as in [7, 1]. Consequently, it is too restrictive to wait for the completion of all pending methods before applying an upgrade. However, objects may reach *quiescent* states when the processor has been released and before any pending process has been activated. Any object which does not deadlock will eventually reach a quiescent state. In particular nonterminating activity is implemented by means of recursion, which ensures at least one quiescent state in each cycle. In the case of process termination or an inner suspension point, Pr is empty. The rule for *object upgrade* applies to quiescent states. Exploiting the implicit inheritance graph, attribute upgrade is handled by a message $getAttr$, similar to $bind$, which recursively extends the object state A and results in a message $gotAttr(\text{A}')$. The new object state A' finally replaces A. The use of equations corresponds to locking the object.

The described runtime mechanism allows the upgrade of active objects. Attributes are collected at upgrade time while code is loaded "on demand". A class may be upgraded several times before the object reaches a quiescent state, so the object may have missed some upgrades. However a single state upgrade suffices to ensure that the object, once upgraded, is a complete instance of the present version of its class. The upgrade mechanism ensures that an object upgrade has occurred before new code is evaluated.

5.3   Type-Safe Execution with Dynamic Class Upgrades

The problem of type-safe execution of programs is now addressed. We prove that errors such as method-not-understood do not occur at runtime, even with the proposed dynamic class construct. A type soundness theorem for Creol without dynamic classes was shown in [15]: *Runtime type errors do not occur for well-typed programs*. The theorem implies that runtime assignments to program variables, object creation, and method invocations are type-correct. The proof is by induction over the length of the execution sequence as given by the operational semantics. However, dynamic upgrades as considered in this paper introduce runtime changes as the state adapts to the upgrades. By reasoning about the type system and operational semantics, the following properties are proved for the class upgrade mechanism of this paper:

Lemma 1. *A well-typed class upgrade does not affect the execution of code of existing processes in an object.*

Lemma 2. *The execution of a method activation from a new version of an object's class will not begin before the object's state is updated.*

Lemma 3. *Let Γ be the typing environment for a well-typed program after a series of upgrades, including the upgrade $\langle C, u \rangle$. The upgrade $\langle C, u \rangle$ is applicable iff the runtime structure satisfies $\Gamma_d(\langle C, u \rangle)$.*

Lemma 4. *The execution of processes introduced in a well-typed upgrade will not cause runtime type errors.*

Lemma 4 follows from Lemmas 2 and 3. Lemmas 1 and 4 show that variable assignments, object creation, and method invocations are type-correct when classes are upgraded, for old and new processes, respectively. A type soundness property for Creol with class upgrades can now be proved by induction over the length of execution sequences, extending the proof for the language without dynamic classes. Lemmas 1 and 4 are used for the application of class upgrades:

Theorem 1 (Type soundness). *Well-typed upgrades do not introduce runtime type errors in well-typed programs.*

6 Related Work

Availability during reconfiguration is an essential feature of many modern distributed applications. Dynamic or online system upgrade considers how running systems may evolve. Recently, several authors have investigated type-safe mechanisms for runtime upgrade of imperative [22], functional [3], and object-oriented [8] languages. These approaches consider the upgrade of single type declarations, procedures, objects, or components in the sequential setting. Reclassification in Fickle [8] is based on a type system which guarantees type safety when an object changes its class. Fickle has been extended to multithreading [7], but restrictions to runtime reclassification are needed; e.g., an object with a non-terminating (recursive) method will not be reclassified.

Version control systems aim at a more modular upgrade support. Some approaches allow multiple module versions to coexist after an upgrade [3,2,9,10,11], while others only keep the last version by doing a global update or "hot-swapping" [19,17,1,5]. The approaches also differ in their treatment of active behavior, which may be disallowed [19,17,10,5], delayed [7,1], or supported [22,11]. Approaches based on global update mostly disallow upgrades of active modules. An upgrade system for type declarations and procedures in active code is proposed in [22] for (sequential) C. Type-safe updates occur at annotated program points found by the type system. However, the approach is synchronous as upgrades which cannot be applied immediately will fail.

Dynamic class constructs support modular upgrades. The approach of Hjálm-týsson and Gray [11] for C++, based on proxy classes which link to the actual classes (reference indirection), supports multiple versions of each class. Existing instances are not upgraded, so the activity in existing objects is uninterrupted. Existing approaches for Java, either using proxies [19] or modifying the Java virtual machine [17], are based on global upgrade and are not applicable to active objects. In [19], each class version supports the same interfaces. New interfaces can only be introduced by adding new classes. In [5] the ordering of upgrades are serialized and in [17] invalid upgrades are handled by exceptions.

Automatic upgrade based on lazy global update is addressed in [1] for distributed objects and in [5] for persistent object stores. Here the object instances of upgraded classes are upgraded, but inheritance and (nonterminating) active code are not addressed, which limits the effect of class upgrade. Our approach supports multiple inheritance, but restricts upgrades to addition and redefinition and may therefore avoid these limitations. Only one version of an upgraded class is kept in the system but active objects may still be upgraded. Upgrade is asynchronous and distributed, and may therefore be temporarily delayed. Moreover, the type system handles upgrade dependencies among distributed objects.

7 Conclusion

In this paper a construct for dynamic class upgrades in Creol is presented, including its type system and operational semantics, which allows method redefinition as well as extending classes with new attributes, methods, superclasses, and interfaces, in the running system. By adding new interfaces, classes may provide new external services, while the redefinition of methods may improve existing ones. Our approach exempts programmers from handling the different version numbers of classes when writing upgrade codes.

To address open distributed systems with concurrent objects, we consider an asynchronous update mechanism where upgrade overtaking is possible in the runtime system, and allow objects of different versions to coexist. A successful introduction of upgrades in this setting requires both type checking and careful timing of when the upgrades are applied. Runtime errors would occur if upgrades are applied at a bad time. The type system captures upgrade dependencies and enforces an ordering of upgrades. If the type checking of an upgrade succeeds, an *effect* system provides a list of dependencies for the upgrade. This list of dependencies is used by the runtime system to ensure that dependent upgrades are applied in an order which preserves type correctness, while independent upgrades may be performed simultaneously. Furthermore, it is shown that well-typed runtime upgrades do not introduce type errors. In future work we plan to extend the dynamic construct proposed in this paper with type-safe mechanisms for removing attributes and method definitions, using similar techniques.

References

1. S. Ajmani, B. Liskov, and L. Shrira. Scheduling and simulation: How to upgrade distributed systems. In *Hot Topics in Op. Sys. (HotOS-IX)*, pages 43–48, 2003.
2. J. L. Armstrong and S. R. Virding. Erlang - an experimental telephony programming language. In *XIII International Switching Symposium*, June 1990.
3. G. Bierman, M. Hicks, P. Sewell, and G. Stoyle. Formalizing dynamic software updating. In *Unanticipated Software Evolution (USE)*, May 2003.
4. T. Bloom. *Dynamic Module Replacement in a Distributed Programming System*. PhD thesis, MIT, 1983. Also available as MIT LCS Tech. Report 303.
5. C. Boyapati *et al.* Lazy modular upgrades in persistent object stores. In *OOPSLA 2003*, pages 403–417. ACM Press, 2003.
6. M. Clavel *et al.* Maude: Specification and programming in rewriting logic. *Theoretical Computer Science*, 285:187–243, Aug. 2002.
7. F. Damiani, M. Dezani-Ciancaglini, and P. Giannini. Re-classification and multithreading: Fickle$_{MT}$. In *Symp. Applied Computing (SAC'04)*. ACM Press, 2004.
8. S. Drossopoulou, F. Damiani, M. Dezani-Ciancaglini, and P. Giannini. More dynamic object re-classification: Fickle$_{II}$. *ACM TOPLAS*, 24(2):153–191, 2002.
9. D. Duggan. Type-Based hot swapping of running modules. In *Intl. Conf. Functional Programming (ICFP-01)*, *ACM SIGPLAN* 36(10), pages 62–73, Sept. 2001.
10. D. Gupta, P. Jalote, and G. Barua. A formal framework for on-line software version change. *IEEE Trans. Software Eng.*, 22(2):120–131, 1996.
11. G. Hjálmtýsson and R. S. Gray. Dynamic C++ classes: A lightweight mechanism to update code in a running program. In *Proc. USENIX Tech. Conf.*, May 1998.
12. C. R. Hofmeister and J. M. Purtilo. A framework for dynamic reconfiguration of distributed programs. Tech. Report CS-TR-3119, Univ. of Maryland, 1993.
13. E. B. Johnsen and O. Owe. A dynamic binding strategy for multiple inheritance and asynchronously communicating objects. *Proc. FMCO'04*, LNCS 3657. Springer, 2005.
14. E. B. Johnsen, O. Owe, and I. Simplot-Ryl. A dynamic class construct for asynchronous concurrent objects. In *Proc. FMOODS*, LNCS 3535. Springer, June 2005.
15. E. B. Johnsen, O. Owe, and I. C. Yu. Creol: A type-safe object-oriented model for distributed concurrent systems. Res. Rep. 327, Ifi, Univ. of Oslo, 2005.
16. J. Kramer and J. Magee. The Evolving Philosophers Problem: Dynamic change management. *IEEE Trans. on Software Engineering*, 16(11):1293–1306, Nov. 1990.
17. S. Malabarba, R. Pandey, J. Gragg, E. Barr, and J. F. Barnes. Runtime support for type-safe dynamic Java classes. In *Proc. ECOOP*, LNCS 1850. Springer, 2000.
18. J. Meseguer. Conditional rewriting logic as a unified model of concurrency. *Theoretical Computer Science*, 96:73–155, 1992.
19. A. Orso, A. Rao, and M. J. Harrold. A technique for dynamic updating of Java software. In *Software Maintenance (ICSM 2002)*, pages 649–658. IEEE Press, 2002.
20. B. C. Pierce. *Types and Programming Languages*. The MIT Press, 2002.
21. C. A. N. Soules *et al.* System support for online reconfiguration. In *Proc. USENIX Tech. Conf.*, pages 141–154, 2003.
22. G. Stoyle, M. Hicks, G. Bierman, P. Sewell, and I. Neamtiu. *Mutatis Mutandis*: Safe and flexible dynamic software updating. In *Proc. POPL*, ACM Press, 2005.

Abstract Interface Behavior of Object-Oriented Languages with Monitors

Erika Ábrahám[1], Andreas Grüner[2], and Martin Steffen[2]

[1] Albert-Ludwigs-University Freiburg, Germany
[2] Christian-Albrechts-University Kiel, Germany

Abstract. We characterize the observable behavior of multi-threaded, object-oriented programs with *re-entrant monitors*. The observable uncertainty at the interface is captured by may- and must-approximations for potential resp. necessary lock ownership. The concepts are formalized in an object calculus. We show the soundness of the abstractions.

Keywords: oo languages, formal semantics, thread-based concurrency, monitors, open systems, observable behavior.

1 Introduction

The behavior of an open system or component can be described by sequences of component-environment interactions. Even if the environment is absent, it must be assumed that the component together with the (abstracted) environment gives a well-formed program adhering to the syntactical and the context-sensitive restrictions of the language at hand. Technically, for an exact representation of the interface behavior, the semantics of the open program needs to be formulated under *assumptions* about the environment, capturing those restrictions. The resulting assumption-commitment framework gives insight to the semantical nature of the language at hand. Furthermore, an independent characterization of possible interface behavior with environment and component abstracted can be seen as a trace logic under the most general assumptions, namely conformance to the inherent restrictions of the language and its semantics.

This paper deals primarily with the following features, which correspond to those of modern class-based object-oriented languages like *Java* [8] or *C#* [6] and which are notoriously hard to capture:

- *types and classes:* the languages are statically typed, and only well-typed programs are considered.
- *references:* each object carries a unique *identity*. New objects are dynamically allocated on the heap.
- *concurrency:* the mentioned languages feature concurrency based on *threads* (as opposed to processes or active objects).
- *monitor synchronization:* objects can play the role of monitors [9][5], guaranteeing that synchronized methods are executed mutually exclusive. Recursion —direct or indirect— via method call requires *re-entrant* monitors.

R. Gorrieri and H. Wehrheim (Eds.): FMOODS 2006, LNCS 4037, pp. 218–232, 2006.

We investigate these issues in a class-based, multi-threaded calculus with monitors. The interface behavior is formulated in an assumption-commitment framework and based on three orthogonal abstractions:

- a static abstraction, i.e., the type system;
- an abstraction of the stacks of recursive method invocations, representing the recursive nature of method calls in a multi-threaded setting;
- finally as the main contribution, an abstraction of *lock ownership*.

The contribution of this paper over our previous work in this field (e.g., [2] dealing with deterministic, single-threaded programs, or [4] considering thread classes) is to capture re-entrant monitor behavior. In comparison with the mentioned work, the setting here is simpler in one respect: We disallow instantiation across the interface here; of course, instantiation as such is supported, only not across the boundary between component and environment.

Incorporating monitors into the formal calculus is not only pragmatically motivated —after all, *Java* and similar languages offer monitor synchronization— but also semantically interesting, because the observable equivalences induced by a language offering synchronized methods and one without are incomparable.

Overview. Section 2 contains syntax and operational semantics of the calculus. Section 3 contains an independent characterization of the interface behavior of an open system, especially capturing the effects of lock ownership. Furthermore, it contains the basic soundness results of the abstractions. Section 4 concludes with related and future work. For a full account of the operational semantics and the type system, we refer to the technical report [3].

2   A Multi-threaded Calculus with Classes

This section presents the calculus, which is based on a multi-threaded object calculus, similar to the one presented in [7] and in particular [10].

2.1   Syntax

The abstract syntax is given in Table 1. A program is given by a collection of classes where a class $c[\![O]\!]$ carries a name c and defines its methods and fields. We generally use o and its syntactic variants as names for objects, c for classes, and n for thread names and when being unspecific. An object $o[c, F, n]$ keeps a reference to the class c it instantiates, stores the current value of the fields or instance variables, and maintains a *lock* n, referring to the name of the thread holding the lock. The special name $\perp_{thread}$ (which is not a value) denotes that the lock is free. Immediately after instantiation, all fields carry the undefined reference $\perp_c$, where c is the (return) type of the field, and the lock is free. A method $\varsigma(self{:}c).\lambda(\vec{x}{:}\vec{T}).t$ provides the method body abstracted over the ς-bound "self" parameter and the formal parameters of the method [1]. We distinguish between synchronized and un-synchronized methods conventionally by superscripts l^s resp. l^u, and just l when unspecific. Besides objects and classes, the dynamic configuration of a program contains threads $n\langle t \rangle$ as active entities.

Table 1. Abstract syntax

$$
\begin{array}{lll}
C ::= \mathbf{0} \mid C \parallel C \mid \nu(n{:}T).C \mid n\langle\!\langle O\rangle\!\rangle \mid n[n, F, n] \mid n\langle t\rangle & \text{program} \\
O ::= F, M & \text{object} \\
M ::= l^u = m, \ldots, l^u = m, l^s = m, \ldots, l^s = m & \text{method suite} \\
F ::= l^u = f, \ldots, l^u = f & \text{fields} \\
m ::= \varsigma(n{:}T).\lambda(x{:}T, \ldots, x{:}T).t & \text{method} \\
f ::= \varsigma(n{:}T).\lambda().v \mid \varsigma(n{:}T).\lambda().\bot_n & \text{field} \\
t ::= v \mid stop \mid let\ x{:}T = e\ in\ t & \text{thread} \\
e ::= t \mid if\ v = v\ then\ e\ else\ e \mid if\ undef(v.l)\ then\ e\ else\ e & \text{expr.} \\
\quad\mid\ v.l(v, \ldots, v) \mid v.l := v \mid currentthread & \\
\quad\mid\ new\ n \mid new\langle t\rangle & \\
v ::= x \mid n & \text{values}
\end{array}
$$

A thread is basically either a value or a *let*-construct, which is used for local declarations and sequencing[1] of expressions, notably method calls (written $v.l(\vec{v})$), the creation of new objects $new\ c$ where c is a (component) class name, and *thread creation* $new\langle t\rangle$. We use f for instance variables or fields, $l = v$ for field variable declaration. Field access is written as $v.l$, and field update as $v'.l := v$. Apart from disallowing instantiation cross the interface between component and environment, we impose the following two restrictions on the language: firstly, we disallow direct access (read or write) to fields across object boundaries. Secondly, we forbid that any occurrence of thread creation $new\langle t\rangle$ contains a self-parameter, i.e., a name occurring bound by ς. The reason is that a new thread must start its life "outside" any monitor.

The available types include *thread* as the type of threads. Furthermore, objects are typed by the name of their class. As auxiliary types we have $T_1 \times \ldots \times T_k \to T$ as the type of methods, and furthermore $[l_1{:}U_1, \ldots, l_k{:}U_k]$ as the type or interface of unnamed objects, and $[\![l_1{:}U_1, \ldots, l_k{:}U_k]\!]$ as the type for classes. For brevity, we omit the definition of the type system, as it is straightforward.

2.2 Operational Semantics

The operational semantics is given in two stages, component internal steps and external ones, the latter describe the interaction at the interface. The external steps are defined in reference to assumption and commitment contexts. The static part of the contexts corresponds to the static type system (cf. again [4]) and takes care that, e.g., only well-typed values are received from the environment.

2.2.1 Internal Steps

Table 2 contains a few typical internal reduction steps (the ones for conditionals, sequencing via let, thread creation, etc., are straightforward), distinguishing between confluent steps, written $\rightsquigarrow$, and other internal transitions, written $\xrightarrow{\tau}$. The CALL$_i$-rules treat internal method calls, i.e., a call to an object contained in the configuration, where for synchronized methods, CALL$_{i_1}^s$ takes the free lock and adds a release-action at the end of the method body. Rule CALL$_{i_2}^s$ describes re-entrant calls. In the call-steps, $M.l(o)(\vec{v})$

---

[1] Sequential composition $t_1; t_2$ of two threads stands for $let\ x{:}T = t_1\ in\ t_2$, where x does not occur free in t_2.

resp. $O.l(o)(\vec{v})$ stands for $t[o/s][\vec{v}/\vec{x}]$, when the method suite $[M]$ resp. the object implementation $[O]$ equals $[\ldots, l = \varsigma(s{:}T).\lambda(\vec{x}{:}\vec{T}).t, \ldots]$. The rule CALL_i^u additional deals with field access. Note that the step is a $\xrightarrow{\tau}$-step, not a confluent one. The above reduction relations are used modulo *structural congruence,* which captures the algebraic properties of parallel composition and the hiding operator.

2.2.2 External Steps

A component exchanges information with the environment via *calls* and *returns.* In the labels, n is the thread that issues the call or returns from the call. Note that there are no separate external labels for object instantiation; we have forbidden cross-border instantiation. Given a label $\nu(\varXi).\gamma'$ where $\varXi$ is a name context, i.e., a sequence of single $\nu(n{:}T)$ bindings and where γ' does not contain any binders; we call γ' the *core* of the label. Note that for incoming labels, $\varXi$ contains only bindings to environment objects and at most one thread name; dually for outgoing communication. Given a label γ, we refer with $\lfloor\gamma\rfloor$ to its core. Furthermore, $thread(\gamma)$ denotes the thread of the label. The definitions are used analogously for send and receive labels. We write shortly γ_c for call and γ_r for return labels.

$$\gamma ::= n\langle call\ o.l(\vec{v})\rangle \mid n\langle return(v)\rangle \mid \nu(n{:}T).\gamma \qquad \text{basic labels}$$
$$a ::= \gamma? \mid \gamma! \qquad\qquad\qquad\qquad\qquad\qquad\qquad \text{receive and send labels}$$

The external semantics is formalized as labeled transitions between judgments of the form $\Delta, \Sigma \vdash C : \Theta, \Sigma$, where Δ, Σ represent the *assumptions* about the environment of the component C and Θ, Σ the *commitments.* The assumptions require the existence (plus static typing information) of *named entities* in the environment. The semantics maintains as invariant that the assumption and commitment contexts are disjoint concerning object and class names, whereas a thread name occurs as assumption iff. it is mentioned in the commitments. By convention, the contexts Σ (and their alphabetic variants) contain exactly all bindings for thread names. This means, as invariant

Table 2. Internal steps

$c[\![F, M]\!] \parallel n\langle let\ x{:}c = new\ c\ in\ t\rangle \rightsquigarrow$

$\qquad c[\![F, M]\!] \parallel \nu(o{:}c).(o[c, F, \bot_{thread}] \parallel n\langle let\ x{:}c = o\ in\ t\rangle) \qquad \text{NEWO}_i$

$c[\![F, M]\!] \parallel o[c, F', n'] \parallel n\langle let\ x{:}T = o.l^u(\vec{v})\ in\ t\rangle \xrightarrow{\tau}$

$\qquad c[\![F, M]\!] \parallel o[c, F', n'] \parallel n\langle let\ x{:}T = O.l^u(o)(\vec{v})\ in\ t\rangle \qquad \text{CALL}_i^u$

$c[\![F, M]\!] \parallel o[c, F', \bot_{thread}] \parallel n\langle let\ x{:}T = o.l^s(\vec{v})\ in\ t\rangle \rightsquigarrow$

$\qquad c[\![F, M]\!] \parallel o[c, F', n] \parallel n\langle let\ x{:}T = M.l^s(o)(\vec{v})\ in\ release(o); t\rangle \qquad \text{CALL}_{i_1}^s$

$c[\![F, M]\!] \parallel o[c, F', n] \parallel n\langle let\ x{:}T = o.l^s(\vec{v})\ in\ t\rangle \rightsquigarrow$

$\qquad c[\![F, M]\!] \parallel o[c, F', n] \parallel n\langle let\ x{:}T = M.l^s(o)(\vec{v})\ in\ t\rangle \qquad \text{CALL}_{i_2}^s$

$o[c, F, n] \parallel n\langle let\ x{:}T = release(o)\ in\ t\rangle \xrightarrow{\tau} o[c, F, \bot_{thread}] \parallel n\langle t\rangle \qquad \text{RELEASE}$

---

we maintain for all judgments $\Delta, \Sigma \vdash C : \Theta, \Sigma$ that Δ, Σ, and Θ are pairwise disjoint. The operational semantics is formulated as transitions between typed judgments $\Delta, \Sigma \vdash C : \Theta, \Sigma \xrightarrow{a} \acute{\Delta}, \acute{\Sigma} \vdash \acute{C} : \acute{\Theta}, \acute{\Sigma}$.

Notation 1. *We abbreviate the triple of name contexts Δ, Σ, Θ as Ξ. Furthermore we understand $\acute{\Delta}, \acute{\Sigma}, \acute{\Theta}$ as $\acute{\Xi}$, etc.*

The open semantics checks the *static* assumptions, i.e., whether at most the names actually occurring in the core of the label are mentioned in the ν-binders of the label, and whether the transmitted values are of the correct types. We write $\Xi \vdash a : T$ for that check, where T is type of the expression in the program that gives rise to the label. We omit the exact definition here (see [3]).

Besides *checking* whether the assumptions are met before a transition, the contexts are *updated* by a transition step, reflecting the change of knowledge.

Definition 1 (Context update). *For an incoming label $a = \nu(\Xi')\lfloor a \rfloor$ where n is a thread name s.t. $\Xi' \vdash n$, we define $\acute{\Xi}$ as:*

$$\acute{\Theta} = \Theta + \Theta', \quad \acute{\Delta} = \Delta + (\Delta', \odot_n), \text{ and } \acute{\Sigma} = \Sigma + \Sigma'.$$

In case $\Xi' \not\vdash n$, the summand $\odot_n$ is omitted. We write $\Xi + a$ for the update of Ξ. The update for outgoing communication is defined dually.

The operational rules of Table 3 use two additional expressions *blocks* and *returns v*. The three CALLI-rules deal with incoming calls. For all three cases, the contexts are *updated* to $\acute{\Xi}$ to include the information concerning new objects and threads. Furthermore, it is *checked* whether the label is type-correct and that the step is possible according to the (updated) assumptions $\acute{\Xi}$. In the rules, $fn(\lfloor a \rfloor)$ refers to the free names of $\lfloor a \rfloor$ (which equal $names(\lfloor a \rfloor)$). Outgoing calls are dealt with in rule CALLO. To distinguish the situation from component-internal calls, the receiver must be part of the environment, expressed by $\Delta \vdash o_r$. Starting with a well-typed component, there is no

Table 3. External steps

$$\frac{a = \nu(\Xi').\ n\langle call\ o_r.l(\vec{v})\rangle?\quad t_{blocked} = let\ x':T' = blocks\ in\ t\quad \acute{\Xi} = \Xi + a\quad \acute{\Xi} \vdash \lfloor a \rfloor : T}{\Xi \vdash \nu(\Xi_1).(C \parallel n\langle t_{blocked}\rangle) \xrightarrow{a} \acute{\Xi} \vdash \nu(\Xi_1).(C \parallel n\langle let\ x:T = o_r.l(\vec{v})\ in\ returns\ x; t_{blocked}\rangle)} \ \text{CALLI}_1$$

$$\frac{a = \nu(\Xi').\ n\langle call\ o_r.l(\vec{v})\rangle?\quad \Delta \vdash \odot_n\quad \acute{\Xi} = \Xi + a\quad \acute{\Xi} \vdash \lfloor a \rfloor : T}{\Xi \vdash C \parallel n\langle stop\rangle \xrightarrow{a} \acute{\Xi} \vdash C \parallel n\langle let\ x:T = o_r.l(\vec{v})\ in\ returns\ x; stop\rangle} \ \text{CALLI}_2$$

$$\frac{a = \nu(\Xi').\ n\langle call\ o_r.l(\vec{v})\rangle?\quad \Xi' \vdash n : thread\quad \acute{\Xi} = \Xi + a\quad \acute{\Xi} \vdash \lfloor a \rfloor : T}{\Xi \vdash C \xrightarrow{a} \acute{\Xi} \vdash C \parallel n\langle let\ x:T = o_r.l(\vec{v})\ in\ returns\ x; stop\rangle} \ \text{CALLI}_3$$

$$\frac{a = \nu(\Xi').\ n\langle call\ o_r.l(\vec{v})\rangle!\quad \Xi' = fn(\lfloor a \rfloor) \cap \Xi\quad \acute{\Xi}_1 = \Xi_1 \setminus \Xi'\quad \Delta \vdash o_r\quad \acute{\Xi} = \Xi + a}{\Xi \vdash \nu(\Xi_1).(C \parallel n\langle let\ x:T = o_r.l(\vec{v})\ in\ t\rangle) \xrightarrow{a} \acute{\Xi} \vdash \nu(\acute{\Xi}_1).(C \parallel n\langle let\ x:T = blocks\ in\ t\rangle)} \ \text{CALLO}$$

need in re-checking now that only values of appropriate types are handed out, as the operational steps preserve well-typedness ("subject reduction"). In addition to the rules of Table 3, there are similar ones for communication via returns (cf. [3]).

Note that the steps of Table 3 are independent of *lock* manipulations, e.g., an incoming call, which hands over the message via one of the CALLI-rules does not attempt to obtain the lock; this is done by the internal steps from Table 2. This *decouples* the responsibilities of component and environment in the spirit of the assumption/commitment set-up. Whether an incoming call can be sent by the environment depends *only* on the past interface interaction and the environment, *but not* on an internal state of the component!

3 Interface Behavior

Next we characterize the possible ("legal") interface behavior as interaction traces between component and environment. The calls and returns of each thread must be "parenthetic", i.e., each return must have a prior matching call, and we must take into account whether the thread is resident inside the component or outside. In particular, we must take into account restrictions due to the fact that the method bodies are executed in *mutual exclusion* wrt. individual objects.

3.1 Balance Conditions

We start with auxiliary definitions concerning the parenthetic nature of calls and returns. Starting from an initial configuration, the operational semantics from Section 2.2 assures strict alternation of incoming and outgoing communication and additionally that there is no return without matching prior call.

Definition 2 (Balance). *Let $s \downarrow_n$ be the projection of trace s onto thread n. The balance of a thread n in a sequence s of labels is given by the rules of Table 4, where the dual rules for balanced$^-$ are omitted. We write $\vdash s : balanced_n$ if $\vdash s : balanced_n^+$ or $\vdash s : balanced_n^-$. We call a (not necessarily proper) prefix of a balanced trace weakly balanced. We write $\vdash s : wbalanced_n^+$ if the trace is weakly balanced in n, i.e., if the projection of the trace on n is weakly balanced, and if the last label is an incoming*

Table 4. Balance

$$\frac{}{\vdash \epsilon : balanced^+} \text{ B-EMPTY}^+$$

$$\frac{\vdash s_1 : balanced^+ \quad \vdash s_2 : balanced^+ \quad s_1, s_2 \neq \epsilon}{\vdash s_1\, s_2 : balanced^+} \text{ B-II}$$

$$\frac{\vdash s : balanced^-}{\vdash \nu(\Xi).n\langle call\ o_r.l(\vec{v})\rangle!\ s\ \nu(\Xi').n\langle return(v)\rangle? : balanced^+} \text{ B-OI}$$

communication or if $s \downarrow_n$ is empty; dually for $\vdash s : wbalanced_n^-$. The function pop (on the projection of a trace onto a thread n) is defined as follows:

1. *pop $s = \bot$, if s is balanced in n.*
2. *pop $(s_1 a s_2) = s_1 a$ if $a = \nu(\Xi).n\langle call\ o_r.l(\vec{v})\rangle?$ and s_2 is $balanced_n^+$.*
3. *pop $(s_1 a s_2) = s_1 a$ if $a = \nu(\Xi).n\langle call\ o_r.l(\vec{v})\rangle!$ and s_2 is $balanced_n^-$.*

We use pop $n\ r$ for pop $(r \downarrow_n)$.

Based on a weakly balanced history, we defined the source and target of a communication event at the end of a trace with the help of the function *pop*.

Definition 3 (Sender and receiver). *Let $r\ a$ be the non-empty projection of a balanced trace onto the thread n. Sender and receiver of label a after history r are defined by mutual recursion and pattern matching over the following cases:*

$$sender(\nu(\Xi).n\langle call\ o_r.l(\vec{v})\rangle!) = \odot_n$$
$$sender(r'\ a'\ \nu(\Xi).n\langle call\ o_r.l(\vec{v})\rangle!) = receiver(r'\ a')$$
$$sender(r'\ a'\ \nu(\Xi).n\langle return(v)\rangle!) = receiver(pop(r'\ a'))$$

$$receiver(r\ \nu(\Xi).n\langle call\ o_r.l(\vec{v})\rangle!) = o_r$$
$$receiver(r\ \nu(\Xi).n\langle return(v)\rangle!) = sender(pop(r))$$

For $\nu(\Xi)n\langle call\ o_r.l(\vec{v})\rangle?$ resp. $\nu(\Xi).n\langle return(v)\rangle?$, the definition is dual.

$\Delta, \Sigma \vdash r \triangleright a : \Theta, \Sigma$ asserts that after r, the action a is enabled. Input enabledness checks whether, given a sequence of past communication labels, an incoming call is possible in the next step; analogously for output enabledness. To be input enabled, one checks against the last matching communication. If there is no such label, enabledness depends on where the thread started:

Definition 4 (Enabledness). *Given $\gamma = \nu(\Xi).n\langle call\ o_r.l(\vec{v})\rangle$. Then call-enabledness of γ after history r and in the contexts Δ, Σ and Θ, Σ is defined as:*

$$\Delta, \Sigma \vdash r \triangleright \gamma? : \Theta, \Sigma \text{ if } pop\ n\ r = \bot \quad and \quad \Delta \vdash \odot_n\ or \tag{1}$$
$$pop\ n\ r = r'\gamma'!$$

$$\Delta, \Sigma \vdash r \triangleright \gamma! : \Theta, \Sigma \text{ if } pop\ n\ r = \bot \quad and \quad \Theta \vdash \odot_n\ or \tag{2}$$
$$pop\ n\ r = r'\gamma'?$$

For return labels $\gamma = \nu(\Xi).n\langle return(v)\rangle$, $\Xi \vdash r \triangleright \gamma!$ abbreviates pop $n\ r = r'\nu(\Xi').n\langle call\ o_2.l(\vec{v})\rangle?$, and dually for incoming returns $\gamma?$.

We further combine enabledness and determining sender and receiver (cf. Definitions 4 and 3) into the notation $\Xi \vdash r \triangleright o_s \xrightarrow{a} o_r$.

3.2   Side Conditions for Monitors

Next we address the restrictions imposed by the fact that the methods are synchronized. We assume in the following that *all* methods are synchronized, unless stated otherwise. We proceed in two stages. The first step in Section 3.2.1 concentrates on individual

Table 5. Potential lock ownership for Θ-locks

$$\frac{\vdash s_2 : balanced \qquad s_2 \neq \epsilon \qquad \Xi \vdash s_1 : \Diamond o}{\Xi \vdash s_1\, s_2 : \Diamond o} \text{ M-}\Diamond$$

$$\frac{receiver(s\gamma_c) = o}{\Xi \vdash s\,\gamma_c? : \Diamond o} \text{ M-I}\Diamond_1 \qquad \frac{receiver(s\gamma_c) \neq o \quad \Xi \vdash s : \Diamond o}{\Xi \vdash s\,\gamma_c? : \Diamond o} \text{ M-I}\Diamond_2$$

$$\frac{\Xi \vdash s : \Diamond o}{\Xi \vdash s\,\gamma_c! : \Diamond o} \text{ M-O}\Diamond$$

threads: given the interaction history of a single thread, we present two abstractions, one characterizing situations where the thread *may* hold the lock of a given object, and a second one where, independent of the scheduling, the thread *must* hold the lock. The second step in Section 3.2.2 takes a global view, i.e., considers all threads, to characterize situations in a trace which are (in-)consistent with the fact that objects act as monitors. The formalization is based on a *precedence* or *causal* relation of events of the given trace. This precedence relation formalizes three aspects that regulate the possible orderings of events in a trace:

mutual exclusion: If a thread has taken the lock of a monitor, interactions of other threads with that monitor must either occur *before* the lock is taken, or *after* it has been released again.

data **dependence:** no value (unless generated new) can be transmitted before it has been received.

control **dependence:** within a single thread, the events are linearly ordered.

The formalization of mutual exclusion is complicated by the fact that the locks are not taken atomically, i.e., we often do not have *immediate* information when the lock is taken and relinquished. Instead we must work with the may- and must-approximations calculated in Section 3.2.1.

3.2.1 Lock Ownership
We start by characterizing when, given a history of interaction of a single thread, it *may* own the lock of an object. The "may"-uncertainty is due to the fact that the actual lock manipulation is separated by the corresponding visible interface interaction by some internal i.e., non-observable reduction steps.

Definition 5 (May lock ownership). *Given a sequence s of interactions of a single thread and a component object o, the judgment $\Xi \vdash s : \Diamond o$ ("after s, the thread of s may own the lock of o.") is given by the rules of Table 5. For environment locks, i.e., when o is an environment object, the definition is dual.*

Rule M-$\Diamond$ states that a strongly balanced tail s_2 can be ignored, lock-wise. The two M-I$\Diamond$-rules deal with incoming calls, depending on the receiver of the communication.

If the call concerns the object o in question, the thread may own the lock afterwards. If the receiver is distinct from o (cf. rule M-I$\Diamond_2$), the thread may own the lock of o, if that was the case already before the call. An outgoing call finally does not affect the $\Diamond$-information.

Now to the *definite* knowledge that a thread owns the lock of a given object.

Definition 6 (Must lock ownership). *Given a sequence s of interactions of a single thread and a component object o, the judgment $\Xi \vdash s : \Box o$ ("after s, the thread of s must own the lock of o.") is given by the rules of Table 6. For environment locks, i.e., when o is an environment object, the definition is dual.*

The first rule M-I$\Box_1$ deals with incoming calls. Since the lock is not acquired atomically, an incoming call alone does not guarantee that the thread owns the callee's lock; it potentially owns it according to rule M-I$\Diamond_1$. If however the lock of an object is necessarily owned before the call, the same is true afterwards. Rule M-I$\Box_2$ deals with incoming returns. As for incoming calls, the lock is owned for sure after the communication, if this was true before already. We need to be careful, however. After the return γ_r in question, the thread may continue *internally* i.e., without performing a further interface communication, and this internal reduction may relinquish the lock! This may be the case if the mentioned internal reduction includes the very last internal steps of a synchronized method call, before the call actually returns at the interface, re-establishing balance. In other words, after $\gamma_r?$, the component may be in a state where internally, the lock has already been released, only that the fact has not yet been manifest at the interface. This is captured in the premise $\Xi \vdash r\gamma_r?\gamma_r'! : \Diamond o$, i.e., the trace $r\gamma_r?$ is *extended* by one additional outgoing return $\gamma_r'!$, and if the thread *may* have the lock after this extended trace, then it must have the lock after $\gamma_r?$.

The M-O$\Box$-rules cover outgoing communication. Remember that outgoing communication leaves the $\Diamond$-information unchanged. For $\Box$-information, this is different and characteristic of the non-atomic lock-handling: an incoming call is the sign that we *may* have the lock of a component object, but only a following outgoing call is the observable sign that the component *must* have the lock.

We write $\Xi \vdash t : \Box_n o$ for $\Xi \vdash (t \downarrow_n) : \Box o$, and analogously for $\Diamond_n o$.

Lemma 1 (Decidability). *Given a weakly balanced trace t, the relations $\Xi \vdash t : \Diamond_n o$ and $\Xi \vdash t : \Box_n o$ are decidable.*

Table 6. Necessary lock ownership for Θ-locks

$$\frac{\Xi \vdash t : \Box o}{\Xi \vdash t\gamma_c? : \Box o} \text{ M-I}\Box_1 \qquad \frac{\Xi \vdash t\gamma_r?\gamma_r'! : \Diamond o \quad \Xi \vdash t : \Box o}{\Xi \vdash t\gamma_r? : \Box o} \text{ M-I}\Box_2$$

$$\frac{\Xi \vdash t : \Diamond o}{\Xi \vdash t\gamma_c! : \Box o} \text{ M-O}\Box_1 \qquad \frac{\Xi \vdash t : \Box o}{\Xi \vdash t\gamma_r! : \Box o} \text{ M-O}\Box_2$$

With decidability at hand we can consider the assertions $\Xi \vdash t : \Diamond_n o$ and $\Xi \vdash t : \Box_n o$ as boolean predicates, and we write $\Xi \vdash t : \neg\Diamond_n o$ for $\Xi \not\vdash t : \Diamond_n o$, and analogously for $\Box$.

Lemma 2 ($\Box$ implies $\Diamond$). *Assume a weakly balanced trace t. If $\Xi \vdash t : \Box_n o$ then $\Xi \vdash t : \Diamond_n o$.*

3.2.2   Mutual Exclusion

So far we concentrated on each thread in isolation. This cannot be the whole story, as mutual exclusion is a global property concerning more than one thread. The formalization is based on a *precedence* relation on the events of a trace. An event is an *occurrence* of a label in a trace, i.e., as usual, events are assumed unique. In the following we do not strictly distinguish (notationally) between labels and events, i.e., we write $\gamma?$ for an event labeled by an incoming communication etc. To formalize the dependencies for mutual exclusion, we need to require that certain events are positioned *before* the lock has been taken, or *after* it has been released. So the following definition picks out relevant events of a trace. In the definition, $\preceq$ denotes the prefix relation. The $\Diamond$-function ("after may") designates the labels *after* the point where the lock may be taken, for a given pair of thread and monitor. The $\Box$-function ("before must") picks out the point before a thread enters the monitor.

Definition 7. *Let t be the projection of a weakly balanced trace onto a thread n. Then the set of events $\Diamond(t, o)$ is given by:*

$$\Diamond(t, o) = \{a \mid longest\,prefix \quad sa \preceq t \quad s.t. \; \Xi \vdash s : \Diamond o\} \, . \tag{3}$$

Furthermore, the set of events $\Box(t, o)$ is given as:

$$\Box(t, o) = \{a_1 \mid \Xi \vdash t : \Box o, \quad longest\,prefix \; sa_1 a_2 \preceq t \quad s.t. \tag{4}$$
$$\Xi \vdash s : \neg\Diamond o, \quad \Xi \vdash sa_1 a_2 : \Box o \,\} \, .$$

We use the following abbreviations: $\Diamond_n(t, o)$ stands for $\Diamond(t \downarrow_n, o)$ and $\Diamond_{\neq n}(t, o) = \bigcup_{n' \neq n} \Diamond(t \downarrow_{n'}, o)$, and analogously for $\Box$.

Note that the "set" given by $\Diamond$ in Definition 7 contains one element or is empty. The same holds for $\Box$.

Based on these auxiliary definitions, we now introduce the three types of dependencies we need to consider. We start with data dependence.

Definition 8 (Data dependence). *Given a trace r, reference o, and input label $\gamma?$, we write $\vdash_\Theta r : \gamma? \twoheadrightarrow^d o$ (in words: "o is potentially data-dependent on event/label $\gamma?$ of trace r"), if $o \in names(\gamma)$, where $r'\gamma?$ is a prefix of r. When given a tuple $\vec{o}$ of names, $\vdash_\Theta r : \vec{\gamma}? \twoheadrightarrow^d \vec{o}$ is meant as asserting $\vdash_\Theta r : \gamma_i? \twoheadrightarrow^d o_i$, for all o_i from $\vec{o}$ (for Δ, the definitions are applied dually).*

$$D_\Theta(r\gamma!) = \{\vec{\gamma}? \rightarrow \gamma!\} \quad where \vdash_\Theta \vec{\gamma}? \twoheadrightarrow^d fn(\gamma!) \cap \Delta(r) \tag{5}$$
$$D_\Theta(r\gamma?) = \{\} \, .$$

The definition states that, from the perspective of the component, arguments of an outgoing communication must either be generated previously by the component, or must have entered the component from the outside. The complexity of the technical definition is explained as follows. First of all, we calculate the dependence in equation (5) only for object references occurring free in the output label; those that occur under a ν-binder are generated by the component itself, and do not constitute a data dependence. For the same reason we consider only those free object references, which originally have been passed to the component during the history; we denote all ν-bound environment objects in r by $\Delta(r)$ (dually for component objects). Finally, each such object in $\gamma!$ may be potentially data dependent on *more* than one incoming label in the history r. It suffices to add *one* data dependence edge, which is non-deterministically chosen.

Definition 9 (Control dependence). *Given a trace ra, where $n = thread(a)$, we write $\vdash r : a' \to^c a$, if $r \downarrow_n = r'a'$ for some label a'. We write $C(ra)$ for $\{a' \to a \mid r \vdash a' \to^c a\}$.*

Note that the set $C(ra)$ contains one element, i.e., one edge, or is empty.

Definition 10 (Mutual exclusion). *Given a trace ra and a component object o, the label a gives rise to the precedence edges wrt. component locks given by:*

$$M_\Theta(r\gamma_c?, o) = \grave{\Diamond}_{\neq n}(r, o) \to \gamma_c? \tag{6}$$
$$M_\Theta(r\gamma_r?, o) = \{\}$$
$$M_\Theta(r\gamma!, o) = \gamma! \to \grave{\Box}_{\neq n}(r, o), \grave{\Diamond}_{\neq n}(r, o) \to \grave{\Box}_n(r\gamma!, o)$$

For environment locks, the definition is dual.

Incoming calls can introduce a dependence with *other* threads n' competing for the concerned lock of the callee. Interactions of a thread n' occurring in the history r *after* n' has applied for the lock (but before $\gamma_c?$) makes evident that n' succeeded in entering the monitor. Hence the corresponding monitor interactions of n' must have happened before the current incoming call succeeds in entering the monitor. Incoming returns do not introduce new dependencies wrt. Θ-locks (short for component locks), since the return releases the corresponding lock or keeps it, but does not acquire a lock nor competes for it.

Outgoing communication, however, does introduce dependencies, as they in many cases indicate that a lock definitely is taken or transiently has been taken since the last interaction of that thread. This introduces two types of dependencies. First, if there are other definite lock owners, then the current action $\gamma!$ must precede the monitor interactions of those successful competitors since the outgoing label is a definite sign that the thread of γ has held the lock of o before that step. This explains the edges $\gamma! \to \grave{\Box}_{\neq n}(r, o)$ in the definition. Secondly, $\gamma!$ does not only indicate that the thread in question had the lock prior to the step (at least transiently), but can also introduce definite lock ownership after the step (in particular, an outgoing call can introduce mustownership). Hence, the monitor interactions of all competitors observed in the trace must precede the point, where the current thread n acquires the lock. This explains the dependence $\grave{\Diamond}_{\neq n}(r, o) \to \grave{\Box}_n(r\gamma_c!, o)$.

Example 1. Consider the trace $t = \gamma_{c_1}? \, \gamma_{c_2}? \, \gamma'_{c_1}! \, \gamma_{r_2}!$, in expanded form

$$t = (\nu o':c)n_1\langle call \; o.l(o')\rangle? \; n_2\langle call \; o.l()\rangle? \; n_1\langle call \; o'.l()\rangle! \; n_2\langle return(o')\rangle! \quad (7)$$

This trace is impossible because if n_1 were to enter the monitor before n_2, which is required by the data dependency, it implied that n_1 kept the lock and n_2 *could not* enter the monitor. This consequence is independent of the scheduling.

Formally, Definitions 8 – 10 yield the following dependencies, when considering the trace after two, three, or four steps, respectively:

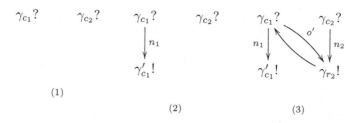

Note that without data dependence from $\gamma_{c_1}?$ to $\gamma_{r_2}!$, the graph is acyclic and the trace possible. Especially, the return $\gamma_{r_2}?$ is possible at the end, even if thread n_1 is guaranteed to hold the lock, since thread n_2 can have performed its monitor interaction before n_1 entered the monitor, only that the return was not yet visible in the trace.   □

3.3 Legal Traces System

Table 7 specifies *legality* of traces; the rules combine all mentioned conditions, type checking, balance, and in particular restrictions due to monitor behavior. We use the same conventions and notations as for the operational semantics (cf. Notation 1). The judgments in the derivation system are of the form

$$G_\Delta; \Delta, \Sigma \vdash r \rhd s : trace \; \Theta, \Sigma; G_\Theta \quad \text{resp.} \quad G; \Xi \vdash r \rhd s : trace \; . \quad (8)$$

In comparison to the judgments used in the operational semantics, the judgment from (8) contains a graph G_Θ as representation of *control, data,* and *mutex*-edges wrt. component locks (cf. Section 3.2.2), and dually G_Δ for environment locks. We adapt Notation 1 appropriately, writing G for the pair (G_Θ, G_Δ).

We write $\Xi \vdash t : trace$, if there exists a derivation of $G_\emptyset; \Xi \vdash \epsilon \rhd t : trace$ according to Table 7, where $G_\emptyset$ is the empty dependence graph. We write $\Xi \vdash_\Delta t : trace$, if there exists a derivation of $G_\emptyset; \Xi \vdash \epsilon \rhd t : trace$, where only the *assumption contexts* are checked in the rules but not the commitments, i.e., the premises $\acute{\Xi} \vdash a : ok$ and $\vdash \acute{G} : ok$ remain in the rules for incoming communication L-CALLI and L-RETI, but for the outgoing communication, the corresponding premises are *omitted* (dually for $\Xi \vdash_\Theta t : trace$).

Now to the rules: As base case, the empty future is always legal, and distinguishing according to the first action a of the trace, the rules check whether a is possible. This check is represented by checking whether the dependencies collected in the pair G are consistent, i.e., that the two graphs are *acyclic*. This is asserted by $\vdash G : ok$. Furthermore, the contexts are updated appropriately, and the rules recur checking the tail of

Table 7. Legal traces (dual rules omitted)

$$\Xi; G \vdash r \rhd \epsilon : trace \qquad \text{L-EMPTY}$$

$$\frac{\begin{array}{c} \Xi \vdash r \rhd o_s \xrightarrow{a} o_r \quad \acute{\Xi} = \Xi + a \quad \acute{\Xi} \vdash a : ok \\ \acute{G}_\Theta = G_\Theta \cup G_\Theta(ra, o_r) \quad \acute{G}_\Delta = G_\Delta \cup G_\Delta(ra, o_s) \quad \vdash \acute{G}_\Delta : ok \\ a = \nu(\Xi').\, n\langle call\ o_r.l(\vec{v})\rangle? \quad \acute{\Xi}; \acute{G} \vdash r\ a \rhd s : trace \end{array}}{\Xi; G \vdash r \rhd a\ s : trace} \text{L-CALLI}$$

$$\frac{\begin{array}{c} \Xi \vdash r \rhd o_s \xrightarrow{a} o_r \quad \acute{\Xi} = \Xi + a \quad \acute{\Xi} \vdash a : ok \\ \acute{G}_\Theta = G_\Theta \cup G_\Theta(ra, o_r) \quad \acute{G}_\Delta = G_\Delta \cup G_\Delta(ra, o_s) \quad \vdash \acute{G}_\Delta : ok \\ a = \nu(\Xi').\, n\langle return(v)\rangle? \quad \acute{\Xi}; \acute{G} \vdash r\ a \rhd s : trace \end{array}}{\Xi; G \vdash r \rhd a\ s : trace} \text{L-RETI}$$

---

the trace. The update for the dependence graph G_Θ given by the union the graph G_Θ before the step with

$$G_\Theta(ra, o) = M_\Theta(ra, o) \cup C(ra) \cup D_\Theta(ra) \tag{9}$$

where the argument o refers to the monitor relevant in that step, i.e., the monitor introduction potential inconsistencies. The definition for G_Δ is dually.

The rules are completely symmetric wrt. incoming and outgoing communication (and the dual rules omitted). L-CALLI for incoming calls works similar to the CALLI-rules in the semantics. The premise $\Delta \vdash r \rhd o_s \xrightarrow{a} o_r : \Theta$ checks whether the incoming call a is enabled and determines the sender and receiver at the same time. The receiver o_r, of course, is mentioned directly, but o_s is calculated from the history r. In case of incoming communication, the relevant monitor for G_Θ is the receiver, and for G_Δ, the sender of the step.

Remember from Section 3.1 that the sender given by, e.g., $sender(r\gamma_c?)$ is not (necessarily) the "*real*" sending object (which remains anonymous), but the last environment object the corresponding thread has entered in the past via an interface action. The sender in this sense is exactly the object, whose lock is relevant when updating/checking the dependencies in G_Δ. A consequence of the clean decoupling of component and environment in the assumption/commitment formulation of the legal traces is, that for incoming communication, the update of the graph G_Θ cannot introduce a cycle: incoming communications are checked for legality using the *assumptions*, not the commitments (cf. Lemma 5).

3.4 Soundness of the Abstractions

The section contains the basic soundness results of the abstractions.

Lemma 3 (Subject reduction). $\Xi \vdash C \overset{s}{\Longrightarrow} \acute{\Xi} \vdash \acute{C}$, *then* $\acute{\Xi} \vdash \acute{C}$. *A fortiori: If* $\Xi \vdash n : T$, *then* $\acute{\Xi} \vdash n : T$.

Lemma 4 (Soundness of lock ownership).

1. $\Xi \vdash C \overset{t}{\Longrightarrow} \acute{\Xi} \vdash \acute{C}$ and $\Xi \vdash t : \Box_n o$, then thread n has the lock of o in $\acute{C}$.

2. If $\Xi \vdash C \overset{t}{\Longrightarrow}$ and $\Xi \vdash t : \Diamond_n o$ and there does not exist an $n' \neq n$ with $\Xi \vdash t : \Box_{n'} o$, then $\Xi \vdash C \overset{t}{\Longrightarrow} \acute{\Xi} \vdash \acute{C}$ for some $\acute{\Xi} \vdash \acute{C}$ s.t. the thread n has the lock of o in $\acute{C}$.

Lemma 5. If $G; \Xi \vdash r : trace$, and $\Xi \vdash r \rhd o_s \overset{\gamma?}{\to} o_r$, and G_Θ is acyclic, then $G_\Theta + G_\Theta(r\gamma?, o_r)$ is acyclic, as well.

Lemma 6 (Soundness of abstractions). Assume $\Xi \vdash C$ and $\Xi \vdash C \overset{t}{\Longrightarrow}$. The (1) $\Xi \vdash_\Theta t : trace$ and (2) $\Xi \vdash_\Delta t : trace$ implies $\Xi \vdash t : trace$.

4 Conclusion

Viswanathan [13] investigates full abstraction in an object calculus with subtyping. The setting is slightly different from the one here, as the paper does not compare a contextual semantics with a denotational one, but a semantics by translation with a direct one. The paper considers neither concurrency nor aliasing. Recently, Jeffrey and Rathke [11] extended their work [10] on trace-based semantics from an object-based setting to a core of *Java*, called *JavaJr*, including classes and subtyping. We plan to extend the language with further features to make it more resembling *Java* or $C^{\#}$. Concerning the concurrency model, one should add thread-coordination using wait- and notify methods. Another interesting direction for extension concerns the type system, in particular to include *subtyping* and *inheritance*. Another direction is to extend the semantics to a *compositional* one; currently, the semantics is open in that it is defined in the context of an environment. However, general composition of open program fragments is not defined. Concentrating on synchronized methods, this paper relied on an interleaving abstraction of the concurrent semantics. More complex interface behavior is expected when considering more general memory models. See e.g. [12] for a recent semantical study of *Java*'s memory model.

Acknowledgements. We thank the anonymous reviewers for their thorough work and their helpful remarks. This work has been financially supported by the NWO/DFG project Mobi-J (RO 1122/9-4) and by the DFG as part of the Transregional collaborative Research Center "Automatic Verification and Analysis of Complex Systems" (SFB/TR 14 AVACS).

References

1. M. Abadi and L. Cardelli. *A Theory of Objects*. Springer, 1996.
2. E. Ábrahám, F. S. de Boer, M. M. Bonsangue, A. Grüner, and M. Steffen. Observability, connectivity, and replay in a sequential calculus of classes. In M. Bosangue, F. S. de Boer, W.-P. de Roever, and S. Graf, editors, *Proceedings of FMCO 2004*, volume 3657 of *LNCS*, pages 296–316. Springer-Verlag, 2005.

3. E. Ábrahám, A. Grüner, and M. Steffen. Abstract interface behavior of object-oriented languages with monitors. Draft technical report, Institut für Informatik und Praktische Mathematik, Christian-Albrechts-Universität zu Kiel, Jan. 2006.
4. E. Ábrahám, A. Grüner, and M. Steffen. Dynamic heap-abstraction for open, object-oriented systems with thread classes (extended abstract). In *Proceedings of CiE'06*, 2006. To appear. A longer version appeared as Technical Report 0601 of the Institute of Computer Science of the University Kiel, January 2006.
5. P. Brinch Hansen. *Operating System Principles*. Prentice Hall, 1973.
6. ECMA International Standardizing Information and Communication Systems. $C^\#$ *Language Specification*, 2nd edition, Dec. 2002. Standard ECMA-334.
7. A. D. Gordon and P. D. Hankin. A concurrent object calculus: Reduction and typing. In U. Nestmann and B. C. Pierce, editors, *Proceedings of HLCL '98*, volume 16.3 of *ENTCS*. Elsevier Science Publishers, 1998.
8. J. Gosling, B. Joy, G. L. Steele, and G. Bracha. *The Java Language Specification*. Addison-Wesley, Second edition, 2000.
9. C. A. R. Hoare. Monitors: An operating system structuring concept. *Communications of the ACM*, 17(10):549–557, 1974.
10. A. Jeffrey and J. Rathke. A fully abstract may testing semantics for concurrent objects. In *Proceedings of LICS '02*. IEEE, Computer Society Press, July 2002.
11. A. Jeffrey and J. Rathke. Java Jr.: A fully abstract trace semantics for a core Java language. In M. Sagiv, editor, *Proceedings of ESOP 2005*, volume 3444 of *LNCS*, pages 423–438. Springer-Verlag, 2005.
12. J. Manson, W. Pugh, and S. V. Adve. The Java memory memory. In *Proceedings of POPL '05*. ACM, Jan. 2005.
13. R. Viswanathan. Full abstraction for first-order objects with recursive types and subtyping. In *Proceedings of LICS '98*. IEEE, Computer Society Press, July 1998.

Mobility Mechanisms in
Service Oriented Computing*

Claudio Guidi and Roberto Lucchi

Department of Computer Science, University of Bologna, Italy
{cguidi, lucchi}@cs.unibo.it

Abstract. The usual context of service oriented computing is characterized by several services offering the same functionalities, new services that are continuosly deployed and other ones that are removed. In this case it can be useful to discover and compose services dynamically at run-time. Orchestration languages provide a mean to deal with service composition, while the problem of fulfilling at run-time the information about the involved services is usually referred to as open-endedness. When designing service-based applications both composition and open endedness play a central role. Such issues are strongly related to mobility mechanisms which make it possible to design applications where services acquire during the execution the necessary information to invoke services. In this paper we discuss the mobility mechanisms for the service oriented computing paradigm. To this end we model a service by means of the notions of interface, location, process and internal state, then we formalize a calculus supporting a specific form of mobility for each of them. We conclude by comparing mobility mechanisms of our calculus with the ones supported by the Web Services technology.

1 Introduction

Service Oriented Computing is an emerging paradigm where services are platform independent autonomous computational entities that, by means of standard protocols, support interoperability thus allowing to design new and more complex services out of simpler ones. Orchestration languages [12, 14, 9] provide a mean to program new services whose functionalities are implemented by exploiting existing services. In particular, the workflow is programmed from the perspective of a single endpoint which orchestrates the invocations of all the involved services and collects all the corresponding results, thus the state of the execution is controlled in a centralized way within the orchestrator process.

The usual context for service oriented computing is characterized by the fact that new services can appear as well as other ones can disappear during the evolution of the system, and by the fact that a number of services offer the same functionalities. In this scenario it can be useful to select at run-time the specific service to be invoked among the available ones. Moreover, there are other cases where it is not possible to statically know the exact location of a

---

* Research partially funded by EU Integrated Project Sensoria, contract n. 016004.

R. Gorrieri and H. Wehrheim (Eds.): FMOODS 2006, LNCS 4037, pp. 233–250, 2006.

service which is to be invoked. For instance, consider the case of a system where an administrative application updates the software product versions of clients; it could be organized as it follows. Each client is equipped of a *client* service which provides the software update functionality, the administrative application is composed by a *software manager* service and an *update* service. The *software manager* service invokes the *update* one by passing the list of clients which have to be updated, then the *update* service invokes the software update functionality of all the listed *client* services. Since it is realistic to suppose that the set of all clients changes during the evolution of the whole system, the *update* service does not know at design time the locations of the clients, thus it needs to acquire them at run-time and in particular when it is invoked by the *software manager* service. The problem of composing services that are not completely known at design time is usually referred to as *open endedness*.

In order to deal with open endedness the paper discusses the mobility mechanisms in service oriented computing. We proceed as follows: i) we define a service by logically classifying the aspects that compose it, ii) we reason on the meaning of supporting the mobility of such aspects, and iii) we present a service-based calculus supporting mobility mechanisms. In particular, we characterize a service by means of four components: the *location*, the *process*, the *interface* and the *internal state*. The location expresses where the service is deployed and then available, the process represents the program which permits to supply the service functionalities, the interface represents the acess points the service can use to interact with other ones and, finally, the internal state represents the information the service internally manages. The definition we propose is not pertaining to a particular technology thus it permits to reason about mobility without referring to a specific technology. We discuss four kinds of mobility: the location mobility, the service functionality mobility, the interface mobility and the internal state mobility. Once having discussed each of them we proceed by presenting a service-based calculus we use to formally describe these mechanisms. Such a calculus, equipped of an operational semantics, is an extension of a previous work [7,6] obtained by introducing the notion of service location. At the end we trace a comparison between the mechanisms we propose and the ones supported by the Web Service technology which is the most credited proposal for service oriented computing. It emerges that the technology supports only internal state mobility and location mobility. In particular, a section is dedicated to investigate the request-response interaction pattern mechanism supported by the Web Service technology which seems to be weaker than the common interpretation of the request-response interaction pattern behavior.

The paper is structured as it follows. Section 2 defines a service and reasons about the meaning of the various forms of mobility that could be supported between services. Section 3 presents the service-based calculus supporting mobility mechanisms and its operational semantics. Section 4 compares the mobility mechanisms we propose with the Web Services technology. Section 5 concludes the paper with some final remarks.

2   Services Formalization and Mobility Mechanisms

This section is devoted for deducing the basic concepts of services and introducing the mobility mechanisms they deal with.

2.1   A Model for Representing Services

A service is a computational entity located at a specific unique *location* (e.g. a URI) which has an *internal state* and is able to perform one or more *functionalities*. A functionality can be a computational process which executes an algorithm, a coordinating process which needs to interact with other services or both. The service communication mechanism is based on peer-to-peer message passing. Every information that needs to be exchanged between two services is to be communicated by means of interaction points. Each service exhibits a set of interaction points, called *operations*, that are exploited for sending and receiving requests to or from other services. Each operation is described by a name and an *interaction modality*. According to [4, 3], there are four kinds of peer-to-peer interaction modality divided into two groups:

- Operations which supply a service functionality, *Input operations*:
  - *One-Way*: it is devoted to receive a request message.
  - *Request-Response*: it is devoted to receive a request message which implies a response message to the invoker.
- Operations which request a service functionality, *Output operations*:
  - *Notification*: it is devoted to send a request message.
  - *Solicit-Response*: it is devoted to send a request message which requires a response message.

The set of all the operations exhibited by a service represents the *interface* of the service. In order to send a request message, a service has to explicit the output operation and the location of the receiver. In other words, the operation expresses *how* to invoke a service whereas the location specifies *where* the service can be accessed.

Let *Loc* be the set of service locations, $\mathcal{O}$ and $\mathcal{O}_R$ be two disjoint sets of operation names, $Sup = \{(o, ow) \mid o \in \mathcal{O}\} \cup \{(o_r, rr) \mid o_r \in \mathcal{O}_R\}$ be the set containing all the input operations where *ow* and *rr* indicate One-Way and Request-Response operations, respectively. Let $Inv=\{(o, n) \mid o \in \mathcal{O}\} \cup \{(o_r, sr) \mid o_r \in \mathcal{O}_R\}$ be the set containing all the output operations where *n* and *sr* denote Notification and Solicit-Response operations. Let $Interfaces = Sup \cup Inv$ be the set of all the possible operations. By definition an operation name unambiguously identifies a couple of operations: a One-Way with a Notification and a Request-Response with a Solicit-Response. This is related to the fact that an operation in *Sup* can be invoked only by the corresponding operation in *Inv* that has the same name.

Formally a service is defined by the following tuple:

$$Service := (I, \mathcal{M}, P_f, l)$$

where $I \subseteq$ *Interfaces* is the interface containing all the operations it can use, $\mathcal{M}$ is the internal state of the service we use to represent all the information it manages (e.g. variables, databases), P_f is the process which expresses the service functionality encoded by exploiting the formalism f and $l \in Loc$ is the location where the service is deployed. We remark that, in order to be as general as possible, in this section we abstract away from the specific formalism f and the representation of the internal state; in the following section such notions will be represented by a specific model.

2.2   Mobility Mechanisms

In this section we describe the mobility mechanisms which deal with open endedness. To this end we exploit the service notion of Section 2.1 and we reason about the meaning of supporting the mobility of each element of the service tuple, that is: internal state mobility, location mobility, interface mobility and service functionality mobility. Since the interaction mechanism is based on message passing, mobility is achieved by communicating service components by means of exchanged messages. This fact has a significant impact on designing issues because mobility must be explicitly programmed by system designers.

– *Internal state mobility:* The mobility of the internal state is strongly related to the message passing communication mechanism. Indeed the content of a sent message is part of the information contained in the internal state of the sender that the receiver acquires and stores in its internal state. In other words a message exchange between two services can be seen as an information mobility from the sender internal state to the receiver one.
– *Location mobility:* Location mobility deals with the possibility to receive a location by means of a message exchange and to exploit it to access the service deployed at that location. This means that a service can acquire at run-time the exact location of a service whose functionalities are known, as in the case of the *update* service discussed in the Introduction section which knows the *client* functionality but not their locations.
– *Interface mobility:* Interface mobility means that a service can acquire at run-time an operation and exhibits it in its interface. In particular, such a kind of mobility deals only with the mobility of the operation name (by definition the interaction modality can be derived by its name). Thus, the service which receives an operation can exhibit it either as an output operation and an input one. Since operations provides access points to the service functionalities, which are supplied by the service by means of its internal process, we consider that the only reasonable usage of an operation acquired at run-time is for exhibiting the related output operation and not the input one. The calculus we propose in the following section allows to exhibit acquired operations only as output operations.
– *Functionality mobility:* Service functionalities are expressed by the internal processes of a service. The mobility of this component implies that a process can be communicated within a message exchange and executed

by the service receiving it. In this case the receiver can enrich its internal functionalities by executing the received process. It is important to highlight the fact that the receiver must be able to execute the received process by exploiting the specific formalism used for encoding it. In this paper we do not discuss such a problem that we consider orthogonal to the mobility mechanisms.

3   A Service-Based Language with Mobility Mechanisms

This section is devoted to model the mobility mechanisms discussed above. In particular, we proceed as it follows: i) we introduce a calculus for representing services accordingly with the model discussed in the previous section, ii) we formalize all the mobility mechanisms by extending step by step the service-based calculus and we describe how services are affected by them.

3.1   The Service-Based Language

Here, we present a service-based calculus which extends OL, defined in our previous works, by means of locations. Such a language allows us to describe systems where each participant is a service[1] and supplies a means for describing service functionalities. For the sake of clarity, we do not take into account asynchronous communication which has been modeled in our previous work. On the other hand, this is an orthogonal aspect which can be separately analyzed w.r.t. mobility mechanisms. Formally, let $InternalLink$ be a set of names ranged over by s, let Var be the set of variables ranged over by x, y, z, k. We denote with $\tilde{x}$ tuples of variables, for instance, we may have $\tilde{x} = \langle x_1, x_2, ..., x_n \rangle$. Let W be a finite ordered non-empty set of indexes, OL is defined by the following grammar:

$$P ::= \mathbf{0} \mid x := e \mid \epsilon \mid \bar{s} \mid \bar{o}@l(\tilde{x}) \mid \bar{o}_r@l(\tilde{x}, \tilde{y})$$
$$\mid P; P \mid P \parallel P \mid \sum_{i \in W}^{+} \epsilon_i; P_i \mid \sum_{i \in W}^{\oplus} \chi_i ? P_i$$
$$\epsilon ::= s \mid o(\tilde{x}) \mid o_r(\tilde{x}, \tilde{y}, P)$$
$$E ::= [P, \mathcal{S}]_l \mid E \parallel E$$

where a service-based system E consists of the parallel composition of services. A service $[P, \mathcal{S}]_l$ is a process P identified by its location $l \in Loc$ whose variables state is $\mathcal{S}$. The variables state of a service is described by a function $\mathcal{S} : Var \to Val \cup \{\perp\}$ from variables to the set $Val \cup \{\perp\}$ ranged over by w. Val, ranged over by v, is a generic set of values on which is defined a total order relation[2]. $\mathcal{S}(x)$ represents the value of variable x in the state $\mathcal{S}$ ($\mathcal{S}(x) = \perp$ means that x is

---

[1] In our previous work we referred to this language as an orchestration language. Usually the term orchestrator means a special service which, in order to supply its functionalities, coordinates other services. Here, we use the term service for indicating both orchestrators and simple services.

[2] We extend such an order relation on the set $Val \cup \{\perp\}$ considering $\perp < v$, $\forall v \in Val$.

not yet initialized), while $\mathcal{S}[v/x]$ denotes the state $\mathcal{S}$ where x holds value v (we use $\mathcal{S}[\tilde{v}/\tilde{x}]$ when dealing with tuples of variables), formally:

$$\mathcal{S}[v/x] = \mathcal{S}' \qquad \mathcal{S}'(x') = \begin{cases} v & \text{if } x' = x \\ \mathcal{S}(x') & \text{otherwise} \end{cases}$$

All the services are executed at different locations, thus they can be composed by using only the parallel operator ($\|$). Processes can be composed in parallel ($|$), sequence (;) and with two different alternative composition operators. The operator $\sum_{i \in W}^{+} \epsilon_i; P_i$ expresses a non-deterministic choice among input guarded processes, that represent exhibited operations, whereas the operator $\sum_{i \in W}^{\oplus} \chi_i?P_i$ expresses a deterministic choice among processes guarded by conditions on variables state (such processes are of the form $\chi?P$ where χ is a logic condition on the state $\mathcal{S}$ associated to P whose syntax is reported in Appendix A). $\mathbf{0}$ represents the null process whereas the processes $x := e$ deals with variable assignment. Processes s and $\bar{s}$ deal with internal service synchronizations which are exploited to coordinate the activities of processes running in parallel. In this case no message is exchanged; this is because the service variables are shared by all the processes running on that service. As far as the operations are concerned, the process $o(\tilde{x})$ represents a One-Way operation where o ranges over $\mathcal{O}$, whereas the process $o_r(\tilde{x}, \tilde{z}, P)$ represents the Request-Response one where o_r ranges over $\mathcal{O}_R$. Namely, $o(\tilde{x})$ represents a One-Way operation whose name is o and the received information are stored in the tuple of variable $\tilde{x}$, while $o_r(\tilde{x}, \tilde{y}, P)$ represents a Request-Response operation named o_r which receives a message, stores the received information in $\tilde{x}$, executes the process P and, at the end, sends the information contained in $\tilde{y}$ as a response message to the invoker. On the contrary, the processes $\bar{o}@l(\tilde{x})$ and $\bar{o}_r@l(\tilde{x}, \tilde{y})$ represent the Notification and the Solicit-Response operations respectively, where o ranges over $\mathcal{O}$ and o_r ranges over $\mathcal{O}_R$. In particular, $\bar{o}@l(\tilde{x})$ invokes the operation o of the service located at l sending the information contained in $\tilde{x}$ whereas $\bar{o}_r@l(\tilde{x}, \tilde{y})$ invokes the operation o_r of the service located at l sending the information contained in $\tilde{x}$ and waits for the response whose information will be stored in $\tilde{y}$.

The semantics of OL is defined in terms of a labelled transition system which describes the evolution of a service-based system. We define $\rightarrow$ as the least relation which satisfies the axioms and rules of Tables 1, 2 and 3. Let $Act_{OL} = \{\bar{o}, o, \bar{o}@l(\tilde{v}), o(\tilde{v}), \bar{o}_r^n(\tilde{v}), o_r^n(\tilde{v}), \bar{o}_r@l(\tilde{v}, \tilde{y})(n), o_r@l(\tilde{v}, \tilde{y})(n), \sigma, \tau\}$ be the set of actions ranged over by γ. σ is a parameterized action of the form $(l, l', op, \tilde{v}, dir)$ where l, l' are service locations, op is an operation name, $\tilde{v}$ are tuples of values and $dir \in \{\uparrow, \downarrow\}$. We exploit dir for discriminating between a request message and a response one. Table 1 deals with the axioms over P where we have introduced the processes $o_r^n(\tilde{x})$ and $\bar{o}_r^n(\tilde{x})$ in order to deal with Request-Response and Solicit-Response mechanisms. The most interesting axiom is the REQUEST one, which describes that when it is invoked, the operation behaves as the process that performs P and, once having completed such a process, performs an output that is consumed by the invoking service. On the contrary, rules SOLICIT and

Table 1. Axioms over P

(IN)

$$(s, \mathcal{S}) \xrightarrow{s} (\mathbf{0}, \mathcal{S})$$

(OUT)

$$(\bar{s}, \mathcal{S}) \xrightarrow{\bar{s}} (\mathbf{0}, \mathcal{S})$$

(NOTIFICATION)

$$(\bar{o}@l(\tilde{x}), \mathcal{S}) \xrightarrow{\bar{o}@l(\tilde{v})} (\mathbf{0}, \mathcal{S}), \tilde{v} = \mathcal{S}(\tilde{x})$$

(ONE-WAY)

$$(o(\tilde{x}), \mathcal{S}) \xrightarrow{o(\tilde{v})} (\mathbf{0}, \mathcal{S}[\tilde{v}/\tilde{x}])$$

(SOLICIT)

$$(\bar{o}_r@l(\tilde{x}, \tilde{y}), \mathcal{S}) \xrightarrow{\bar{o}_r@l(\tilde{v}, \tilde{y})(n)} (o_r^n(\tilde{y}), \mathcal{S}), \tilde{v} = \mathcal{S}(\tilde{x})$$

(REQUEST)

$$(o_r(\tilde{x}, \tilde{y}, P), \mathcal{S}) \xrightarrow{o_r@l(\tilde{v}, \tilde{y})(n)} (P; \bar{o}_r^n(\tilde{y}), \mathcal{S}[\tilde{v}/\tilde{x}])$$

(RESPONSE-OUT)

$$(\bar{o}_r^n(\tilde{x}), \mathcal{S}) \xrightarrow{\bar{o}_r^n(\tilde{v})} (\mathbf{0}, \mathcal{S}), \tilde{v} = \mathcal{S}(\tilde{x})$$

(RESPONSE-IN)

$$(o_r^n(\tilde{x}), \mathcal{S}) \xrightarrow{o_r^n(\tilde{v})} (\mathbf{0}, \mathcal{S}[\tilde{v}/\tilde{x}])$$

RESPONSE-IN deal with Solicit-Response behaviour where, initially, a message is sent and then the service, by means of the process $o_r^n(\tilde{x})$, waits for the response.

Table 2 deals with the rules over P where rule ASSIGN deals with variable assignment within the services; $e \hookrightarrow_S v$ means that the evaluation process of the expression e within state $\mathcal{S}$ reduces to v. Rule INT-SYNC deals with internal synchronization and CONGRP with internal structural congruence denoted by $\equiv_P$. PAR-INT and SEQ describe the behaviour of processes composed in parallel and sequentially respectively, whereas CHOICE1 and CHOICE2 describe the behavior of the two alternative composition operators. The former one non-deterministically selects an input guarded process among the ones listed in the choice operator, while the latter one is the deterministic choice depending on the internal state of the service where the satisfaction relation for $\vdash$ is reported in Appendix A. In Table 3 the rules at the level of service-based systems are considered. Rule ONE-WAYSYNC deals with the synchronization on a One-Way operation between two services whereas rules REQ-SYNC and RESP-SYNC deal with the request and the response message exchanges between a Solicit-Response operation and a Request-Response one. Rule REQ-SYNC exploits a fresh label n which is generated in order to univocally link the response synchronization defined in rule RESP-SYNC. PAR-EXT deals with external parallel composition and CONGRE is for external structural congruence denoted by $\equiv$. INT-EXT expresses the fact that a service behaves in accordance with its internal processes.

Now, we remind the service formalization presented in section 2 where a service is represented by the tuple $(I, \mathcal{M}, P_f, l)$ and we show how an OL service $[P, \mathcal{S}]_l$ is related to it:

- $\mathcal{M}$ is modeled by $\mathcal{S}$.
- l represents the location within both the service model and the OL language.
- P_f is represented by a process P in OL where the formalism f corresponds to OL.
- I represents the interface of a service and it is not explicitly modeled in OL but it can be extracted from the process P. Indeed, by considering a service $[P, \mathcal{S}]_l$, its interface I is defined by the function $\Theta(P)$ where Θ is inductively defined by the following rules:

Table 2. Rules over P

(Assign)
$$\frac{e \hookrightarrow_S v}{(x := e, S) \xrightarrow{\tau} (\mathbf{0}, S[v/x])}$$

(Int-Sync)
$$\frac{(P,S) \xrightarrow{s} (P',S) \,,\, (Q,S) \xrightarrow{\bar{s}} (Q',S)}{(P \mid Q, S) \xrightarrow{\tau} (P' \mid Q', S)}$$

(CongrP)
$$\frac{P \equiv_P P' \,,\, (P',S) \xrightarrow{\gamma} (Q',S'), \; Q' \equiv_P Q}{(P,S) \xrightarrow{\gamma} (Q,S')}$$

(Par-Int)
$$\frac{(P,S) \xrightarrow{\gamma} (P',S')}{(P \mid Q, S) \xrightarrow{\gamma} (P' \mid Q, S')}$$

(Seq)
$$\frac{(P,S) \xrightarrow{\gamma} (P',S')}{(P;Q,S) \xrightarrow{\gamma} (P';Q,S')}$$

(Choice 1)
$$\frac{(\epsilon_i; P_i, S) \xrightarrow{\gamma} (P',S') \quad i \in W}{(\sum_{i \in W}^{+} \epsilon_i; P_i, S) \xrightarrow{\gamma} (P',S')}$$

(Choice 2)
$$\frac{S \vdash \chi_i \quad S \nvdash \chi_j, j \in W, j < i}{(\sum_{i \in W}^{\oplus} \chi_i ? P_i, S) \xrightarrow{\tau} (P_i, S)}$$

(Structural Congruence over P)

$$P \mid \mathbf{0} \equiv_P P \quad \mathbf{0}; P \equiv_P P \quad (P \mid Q) \equiv_P (Q \mid P) \quad (P \mid Q) \mid R \equiv_P P \mid (Q \mid R)$$

1. $\Theta(\mathbf{0}) = \phi$
2. $\Theta(x := e) = \phi$
3. $\Theta(s) = \phi$
4. $\Theta(\bar{s}) = \phi$
5. $\Theta(\bar{o}@l(\tilde{x})) = \{(o,n)\}$
6. $\Theta(\bar{o}_r@l(\tilde{x},\tilde{y})) = \{(o_r, sr)\}$
7. $\Theta(o(\tilde{x})) = \{(o, ow)\}$
8. $\Theta(o_r(\tilde{x},\tilde{y},P)) = \{(o_r, rr)\} \cup \Theta(P)$
9. $\Theta(o_r^n(\tilde{x})) = \phi$
10. $\Theta(\bar{o}_r^n(\tilde{x})) = \phi$
11. $\Theta(P;P') = \Theta(P) \cup \Theta(P')$
12. $\Theta(P \mid P') = \Theta(P) \cup \Theta(P')$
13. $\Theta(\sum_{i \in W}^{+} \epsilon_i; P_i) = \bigcup_{i \in W} \Theta(\epsilon_i; P_i)$ 14. $\Theta(\sum_{i \in W}^{\oplus} \chi_i ? P_i) = \bigcup_{i \in W} \Theta(P_i)$

It is worth noting that the interface $\Theta(P)$, during the evolution of a service $[P,S]_l$, is monotonically reduced dependently on the consumption of P. Indeed, let us consider the simple example which follows where, for the sake of brevity, we abstract away from the internal states:

$$[\bar{a}(x), S]_l \parallel [a(y), S']_{l'} \xrightarrow{\sigma} [\mathbf{0}, S]_l \parallel [\mathbf{0}, S']_{l'}$$

Before the synchronization the interfaces of the two services are $I_l = \{(a,n)\}$ and $I_{l'} = \{(a,ow)\}$ respectively, whereas after the synchronization they are $I_l = \phi$ and $I_{l'=\phi}$.

3.2   Internal State Mobility

As we have noticed in section 2 the internal state mobility is strongly related to the message passing communication mechanism. Considering Table 1 and

Table 3. Rules over E

(ONE-WAYSYNC)

$$\frac{[P,\mathcal{S}]_l \overset{\bar{o}@l'(\tilde{v})}{\rightarrow} [P',\mathcal{S}']_l \, , \, [Q,T]_{l'} \overset{o(\tilde{v})}{\rightarrow} [Q',T']_{l'}}{[P,\mathcal{S}]_l \parallel [Q,T]_{l'} \overset{\sigma}{\rightarrow} [P',\mathcal{S}']_l \parallel [Q',T']_{l'}} \, , \sigma = (l,l',o,\tilde{v},\uparrow)$$

(REQ-SYNC)

$$\frac{[P,\mathcal{S}]_l \overset{\bar{o}_r@l'(\tilde{v},\tilde{y})(n)}{\rightarrow} [P',\mathcal{S}']_l \, , \, [Q,T]_{l'} \overset{o_r@l(\tilde{v},\tilde{y})(n)}{\rightarrow} [Q',T']_{l'}}{[P,\mathcal{S}]_l \parallel [Q,T]_{l'} \overset{\sigma}{\rightarrow} [P',\mathcal{S}']_l \parallel [Q',T']_{l'}} \, , n \; fresh, \sigma = (l,l',o_r,\tilde{v},\uparrow)$$

(RESP-SYNC)

$$\frac{[P,\mathcal{S}]_l \overset{\bar{o}_r^n(\tilde{v})}{\rightarrow} [P',\mathcal{S}']_l \, , \, [Q,T]_{l'} \overset{o_r^n(\tilde{v})}{\rightarrow} [Q',T']_{l'}}{[P,\mathcal{S}]_l \parallel [Q,T]_{l'} \overset{\sigma}{\rightarrow} [P',\mathcal{S}']_l \parallel [Q',T']_{l'}} \, , \sigma = (l,l',o_r,\tilde{v},\downarrow)$$

(PAR-EXT)	(CONGRE)	(INT-EXT)
$$\frac{E_1 \overset{\gamma}{\rightarrow} E_1'}{E_1 \parallel E_2 \overset{\gamma}{\rightarrow} E_1' \parallel E_2}$$	$$\frac{E_1 \equiv E_1' \, , \, E_1' \overset{\gamma}{\rightarrow} E_2', \, E_2' \equiv E_2}{E_1 \overset{\gamma}{\rightarrow} E_2}$$	$$\frac{(P,\mathcal{S}) \overset{\gamma}{\rightarrow} (P',\mathcal{S}')}{[P,\mathcal{S}]_l \overset{\gamma}{\rightarrow} [P',\mathcal{S}']_l}$$

(STRUCTURAL CONGRUENCE OVER E)

$$\frac{P \equiv_P Q}{[P,\mathcal{S}]_l \equiv [Q,\mathcal{S}]_l} \qquad E_1 \parallel E_2 \equiv E_2 \parallel E_1 \qquad E_1 \parallel (E_2 \parallel E_3) \equiv (E_1 \parallel E_2) \parallel E_3$$

Table 3, such a kind of mobility is expressed by the rules which deal with operation processes. In particular, let us consider rules NOTIFICATION and ONE-WAY in order to clarify how it works. In the former the internal state information $\tilde{v}$ contained within the variables $\tilde{x}$ are sent by exploiting a message whereas in the latter the received information $\tilde{v}$ are stored into the variables $\tilde{x}$ contained within the internal state of the receiver. Rule ONE-WAYSYNC of Table 3 couples the two axioms by correlating the receiver location to that explicited within the notification process and σ is a formal representation of the exchanged message. Summarizing, internal state mobility is modeled as a an information exchange between the internal state of the sender and the internal state of the receiver. Such a mobility mechanism is the cornerstone of service-based systems and supplies the basic layer on which the other mobility mechanisms can be implemented.

3.3 Location Mobility

In order to deal with location mobility here we modify the syntax of OL by replacing the processes $\bar{o}@l(\tilde{x})$ and $\bar{o}_r@l(\tilde{x},\tilde{y})$ with the new processes which follow:

$$P ::= \ldots \mid \bar{o}@z(\tilde{x}) \mid \bar{o}_r@z(\tilde{x},\tilde{y}) \mid \ldots$$

where z is a variable. These novelties allow us to dynamically bind the receiver location when performing the Notification and Solicit-Response operations by evaluating the content of variable z. The semantics of axioms NOTIFICATION and SOLICIT of Table 1 change as it follows:

(NOTIFICATION)

$$(\bar{o}@z(\tilde{x}), \mathcal{S}) \xrightarrow{\bar{o}@l(\tilde{v})} (\mathbf{0}, \mathcal{S}), \begin{array}{l} \tilde{v} = \mathcal{S}(\tilde{x}) \\ l = \mathcal{S}(z) \end{array}$$

(SOLICIT)

$$(\bar{o}_r@z(\tilde{x}, \tilde{y}), \mathcal{S}) \xrightarrow{\bar{o}_r@l(\tilde{v}, \tilde{y})(n)} (o_r^n(\tilde{y}), \mathcal{S}), \begin{array}{l} \tilde{v} = \mathcal{S}(\tilde{x}) \\ l = \mathcal{S}(z) \end{array}$$

Variable z is evaluated when the processes are executed. This mechanism allows us to design a service which does not know *a priori* the locations of the services to be invoked that can be acquired during the execution. In order to clarify such a behaviour let us consider the business scenario example depicted in Fig. 1 where a customer purchases a good invoking a shopping service, the shopping service invokes a bank service for performing the payment and the bank service invokes the customer that receives the invoice. In Fig. 1 we have exploited an informal graphical representation where services are represented by circles, the symbol @*uri* expresses the fact that the service is available at the location *uri*, the input operations exhibited by a service are represented by a black line whose name is shown within a rectangle and the arrows represent a message exchange.

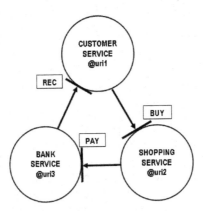

Fig. 1. Business scenario example

In the following we formalize such a scenario by supposing that the bank service does not know the location of the customer:

$$System ::= [z_1 := uri2; add := uri1; inv := \bot; \overline{BUY}@z_1(add); REC(inv), \mathcal{S}_c]_{uri1}$$
$$\| [z_2 := uri3; fwadd := \bot; BUY(fwadd); \overline{PAY}@z_2(fwadd), \mathcal{S}_s]_{uri2}$$
$$\| [z_3 := \bot; invoice = msg; PAY(z_3); \overline{REC}@z_3(invoice), \mathcal{S}_b]_{uri3}$$

The shopping service located (at $uri2$) receives on the One-Way operation BUY the location of the customer ($uri1$) and stores it within the variable $fwadd$. Moreover, it forwards it to the bank service by exploiting the Notification operation $\overline{PAY}$. The bank service (at $uri3$) receives on PAY the customer location and then exploits it for invoking the REC operation of the customer sending the invoice represented by the value msg. Finally, the customer stores the received invoice within the variable inv.

Location mobility is built on top of the internal state mobility because acquired locations are stored within the internal state. Such a kind of mobility allows us to design flexible services which bind their output operations at run-time.

3.4   Interface Mobility

In order to deal with interface mobility here we modify the syntax of OL by replacing the output operation processes with the new processes that follow:

$$P ::= \ldots \mid \bar{k}@z(\tilde{x}) \mid \bar{k}@z(\tilde{x}, \tilde{y}) \mid \ldots$$

where z and k are variables. As far as the output operations are concerned, the operation names are evaluated at run-time by considering the value of an internal state variable (k). The new semantics of axioms NOTIFICATION and SOLICIT is as follows:

(NOTIFICATION)   (SOLICIT)

$$(\bar{k}@z(\tilde{x}), \mathcal{S}) \xrightarrow{\bar{o}@l(\tilde{v})} (\mathbf{0}, \mathcal{S}), \begin{array}{l} o = \mathcal{S}(k) \\ \tilde{v} = \mathcal{S}(\tilde{x}) \\ l = \mathcal{S}(z) \end{array} \qquad (\bar{k}@z(\tilde{x}, \tilde{y}), \mathcal{S}) \xrightarrow{\bar{o}_r@l(\tilde{v}, \tilde{y})(n)} (o_r^n(\tilde{y}), \mathcal{S}), \begin{array}{l} o_r = \mathcal{S}(k) \\ \tilde{v} = \mathcal{S}(\tilde{x}) \\ l = \mathcal{S}(z) \end{array}$$

Furthermore, we modify some rules for the inductive definition of Θ which allows us to extract the service interface. In particular, we modify the rules 5 and 6 which deal with the output operations:

5. $\Theta(\bar{k}@z(\tilde{x}), \mathcal{S}) \quad = \begin{cases} \{(\mathcal{S}(k), n)\} \; \text{if } \mathcal{S}(k) \neq \bot \wedge \mathcal{S}(k) \in \mathcal{O} \\ \phi \quad otherwise \end{cases}$

6. $\Theta(\bar{k}@z(\tilde{x}, \tilde{y}), \mathcal{S}) = \begin{cases} \{(\mathcal{S}(k), sr)\} \; \text{if } \mathcal{S}(k) \neq \bot \wedge \mathcal{S}(k) \in \mathcal{O}_R \\ \phi \quad otherwise \end{cases}$

It is worth noting that now the interface depends also by the internal state[3]. This is due to the fact that operation names are contained within variables. The condition $\mathcal{S}(k) \neq \bot$ guarantees that the interface contains only the known operations.

By exploiting the new output operation processes it is possible to design separately the functionalities which deal with output operations from the actual interface of the service. Let us consider the example of Fig. 1 where, now, we suppose that the bank service does not know $a\ priori$ both the location and the one-way operation of the customer:

$System ::= [z_1 := uri2; add := uri1; opr_1 := \text{REC}; inv := \bot$
$\quad ; \overline{\text{BUY}}@z_1(\langle add, opr_1\rangle); \text{REC}(inv), \mathcal{S}_c]_{uri1}$
$\quad \parallel [z_2 := uri3; fwadd := \bot; opr_2 := \bot$
$\quad ; \text{BUY}(\langle fwadd, opr_2\rangle); \overline{\text{PAY}}@z_2(\langle fwadd, opr_2\rangle), \mathcal{S}_s]_{uri2}$
$\quad \parallel [z_3 := \bot; k_3 := \bot; invoice = msg; \text{PAY}(z_3, k_3); \overline{k_3}@z_3(invoice), \mathcal{S}_b]_{uri3}$

---

[3] Namely, the domain of Θ now considers also the internal state $\mathcal{S}$. For the sake of brevity, we do not show all the rules because they are not affected by the state.

The bank service indeed, receives from the shopping service both the location and the name of the operation of the customer and stores it in l_3 and k_3 respectively. The customer sends, by means of the variable opr_1, the operation REC on which it will wait for receiving the invoice. The example shows how is possible to design a service (in the example the bank one) with a functionality which deals with an output operation without statically knowing its interface. This fact has some implications on the service interface. By considering the new rules for Θ, the interface can also dynamically includes new operations. The interface of the bank service indeed, is $I = \{(PAY, ow)\}$ before receiving a message on the PAY operation and $I = \{(REC, n)\}$ after the reception of the customer operation.

3.5   Service Functionality Mobility

In order to deal with service functionality mobility we extend the OL language by introducing the following process:

$$P ::= \dots \mid \mathbf{run}(x)$$

$\mathbf{run}(x)$ allows us to execute the code contained within the variable x. The semantics of such a primitive is expressed by a new rule that must be added to those presented in Table 2:

(RUN)
$$(\mathbf{run}(x), \mathcal{S}) \xrightarrow{\tau} (\mathcal{S}(x), \mathcal{S})$$

Since the received code can be formed by operation processes, we add a new rule for inductively defining the function Θ which allows us to extract the interface of the service:

13. $\Theta(\mathbf{run}(x), \mathcal{S}) = \begin{cases} \Theta(\mathcal{S}(x)) & if\ \mathcal{S}(k) \neq \perp \\ \phi & otherwise \end{cases}$

Service functionality mobility directly deals with code mobility. In particular it allows us to design services where a specific part of its functionalities are unknown at design time and they are acquired during the execution of the service. In order to clarify this aspect let us consider the example of the shopping service again. Now, we suppose that the customer that wants to interact with the shopping service does not know *a priori* the conversation rules to follow. In other words, the customer does not know that it has to exhibit the REC operation in order to receive the invoice from the bank service.

$System ::= [z_1 := uri2; add := uri1; code_1 := \perp$
$\quad ; \overline{BUY}@z_1(add, code_1); \mathbf{run}(code_1), \mathcal{S}_c]_{uri1}$
$\quad \| [z_2 := uri3; fwadd := \perp; code_2 := "inv := \perp; REC(inv)"$
$\quad ; BUY(fwadd, code_2, \mathbf{0}); \overline{PAY}@z_2(fwadd), \mathcal{S}_s]_{uri2}$
$\quad \| [z_3 := \perp; invoice = msg; PAY(z_3); \overline{REC}@z_3(invoice), \mathcal{S}_b]_{uri3}$

Here, the customer invokes the operation BUY of the shopping service which is modeled as a Request-Response operation. The customer receives as a response a piece of code and stores it within the variable $code_1$, then it executes it by exploiting the primitive $run(code_1)$. After the execution of the code stored within $code_1$ the system behaves as the example presented in the location mobility section. It is worth noting that the customer receives the input operation REC which enriches at run-time its interface similarly to the case of the interface mobility. Even if the two kind of mobility could appear similar w.r.t. the effects on the interface, they are different from a system design point of view. In the case of interface mobility the designer must specify that an input operation has to be performed without knowing its name, on the contrary in the case of service functionality mobility the designer does not know the process which will be executed. Furthermore, by exploiting the primitive $run(x)$ it is possible to enrich the service interface also with both input and output operations. In the example indeed, the customer service interface is enriched with the operation (REC, ow) which is an input one.

Some considerations about code mobility issues are necessary. On the one hand when a service executes a process which has been acquired at run-time, it does not know how it behaves. On the other hand, when programming a process which will be executed by another service the internal behavior of such a service is not known. This fact implies a number of issues. First of all, internal processes share the variables state thus the acquired process could interfere with the behavior of the other ones. Moreover, an acquired process could exploit a certain name s to perform internal synchronizations but the same name could be already used by other internal processes, thus altering also in this case the behavior of the other processes. A formal analysis of these issues is out of the scope of this paper but we consider that, to avoid at least the issues listed above, a mechanisms which syntactically renames all the variables and names of the acquired process which interferes with the ones of the internal processes is necessary before executing it.

4   Web Services Technology

In this section we discuss the mobility mechanisms presented in the previous sections w.r.t. Web Services technology. Furthermore, we discuss a particular hidden mobility related to the Request-Response operation.

4.1   Web Service Mobility Mechanisms

- **Internal state mobility:** Since Web Services are a message passing technology, they fully support the internal state mobility as we have formalized it in Section 3. In particular, an information exchange between two services is an XML document whose schema is defined within the SOAP [16] specification.
- **Location mobility:** As we have shown in Section 3 location mobility is strictly related to the communication mechanisms of the internal process that we have formalized by exploiting OL. Although that Web Services are platform independent and there is not a standard formalism for describing

the internal process, here we consider orchestration languages as a class of languages which can be used for expressing it. Indeed, they deal with service coordination aspects which are fundamental to the end of location mobility. In particular, we consider WS-BPEL because it is the most credited proposal for orchestration. It supports compositional operators as parallel, sequence and choice and it has specific primitives to interact with other services which resemble the input and output operation processes of the OL calculus. WS-BPEL supports location mobility by managing endpoints within its internal variables. An endpoint, which is defined within WS-Addressing [15] specification, is a data structure which contains all the information required for invoking a service, that is the operation and the location.

- **Interface mobility:** The interface mobility that we have formalized in Section 3 is strictly related to the communication mechanisms of the internal process. Following the same approach of location mobility we consider WS-BPEL. As previously mentioned, WS-BPEL is able to manage endpoints which contain the information related to the operations. However it does not support interface mobility because the operations it exploits for invoking and receiving messages are defined statically at design time and they cannot be bound at run-time. To the best of our knowledge interface mobility is not supported by the Web Services technology even if it is possible to consider other solutions that indirectly allows us to achieve it. Let us consider WSDL specification [18] that is an XML-based language which allows to specify the operations (One-Way, Request-Response, Notification and Solicit-Response) exhibited by a service[4]. Several programming languages at a low-level w.r.t. the orchestration ones are equipped of libraries which permit to simplify the service composition. In particular, there exist libraries in Java [2, 1, 13] that, given a WSDL document, automatically produce the corresponding classes which allow us to invoke all the operations supplied by the Web service described in that document. In this case we can guess that by exploiting such languages and libraries we can also support interface mobility.

- **Service functionality mobility:**To the best of our knowledge Web Services technology does not explicitly support such a kind of mobility. Nevertheless we trace a comparison between service functionality mobility and some languages for describing conversational behaviours of service-based systems as, for instance, WS-CDL [17]. Such languages are exploited for describing the communication protocols services have to follow in order to participate to a given service-based system. We can imagine that a service which is willing to access that system could download the related WS-CDL document and extracts a piece of code which allows it to follows the protocol.

---

[4] A WSDL interface could be modeled by exploiting the service interface I defined in section 2 but there are some relevant issues to take into account: a WSDL document is statically defined and can not change dynamically during the evolution of the service by adding or removing some of the exhibited operations and, generally, Notification and Solicit-Response operations are unused.

4.2   The Hidden Mobility of the Request-Response

In this section we discuss the Request-Response interaction mechanism and in particular we compare the one we propose with the one supported by the Web Services technology. Usually the request-response interaction pattern has been intended as a powerful mechanism which is able to relate the two message exchanges involved within a Request-Response as modeled in our calculus and in [10, 11]. In particular, these proposals formalize the Request-Response behaviour by joining the output operation process with the input one. As far as our proposal is concerned, in Table 3 we have exploited a fresh label n in order to couple the two processes.

In the Web Services technology the Request-Response interaction is not supported at the service application level but, as specified by the WSDL recommendation, it has to be supplied by the communication infrastructure (e.g. HTTP) which exploits the service locations to bind the two message exchanges instead of the service processes involved in the interactions as in our calculus. This means that if a service invokes two times a Request-Response operation at the same service location the two responses could be swapped with each other. Example 1, which follows, reveals that the interaction mechanism supported by the Web Services technology is weaker than the one previously proposed.

Table 4 reports the semantics rules governing the Request-Response interaction pattern á la Web Services. As it emerges by the semantics rules, there exists a hidden form of location mobility that is used by the infrastructure to support the response phase. Indeed, the infrastrure keeps the location invoker and uses it when the response is to be sent. Such a semantics, that we consider faithful w.r.t. the Web Services technology, represents a meaningful contribute towards the formal reasoning of the current technology features and lacks.

Example 1. Let us consider the following example where a service, say A, provides a functionality which computes, given two numbers a and b, $|a| - |b|$. Such

Table 4. Modified rules for Request-Response

(SOLICIT)

$$(\bar{o}_r@l(\tilde{x}, \tilde{y}), \mathcal{S}) \xrightarrow{\bar{o}_r@l(\tilde{v}, \tilde{y})} (o_r@l(\tilde{y}), \mathcal{S}), \tilde{v} = \mathcal{S}(\tilde{x})$$

(REQUEST)

$$(o_r(\tilde{x}, \tilde{y}, P), \mathcal{S}) \xrightarrow{o_r@l(\tilde{v}, \tilde{y})} (P; \bar{o}_r@l(\tilde{y}), \mathcal{S}[\tilde{v}/\tilde{x}])$$

(RESPONSE-OUT)

$$(\bar{o}_r@l(\tilde{x}), \mathcal{S}) \xrightarrow{\bar{o}_r@l(\tilde{v})} (0, \mathcal{S}), \tilde{v} = \mathcal{S}(\tilde{x})$$

(RESPONSE-IN)

$$(o_r@l(\tilde{x}), \mathcal{S}) \xrightarrow{o_r@l(\tilde{v})} (0, \mathcal{S}[\tilde{v}/\tilde{x}])$$

(REQ-SYNC)

$$\frac{[P, \mathcal{S}]_l \xrightarrow{\bar{o}_r@l'(\tilde{v}, \tilde{y})} [P', \mathcal{S}']_l \ , \ [Q, T]_{l'} \xrightarrow{o_r@l(\tilde{v}, \tilde{y})} [Q', T']_{l'}}{[P, \mathcal{S}]_l \parallel [Q, T]_{l'} \xrightarrow{\sigma} [P', \mathcal{S}']_l \parallel [Q', T']_{l'}} , \sigma = (l, l', o, \tilde{v}, \uparrow)$$

(RESP-SYNC)

$$\frac{[P, \mathcal{S}]_l \xrightarrow{\bar{o}_r@l'(\tilde{v})} [P', \mathcal{S}']_l \ , \ [Q, T]_{l'} \xrightarrow{o_r@l(\tilde{v})} [Q', T']_{l'}}{[P, \mathcal{S}]_l \parallel [Q, T]_{l'} \xrightarrow{\sigma} [P', \mathcal{S}']_l \parallel [Q', T']_{l'}} , \sigma = (l, l', o, \tilde{v}, \downarrow)$$

a service exploits another service, located at l, which supplies the absolute value and the subtraction functionality supplied by means of the Request-Response operations ABS and SUB, respectively. Let OP be the Request-Response operation A uses to supply its functionality, the service could be programmed as it follows (we do not describe the variables state since its initial configuration does not alterate the behaviour):

$$A ::= OP(\langle a, b\rangle, res, P)$$
$$P ::= (\overline{ABS}(a, absA)@l \mid \overline{ABS}(b, absB)@l); \overline{SUB}(\langle absA, absB\rangle, res)@l$$

In the case the Request-Response mechanisms is the one modeled by rules of Table 4, there exists an execution path where the responses of the two ABS invocations can be swapped and then, in this case, the OP response is $|b| - |a|$ instead of the expected value $|a| - |b|$. On the contrary, in the case the Request-Response mechanism is modeled as in section 3 such a behavior is not allowed.

5   Conclusion

In this work we have discussed the mobility aspects of service-oriented computing. We have caught the essence of a service by modeling it as a tuple of four basic components (state, location, interface, process) and we have discussed a specific form of mobility for each of them. Namely, we have modeled such a tuple by extending a formal language defined in our previous works that has been exploited as a formal workbench for highlighting the peculiarities of each kind of mobility. Finally, we have analyzed the Web Services technology in order to show which kinds of mobility are actually supported. The discussion about Web Services shows that only the internal state mobility, by means of message passing communication mechanism, and the location mobility are supported by this technology. On the other hand, interface mobility and service functionality mobility raise some interesting issues from the system design point of view. In this sense our formal investigation could be a good starting point for enriching the actual technologies with these new kinds of mobility. Moreover, we have modeled the behavior of the Request-Response interactions supported by the Web Services by discussing how it seems to be weaker than the one we propose in our model.

The contribute of this paper is twofold, on the one hand we have formalized the mobility aspects of service oriented computing and on the other hand we have discussed them by analyzing the current technology state of the art. To the best of our knowledge this is the first attempt to strictly formalize mobility aspects of the service oriented computing paradigm. There are several works which exploit other formalisms like pi-calculus [10, 5] and Petri-nets [8] for dealing with service-based composition but a comprehensive investigation on mobility does not exist.

In our previous work we have defined a formal framework devoted to represent the peculiarities of choreography and orchestration languages and their interdependencies. It emerges that orchestration is a further developement step w.r.t. the choreography which defines the conversation rules among participants. A conformance notion captures such a relationship and permits to verify whether an orchestrated system behaves accordingly with a given choreography. In this paper we have enriched the orchestration language (here called service-based language) with mobility aspects and, as a future work, we plan on the one hand to rephrase the choreography language and the conformance notion by considering the issues raised by mobility mechanisms and, on the other hand, we intend to enrich our formal framework by introducing other fundamental aspects like sessions.

References

1. Apache. *Axis (Java2WSDL)*. [http://ws.apache.org/axis/index.html].
2. Apache. *Axis (WSDL2Java)*. [http://ws.apache.org/axis/index.html].
3. A. Barros and E. Borger. A compositional framework for service interaction patterns and interaction flows. In *Proc. of International conference on formal engineering methods (ICFM 2005)*, LNCS, pages 5–35. Springer Verlag, 2005.
4. A. Barros, M. Dumas, and A. H.M. ter Hofstede. Service interaction patterns: Towards a reference framework for service-based business process interconnection. *Tech. Report FIT-TR-2005-02,Faculty of information Technology, Queensland University of technology, Brisbane, Australia, March 2005*.
5. L. Bocchi, C. Laneve, and G. Zavattaro. A Calculus for Long-Running Transactions. In *FMOODS*, volume 2884 of *LNCS*, pages 124–138. Springer Verlag, 2003.
6. Nadia Busi, Roberto Gorrieri, Claudio Guidi, Roberto Lucchi, and Gianluigi Zavattaro. Choreography and orchestration conformance for system design. In *Proc. of 8th International conference on Coordination Models and Languages (Coordination 2006), To appear*.
7. Nadia Busi, Roberto Gorrieri, Claudio Guidi, Roberto Lucchi, and Gianluigi Zavattaro. Choreography and orchestration: A synergic approach for system design. In *ICSOC*, pages 228–240, 2005.
8. Remco Dijkman and Marlon Dumas. Service-oriented Design: a Multi-viewpoint Approach. *Int. J. Cooperative Inf. Syst.*, 13(4):337–368, 2004.
9. F. Leymann. Web Services Flow Language (WSFL 1.0). [http://www-4.ibm.com/software/solutions/webservices/pdf/WSFL.pdf], Member IBM Academy of Technology, IBM Software Group, 2001.
10. R. Lucchi and M. Mazzara. A pi-calculus based semantics for WS-BPEL. *Journal of Logic and Algebraic Programming*. Elsevier Press. To appear.
11. J. Misra and W. Cook. Computation orchestration. *Software and Systems modeling*. To appear.
12. OASIS. *Web Services Business Process Execution Language Version 2.0, Working Draft*. [http://www.oasis-open.org/committees/download.php/10347/wsbpel-specification-draft-120204.htm].
13. Sun microsystems. *Java Web Services Developer Pack*. [http://java.sun.com/webservices/downloads/webservicespack.html].
14. S. Thatte. XLANG: Web Services for Business Process Design. [http://www.gotdotnet.com/team/xml_wsspecs/xlang-c/default.htm], Microsoft Corporation, 2001.
15. W3C member submission 10 august, 2004. *Web Services Addressing*. [http://www.w3.org/submission/ws-addressing/].

16. World Wide Web Consortium. *SOAP Version 1.2 Part 1: Messaging Framework.*
    [http://www.w3.org/TR/soap12-part1/].
17. World Wide Web Consortium. *Web Services Choreography Description Language
    Version 1.0. Working draft 17 December 2004.* [http://www.w3.org/TR/2004/
    WD-ws-cdl-10-20041217/].
18. World Wide Web Consortium. *Web Services Description Language (WSDL) 1.1.*
    [http://www.w3.org/TR/wsdl].

A   Syntax of χ and Satisfaction Relation for $\vdash$

The syntax of χ is

$$\chi ::= x \leq e \mid e \leq x \mid \neg \chi \mid \chi \wedge \chi$$

where e denotes an expression which can contain variables references and which
can be evaluated into a value v or, when some variables within the expression
are not instantiated, into the symbol $\bot$.

The satisfaction relation for $\vdash$ is defined by the following rules:

1. $\mathcal{S}(x) = \bot \Rightarrow \mathcal{S} \vdash (x \leq \bot \wedge \bot \leq x)$
2. $e \hookrightarrow_\mathcal{S} v, \mathcal{S}(x) \leq v \Rightarrow \mathcal{S} \vdash x \leq e$
3. $e \hookrightarrow_\mathcal{S} v, v \leq \mathcal{S}(x) \Rightarrow \mathcal{S} \vdash e \leq x$
4. $\mathcal{S} \vdash \chi' \wedge \mathcal{S} \vdash \chi'' \Rightarrow \mathcal{S} \vdash \chi' \wedge \chi''$
5. $\neg(\mathcal{S} \vdash \chi) \Rightarrow \mathcal{S} \vdash \neg \chi$

We highlight the fact that rule 1 states that when a variable x is defined with
value $\bot$ the only condition which can be satisfied on such a state is $x = \bot$.

Theoretical Foundations of Scope-Based Compensable Flow Language for Web Service*

Geguang Pu[1], Huibiao Zhu[1], Zongyan Qiu[2],
Shuling Wang[2], Xiangpeng Zhao[2], and Jifeng He[1]

[1] Software Engineering Institute
East China Normal University, Shanghai, China, 200062
[2] LMAM and Department of Informatics, School of Mathematical Sciences
Peking University, Beijing, China, 100871

Abstract. Web Services have become more and more important in these years, and BPEL4WS is a de facto standard for the web service composition and orchestration. In this paper, we propose a language *BPEL0* to capture the important features of BPEL4WS, with the scope-based compensation handling mechanism, which allow the users to specify the compensation behaviors of processes in application-specific manners. The operational semantics of *BPEL0* is formalized, with some key concepts related to compensation handling, i.e., the compensation closure and compensation context. Based on the achieved semantics, the concept of bisimulation in hierarchy structure is investigated, which is used to define the equivalence between *BPEL0* programs.

1 Introduction

Web services and other web-based applications have been becoming more and more important in practice. In this blooming field, various web-based business process languages are introduced, such as XLANG [19], WSFL [13], BPEL4WS (BPEL) [9], and StAC [6], which are designed for the description of services composed by a set of processes across the Internet. Their goal is to achieve the universal interoperability between applications by using web standards, as well as to specify the technical infrastructure for carrying out business transactions. However, BPEL has become the de facto standard for specifying and executing workflow specification for web service composition.

The important feature of BPEL is that it supports the stateful, long-running interactions involving two or more parties. Therefore, it provides the ability to define fault and compensation handing in application-specific manner, resulting in a feature called *Long-Running (Business) Transactions (LRTs)*. The concept *compensation* is due to the use of Sagas [11] and open nested transactions [15].

Aimed to be a language for web service composition and LRTs, BPEL provides a special form of compensation mechanism, with the *scope-based* fault and

---

* The authors at East China Normal University were supported by National Basic Research Program of China (No. 2002CB312001). The authors at Peking University were supported by National Natural Science Foundation of China (No. 60573081).

R. Gorrieri and H. Wehrheim (Eds.): FMOODS 2006, LNCS 4037, pp. 251–266, 2006.
© IFIP International Federation for Information Processing 2006

compensation handling. The mechanism adopted by BPEL is very flexible and powerful, and of course, it causes the complexity of the BPEL and increases the difficulty of the usage. As a result, not surprisingly, the formal semantics of scope-based workflow language, such as BPEL, is not very clear at present.

In this paper, we focus on the theoretical foundation of scope-based flow languages, and propose a language called *BPEL0* which can be regarded as the foundation of BPEL. The operational semantics of *BPEL0* is carefully studied, and with the help of the key concepts of *compensation closure* and *compensation context*, *BPEL0* clearly illustrates how the scope-based compensation mechanism works. For the discussion of the equivalence of *BPEL0* programs, which not only includes the normal programs, but also contains the compensation programs, we propose the concept of bisimulation in hierarchy structure, which reflects the scope-based compensation mechanism, as the scopes in *BPEL0* are allowed to be nested arbitrarily.

This paper is organized as follows. Section 2 introduces the *BPEL0* language with its informal illustrations. Section 3 presents the semantics of *BPEL0*. Section 4 studies the equivalence of *BPEL0* by means of bisimulation in hierarchy structure. Section 5 discusses the related work on compensational workflow language. The last section gives the conclusion and future work.

2   The *BPEL0* Language

The design of *BPEL0* is enlightened by BPEL, where the complicated XML syntactical style of BPEL is abandoned, but all the important features are included. *BPEL0* process is constructed by activities, as shown in BPEL. The syntax of *BPEL0* is as follows:

$$BA \ ::= \ \mathsf{skip} \ | \ \bar{x} := \bar{e} \ | \ \mathsf{wait} \ t \ | \ \mathsf{rec} \ a \ x \ | \ \mathsf{rep} \ a \ v \ | \ \mathsf{inv} \ a \ x \ y \ | \ \mathsf{throw} \ | \ \epsilon$$

$$A \quad ::= \ BA \ | \ A; \ A \ | \ A \triangleleft b \triangleright A \ | \ b * A \ |$$
$$\qquad \quad g \to A \| g \to A \ | \ LA \ \|_L \ LA \ | \ A \sqcap A \ | \ \{A ? C : F\}_n$$

$$LA \ ::= \ b \ \{\breve{l}_1, \breve{l}_2\} \circ A \ | \ A \circ \{b_1 \triangleright \hat{l}_1, \ b_2 \triangleright \hat{l}_2\}$$

$$g \quad ::= \ \mathsf{rec} \ a \ x \ | \ \mathsf{wait} \ t$$

$$C, F \ ::= \ \uparrow n \ | \ldots \quad (\text{similar to } A)$$

$$BP \ ::= \ \{ \! | A : F \! | \}$$

Basic Activities. The basic activity skip does nothing and terminates immediately. $\bar{x} := \bar{e}$ is a multiple assignment which modifies the global state of the business process. Activity wait t makes the process to wait for a given time period t. Activities rec a x and rep a v communicate with the environment of the business process, while inv a x y calls a web service offered by its environment, with two kinds of functions: synchronous request/response or asynchronous one-way operation. Here we assume inv is a two-way operation. The behavior of one-way inv is similar to that of activity skip.

Activity throw generates a fault from inside the business process explicitly. We assume any fault produced in an activity can be captured by its corresponding fault handler when the fault handler does exist. We use ϵ to denote the empty text.

Sequential, Conditional, and Iterative Activities. $A; B$ is the sequential composition of activities A and B. The behavior of the conditional $A \lhd b \rhd B$ is the same as that of A if boolean variable b is evaluated to true, otherwise, it is the same as B. Activity $b * A$ supports repeated performance of the specified activity A, until the given boolean condition b no longer holds.

Choice Activities. BPEL0 provides two kinds of choice: the external choice $g_1 \rightarrow A \parallel g_2 \rightarrow B$ and the internal choice $A \sqcap B$. In BPEL, there is only the external choice, which awaits the occurrence of one of a set of events and then performs the activity associated with the event that occurred. We added the internal choice into BPEL0 to facilitate the reasoning about programs.

Flow and Link Activities. Flow activity $A \parallel_L B$ executes activities A and B in parallel, where A and B are synchronized over the link set L.

The link construct is a mechanism in BPEL to provide additional synchronization in flow activities. Each link must have exactly one activity within the flow as its source and exactly one activity as its target. The source and target of a link may be nested in arbitrary depth within the flow activity, except for the boundary-crossing restrictions [9]. To model this, two link structures $A \circ \{b_1 \rhd \hat{l}_1, \ b_2 \rhd \hat{l}_2\}$ and $b \ \{\check{l}_1, \check{l}_2\} \circ A$ are introduced into BPEL0. In fact, an activity can be the source or target of an arbitrary number of links in BPEL. We make them two here to simplify the discussion, which can be generalized.

$A \circ \{b_1 \rhd \hat{l}_1, \ b_2 \rhd \hat{l}_2\}$ denotes that A is the source of l_1 and l_2 which are assigned boolean values b_1 and b_2 when A completes, while in $b \ \{\check{l}_1, \check{l}_2\} \circ B$, B is the target of l_1 and l_2 with condition b. We use $\hat{l}$ and $\check{l}$ to stand for the source and target of link l respectively. Consider the following example:

$$\check{l} \circ A \parallel_{\{l\}} B \circ \{true \rhd \hat{l}\}$$

Though activities A and B can execute in parallel if there were no link l, but now, they cannot, because the target activities of links have to wait until the link make its condition becoming true. Thus, only when B finishes and stores $true$ into link l, activity A can perform its execution because link l enables its condition. Therefore, the behavior of this program is like $B; A$. Essentially speaking , the flow activity in BPEL0 provides a kind of synchronization similar to the shared variable.

Suppose $l \in L$, we make l a variable recording the status of the link l. The value of l is from the three-values set $\{true, false, \oslash\}$, where $\oslash$ denotes that the status of l is not determined. The following table shows the results of the conjunction operator for the values of a link variable. Other boolean operators are defined similarly.

$\wedge$	$true$	$false$	$\oslash$
$true$	$true$	$false$	$\oslash$
$false$	$false$	$false$	$\oslash$
$\oslash$	$\oslash$	$\oslash$	$\oslash$

Scope Activity with Compensation and Fault Handlers. The interesting feature in BPEL0 (same as in BPEL) is its scope activity, which provides fault and compensation handlers, and both of them are important to support the Long-Running Transactions. Similar to BPEL, the compensation mechanism in *BPEL0* is:

Scope-based (not activity-based). The compensation handlers can only be attached to the scopes.

Fault triggered. A compensation handler can only be invoked directly or indirectly by some fault handler, which is triggered by a fault in the execution.

Fully programmable. The compensation handlers are named. The installed handlers can be invoked in any order, interweaved with any other activities.

$\{A ? C : F\}_n$ denotes a scope with the name n. A is its primary activity, while C and F are its compensation handler and fault handler respectively. The execution of a scope is the execution of its primary activity. The compensation handler is installed with the same name as its scope when the primary activity completes its execution (terminates successfully). An installed compensation handler n is invoked by activity $\uparrow n$, which can only appear in the fault handler or compensation handler of the scope immediately enclosing the scope named n. As mentioned earlier, we suppose that any fault can be caught by the fault handler of the immediately enclosing scope.

Business Process. A complete program in *BPEL0* is in the form of a business process $\{\!|A : F|\!\}$, which is actually an outmost scope without name and compensation handler. If A completes successfully, the whole business process completes as well. While fault handler F terminates successfully when it catches the fault occurring in A, the whole business is still regarded as completed. The last case in which F terminates with a fault denotes that the whole business process terminates abnormally.

The *BPEL0* language provides almost all the features offered by BPEL except the event handlers. We present the comparison for *BPEL0* and BPEL in [18].

3   Semantics

This section formalizes the operational semantics of *BPEL0*. In the semantics, the configuration is defined as a tuple:

$$\langle A, \sigma, \alpha, \beta \rangle \in (Activity \cup \{\boxtimes\}) \times State \times Compensation \times Compensation$$

where *Activity* is the set of program texts consisted of *BPEL0* activities or a termination mark $\boxtimes$, *State* is the set of functions from variables to values. As variables are defined in scopes, we suppose each variable is qualified with the scope name it belongs to. This means all variables are distinct in the state no matter how the scopes are nested.

The compensation context set *Compensation* is the key to deal with the scope-based compensational flow language. Contexts $\alpha, \beta \in Compensation$ are sequences of compensation closures of the form $(C_n : \alpha_1)$, where n is the same name as the scope where the handler C is defined, and α_1 is still a compensation context. When handler C is invoked, it runs in company with the context α_1.

There are two compensation contexts α and β in the configuration. As mentioned earlier, the compensation handler C in scope $\{P\,?\,C\,{:}\,F\}_n$ is installed only when P completes. We use α to record the accumulated compensation handlers installed in the immediately enclosing scope before the current scope starts. We call α *static compensation context*. On the other hand, β records the accumulated compensation closures during the execution of P, which can be changed with the execution of P. We denote β as the *active compensation text*. The following example illustrates the difference between α and β.

$$\{\underbrace{\{P_1\,?\,C_1\,{:}\,F_1\}_{n_1}; A;}_{\alpha}\overbrace{\{P_2}^{\beta}\,?\,C_2\,{:}\,F_2\}_{n_2}; \{P_3\,?\,C_3\,{:}\,F_3\}_{n_3}\,?\,C\,{:}\,F\}_n$$

In this example, when P_2 is executing, β records the compensation closures installed in the execution of P_2, while α records the context for the scope n. When the control enters scope n_3, β will be reset empty and start to record the context accumulated in the execution of P_3 in scope n_3.

$\langle \epsilon,\ \sigma,\ \alpha,\ \langle\rangle \rangle$ is a terminated configuration. As a process might complete (terminate successfully) or fail (terminate with a fault), we use $\langle \boxtimes,\ \sigma,\ \alpha,\ \langle\rangle \rangle$ to denote the failure configuration.

We distinguish three kinds of events: visible event a, time elapsing event $\sqrt{}$, and silent event τ. The visible event set mainly contains the events communicating with the external environment. The time elapsing event denotes the time elapses one time-unit in the real world. The silent event stands for a silent action of the corresponding activity. We assume that when a fault occurs in program P, the event η with fault transition belongs to $\{\tau, a\}$, which leads to make the control flow enter the fault handler from the primary activity. For simplicity, we use symbol δ to stand for an activity in $\{\tau, a, \sqrt{}\}$.

Because compensation text α is a sequence, we list some operators to deal with sequences, which will be used later.

$$a_0 \cdot \langle a_1, \ldots, a_n \rangle = \langle a_0, a_1, \ldots, a_n \rangle \quad \Big| \quad \langle\rangle \parallel \langle a_0, a_1, \ldots, a_n \rangle = \langle a_0, a_1, \ldots, a_n \rangle$$
$$hd(\langle a_1, a_2, \ldots, a_n \rangle) = a_1 \quad \Big| \quad tl(\langle a_1, a_2, \ldots, a_n \rangle) = \langle a_2, \ldots, a_n \rangle$$
$$\langle a_1, , \ldots, a_n \rangle {}^\frown \langle b_1, \ldots, b_m \rangle = \langle a_1, \ldots, a_n, b_1, \ldots, b_m \rangle$$

The operator $\parallel$ on sequence denotes two sequences are composed in parallel. If one part of parallel sequence is empty, then this part can be omitted.

3.1 Basic Activities

The semantics of basic activities are listed as follows:

$$\langle \text{skip},\ \sigma,\ \alpha,\ \langle\rangle \rangle \xrightarrow{\tau} \langle \epsilon, \sigma,\ \alpha,\ \langle\rangle \rangle$$
$$\langle \text{inv } a\ x\ y,\ \sigma,\ \alpha,\ \langle\rangle \rangle \xrightarrow{\sqrt{}} \langle \text{inv } a\ x\ y,\ \sigma,\ \alpha,\ \langle\rangle \rangle$$
$$\langle \text{inv } a\ x\ y,\ \sigma,\ \alpha,\ \langle\rangle \rangle \xrightarrow{a.v} \langle \epsilon,\ \sigma[y \mapsto v],\ \alpha,\ \langle\rangle \rangle$$
$$\langle \text{rec } a\ x,\ \sigma,\ \alpha,\ \langle\rangle \rangle \xrightarrow{\sqrt{}} \langle \text{rec } a\ x,\ \sigma,\ \alpha,\ \langle\rangle \rangle$$
$$\langle \text{rec } a\ x,\ \sigma,\ \alpha,\ \langle\rangle \rangle \xrightarrow{a.v} \langle \epsilon,\ \sigma[x \mapsto v],\ \alpha,\ \langle\rangle \rangle$$
$$\langle \text{rep } a\ x,\ \sigma,\ \alpha,\ \langle\rangle \rangle \xrightarrow{\sqrt{}} \langle \text{rep } a\ x,\ \sigma,\ \alpha,\ \langle\rangle \rangle$$
$$\langle \text{rep } a\ x,\ \sigma,\ \alpha,\ \langle\rangle \rangle \xrightarrow{\tau} \langle \epsilon,\ \sigma,\ \alpha,\ \langle\rangle \rangle$$

$$\langle \bar{x} := \bar{e},\ \sigma,\ \alpha,\ \langle\rangle\rangle \xrightarrow{\tau} \langle \epsilon,\ \sigma[\bar{x} \mapsto \sigma(\bar{e})],\ \alpha,\ \langle\rangle\rangle$$

$$\langle \text{wait } t,\ \sigma,\ \alpha,\ \langle\rangle\rangle \xrightarrow{\checkmark} \langle \text{wait } t-1,\ \sigma,\ \alpha,\ \langle\rangle\rangle \quad t > 1$$

$$\langle \text{wait } 1,\ \sigma,\ \alpha,\ \langle\rangle\rangle \xrightarrow{\checkmark} \langle \epsilon,\ \sigma,\ \alpha,\ \langle\rangle\rangle$$

$$\langle \text{inv } a\ x\ y,\ \sigma,\ \alpha,\ \langle\rangle\rangle \xrightarrow{a} \langle \boxtimes,\ \sigma,\ \alpha,\ \langle\rangle\rangle$$

$$\langle \text{rec } a\ x\ y,\ \sigma,\ \alpha,\ \langle\rangle\rangle \xrightarrow{a} \langle \boxtimes,\ \sigma,\ \alpha,\ \langle\rangle\rangle$$

$$\langle \text{rep } a\ x,\ \sigma,\ \alpha,\ \langle\rangle\rangle \xrightarrow{a} \langle \boxtimes,\ \sigma,\ \alpha,\ \langle\rangle\rangle$$

The last three rules for the basic activities show that, a fault might take place when *BPEL0* process communicates with the environment. Note that the basic activities do not embed any scope. Therefore, the active compensation context is empty for each of them.

3.2   Composition Activities

Sequence. Compared with the sequential composition in traditional programming languages, one interesting rule here is that when a fault takes place in activity A, the whole structure $A; B$ goes into the fault state immediately, where the active compensation text β is reset empty.

$$\langle \epsilon; A,\ \sigma,\ \alpha,\ \beta \rangle \xrightarrow{\tau} \langle A,\ \sigma,\ \alpha,\ \beta \rangle \qquad \frac{\langle A,\ \sigma,\ \alpha,\ \beta\rangle \xrightarrow{\delta} \langle A',\ \sigma',\alpha',\ \beta'\rangle}{\langle A; B,\ \sigma,\ \alpha,\ \beta \rangle \xrightarrow{\delta} \langle A'; B,\ \sigma',\ \alpha',\ \beta'\rangle}$$

$$\frac{\langle A,\ \sigma,\ \alpha,\ \beta\rangle \xrightarrow{\eta} \langle \boxtimes,\ \sigma,\ \alpha,\ \langle\rangle\rangle}{\langle A; B,\ \sigma,\ \alpha,\ \beta \rangle \xrightarrow{\eta} \langle \boxtimes,\ \sigma,\ \alpha,\ \langle\rangle\rangle}$$

For switch, iteration, external and internal choice, their transition rules can be found in [18].

Link. Link structure provides the synchronization mechanism in parallel composition of *BPEL0*.

$$\frac{\langle A,\ \sigma,\ \alpha,\ \beta\rangle \xrightarrow{\delta} \langle A',\ \sigma',\ \alpha',\ \beta'\rangle}{\langle A \circ \{b_1 \triangleright \hat{l}_1,\ b_2 \triangleright \hat{l}_2\},\ \sigma,\ \alpha,\ \beta\rangle \xrightarrow{\delta} \langle A' \circ \{b_1 \triangleright \hat{l}_1,\ b_2 \triangleright \hat{l}_2\},\ \sigma',\ \alpha',\ \beta'\rangle}$$

$$\langle \epsilon \circ \{b_1 \triangleright \hat{l}_1,\ b_2 \triangleright \hat{l}_2\},\ \sigma,\ \alpha,\ \beta\rangle \xrightarrow{\tau} \langle \epsilon,\ \sigma[l_1 \mapsto \sigma(b_1),\ l_2 \mapsto \sigma(b_2)],\ \alpha,\ \langle\rangle\rangle$$

$$\frac{\langle A,\ \sigma,\ \alpha,\ \beta\rangle \xrightarrow{\eta} \langle \boxtimes,\ \sigma',\alpha',\ \langle\rangle\rangle}{\langle A \circ \{b_1 \triangleright \hat{l}_1,\ b_2 \triangleright \hat{l}_2\},\ \sigma,\ \alpha,\ \beta\rangle \xrightarrow{\eta} \langle \boxtimes,\ \sigma[l_1 \mapsto false,\ l_2 \mapsto false],\ \alpha,\ \langle\rangle\rangle}$$

$$\frac{\sigma(b\{\check{l}_1,\ \check{l}_2\}) = true}{\langle b\{\check{l}_1,\ \check{l}_2\} \circ A,\ \sigma,\ \alpha,\ \beta\rangle \xrightarrow{\tau} \langle A,\ \sigma,\ \alpha,\ \beta\rangle}$$

$$\frac{\sigma(b\{\check{l}_1,\ \check{l}_2\}) = false}{\langle b\{\check{l}_1,\ \check{l}_2\} \circ A,\ \sigma,\ \alpha,\ \beta\rangle \xrightarrow{\tau} \langle \boxtimes,\ \sigma,\ \alpha,\ \langle\rangle\rangle}$$

Note that when a fault occurs in source link structure $A \circ \{b_1 \triangleright \hat{l}_1,\ b_2 \triangleright \hat{l}_2\}$, it enters the fault state with assigning *false* to all its link variables. This mechanism ensures that the target link structure can work well, even though its corresponding source link structure has a fault. If the valuation of the boolean variable in the target link is *false*, a standard fault will be thrown immediately. This rule reflects the *non dead-path-elimination semantics* in the flow structure of the BPEL.

Scope. Scope activity is one of the most important features in *BPEL0*. By means of the compensation and fault handlers with the scope activity, *BPEL0* can deal with very complicated long running transactions in business process.

$$\frac{\langle A,\ \sigma,\ \beta,\ \gamma \rangle \xrightarrow{\delta} \langle A',\ \sigma',\ \beta',\ \gamma' \rangle}{\langle \{A\,?\,C\!:\!F\}_n,\ \sigma,\ \alpha,\ \beta \rangle \xrightarrow{\delta} \langle \{A'\,?\,C\!:\!F\}_n,\ \sigma',\ \alpha,\ \beta' \rangle}$$

$$\langle \{\epsilon\,?\,C\!:\!F\}_n, \sigma,\ \alpha,\ \beta \rangle \xrightarrow{\tau} \langle \epsilon,\ \sigma,\ (C_n\!:\!\beta)\cdot\alpha, \langle\rangle \rangle$$

$$\frac{\langle A,\ \sigma,\ \beta,\ \gamma \rangle \xrightarrow{\eta} \langle \boxtimes,\ \sigma,\ \beta,\ \gamma' \rangle}{\langle \{A\,?\,C\!:\!F\}_n,\ \sigma,\ \alpha,\ \beta \rangle \xrightarrow{\eta} \langle F,\ \sigma,\ \beta, \langle\rangle \rangle}$$

The relation between static and active compensation contexts embodied in scope activity is that the active compensation context of $\{A\,?\,C\!:\!F\}_n$ is exactly the static compensation context of activity A.

The primary activity A is executed with an empty context initially. When it completes, a compensation closure is created, and put in the front of α. A sequence of compensation closures will accumulate in this way. When primary activity A fails, the execution switches to the fault handler, and the termination status of the fault handler F is the termination status of the scope. The fault handler can do anything to the state and the environment. Basically, it has the responsibility to recover the process back to a normal state. Note that the fault handler resets its active compensation context empty again before it starts its computing task.

Business Process. A business process is just like the scope activity except lacking of compensation handler. As business process can be regarded as the outmost scope activity, its static compensation text always keeps empty. The following rules are similar to those of scope activity.

$$\frac{\langle P,\ \sigma,\ \beta,\ \gamma \rangle \xrightarrow{\delta} \langle P',\ \sigma',\ \beta',\ \gamma' \rangle}{\langle \{\!|P:F|\!\},\ \sigma,\ \langle\rangle,\ \beta \rangle \xrightarrow{\delta} \langle \{\!|P':F|\!\},\ \sigma',\ \langle\rangle,\ \beta' \rangle}$$

$$\langle \{\!|\epsilon:F|\!\},\ \sigma,\ \langle\rangle,\ \beta \rangle \xrightarrow{\tau} \langle \epsilon,\ \sigma',\ \langle\rangle,\ \langle\rangle \rangle$$

$$\frac{\langle P,\ \sigma,\ \beta,\ \gamma \rangle \xrightarrow{\eta} \langle \boxtimes,\ \sigma,\ \beta,\ \gamma' \rangle}{\langle \{\!|P:F|\!\},\ \sigma,\ \langle\rangle,\ \beta \rangle \xrightarrow{\eta} \langle F,\ \sigma,\ \beta,\ \langle\rangle \rangle}$$

Flow (Parallel). The activities in flow structure are synchronized by the link set defined within parallel activity. The flow activity obeys the following rules:

$$\frac{\langle A,\ \sigma,\ \alpha_A,\ \beta_A \rangle \xrightarrow{\delta} \langle A',\ \sigma',\ \alpha'_A,\ \beta'_A \rangle \ \text{and}\ \delta \neq \surd}{\langle A\,\|_L\,B,\ \sigma,\ (\alpha_A\,\|\,\alpha_B)\cdot\alpha,\ \beta_A\,\|\,\beta_B \rangle \xrightarrow{\delta} \langle A'\,\|_L\,B,\ \sigma',\ (\alpha'_A\,\|\,\alpha_B)\cdot\alpha,\ \beta'_A\,\|\,\beta_B \rangle}$$

$$\frac{\langle B,\ \sigma,\ \alpha_B,\ \beta_B \rangle \xrightarrow{\delta} \langle B',\ \sigma',\ \alpha'_B,\ \beta'_B \rangle \ \text{and}\ \delta \neq \surd}{\langle A\,\|_L\,B,\ \sigma,\ (\alpha_A\,\|\,\alpha_B)\cdot\alpha,\ \beta_A\,\|\,\beta_B \rangle \xrightarrow{\delta} \langle A\,\|_L\,B',\ \sigma',\ (\alpha_A\,\|\,\alpha'_B)\cdot\alpha,\ \beta_A\,\|\,\beta'_B \rangle}$$

$$\frac{\langle A,\ \sigma,\ \alpha_A,\ \beta_A \rangle \xrightarrow{\surd} \langle A',\ \sigma',\ \alpha'_A,\ \beta'_A \rangle \ \text{and}\ \langle B,\ \sigma,\ \alpha_B,\ \beta_B \rangle \xrightarrow{\surd} \langle B',\ \sigma',\ \alpha'_B,\ \beta'_B \rangle}{\langle A\,\|_L\,B,\ \sigma,\ (\alpha_A\,\|\,\alpha_B)\cdot\alpha,\ \beta_A\,\|\,\beta_B \rangle \xrightarrow{\surd} \langle A'\,\|_L\,B',\ \sigma',\ (\alpha'_A\,\|\,\alpha'_B)\cdot\alpha,\ \beta'_A\,\|\,\beta'_B \rangle}$$

The operator $\|$ on ϵ and $\boxtimes$ is defined in the following table:

$\|$	ϵ	$\boxtimes$
ϵ	ϵ	$\boxtimes$
$\boxtimes$	$\boxtimes$	$\boxtimes$

Only when all of activities in the flow complete, the flow activity completes. Note that there is an interesting thing about a fault occurring in one branch of the flow activity. If one branch in a flow fails, the other branches can run until they complete or fail. This seems a little unreasonable in real system, because all branches are supposed to be terminated when one of the branch in flow fails. In the next section, the concept of *forced termination* is introduced to modify the semantics provided here in order to conform to the behavior of fault in the real system.

Operation $\uparrow n$ looks up the compensation closure with the name n in the current compensation context. If no closure with the name is found, it acts like skip, otherwise, the handler in the closure is executed in company with its context:

$$\langle \uparrow n, \sigma, \alpha, \langle\rangle \rangle \xrightarrow{\tau} \langle gp(n,\alpha), \sigma, ge(n,\alpha), \langle\rangle \rangle$$

The lookup rules for parallel operator are as follows:

$$gp(n, (\alpha' \| \alpha'') \cdot \alpha) = gp(n, \alpha'^\frown \alpha''^\frown \alpha) \quad \text{and} \quad ge(n, (\alpha' \| \alpha'') \cdot \alpha) = ge(n, \alpha'^\frown \alpha''^\frown \alpha)$$

where $gp(n, \alpha)$ and $ge(n, \alpha)$ extract the process and the context of the compensation closure with name n from α, respectively (where $n \neq m$):

$$gp(n, \langle\rangle) = \text{skip}$$
$$gp(n, (C_n : \beta) \cdot \alpha') = C$$
$$gp(n, (C_m : \beta) \cdot \alpha') = gp(n, \alpha')$$

$$ge(n, \langle\rangle) = \langle\rangle$$
$$ge(n, (C_n : \beta) \cdot \alpha') = \beta$$
$$ge(n, (C_m : \beta) \cdot \alpha') = ge(n, \alpha')$$

3.3   Forced Termination

In a BPEL flow activity, when one branch fails, the fault handler of the innermost enclosing scope begins its behavior by implicitly terminating all other (concurrent) activities in the scope, and then starts the execution of its body. This is called the *forced termination*. To deal with this mechanism, a new termination mark $\boxtimes$ is introduced to describe this new kind of termination.

We have to add some rules to handle the forced termination. First of all, all basic actives will be allowed to complete their work as before and their completion can be regarded as a forced termination as well. We use P_{ba} to denote any basic activity, such as rec, inv etc.

$$\frac{\langle P_{ba}, \sigma, \alpha, \langle\rangle \rangle \xrightarrow{\delta} \langle \epsilon, \sigma', \alpha, \langle\rangle \rangle}{\langle P_{ba}, \sigma, \alpha, \langle\rangle \rangle \xrightarrow{\delta} \langle \boxtimes, \sigma', \alpha, \langle\rangle \rangle}$$

A rule for sequential composition is added:

$$\frac{\langle A, \sigma, \alpha, \beta \rangle \xrightarrow{\delta} \langle \boxtimes, \sigma', \alpha, \langle\rangle \rangle}{\langle A; B, \sigma, \alpha, \beta \rangle \xrightarrow{\delta} \langle \boxtimes, \sigma', \alpha, \langle\rangle \rangle}$$

A rule for link construct is added:

$$\frac{\langle A,\ \sigma,\ \alpha,\ \beta\rangle \xrightarrow{\ \delta\ } \langle \boxtimes,\ \sigma',\alpha,\ \langle\rangle\rangle}{\langle A \circ \{b_1 \triangleright \hat{l}_1,\ b_2 \triangleright \hat{l}_2\},\ \sigma,\ \alpha,\ \beta\rangle \xrightarrow{\ \delta\ } \langle \boxtimes,\ \sigma'[l_1 \mapsto false,\ l_2 \mapsto\ false],\ \alpha,\ \langle\rangle\rangle}$$

A new rule for scope is added as well.

$$\frac{\langle P,\ \sigma,\ \beta,\ \gamma\rangle \xrightarrow{\ \delta\ } \langle \boxtimes,\ \sigma',\ \beta,\ \langle\rangle\rangle}{\langle \{P\,?\,C\,{:}\,F\}_n,\ \sigma,\ \alpha,\ \beta\rangle \xrightarrow{\ \delta\ } \langle \boxtimes,\ \sigma',\ \alpha,\ \langle\rangle\rangle}$$

At last, we should modify the results of operator $\parallel$ while $\boxtimes$ is added

$\parallel$	ϵ	$\boxtimes$	$\boxtimes$
ϵ	ϵ	$\boxtimes$	$\boxtimes$
$\boxtimes$	$\boxtimes$	$\boxtimes$	$\boxtimes$
$\boxtimes$	$\boxtimes$	$\boxtimes$	$\boxtimes$

Example 1. (Forced Termination) Consider a *BPEL0* program $P = \{\{A_1\,?\,C_1:$ $F_1\}_{n_1}; A_2; A_3 \parallel_{\{\}} A_4; A_5; A_6\,?\ \mathsf{skip}:\ ^\uparrow n\}_n$, where A_i $(i\ =\ 1...6)$ are all basic activities. Suppose a fault occurs in the execution of A_2, and all the other basic activities can complete. Using the semantic rules above, we can reason about the execution of P. For simplicity, we use some abbreviations $P_1 = \{A_1\,?\,C_1:F_1\}_{n_1}$, $P_{11} = \{A_1\,?\,C_1:F_1\}_{n_1}; A_2; A_3$ and $P_{12} = A_4; A_5; A_6$. In the following , we use $\longrightarrow^*$ to denote zero or multiple transitions.

When there is no forced termination:

(1) $\langle P_1, \sigma, \langle\rangle, \langle\rangle\rangle \longrightarrow^* \langle \epsilon, \sigma', (C_n:\langle\rangle), \langle\rangle\rangle$
(2) $\langle P_{11}, \sigma, \langle\rangle, \langle\rangle\rangle \longrightarrow^* \langle \boxtimes, \sigma'', (C_n:\langle\rangle), \langle\rangle\rangle$
(3) $\langle P_{12}, \sigma, \langle\rangle, \langle\rangle\rangle \longrightarrow^* \langle \epsilon, \sigma'', \langle\rangle, \langle\rangle\rangle$
(4) $\langle P_{11} \parallel_{\{\}} P_{12}, \sigma, \langle\rangle, \langle\rangle\rangle \longrightarrow^* \langle \boxtimes, \sigma'', (C_n:\langle\rangle), \langle\rangle\rangle$
(5) $\langle P, \sigma, \langle\rangle, \langle\rangle\rangle \longrightarrow^* \langle ^\uparrow n, \sigma'', (C_n:\langle\rangle), \langle\rangle\rangle$
(6) $\langle P, \sigma, \langle\rangle, \langle\rangle\rangle \longrightarrow^* \langle C_n, \sigma'', \langle\rangle, \langle\rangle\rangle$

Now we take the forced termination into account:

(1) $\langle P_1, \sigma, \langle\rangle, \langle\rangle\rangle \longrightarrow^* \langle \epsilon, \sigma', (C_n:\langle\rangle), \langle\rangle\rangle$
(2) $\langle P_{11}, \sigma, \langle\rangle, \langle\rangle\rangle \longrightarrow^* \langle \boxtimes, \sigma'', (C_n:\langle\rangle), \langle\rangle\rangle$
(3) $\langle P_{12}, \sigma, \langle\rangle, \langle\rangle\rangle \longrightarrow \langle \epsilon; A_2; A_3, \sigma_1, \langle\rangle, \langle\rangle\rangle$
(4) $\langle P_{12}, \sigma, \langle\rangle, \langle\rangle\rangle \longrightarrow^* \langle \boxtimes, \sigma_1, \langle\rangle, \langle\rangle\rangle$
(5) $\langle P_{11} \parallel_{\{\}} P_{12}, \sigma, \langle\rangle, \langle\rangle\rangle \longrightarrow^* \langle \boxtimes, \sigma'', (C_n:\langle\rangle), \langle\rangle\rangle$

From the second deduction, we can see that when a branch in a parallel process fails, the other activities that are currently active are forced to terminate by means of force termination rules.

4   Bisimulation

The behavior of a program can be represented in terms of execution steps. Two syntactically different programs may have the same observable behavior. Thus, a reasonable abstraction is desirable in defining program equivalence via operational semantics. Bisimulation is a useful approach in defining program equivalence. Algebraic laws can be explored using the formalized bisimulation.

Here are some auxiliary definitions for the definition of bisimulation.

Definition 1. *The transition relation $\overset{id}{\Longrightarrow}$ is defined as:*

$$\langle P, \sigma, \alpha, \beta \rangle \overset{id}{\Longrightarrow} \langle P', \sigma, \alpha, \beta \rangle$$
$$=_{df} \exists n, P_1, \ldots, P_n \bullet \langle P, \sigma, \alpha, \beta \rangle \overset{\eta_1}{\longrightarrow} \langle P_1, \sigma, \alpha, \beta \rangle \ldots \overset{\eta_n}{\longrightarrow} \langle P_n, \sigma, \alpha, \beta \rangle$$
$$\text{and} \quad P_n = P'$$

where $\overset{\eta_i}{\longrightarrow}$ can be of the form $\overset{\tau}{\longrightarrow}$ or $\overset{a}{\longrightarrow}$. □

Definition 2. *The transition relation $\overset{\delta}{\Longrightarrow}$ ($\delta \in \{\tau, a, \surd\}$) is defined as:*

$$\langle P, \sigma, \alpha, \beta \rangle \overset{\delta}{\Longrightarrow} \langle P', \sigma', \alpha', \beta' \rangle$$
$$=_{df} \begin{cases} \langle P, \sigma, \alpha, \beta \rangle \overset{\delta}{\longrightarrow} \langle P', \sigma', \alpha', \beta' \rangle & \text{or} \\ \exists P_1 \bullet \langle P, \sigma, \alpha, \beta \rangle \overset{id}{\Longrightarrow} \langle P_1, \sigma, \alpha, \beta \rangle \overset{\delta}{\longrightarrow} \langle P', \sigma', \alpha', \beta' \rangle \end{cases}$$

In a *BPEL0* program configuration, the third element stores a sequence of programs. This gives the complexity of defining bisimulation for the programs. In order to deal with the definition, we firstly introduce the concept of 0-*Bisimulation*, which forms the basis for defining program equivalence.

Definition 3. *(0-Bisimulation) A symmetric relation R is a 0-Bisimulation if and only if* $\forall \langle P, \sigma, \alpha, \beta \rangle \, R \, \langle Q, \sigma, \alpha_1, \beta_1 \rangle$

(1) if $\langle P, \sigma, \alpha, \beta \rangle \overset{\surd}{\Longrightarrow} \langle P', \sigma', \alpha', \beta' \rangle$,

    then $\exists Q', \alpha_1', \beta_1' \bullet \langle Q, \sigma, \alpha_1, \beta_1 \rangle \overset{\surd}{\Longrightarrow} \langle Q', \sigma', \alpha_1', \beta_1' \rangle$ and
        $\langle P', \sigma', \alpha', \beta' \rangle \, R \, \langle Q', \sigma', \alpha_1', \beta_1' \rangle$

(2) if $\langle P, \sigma, \alpha, \beta \rangle \overset{\eta}{\Longrightarrow} \langle P', \sigma', \alpha', \beta' \rangle$ ($\eta \in \{\tau, a\}$),

  (2-1) if $\sigma \neq \sigma'$, then

      $\exists Q', \alpha_1', \beta_1' \bullet \langle Q, \sigma, \alpha_1, \beta_1 \rangle \overset{\eta}{\Longrightarrow} \langle Q', \sigma', \alpha_1', \beta_1' \rangle$ *and*
         $\langle P', \sigma', \alpha', \beta' \rangle \, R \, \langle Q', \sigma', \alpha_1', \beta_1' \rangle$

  (2-2) if $\sigma = \sigma'$, then

     either $\langle P', \sigma', \alpha', \beta' \rangle \, R \, \langle Q, \sigma, \alpha_1, \beta_1 \rangle$

     or $\exists Q', \alpha_1', \beta_1' \bullet \langle Q, \sigma, \alpha_1, \beta_1 \rangle \overset{\eta}{\Longrightarrow} \langle Q', \sigma', \alpha_1', \beta_1' \rangle$ and
         $\langle P', \sigma', \alpha', \beta' \rangle \, R \, \langle Q', \sigma', \alpha_1', \beta_1' \rangle$

(3) if $\langle P, \sigma, \alpha, \beta \rangle \overset{\eta}{\longrightarrow} \langle \boxtimes, \sigma', \alpha', \langle \rangle \rangle$ ($\eta \in \{\tau, a\}$),

    then $\exists \alpha_1' \bullet \langle Q, \sigma, \alpha, \beta \rangle \overset{\eta}{\longrightarrow} \langle \boxtimes, \sigma', \alpha_1', \langle \rangle \rangle$ □

Item (1) indicates that if process P makes time transition, so does the process Q and the two result configurations are also 0-bisimilar.

Item (2) stands for the case of atomic-like transitions. It can be divided into two types. If the two states before and after the transition are different, the bisimilarity analysis is similar to item (1). The second type models the case that the two states are the same. For this sub case, although process P has made transitions, process Q may not make further transitions and the result configuration of P is directly bisimilar to the configuration of process Q. On the other hand, process Q may also need to do atomic-like transition and the result configurations of process P and Q after transitions are bisimilar.

Item (3) represents the failure case. If a process makes a failure transition, the corresponding process must also make a failure transition.

Definition 4. *(1) Configurations* $\langle P_1, \sigma, \alpha_1, \beta_1 \rangle$ *and* $\langle P_2, \sigma, \alpha_2, \beta_2 \rangle$ *are 0-bisimilar, written as* $\langle P_1, \sigma, \alpha_1, \beta_1 \rangle \approx_0 \langle P_2, \sigma, \alpha_2, \beta_2 \rangle$, *if there exists a 0-bisimulation relation* R *such that* $\langle P_1, \sigma, \alpha_1, \beta_1 \rangle \, R \, \langle P_2, \sigma, \alpha_2, \beta_2 \rangle$.

(2) Programs P *and* Q *are 0-bisimilar, written as* $P \approx_0 Q$, *if* $\forall \sigma, \alpha_1, \alpha_2, \beta_1, \beta_2$ •
$\langle P, \sigma, \alpha_1, \beta_1 \rangle \approx_0 \langle Q, \sigma, \alpha_2, \beta_2 \rangle$. □

This definition indicates that $\approx_0$ is the largest relation for 0-bisimulation over configurations. Further, the concept of 0-bisimulation has also been extended to the domain of processes.

Now we give the definition of the *simple compensation sequence*:

(1) $\langle \, \rangle$ is a simple compensation sequence;
(2) $(C_1 : \alpha_1)\widehat{\,} \ldots \widehat{\,} (C_n : \alpha_n)$ is a simple compensation sequence if $\alpha_1, \ldots, \alpha_n$ are also simple compensation sequences.

Example 2. Let $\alpha = (C_1 : \alpha_1)\widehat{\,}(C_2 : \alpha_2)\widehat{\,}(C_3 : \langle \, \rangle)$,
$\alpha_1 = (C_4 : \alpha_4)\widehat{\,}(C_5 : \langle \, \rangle)$ and $\alpha_2 = (C_6 : \alpha_6)\widehat{\,}(C_7 : \langle \, \rangle)\widehat{\,}(C_8 : \alpha_8)$,
$\alpha_4 = (C_9 : \langle \, \rangle)\widehat{\,}(C_{10} : \langle \, \rangle)$,
$\alpha_6 = (C_{11} : \langle \, \rangle)\widehat{\,}(C_{12} : \langle \, \rangle)\widehat{\,}(C_{13} : \langle \, \rangle)$ and $\alpha_8 = (C_{14} : \langle \, \rangle)\widehat{\,}(C_{15} : \langle \, \rangle)$

From the above definition, we know α is a simple compensation sequence. □

Consider a simple compensation sequence $\alpha = (C_1 : \alpha_1)\widehat{\,} \ldots \widehat{\,} (C_n : \alpha_n)$. In order to describe its full structure, we translate the nested sequence structure of α into a tree structure; namely $tree(\alpha)$:

(1) if $\alpha = \langle \, \rangle$, then $tree(\alpha)$ is just one node;
(2) if $\alpha = (C_1 : \alpha_1)\widehat{\,} \ldots \widehat{\,} (C_n : \alpha_n)$, then there are n branches for the root of the tree, the names for the n edges from left to right are $C_1, \ldots \ldots, C_n$. Further, the root of $tree(\alpha_i)$ is just another node of edge C_i.

The tree structure of α in *Example 2* is shown in the left tree below. It clearly illustrates the structure of the compensation sequence. Regarding the tree for

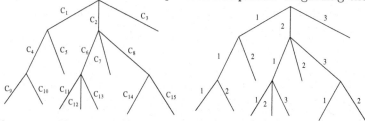

a simple compensation sequence, we now assign a number for each edge (called edge number). For a given edge, consider all the edges starting from the upper point of the given edge. The edge number for a given edge is i if the given edge is the i-th edge starting from left to right. The edge number for each edge in *Example 2* is shown in the right tree above.

The $path(\alpha)$ for any simple compensation sequence β is defined as:

$$path(\alpha) =_{df} \{ i_1 {}^\frown \dots {}^\frown i_n \mid \exists \text{ edge } C \bullet i_1, \dots, i_n \text{ are the edge number}$$
$$\text{from the root of } tree(\alpha) \text{ to the exact edge } C \}$$

The sequence $i_1 {}^\frown \dots {}^\frown i_n$ dynamically indices to the exact edge in $tree(\alpha)$. Therefore, we will use $\alpha[i_1 {}^\frown \dots {}^\frown i_n]$ to represent the corresponding edge in $tree(\alpha)$, which stands for a program. For example, in the simple compensation sequence α of *Example 2*, $2{}^\frown 1{}^\frown 2$ will identify program C_{12}.

Two sequences α_1 and α_2 are called structural equivalence, written as $\alpha_1 \approx_s \alpha_2$, if $path(\alpha_1) = path(\alpha_2)$.

However, not all compensation sequences are simple. For example, let $\alpha = ((C_1 : \langle \rangle) \parallel (C_2 : (C_3 : \langle \rangle))){}^\frown (C_4 : \langle \rangle)$. It is easy to see that α is not simple.

To illustrate the further structure for compensation, we introduce a function $mul(\alpha)$, which contains all the simple compensation sequences for compensation sequence α:

$$mul(\langle \rangle) =_{df} \{ \langle \rangle \}$$
$$mul((C_1 : \alpha_1){}^\frown x) =_{df} \{ (C_1 : u){}^\frown t \mid u \in mul(\alpha_1) \wedge t \in mul(x) \}$$
$$mul((x \parallel y){}^\frown z) =_{df} mul(x{}^\frown y{}^\frown z) \cup mul(y{}^\frown x{}^\frown z)$$

Now we introduce the concept of k-bisimulation ($k \geq 1$). Together with 0-bisimulation, they form the basis in defining program equivalence.

Definition 5. *(k-Bisimulation)* *A symmetric relation R is a k-Bisimulation ($k \geq 1$) if and only if for any $\langle P, \sigma, \alpha, \beta \rangle\, R\, \langle Q, \sigma, \alpha_1, \beta_1 \rangle$*

(0) $Equiv(\alpha, \alpha_1, k - 1);$

(1) if $\langle P, \sigma, \alpha, \beta \rangle \overset{\checkmark}{\Longrightarrow} \langle P', \sigma', \alpha', \beta' \rangle,$

    then $\exists Q', \alpha_1', \beta_1' \bullet \langle Q, \sigma, \alpha_1, \beta_1 \rangle \overset{\checkmark}{\Longrightarrow} \langle Q', \sigma', \alpha_1', \beta_1' \rangle$ *and*
             $\langle P', \sigma', \alpha', \beta' \rangle\, R\, \langle Q', \sigma', \alpha_1', \beta_1' \rangle$ *and*
             $Equiv(\alpha', \alpha_1', k - 1);$

(2) if $\langle P, \sigma, \alpha, \beta \rangle \overset{\eta}{\Longrightarrow} \langle P', \sigma', \alpha', \beta' \rangle$ *($\eta \in \{\tau, a\}$),*

  (2-1) if $\sigma \neq \sigma',$ *then*

      $\exists Q', \alpha_1', \beta_1' \bullet \langle Q, \sigma, \alpha_1, \beta_1 \rangle \overset{\eta}{\Longrightarrow} \langle Q', \sigma', \alpha_1', \beta_1' \rangle$ *and*
          $\langle P', \sigma', \alpha', \beta' \rangle\, R\, \langle Q', \sigma', \alpha_1', \beta_1' \rangle$ *and*
          $Equiv(\alpha', \alpha_1', k - 1);$

  (2-2) if $\sigma = \sigma',$ *then*

      either $\langle P', \sigma', \alpha', \beta' \rangle\, R\, \langle Q, \sigma, \alpha_1, \beta_1 \rangle$ *and* $Equiv(\alpha', \alpha_1, k - 1);$
      or $\exists Q', \alpha_1', \beta_1' \bullet \langle Q, \sigma, \alpha_1, \beta_1 \rangle \overset{\eta}{\Longrightarrow} \langle Q', \sigma', \alpha_1', \beta_1' \rangle$ *and*
            $\langle P', \sigma', \alpha', \beta' \rangle\, R\, \langle Q', \sigma', \alpha_1', \beta_1' \rangle$ *and*
            $Equiv(\alpha', \alpha_1', k - 1);$

(3) if $\langle P, \sigma, \alpha, \beta \rangle \xrightarrow{\eta} \langle \boxtimes, \sigma', \alpha', \langle \rangle \rangle$ *($\eta \in \{\tau, a\}$),*

  then $\exists \alpha_1' \bullet \langle Q, \sigma, \alpha, \beta \rangle \xrightarrow{\eta} \langle \boxtimes, \sigma', \alpha_1', \langle \rangle \rangle$ *and* $Equiv(\alpha', \alpha_1', k - 1)$;

where

  (a) $Equiv(\alpha_1, \alpha_2, n) =_{df} \forall u \in mul(\alpha_1) \bullet \exists v \in mul(\alpha_2) \bullet equiv(u, v, n) \wedge$
    $\forall v \in mul(\alpha_2) \bullet \exists u \in mul(\alpha_1) \bullet equiv(v, u, n)$

  (b) $equiv(u, v, n) =_{df} u \approx_s v \wedge \forall t \in path(u) \bullet u[t] \approx_n v[t]$ □

Here, $equiv(u, v, n)$ indicates that the two simple compensation sequences u and v are structural equivalent (described by $u \approx_s v$). Further, it also indicates that every program in $tree(u)$ is n-bisimilar to the corresponding program in $tree(v)$.

Regarding $Equiv(\alpha_1, \alpha_2, n)$, α_1 and α_2 may not be simple compensation sequences. We use $mul(\alpha_1)$ and $mul(\alpha_2)$ to record all the simple compensation sequences generated from α_1 and α_2 respectively. Further, for every simple compensation sequence u in $mul(\alpha_1)$, there should exist a simple compensation sequence v in $mul(\alpha_2)$ such that $equiv(u, v, n)$ is satisfied and vice-versa. Therefore, $Equiv(\alpha_1, \alpha_2, n)$ stands for the n-bisimilarity for α_1 and α_2.

The key point of k-bisimulation ($k \geq 1$) is as follows. As mentioned earlier, the third element of a configuration is a sequence recording a set of programs in tree structure. In k-bisimulation ($k \geq 1$), for the sequences appearing as the third elements in the two bisimilar configurations before and after the transition, their structures should be the same. Further, before a transition (or after a transition), the corresponding processes recorded in the two sequences of two k-bisimilar configurations should be $(k - 1)$-bisimilar. This shows the difference of k-bisimulation and 0-bisimulation, which is shown in item (0) and the extra information (i.e., function $Equiv(\ )$) in other items in the definition of k-bisimulation.

Definition 6. *(1) Configurations* $\langle P_1, \sigma, \alpha_1, \beta_1 \rangle$ *and* $\langle P_2, \sigma, \alpha_2, \beta_2 \rangle$ *are* k-*bisimilar* *($k \geq 1$), written as* $\langle P_1, \sigma, \alpha_1, \beta_1 \rangle \approx_k \langle P_2, \sigma, \alpha_2, \beta_2 \rangle$, *if there exists a* k-*bisimulation relation* R *such that* $\langle P_1, \sigma, \alpha_1, \beta_1 \rangle R \langle P_2, \sigma, \alpha_2, \beta_2 \rangle$.

(2) Programs P *and* Q *are* k-*bisimilar ($k \geq 1$), the fact is written as* $P \approx_k Q$, *if* $\forall \sigma, \alpha_1, \alpha_2, \beta_1, \beta_2 \bullet Equiv(\alpha_1, \alpha_2, k - 1) \implies \langle P, \sigma, \alpha_1, \beta_1 \rangle \approx_k \langle Q, \sigma, \alpha_2, \beta_2 \rangle$ □

From definition 5 and 6, k-bisimulation relies on $(k - 1)$-bisimulation. Thus, 0-bisimulation is the basis for the definition of all k-bisimulations (for $k \geq 1$). Therefore, n-bisimulation ($n \geq 0$) forms a *hierarchy* structure.

Lemma 1. *If* $P \approx_k Q$, *then* $P \approx_{k-1} Q$ *($k \geq 1$).*   □

Definition 7. *(Program equivalence)* $\approx =_{df} \bigcap_{n \geq 0} \approx_n$ □

Two programs are equivalent, if they are n-bisimilar for any n ($n \geq 0$).

Theorem 1. $\approx$ *is a congruence.*   □

This theorem indicates that "program equivalence" relation $\approx$ is preserved by all *BPEL0* processes.

5   Related Work

In recent years, many efforts have been attempted to formalize various workflow languages [1, 3, 6, 5], especially with some kinds of *compensation* concepts, which root to the Sagas and open nested transactions, and have been studied for a long time in the transaction processing world.

M. Mazzara *et al.* suggested to merge the fault and compensation handling into a general framework of even handling [14], and presented an operational semantics for their CCS-like language. In paper [12], Koshkina *et al.* analyzed the link structure carefully in BPEL, and presented a language called BPEL-calculus (a CCS-like language as well) to model and verify BPEL specifications. But they omitted the compensation and fault handling mechanisms totally.

In a recent paper [7], Bruni *et al.* presented the operational semantics for a series of languages, embodying the concept of *compensation*. However, the compensation in these languages is basic-activity-oriented (each basic activity is in company with a compensation) with no name. The compensation is triggered by a special command, and always executed in the reverse order with respect to the installation. Compared to the work of paper [6], Butler *et al.* presented a language called StAC (Structured Activity Compensation), where the semantics of StAC was defined on its semantic language. The paper [8] illustrated the link and difference between the two languages proposed by Bruni [7] and Butler [6] respectively. Our previous work [16] studied the semantics of the fault and compensation handling in BPEL specification, and presented a simple language to catch the features of BPEL related to fault and compensation handling. The big step semantics are adopted by most researchers when studying the compensation mechanism in workflow language.

Some research groups aim to model and verify the BPEL4WS program, such as [10, 3]. In paper [10], authors presented a set of tools and techniques for analyzing interactions of composite web services which are specified in BPEL. The BPEL specifications are translated into an intermediate representation, and then verified using SPIN. In paper [17], we adopted a similar approach to use model checker UPPAAL [4] to verify the properties of BPEL program including timed properties. But we find no work on verifying BPEL specification with the features of the compensation and fault handling.

Of course there are much more informal work on workflow languages, and especially on BPEL. For example, [1] proposed a general framework to evaluate the capabilities and limitations of BPEL. Paper [2] presented an informal analysis from a pattern-based view on workflow language. But their work did not provide the patterns related to fault and compensation handling as well.

6   Conclusion

BPEL is one of the most important business process modelling languages, aimed to specify the business services which are formed by distributed, interoperational and heterogeneous components over networks. One distinct feature of BPEL is its scope-based compensation handling and fully programmable compensation mechanism, which allows users to specify the compensation behaviors of processes in application-specific manners.

In this paper, we proposed a language *BPEL0* based on BPEL, and regard it as a foundation to study the scoped-base compensation languages. With the help of the key concepts of *compensation closure* and *compensation context*, the semantics of *BPEL0* has been carefully studied. Based on the semantics, the concept of bisimulation in hierarchy structure has been studied , which can be used to define the equivalence between *BPEL0* programs

Based on this work, an execution engine of *BPEL0* is being developed, and we also hope to study the verification of *BPEL0* relying on the semantic framework proposed here, which can be added into the developing of execution engine. As one future work as well, we will consider the design patterns provided by *BPEL0*, especially the patterns with compensation handling by means of our defined bisimulation relation.

References

1. W. Aalst, M. Dumas, and A. Hofstede, and P. Wohed, Analysis of web services composition languages: The case of BPEL4WS. In *Proc. of ER'03*, LNCS 2813, pp 200-215, Springer, 2003.
2. W. Aalst, A. Hofstede. YAWL: yet another workflow language. In *Inf. Syst.*, Vol.30(4), pp 245-275, 2005.
3. B. Benatallah and R. Hamadi. A Petri net-based model for web service composition. *Proc. of ADC'03*, pp 191-200, Australian Computer Society, 2003.
4. J. Bengtsson, K. G. Larsen, F. Larsson, P. Pettersson, and Y. Wang. UPPAAL - a tool suite for automatic verification of real-time systems. In *Hybrid Systems III: Verification and Control*, pp 232-243, Springer, 1996.
5. A. Brogi, C. Canal, E. Pimentel, and A. Vallecillo. Formalizing web services choreographies. In *Pro. of WS-FM'04*, 2004.
6. M. Butler and C. Ferreira. An operational semantics for StAC, a language for modelling long-running business transactions. In *Proc. of Coordination'04*, LNCS 2949, pp 87-104, Springer, 2004.
7. R. Bruni, H. Melgratti, and U. Montanari, Theoritical Foundations for Compensation in Flow Composition Languages, In *Proc. of ACM POPL'05*, 2005.
8. R. Bruni, M. Butler, C. Ferreira, C. A. R. Hoare, H. C. Melgratti, U. Montanari. Comparing Two Approaches to Compensable Flow Composition. In *Proc. of CONCUR'05*, pp 383-397, 2005.
9. BPEL4WS, *Business Process Execution Language for Web Service*. http://www.siebel.com/bpel, 2003.
10. X. Fu, T. Bultan, and J. Su. Analysis of interacting BPEL web services. In *Proc. of WWW'04*, pp 621-630, 2004.
11. H. Garcia-Molina and K. Salem. Sagas. In *Proc. of ACM SIGMOD'87*, pp 249-259, ACM Press, 1987.
12. M. Koshkina and F. Breugel. Modelling and verifying web service orchestration by means of the concurrency workbench. In *ACM SIGSOFT Software Engineering Notes, 29(5)*, 2004.

13. F. Leymann. *WSFL: Web Serices Flow Languag.* http://www-3.ibm.com/software/solutions/webservices/pdf/WSDL.pdf.

14. M. Mazzara and R. Lucchi. A framework for generic error handling in business process. In *Proc. of WS-FM'04*, ENTCS Vol. 105, pp 133-145, Elsevier, 2004.

15. J. Moss. Nested Transactions: An Approach to Reliable Distributed Computing. PhD thesis, Dept. of Electrical Eng. and Computer Sci., MIT, 1981.

16. Qiu Zongyan, Wang Shuling, Pu Geguang and Zhao Xiangpeng. Semantics of BPEL4WS-like Fault and Compensation Handling . In *Proc. of Formal Methods'05*, pp 350-365, Springer, 2005.

17. Pu Geguang, Zhao Xiangpeng, Wang Shuling, and Qiu Zongyan. Towards the semantics and verification of BPEL4WS. In *Proc. of WS-FM05*, 2005.

18. Pu Geguang, Zhu Huibiao, Qiu Zongyan, Wang Shuling, Zhao Xiangpeng, and He Jifeng. Theoretical Foundations of Scope-based Compensation Flow Language for Web Service. Research Report 67, School of Mathematical Sciences, Peking University, 2005.

19. S. Thatte. *XLANG: Web Service for Business Process Design.* http://www.gotdotnet.com/team/xml_wsspecs/xlang-c/default.html.

Author Index

Lecture Notes in Computer Science

For information about Vols. 1–3921

please contact your bookseller or Springer

Vol. 3975: S. Mehrotra, D.D. Zeng, H. Chen, B. Thuraisingham, F.-Y. Wang (Eds.), Intelligence and Security Informatics. XXII, 772 pages. 2006.

Vol. 3973: J. Wang, Z. Yi, J.M. Zurada, B.-L. Lu, H. Yin (Eds.), Advances in Neural Networks - ISNN 2006, Part III. XXIX, 1402 pages. 2006.

Vol. 3972: J. Wang, Z. Yi, J.M. Zurada, B.-L. Lu, H. Yin (Eds.), Advances in Neural Networks - ISNN 2006, Part II. XXVII, 1444 pages. 2006.

Vol. 3971: J. Wang, Z. Yi, J.M. Zurada, B.-L. Lu, H. Yin (Eds.), Advances in Neural Networks - ISNN 2006, Part I. LXVII, 1442 pages. 2006.

Vol. 3970: T. Braun, G. Carle, S. Fahmy, Y. Koucheryavy (Eds.), Wired/Wireless Internet Communications. XIV, 350 pages. 2006.

Vol. 3968: K.P. Fishkin, B. Schiele, P. Nixon, A. Quigley (Eds.), Pervasive Computing. XV, 402 pages. 2006.

Vol. 3967: D. Grigoriev, J. Harrison, E.A. Hirsch (Eds.), Computer Science – Theory and Applications. XVI, 684 pages. 2006.

Vol. 3966: Q. Wang, D. Pfahl, D.M. Raffo, P. Wernick (Eds.), Software Process Change. XIV, 356 pages. 2006.

Vol. 3965: M. Bernardo, A. Cimatti (Eds.), Formal Methods for Hardware Verification. VII, 243 pages. 2006.

Vol. 3964: M. Ü. Uyar, A.Y. Duale, M.A. Fecko (Eds.), Testing of Communicating Systems. XI, 373 pages. 2006.

Vol. 3963: O. Dikenelli, M.-P. Gleizes, A. Ricci (Eds.), Engineering Societies in the Agents World VI. X, 303 pages. 2006. (Sublibrary LNAI).

Vol. 3962: W. IJsselsteijn, Y. de Kort, C. Midden, B. Eggen, E. van den Hoven (Eds.), Persuasive Technology. XII, 216 pages. 2006.

Vol. 3960: R. Vieira, P. Quaresma, M.d.G.V. Nunes, N.J. Mamede, C. Oliveira, M.C. Dias (Eds.), Computational Processing of the Portuguese Language. XII, 274 pages. 2006. (Sublibrary LNAI).

Vol. 3959: J.-Y. Cai, S. B. Cooper, A. Li (Eds.), Theory and Applications of Models of Computation. XV, 794 pages. 2006.

Vol. 3958: M. Yung, Y. Dodis, A. Kiayias, T. Malkin (Eds.), Public Key Cryptography - PKC 2006. XIV, 543 pages. 2006.

Vol. 3956: G. Barthe, B. Grégoire, M. Huisman, J.-L. Lanet (Eds.), Construction and Analysis of Safe, Secure, and Interoperable Smart Devices. IX, 175 pages. 2006.

Vol. 3955: G. Antoniou, G. Potamias, C. Spyropoulos, D. Plexousakis (Eds.), Advances in Artificial Intelligence. XVII, 611 pages. 2006. (Sublibrary LNAI).

Vol. 3954: A. Leonardis, H. Bischof, A. Pinz (Eds.), Computer Vision – ECCV 2006, Part IV. XVII, 613 pages. 2006.

Vol. 3953: A. Leonardis, H. Bischof, A. Pinz (Eds.), Computer Vision – ECCV 2006, Part III. XVII, 649 pages. 2006.

Vol. 3952: A. Leonardis, H. Bischof, A. Pinz (Eds.), Computer Vision – ECCV 2006, Part II. XVII, 661 pages. 2006.

Vol. 3951: A. Leonardis, H. Bischof, A. Pinz (Eds.), Computer Vision – ECCV 2006, Part I. XXXV, 639 pages. 2006.

Vol. 3950: J.P. Müller, F. Zambonelli (Eds.), Agent-Oriented Software Engineering VI. XVI, 249 pages. 2006.

Vol. 3947: Y.-C. Chung, J.E. Moreira (Eds.), Advances in Grid and Pervasive Computing. XXI, 667 pages. 2006.

Vol. 3946: T.R. Roth-Berghofer, S. Schulz, D.B. Leake (Eds.), Modeling and Retrieval of Context. XI, 149 pages. 2006. (Sublibrary LNAI).

Vol. 3945: M. Hagiya, P. Wadler (Eds.), Functional and Logic Programming. X, 295 pages. 2006.

Vol. 3944: J. Quiñonero-Candela, I. Dagan, B. Magnini, F. d'Alché-Buc (Eds.), Machine Learning Challenges. XIII, 462 pages. 2006. (Sublibrary LNAI).

Vol. 3943: N. Guelfi, A. Savidis (Eds.), Rapid Integration of Software Engineering Techniques. X, 289 pages. 2006.

Vol. 3942: Z. Pan, R. Aylett, H. Diener, X. Jin, S. Göbel, L. Li (Eds.), Technologies for E-Learning and Digital Entertainment. XXV, 1396 pages. 2006.

Vol. 3941: S.W. Gilroy, M.D. Harrison (Eds.), Interactive Systems. XI, 267 pages. 2006.

Vol. 3940: C. Saunders, M. Grobelnik, S. Gunn, J. Shawe-Taylor (Eds.), Subspace, Latent Structure and Feature Selection. X, 209 pages. 2006.

Vol. 3939: C. Priami, L. Cardelli, S. Emmott (Eds.), Transactions on Computational Systems Biology IV. VII, 141 pages. 2006. (Sublibrary LNBI).

Vol. 3936: M. Lalmas, A. MacFarlane, S. Rüger, A. Tombros, T. Tsikrika, A. Yavlinsky (Eds.), Advances in Information Retrieval. XIX, 584 pages. 2006.

Vol. 3935: D. Won, S. Kim (Eds.), Information Security and Cryptology - ICISC 2005. XIV, 458 pages. 2006.

Vol. 3934: J.A. Clark, R.F. Paige, F.A. C. Polack, P.J. Brooke (Eds.), Security in Pervasive Computing. X, 243 pages. 2006.

Vol. 3933: F. Bonchi, J.-F. Boulicaut (Eds.), Knowledge Discovery in Inductive Databases. VIII, 251 pages. 2006.

Vol. 3931: B. Apolloni, M. Marinaro, G. Nicosia, R. Tagliaferri (Eds.), Neural Nets. XIII, 370 pages. 2006.

Vol. 3930: D.S. Yeung, Z.-Q. Liu, X.-Z. Wang, H. Yan (Eds.), Advances in Machine Learning and Cybernetics. XXI, 1110 pages. 2006. (Sublibrary LNAI).

Vol. 3929: W. MacCaull, M. Winter, I. Düntsch (Eds.), Relational Methods in Computer Science. VIII, 263 pages. 2006.

Vol. 3928: J. Domingo-Ferrer, J. Posegga, D. Schreckling (Eds.), Smart Card Research and Advanced Applications. XI, 359 pages. 2006.

Vol. 3927: J. Hespanha, A. Tiwari (Eds.), Hybrid Systems: Computation and Control. XII, 584 pages. 2006.

Vol. 3925: A. Valmari (Ed.), Model Checking Software. X, 307 pages. 2006.

Vol. 3924: P. Sestoft (Ed.), Programming Languages and Systems. XII, 343 pages. 2006.

Vol. 3923: A. Mycroft, A. Zeller (Eds.), Compiler Construction. XIII, 277 pages. 2006.

Vol. 3922: L. Baresi, R. Heckel (Eds.), Fundamental Approaches to Software Engineering. XIII, 427 pages. 2006.